SECOND EDITION

Families &
CHANGE

This book is dedicated to Us—
who have worked together since 1976.
It is seldom we have such
special and productive relationships—
valued friends and colleagues.

SECOND EDITION

Families &
CHANGE
Coping With Stressful
Events and Transitions

Patrick C. McKenry / Sharon J. Price

Editors

Sage Publications, Inc.
International Educational and Professional Publisher
Thousand Oaks ■ London ■ New Delhi

For information:

Sage Publications, Inc.
2455 Teller Road
Thousand Oaks, California 91320
E-mail: order@sagepub.com

Sage Publications Ltd.
6 Bonhill Street
London EC2A 4PU
United Kingdom

Sage Publications India Pvt. Ltd.
M-32 Market
Greater Kailash I
New Delhi 110 048 India

Printed in the United States of America

Library of Congress Cataloging-in-Publication Data

Main entry under title:

Families and change : Coping with stressful events and transitions / by
    Patrick C. McKenry and Sharon J. Price [editors]. — 2nd ed.
        p. cm.
    Includes bibliographical references and index.
    ISBN 0-7619-1972-4 (cloth)
    ISBN 0-7619-1973-2 (pbk.)
    1. Family—United States. 2. Social problems—United States. 3.
Social change—United States. I. McKenry, Patrick C. II. Price, Sharon J.
    HQ534 .F35 2000
    306.85'0973—dc21   00-009215

        02   03   05   06   07   7   6   5

Acquiring Editor: Jim Brace-Thompson
Editorial Assistant: Anna Howland
Production Editor: Denise Santoyo
Editorial Assistant: Candice Crosetti
Typesetter/Designer: Tina Hill
Indexer: Teri Greenberg
Cover Designer: Candice Harman

Contents

Preface

The second edition of *Families and Change: Coping With Stressful Events and Transitions* presents a synthesis and analysis of the vast literature that has emerged in recent years detailing families' responses to various transitions and other stressful life events. Scholarly interest in family stressors is not new. The social and behavioral sciences evolved during the Progressive Era (1890-1920) out of an interest in the social problems facing families as a result of industrialization and urbanization. The interest at this time was in social reform and the use of research to solve these problems. During the 1920s and 1930s, scholars began to focus on the internal dynamics of families. Because of disillusionment with the effects of social reform programs and the growing depersonalization of mass society, there was an increasing interest in the well-being and personal adjustment of families and individuals. Researchers became interested in healthy lifestyles, mental health, and child development. Both family sociology and family therapy developed at this time (Cole & Cole, 1993).

Two major societal disruptions—the Great Depression and World War II—prompted further attention to how families cope with unprecedented change. Angell (1936) and Cavan and Ranck (1938) both identified various family characteristics that mediated the impact of the effects of the depression—that is, family organization, integration, and adaptability. These findings remain largely unchallenged today (Boss, 1987). Hill (1949), in his study of wartime family separations, developed a framework for assessing family crisis: the ABC-X Model. This framework, with its emphasis on the family resources and definitions that mediate the extent of the stress or crisis response, serves today as the basis for most stress and coping theoretical models. The 1950s represented a focus on both the integrity of the American family as an institution and traditional family patterns. The social and political revolution of the 1960s, however, and the technological changes accompanying the greater industrialization and urbanization of the 1970s, 1980s, and 1990s have resulted in a proliferation of research on families' coping and adaptation to a myriad of changes and new problems.

Between the time when the first edition of this text was published (1994) and the present, our society has witnessed major and significant changes. For example, technology has produced major and unimagined changes in the lives of families; these changes appear to have only begun the long-term impact they are expected to have. Families in the United States live in a faster-paced society with an increase in demands on both adults and children. For example, families are striving for continuing improvement in their quality of life while also experiencing uncertainty about job security and advancement; both parents usually must work outside the home; and women and ethnic minorities are still facing economic discrimination. Quality day care and health care are increasingly viewed as beyond the reach of many, and an increasing population has resulted in transportation problems, pollution, and a shortage of some resources. Therefore, families, which were once havens for individuals who were stressed by external problems, are increasingly challenged to meet individual and family needs.

It is evident, however, that many of our colleagues are involved in developing knowledge, as well as teaching classes, in areas that focus on the stressors confronting families. For example, before the development of the first edition of *Families and Change*, we conducted an extensive review of more than 400 randomly selected undergraduate and graduate college and university catalogs. These institutions ranged from small, private, liberal arts colleges to large, land-grant/research universities. We found that more than 60% of these institutions offered courses that dealt with family problems, stress, and/or change. These courses were found in departments of social work, home economics/human ecology, sociology, human services, psychology, human development, family science, family relations, child and family development, health, professional studies, and criminology. We also informally surveyed instructors of such courses at various institutions and discovered that texts representing a compilation of recent research findings in this area were almost nonexistent. This information was combined with extensive feedback from instructors and students who used the first edition of *Families and Change* and from our publisher, who prodded us to develop a second edition.

Thus, the purpose of this second edition (as with the first) is to provide a volume appropriate for the study of various family problems, stressors, and changes prevalent in today's society. This text represents an integration of research, theory, and application, drawing on the interdisciplinary scholarship in each topic area. In addition, special attention is given to issues of special populations, for they are often disproportionately affected by these stressors. This book is intended to serve as a basic or supplementary text for undergraduate and introductory graduate courses on family or social problems. This book will also be useful to professionals, novices, and those with considerable experience, especially in social work, education, and public health, who are increasingly working with family problems.

Each chapter follows a similar outline, providing students with an overview of our current understanding of selected family transitions and stressors as well as possible mechanisms of intervention. However, each author was also afforded the opportunity to present his or her area of expertise in the manner that he or she viewed as appropriate.

The chapters in the book represent both predictable and unpredictable problems or stressors. Predictable family problems would include those stressors that are inherently stressful even though they are foreseen. We take the position that all forms of abrupt or disjunctive changes, although moderated or buffered by the family's coping resources, are likely to be stress producing. Such predictable or normative changes include marriage, parenting, aging, death, and dying. Other problems are potentially more traumatic because of the very fact that they cannot be predicted. These would include physical illness, mental illness, substance abuse, violence, economics, divorce, and remarriage. We also included three chapters that focus on special populations: black Americans, immigrant families, and gay and lesbian families. We take the position that many of these problems are interrelated and that they often combine to produce stress-related responses. For example, stress related to economic issues may lead to marital problems, including violence; this may then initiate a cycle of divorce, personal and economic disorganization, and remarriage. Also, we assume that family problems, change, and stress responses are not necessarily "bad" for the family. The disequilibrium that develops requires new methods for handling problems. Out of this situation may arise new and creative solutions that are superior to those that were present before the problem occurred. This experience may enable the family to handle future crises in a superior manner, and it may result in greater individual and group satisfaction with family life.

Not all family stressors could be reviewed because of page constraints. The topics chosen represent major social issues today and have received considerable social, professional, and research attention. Some family problems that met these criteria were not included as separate chapters because they are components of other chapters.

We begin the text with a conceptual overview of the research on family problems, stressors, change, and coping. The nature and origin of the problems and changes facing families today are delineated, noting that, while many of today's problems are not new, the extent of change in American society is unprecedented. The history of systematic inquiry into family problems and change is traced to individual physiological stress studies in the late 17th century; these studies of individuals have evolved into today's focus on whole-family interaction. A social systems approach is presented as the integrating framework for studying families under stress. This paradigm views families as dynamic mechanisms, always in the process of growth and adaptation as they deal with change and stressor events.

In Chapter 2, Ronald Sabatelli and Jeanne Joseph Chadwick focus on why and how many couples who start their relationships with high hopes and the firm conviction that their relationship is special experience marital distress to the degree that the marriage ends. These authors explore factors that contribute to the deconstruction of these relationships (i.e., how couples fail to navigate the ordinary difficulties confronting lifetime partnerships to the point that they wind up believing that their formerly special relationships can no longer be salvaged). In other words, they explore why many couples make the journey from intimacy and hope to hostility and despair. There is also a section on research implications for application, a description of various programs that focus on helping couples manage conflicts and enhance their communication skills.

Chapter 3, by Barbara Newman, addresses the challenges of parenting infants and young children (i.e., parental role strain and parental stress). Furthermore, she focuses on four themes of family life that illustrate how the presence of infants and young children serves as a source of stress. These are (a) the transition to parenthood, (b) parental separation anxiety, (c) managing child care arrangements, and (d) coping with sibling conflicts. These stressors are viewed as normative stressors and are likely to be faced by most families. In addition, factors such as poverty or underemployment, serious marital conflict, and chronic physical or mental health conditions also are viewed as having an impact on the stress related to parenting.

Gary Peterson and Kathleen Mathieson in Chapter 4 also review parental stress in an effort to integrate the existing research in this area with concepts that are central to family stress theory. In this chapter, the authors address (a) why the experience of parental stress may be universal, (b) why parental stress varies widely within the larger population of mothers and fathers, (c) why parents differ in their capacities to cope with and adapt to parental stress, and (d) what linkages exist between parental stress and the adjustment of children. The application of family stress concepts to the existing research on parental stress helps one understand a wide range of circumstances varying from highly disruptive crisis, to chronic stress, to more normative challenges. It also increases our understanding about how parental stress applies to both the individual and families.

In Chapter 5, Adam Davey focuses on how families cope with aging members. In this chapter, he describes (a) some of the many and considerable changes in the aging of the population in the United States, (b) the enormous changes that families have faced in post–World War II United States, and (c) the intersection of aging and family relationships. He also presents several theoretical models (appropriate for research and intervention) that contribute to our understanding of the family context of aging and adaptation. A life-span framework is used to organize these changes and demands, particularly as applied to family caregiving and intergenerational relationships using the stress process model and contingent exchange theory. In addition, the areas that are viewed as most pressing regarding the resiliency of individual and family development are highlighted.

Colleen Murray discusses family experiences with death, dying, and bereavement in Chapter 6. She notes that the death of a family member is widely considered the most stressful life event that families face. Although a predictable and hence normative event, the death of a family member is not viewed as normal by society, including many researchers and clinicians, and it is often treated as a problem rather than something that can result in growth and strength. Adapting to the loss of a family member is hampered by a lack of cultural support for the bereaved, a minimum of rituals surrounding death, and poorly defined roles for the chronically ill or the bereaved. The author conceptualizes the reaction to the death of a family member as a process, not an event, that does not always follow a linear progression. A social systems perspective is used to describe family reactions, noting that the family responds as a unit to the death of a family member and that a variety of systemic characteristics may influence the outcome for families. Gender, culture, and religion also are identified as important mediating factors in the grief process.

Thomas Campbell discusses the interrelationship between health and families in Chapter 7. This area is particularly relevant in view of the tremendous pressures, changes, and crises confronting this health care system, and, subsequently, families. The chapter takes a systemic, bidirectional (bio-psychosocial) approach in analyzing the role that families play in individual physical health; that is, not only does illness influence families, but families very much influence the health status of their members. From health promotion to intervention, families are seen as the most important context for health and illness. Healthy and unhealthy behaviors are developed and maintained or changed within the family. In addition, families are the most important source of stress and social support, both of which have a profound effect on the development and course of physical illness. Finally, he stresses the need for greater emphasis in this area by researchers, clinicians, educators involved in programs for family and health professionals, and health care policymakers.

Richard Gelles in Chapter 8 discusses the incidence and etiology of various forms of family violence. Estimates of the extent of family violence suggest that it is pervasive in American society. The author goes beyond individual explanations to discuss various societal factors that are related to family violence, including gender, race, socioeconomic status, stress, social isolation, and intergenerational patterns. More theoretically, models from psychology, sociology, and biology are used to provide the systems context for family violence. Drawing on the research literature, the most promising preventive measures would focus on eliminating norms that legitimize and glorify violence, reducing violence-provoking stress created by society, integrating families into a network of kin and community, changing the sexist character of our society, and breaking the cycle of violence in families.

In Chapter 9, Michael Farrell and Grace Barnes address the issue of substance abuse and family stress, with an emphasis on adolescence. They examine the historical trends in adolescent alcohol and drug abuse, including racial and ethnic differences. In addition, they review recent advances in theory and research on the role that families play in adolescent alcohol and drug use and on how adolescent alcohol and drug abuse contribute to stress within families. Finally, they discuss the part that families can play in interventions to prevent substance abuse.

Like Campbell, Stephen Gavazzi and Angie Schock in Chapter 10 view mental illness as a bidirectional phenomenon. Families play a role in the etiology of mental disorders, and they are severely affected by the mental illness of a family member. The stressors and strains of families with mentally ill family members are often referred to as burdens, consisting of resource contribution (e.g., payment of medical expenses and provision of transportation), stigma, and psychological costs (e.g., lower self-esteem, reduced social contacts, job loss, and family relationship difficulties). The authors note that, traditionally, families have been neglected and even blamed by practitioners, who have focused only on the treatment of the individual and on the role that family interaction has played in the etiology of the disorder.

In Chapter 11, Jonathan Fox and Suzanne Bartholomae address the issues of economic stress and families. The authors emphasize that most families possess limited resources and, therefore, must manage them in an effort to meet their needs and desires. The level and management of these resources, however, can be sources of stress or comfort. Stress is often related to disagreement over the use of resources and concern about their availability. They also examine normative economic stressors, economic demands at different stages of the life cycle, the dangers of debt accumulation, and planning for retirement.

In Chapter 12, David Demo, Mark Fine, and Lawrence Ganong discuss divorce as a family process that differs significantly for husbands, wives, and children; thus, the perceptions of all three must be considered to understand this common transition. Although divorce is often viewed as a serious problem that results in severe long-term adjustment problems, the authors suggest that while some women and children are at risk for long-term negative consequences of divorce, this assumption cannot be applied to all. Rather, recent studies of larger and more representative samples suggest moderate and short-term effects for adults and children. The authors also propose intervention strategies that may facilitate divorce adjustment.

Margaret Crosbie-Burnett and Katrina McClintic discuss remarriage and recoupling as a stressor event in Chapter 13. This chapter presents demographic data on remarriage as well as a model explaining family stress and coping in remarried families. This model, based on the ABC-X Model, has both sociological and psychological components and focuses on the role of hardships and pileups, resources, perception, and adaptation to the recoupling. The authors emphasize the need for changes in law, education, and therapy to address the unique needs of remarried families.

In Chapter 14, Velma McBride Murry addresses the unique stressors and challenges experienced by black American families in a largely racist society. Although considerable progress has occurred over the last 100 years, there are still serious issues in a culture that values white over black and where whites are viewed as the "norm" to which blacks should aspire. Murry proposes that black families from different social classes and backgrounds need to be acknowledged, in contrast to viewing all black families as the same. She uses major theories, including traditional family stress models, to explain the experience of black families. In addition, she confronts the economic issues, disproportionate sex ratios, issues in marital relationships, and parenting issues in black families. In summary, she proposes the development of new and revised theoretical frameworks for the study of black families and the need for policy and intervention efforts that are derived from both empirical and theoretical formulations.

In Chapter 15, Hector Balcazar and Zhenchao Qian discuss the unique stressors of immigrant families. These stressors are often the result of the processes of transformation and the multiple challenges that confront immigrant families. These may include the inability to speak English, underemployment and unemployment, being identified as a racial minority, cultural and generation gaps, issues surrounding acculturation, and homesickness. Despite these stressors, immigrant groups uphold the value of preserving the family structure and its function as a core element of their existence in a new country. These authors also discuss the unique stressors for immigrant children and children of immigrants.

Karen Wilcox and Katherine Allen write about an often-neglected area, gay and lesbian families, in Chapter 16. These authors stress the importance of studying these families as our society is increasingly bringing issues related to different lifestyles, particularly through popular writing and the media. In this chapter, the authors address the various issues that affect both individuals and families; family-related stressors and strengths associated with revealing that one is gay or lesbian; and issues of partnership and parenting that are central to adult life, regardless of sexual orientation. They also address the strengths and stressors associated with the aging process for gay men and lesbians. Finally, they propose intervention strategies, policy implications, and future directions for research and advocacy relevant to strengthening families with gay, lesbian, bisexual, and transgendered members.

REFERENCES

Angell, R. C. (1936). *The family encounters the depression.* New York: Scribner.
Boss, P. (1987). Family stress. In M. B. Sussman & S. K. Steinmetz (Eds.), *Handbook of marriage and the family* (pp. 695-724). New York: Plenum.
Cavan, R. S., & Ranck, K. H. (1938). *The family and the depression.* Chicago: University of Chicago Press.
Cole, C. L., & Cole, A. L. (1993). Family therapy theory implications for marriage and family enrichment. In P. G. Boss, W. J. Doherty, R. LaRossa, W. R. Schumm, & S. K. Steinmetz (Eds.), *Sourcebook of family theories and methods: A contextual approach* (pp. 525-530). New York: Plenum.
Hill, R. (1949). *Families under stress.* New York: Harper & Row.

Acknowledgments

The support, advice, and encouragement of colleagues and friends were instrumental in the conceptualization and production of this text. We would like to express our appreciation to Al Davis, Pat's department head, and Lynda Walters, Sharon's interim department head. Both have been supportive through the years—administratively and personally. We would also like to thank the many instructors and students who provided feedback and asked us to update this text.

The authors of this volume deserve a very special thank you. We are very grateful for their thoughtful and well-written contributions. Their enthusiasm for this project and their timely revisions (without too much prodding) certainly helped make the project less onerous.

We also are very indebted to our graduate assistants who made it possible for us to meet deadlines: specifically, Kate Fogarty, Roy Fish, and Hyoun Kim, who worked endless hours. We also want to thank Linda Crosby, who came to our rescue at the last minute.

In addition, we offer a special thank you to David Coker (Sharon's husband), who has been our cheering section through the development of four books. He added a sense of humor, made sure we were fed, and kept the bar stocked—all valuable contributions.

1

Families Coping
With Problems and Change

A Conceptual Overview

PATRICK C. MCKENRY
SHARON J. PRICE

American families today are experiencing unprecedented change and are coping with a variety of problems, both old and new (Cherlin, 1996; Settles, 1999). It is impossible to read extensively in either scholarly or lay publications without encountering a discussion of stress in American society.

Technology accompanying industrialization and urbanization, with increased population density, frequently is identified as making daily life more complex and impersonal. Gender roles have blurred, traditional values are being questioned, and even traditional definitions and conceptualizations of "family" have changed in response to the increasing options of postmodern society. Feminists and others have challenged prevailing assumptions about families by raising questions about family boundaries, equity in family relationships, and the viability of a monolithic family form.

The "ideal of progress" that emerged with industrialization proclaimed that scientific advances would always make life progressively better (Naisbitt & Aburdene, 1990). However, while American families generally have experienced continuing improvement in their quality of life, threats to economic stability still exist. A changing economy has introduced uncertainty into the lives of many family members; job security and advancement are less certain, even to those who have formal preparation for a career. For example, many have made the transition from a "9-to-5" job to 5 to 9 jobs in a lifetime.

Both parents usually must work outside the home, women and ethnic minorities still face economic discrimination, and the percentage of families in poverty has actually increased since the 1970s. Quality day care and adequate health care have become luxuries beyond the reach of many families. Overpopulation accompanying industrialization has resulted in transportation problems, pollution, and a shortage of resources. Societal alienation has resulted in a steady increase in major mental disorders and related self-destructive behaviors, including drug and alcohol abuse, suicide, and violence.

Families, which were once havens for individuals who were stressed by external pressures, increasingly are challenged to meet individual emotional needs. There is decreasing time for leisure because most persons, including adolescents, are working longer hours outside the home or are otherwise heavily involved in extrafamilial activities.

Families are faced with many unique problems as a result of societal change. For example, technology has facilitated an increasing life span, but it has also brought about a growing aged population with whom overextended and geographically mobile families must cope. Young family members must contend with the realization that there are fewer opportunities and resources available to them as compared with their parents. And the fluidity of family structures requires most families to deal with several family structural transitions during the life course (Price, McKenry, & Murphy, 2000; Teachman, Polonko, & Scanzoni, 1999).

Change results in stress responses whether that change is "good" or "bad." The impact of the change is dependent on the family's coping ability. Boss (1988) defines *family stress* as pressure or tension in the family system; it is a disturbance of the family's steady state, yet it is normal and even desirable at times. Life transitions and events often provide an essential condition for psychological development. Family stress is perceived as inevitable because people, and hence families, develop and change over time. With change comes disturbance and pressure—what is termed *stress*. Changes affecting families also occur externally (e.g., unemployment or natural disasters), and these also create stress within the family system. Change becomes problematic only when the degree of stress in the family system reaches a level at which family members and/or the family system become dissatisfied or show symptoms of disturbance.

The Study of Family Stress and Coping

In comparison with the long history of research in the general area of stress and coping, theoretical and clinical interest in family stress, problems, and coping styles is a rather recent phenomenon (Cowan, Cowan, & Schulz, 1996; McCubbin, Cauble, & Patterson, 1982). Research on family stress and coping has gradually evolved from various disciplines that have examined stress and coping from more of an individualistic perspective.

According to the *Oxford English Dictionary,* the term *stress* can be traced back to the early 14th century when *stress* had several distinct meanings, including hardship, adversity, and affliction (Rutter, 1983). Even among stress researchers today, *stress* is variably defined as a stimulus, an inferred inner state, and an observable response to a stimulus or situation; there is also debate concerning the extent to which stress is chemical, environmental, or psychological in nature (Frankenhaeuser, 1994; Lazarus & Folkman, 1984; Sarafino, 1990).

In the late 17th century, Hooke used *stress* in the context of physical science, although the usage was not made systematic until the early 19th century. Stress and strain were first conceived as a basis of ill health in the 19th century (Lazarus & Folkman, 1984). In the 20th century, Cannon (1932) laid the foundation for systematic research on the effects of stress in detailed observations of bodily changes. He showed that stimuli associated with emotional arousal (e.g., pain, hunger, cold) caused changes in basic physiological functioning (Dohrenwend & Dohrenwend, 1974). Selye (1978) was the first researcher to define and measure stress adaptations in the human body. He defined *stress* as an orchestrated set of bodily defenses against any form of noxious stimuli (General Adaptation Syndrome). In the 1950s, social scientists became interested in his conceptualization of stress, and even today Selye's seminal work underlies much of the scholarly interest in stress and coping (Lazarus & Folkman, 1984; Lovallo, 1997).

Meyer, in the 1930s, taught that life events may be an important part of the etiology of a disorder and that the most normal and necessary life events may be potential contributors to pathology (Dohrenwend & Dohrenwend, 1974). More recently, Holmes and Rahe (1967) have used the Meyerian perspective to study life events and their connection to the onset and progression of illness. Through their Schedule of Recent Events, which includes many family events, Holmes and Rahe have related the accumulation of life changes and those of greater magnitude to a higher chance of associated illness or disease.

In the social sciences, both sociology and psychology have long histories of study related to stress and coping. Sociologists Marx, Weber, and Durkheim wrote extensively about "alienation." Alienation was conceptualized as synonymous with powerlessness, meaninglessness, and self-estrangement, clearly under the general rubric of stress (Lazarus & Folkman, 1984).

In psychology, stress was implicit as an organizing framework for thinking about psychopathology, especially in the theorizing of Freud and later psychodynamically oriented writers. Freudian psychology also highlighted the process of coping and established the basis for a developmental approach that considered the effect of life events on later development and the gradual acquisition of resources over the life cycle. Early psychologists used anxiety to denote stress, and it was seen as a central component in psychopathology through the 1950s. The reinforcement learning theorists (e.g., Spence, 1956) viewed anxiety as a classically conditioned response that led to unserviceable (pathological) habits of anxiety reduction. Existentialists (e.g., May, 1950) also focused on anxiety as a major barrier to self-actualization (Lazarus & Folkman, 1984). Developmentalists (e.g., Erikson, 1963) have put forth vari-ous stage models that demand that a particular crisis be negotiated before the individual can cope with subsequent developmental stages. Personal coping resources accrued during the adolescent/young adult years are thought to be integrated into the self-concept and shape the process of coping throughout adulthood (Moos, 1986). Crisis theorists (e.g., Caplan, 1964) conceptualized these life changes as crises, with the assumption that disequilibrium may pro-voke stress in the short run but can promote the development of new skills in the long run.

Since the 1960s, there has been growing interest in coping responses in adaptational outcomes. Researchers have attempted to delineate the coping strategies that individuals and families employ in successfully managing stress (Coelho, Hamburg, & Adams, 1974; McCubbin, 1979; Moos, 1976). Coping in the study of families involves the integration of both sociological and psychological perspectives. Lazarus' (1966) psychological taxonomy emphasized two major categories of coping responses: (a) direct actions and (b) palliative modes (the use of thought or actions to relieve the emotional im-pact of stress). The sociological perspective of coping underscores the impor-tance of individual and family resources, such as cohesion and adaptability, in the management of stress (e.g., Burr, 1973; Hill, 1949).

Many researchers from a variety of disciplines have presented data that support the relationship between social support and the ability to adjust to and cope with crises and change. Caplan (1964, 1974) notes that social sup-port allows individuals to adapt more easily to change and appears to protect them from the typical physiological and psychological health consequences of life stress (McCubbin et al., 1982). From this line of research, others have attempted to explore the contribution of other variables and processes as moderators of the stressor–stress response relationship. In the study of family stress and coping per se, much of the work has used some variation of Hill's (1949) social system model of family stress.

Family Stress Theory

Social Systems Perspective

Family theorists typically have used a social systems approach in their conceptualization of families under stress. Thus, families are viewed as living organisms with both symbolic and real structures. They have boundaries to maintain and a variety of instrumental and expressive functions to perform to ensure growth and survival (Boss, 1988). As with any social system, families strive to maintain a steady state. Families are the products of both subsystems (e.g., individual members, dyads) and suprasystems (e.g., community, culture, nation).

Although most general stress theories have focused only on the individual, the primary interest of family stress theory is the entire family unit. System theory states that the system is more than the sum of its parts (Hall & Fagan, 1968). In terms of families, this means that the collection of family members is not only a specific number of people but also an aggregate of particular relationships and shared memories, successes, failures, and aspirations (Boss, 1988). However, systems theory is also interested in studying the individual to more completely understand a family's response to stress.

A social systems approach allows the researcher to focus beyond the family and the individual to the wider social system (suprasystem). Families do not live in isolation; they are part of the larger social context. This external environment in which the family is embedded is referred to as the "ecosystem," according to social systems theory. This ecosystem consists of historical, cultural, economic, genetic, and developmental influences (Boss, 1988). Thus, the family's response to a stressor event is influenced by the particular historical period in which it lives, its cultural identification, the economic conditions of society, its genetic stamina and resistance, and its stage in the family life cycle.

ABC-X Model

The foundation for a social systems model of family stress lies in Hill's (1949) classic research on war-induced separation and reunion. Although

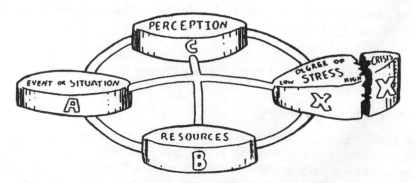

Figure 1.1. ABC-X Model of Family Crisis
SOURCE: Hill, R. (1958, February). Social stresses on the family: Generic features of families under stress. *Social Casework*, pp. 139-150. Used with permission.

his ABC-X formulation has been expanded (McCubbin & Patterson, 1982; Patterson, 1988), it has withstood careful assessment and is still the basis for analyzing family stress and coping (McCubbin & Patterson, 1985). This family stress framework may be stated as follows:

> A (the provoking or stressor event), interacting with B (the family's resources or strengths), interacting with C (the definition or meaning attached to the event by the family), produces X (stress or crisis).

The main idea is that the X factor is influenced by several other moderating or buffering phenomena. Stress or crisis is not seen as inherent in the event itself but, conceptually, as a function of the response of the disturbed family to the stressor (Burr, 1973; Hill, 1949) (see Figure 1.1).

Stressor Events

A stressor event is an occurrence that provokes a variable amount of change in the family system. Anything that changes some aspect of the system such as the boundaries, structures, goals, processes, roles, or values can produce stress. This variable denotes something different from the routine changes within a system that are expected as part of its regular, ordinary operation. This variable is dichotomous; that is, it is an event not changing the system or one changing the system (Burr, 1982). The stressor event by definition has the potential to raise the family's level of stress. However, the degree of stress is dependent on the magnitude of the event as well as other moderating factors to be discussed. Also, both positive and negative events can be stressors. Life events research has clearly indicated that normal or positive changes can increase an individual's risk for illness. In addition, stressor events do not necessarily increase stress levels to the point of crisis; the family's stress level can be managed and the family can return to a new equilibrium.

Researchers have attempted to describe various types of stressor events (e.g., Boss, 1988; Hansen & Hill, 1964; Rees & Smyer, 1983). Lipman-Blumen (1975) has described family stressor events in terms of 10 dimensions: (a) internal versus external, (b) pervasive versus bounded, (c) precipitate onset versus gradual, (d) intense versus mild, (e) transitory versus chronic, (f) random versus expectable, (g) natural generation versus artificial, (h) scarcity versus surplus, (i) perceived insolvable versus solvable, and (j) substantive content. The type of event may be highly correlated with the family's ability to manage stress. (These dimensions are defined in Table 1.1.) Other researchers (e.g., McCubbin, Patterson, & Wilson, 1981; Pearlin & Schooler, 1978) have classified stressor events in terms of their intensity or hardship on the family.

One dichotomous classification that is often used by family stress researchers and clinicians is normal or predictable events versus nonnormative or unpredictable or situational events. Normal events are part of everyday life and represent transitions inherent in the family life cycle, such as the birth or death of a family member, child's school entry, and retirement. Normative stressor events by definition are of short duration. Although predictable and normal, such lifecycle events have the potential to change a family's level of stress because they disturb system equilibrium. These events lead to crisis only if the family does not adapt to the changes brought about by these events (Carter & McGoldrick, 1989).

Nonnormative events are the product of some unique situation that could not be predicted and is not likely to be repeated. Examples of nonnormative events would include natural disasters, loss of a job, or an automobile accident. Unexpected events that are not disastrous, such as promotion or winning the lottery, may also be stressful for families. Although these events are positive, they do change or disturb the family's routine and thus have the potential of raising the family's level of stress (Boss, 1988).

There has been much recent interest in the study of isolated versus accumulated stressors. Specifically, life event scholars (e.g., Holmes & Rahe, 1967; McCubbin et al., 1981; Sarason, Johnson, & Siegel, 1978) suggest that it is

TABLE 1.1 10 Dimensions of Family Stressor Events

1. *Internality versus Externality:* Refers to whether the source of the crisis was internal or external to the social system affected.

2. *Pervasiveness versus Boundedness:* Refers to the degree to which the crisis affects the entire system or only a limited part.

3. *Precipitate Onset versus Gradual Onset:* Marks the degree of suddenness with which the crisis occurred (i.e., with or without warning).

4. *Intensity versus Mildness:* Involves the degree of severity of the crisis.

5. *Transitoriness versus Chronicity:* Refers to the degree to which the crisis represents a short- or long-term problem.

6. *Randomness versus Expectability:* Marks the degree to which the crisis could be expected or predicted.

7. *Natural Generation versus Artificial Generation:* Connotes the distinction between crises that arise from natural conditions and those that come about through technological or other human-made effects.

8. *Scarcity versus Surplus:* Refers to the degree to which the crisis represents a shortage or overabundance of vital commodities—human, material, and nonmaterial.

9. *Perceived Solvability versus Perceived Insolvability:* Suggests the degree to which those individuals involved in the crisis believe the crisis is open to reversal or some level of resolution.

10. *Substantive Content:* (This dimension differs from the previous nine in that it subsumes a set of subject areas, each of which may be regarded as a separate continuum graded from low to high.) Using this dimension, the analyst can determine whether the substantive nature of the crisis is primarily in the political, economic, moral, social, religious, health, or sexual domains or any combination thereof.

SOURCE: Adapted from Lipman-Blumen (1975).

the accumulation of several stressor events rather than the nature of one isolated event that determines a family's level of stress. The clustering of stressor events (normative and/or nonnormative) is termed *stress pileup.* An event rarely happens to a family in total isolation. Normal developmental changes are always taking place, and nonnormative events tend to result in other stressors; for example, the loss of a job may result in moving or marital disruption. By focusing only on certain events or stressors, researchers may fail to capture the complexity in the range and clustering of stressors (Pearlin, 1991).

More recently, researchers have offered an alternative perspective on stressor events. Instead of assessing major life events that tend to be extreme in nature and are fairly low in base-rate occurrence (Fisher, Fagot, & Leve, 1998), researchers are focusing on daily stressors or hassles and ongoing strains and their relationship to stress outcomes. Daily hassles not only parallel major life events in their potential to engender stress but have an even stronger relationship than traditional life events measures in predicting physical health (Derogatis & Coons, 1993; Gruen, 1993).

Resources

The family's resources buffer or moderate the impact of the stressor event on the family's level of stress. Hansen (1965) uses the term *vulnerability* to denote the difference in families' physical and emotional responses to stressful stimuli (Gore & Colten, 1991). This moderator denotes variation in a family's ability to prevent a stressor event or change from creating disruptiveness in the system (Burr, 1973). When members have sufficient appropriate resources, they are less likely to view a stressful situation as problematic. McCubbin and Patterson (1985) define *resources* as traits, characteristics, or abilities of (a) individual family members, (b) the family system, and (c) the community that can be used to meet the demands of a stressor event. Individual or personal resources include finances (economic well-being), education (problem solving and information), health (physical and emotional well-being), and psychological resources (self-esteem).

Family system resources refer to internal attributes of the family unit that protect the family from the impact of stressors and facilitate family adaptation during family stress, family crisis, or both. Family cohesion (bonds of unity) and adaptability (ability to change) (Olson, Russell, & Sprenkle, 1979, 1983) have received the most research attention. These two dimensions are the major axes of the Circumplex Model (Olson et al., 1979). This model suggests that families who function moderately along the dimensions of cohesion and adaptability are likely to make a more successful adjustment to stress (Olson, Russell, & Sprenkle, 1980). However, it should be noted that the family literature contains studies and writings that qualify or refute the curvilinear interpretation of the relationship between adaptability and cohesion and effective functioning; instead, these studies support a linear relationship between these two dimensions and effective outcomes (Anderson & Gavazzi, 1990).

Community resources refer to those capabilities of people or institutions outside the family on which the family can draw for dealing with stress. Social support is one of the most important community resources, although it can, of course, be provided by individual family members. Social support may be viewed as information disseminated to facilitate problem solving and as the development of new social contacts who provide help and assistance.

Social support offers information at an interpersonal level that provides (a) emotional support, (b) esteem support, and (c) network support (Cobb, 1976). In general, social support serves as a protector against the effects of stressors and promotes recovery from stress or crisis. Increasingly, the concept of community resources has been broadened to include the resources of cultural groups; for example, ethnic minority families are thought to be characterized by more elaborate and efficient patterns of social support (Hill, 1999; McCubbin, Futrell, Thompson, & Thompson, 1998).

Definition of the Event/Perceptions

The impact of the stressor event on the family's level of stress is also moderated by the definition or meaning the family gives to the event. This variable is also synonymous with family appraisal, perception, and assessment of the event. Thus, subjective definitions can vary from the positive view that circumstances are a challenge and an opportunity for growth to the negative view that things are hopeless, too difficult, or unmanageable (McCubbin & Patterson, 1985). Empirical findings suggest that an individual's cognitive appraisal of life events strongly influences the response (Lazarus & Launier, 1978).

This concept has a long tradition in social psychology in terms of the self-fulfilling prophecy that if something is perceived as real, it is real in its consequences (Burr, 1982). Families who are able to redefine a stressor event more positively (i.e., reframe it) appear to be better able to cope and adapt. By redefining the stressor event, families are able to (a) clarify the issues, hardships, and tasks to render them more manageable and more responsive to problem-solving efforts; (b) decrease the intensity of the emotional burdens associated with stressors; and (c) encourage the family unit to carry on with its fundamental tasks of promoting individual members' social and emotional development (McCubbin & Patterson, 1985).

Lazarus and Launier (1978) have discussed the impact of an individual's learned cognitive attributional style on the stress response; this work has been applied to the study of families as well (e.g., Boss, 1988). For example, a family may respond to an event in terms of "learned helplessness," thereby increasing its vulnerability as a result of low self-esteem and feelings of hopelessness. Such a family would react to the unemployment of a spouse by failing to look for another job or supporting that family member in the search for another job.

It has long been thought that men and women inherently differ in their susceptibility and reaction to stressor events, with women being more likely to experience stress from relationship-oriented events and men, from external events that threatened the family or their good provider role (Gore & Colten, 1991). Thoits (1991) uses identity theory to suggest that men and women are more likely to experience stress when an important identity, such as one's traditional family gender role, is threatened. Evidence has accumulated that challenges the notion of gender differences in response to stressor events. With changing gender roles, men's distress is as affected by relationships with partners as is women's, and women's distress is as affected by the quality of their job experiences as is men's (Barnett, 1993).

Stress and Crisis

According to social systems theory, stress represents a change in the family's steady state. Stress is the response of the family to the demands experienced as a result of a stressor event. Stress is not inherently bad; it becomes problematic when the degree of stress in the family system reaches a level at which the family becomes disrupted or individual members become dissatisfied or display physical or emotional symptoms. The degree of stress ultimately depends on the family's definition of the stressor event as well as the adequacy of the family's resources to meet the demands of the change associated with the stressor event.

The terms *stress* and *crisis* have been used inconsistently in the literature. In fact, many researchers have failed to make a distinction between the two. Boss (1988) makes a useful distinction when she defines crisis as (a) a disturbance in the equilibrium that is so overwhelming, (b) pressure that is so severe, or (c) change that is so acute that the family system is blocked, immobilized, and incapacitated. When a family is in a crisis state, at least for a time it does not function adequately. Family boundaries are no longer maintained, customary roles and tasks are no longer performed, and family members are no longer functioning at optimal physical or psychological levels. The family has thus reached a state of acute disequilibrium and is immobilized.

Family stress, on the other hand, is merely a state of changed or disturbed equilibrium. Family stress, therefore, is a continuous variable (degree of stress), whereas family crisis is a dichotomous variable (either in crisis or not). A crisis does not have to permanently break up the family system. It may only temporarily immobilize the family system and then lead to a different level of functioning than that experienced before the stress level escalated to the point of crisis. Many family systems, in fact, become stronger after they have experienced and recovered from crisis (Boss, 1988).

Coping

Family stress researchers have increasingly shifted their attention from crisis and family dysfunction to the process of coping. Researchers have become more interested in explaining why some families are better able to manage and endure stressor events than others, rather than documenting the frequency and severity of such events. In terms of intervention, this represents a change from crisis intervention to prevention (Boss, 1988; McCubbin et al., 1980).

The study of family coping has drawn heavily from cognitive psychology (e.g., Lazarus, 1976; Lazarus & Folkman, 1984) as well as sociology (e.g., Pearlin & Schooler, 1978). Cognitive coping strategies refer to the ways in which individual family members alter their subjective perceptions of stressful events. Sociological theories of coping emphasize a wide variety of actions directed at either changing the stressful situation or alleviating distress by manipulating the social environment (McCubbin et al., 1980). Thus, family coping has been conceptualized in terms of three types of responses: (a) direct action (e.g., acquiring resources and learning new skills), (b) intrapsychic (e.g., reframing the problem), and (c) controlling the emotions generated by the stressor (e.g., social support or the use of alcohol) (Boss, 1988; Lazarus & Folkman, 1984; Pearlin & Schooler, 1978). These responses can be used individually, consecutively, or, more commonly, in various combinations. Specific coping strategies are not inherently adaptive or maladaptive; they are very much situation specific. Flexible access to a range of responses appears to be more effective than the use of any one response (Moos, 1986).

Coping interacts with both family resources and perceptions as defined by the "B" and "C" factors of the ABC-X Model. However, coping actions are different from resources and perceptions. Coping represents what people do—their concrete efforts to deal with a stressor (Pearlin & Schooler, 1978). Having a resource or a perception of an event does not imply whether or how a family will react (Boss, 1988; Lazarus & Folkman, 1984).

Although coping is sometimes equated with adaptational success (i.e., a product), from a family systems perspective, coping is a process, not an outcome per se. *Coping* refers to all efforts expended to manage a stressor regardless of the effect (Lazarus & Folkman, 1984). Thus, the family strategy of coping is not instantly created but is progressively modified over time. Because the family is a system, coping behavior involves the management of various dimensions of family life simultaneously: (a) maintaining satisfactory internal conditions for communication and family organization, (b) promoting member independence and self-esteem, (c) maintaining family bonds of coherence and unity, (d) maintaining and developing social supports in transactions with the community, and (e) maintaining some efforts to control the impact of the stressor and the amount of change in the family unit (McCubbin et al., 1980). Coping is thus a process of achieving balance in the family system that facilitates organization and unity and promotes individual growth and development. This is consistent with systems theory, which suggests that the families who most effectively cope with stress are strong as a unit as well as in individual members (Buckley, 1967).

Boss (1988) cautions that coping should not be perceived as maintaining the status quo; rather, the active managing of stress should lead to progressively new levels of organization as systems are naturally inclined toward greater complexity. In fact, sometimes it is better for a family to "fail to cope" even if that precipitates a crisis. After the crisis, the family can reorganize into a better functioning system. For example, a marital separation may be very painful for a family, but it may be necessary to allow the family to grow in a different, more productive direction.

In addition to serving as a barrier to change and growth, coping also can serve as a source of stress. There are three ways that coping itself may be a source of additional hardship (Roskies & Lazarus, 1980). One way is by indirect damage to the family system. This occurs when a family member inadvertently behaves in such a way that puts the family in a disadvantaged position. For example, a father may become ill from overwork to ease his family's economic stress. The second way that coping can serve as a source of stress is through direct damage to the family system. For example, family members may use an addictive behavior or violence to personally cope; this will be disruptive to the family system. The third way that coping may increase family stress is by interfering with additional adaptive behaviors that could help preserve the family. For example, denial of a problem may preclude getting necessary help and otherwise addressing the stressor event (McCubbin et al., 1980).

Adaptation

Another major interest of family stress researchers has been the assessment of how families are able to "recover" from stress or crisis. Drawing from Hansen's (1965) work, Burr (1973) described this process in terms of a family's "regenerative power," denoting a family's ability to recover from stress or crisis. According to McCubbin and Patterson (1982), the purpose of postcrisis or poststress adjustment is to reduce or eliminate the disruptiveness in the family system and restore homeostasis. However, these authors also note that family disruption has the potential of maintaining family relations and stimulating desirable change. Because system theorists (e.g., Buckley, 1967) hold that all systems naturally evolve toward greater complexity, it may be inferred that family systems initiate and capitalize on externally produced change in order to grow. Therefore, reduction of stress or crisis alone is an incomplete index of a family's adjustment to crisis or stress.

McCubbin and Patterson (1982) use the term *adaptation* to describe a desirable outcome of a crisis or stressful state. *Family adaptation* is defined as the degree to which the family system alters its internal functions (behaviors, rules, roles, perceptions) and/or external reality to achieve a system (individual or family)-environment fit. Adaptation is achieved through reciprocal relationships in which (a) system demands (or needs) are met by resources from the environment and (b) environmental demands are satisfied through system resources (Hansen & Hill, 1964).

According to McCubbin and Patterson (1982), demands include normative and nonnormative stressor events as well as the needs of individuals (e.g., intimacy), families (e.g., launching of children), and social institutions and communities (e.g., governmental authority). Resources include individual (e.g., education and psychological stability), family (e.g., cohesion and adaptability), and environmental (e.g., social support and medical services) attributes.

Adaptation is different from adjustment. Adjustment is a short-term response by a family that changes the situation only momentarily. Adaptation implies a change in the family system that evolves over a longer period of time or is intended to have long-term consequences involving changes in family roles, rules, patterns of interaction, and perceptions (McCubbin & Patterson, 1982).

McCubbin and Patterson (1982) have expanded Hill's (1949) ABC-X Model by adding postcrisis/poststress factors to explain how families achieve a satisfactory adaptation to stress or crisis. Their model consists of the ABC-X Model followed by their "Double ABC-X" configuration. (See Figure 1.2.)

McCubbin and Patterson's (1982) "Double A" factor refers to the stressor pileup in the family system. This includes three types of stressors. The family must deal with unresolved aspects of the initial stressor event, the changes and events that occur regardless of the initial stressor (e.g., changes in family

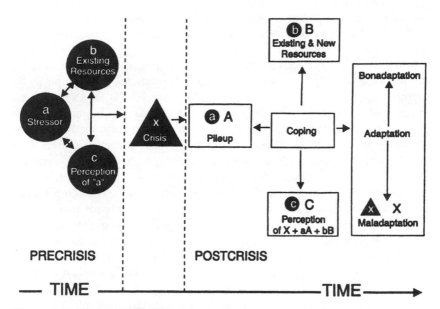

Figure 1.2. Double ABC-X Model
SOURCE: From McCubbin, H. I., & Patterson, J. M. (1982). *Family stress, coping, and social support.*
Reprinted by courtesy of Charles C Thomas, Publisher, Springfield, Illinois.

membership), and the consequences of the family's efforts to cope with the
hardships of the situation (e.g., intrafamily role changes).

The family's resources, the "Double B" factor, are of two types. The first
are those resources that are already available to the family and that minimize
the impact of the initial stressor. The second are those coping resources (personal, family, and social) that are strengthened or developed in response to
the stress or crisis situation.

The "Double C" factor refers to (a) the perception of the initial stressor
event and (b) the perception of the stress or crisis. The perception of the stress
or crisis situation includes the family's view of the stressor and related hardships and the pileup of events as well as the meaning that families attach to the
total family situation. The family's postcrisis/poststress perceptions involve
religious beliefs, redefining (reframing) the situation, and endowing the situation with meaning.

The "Double X" factor includes the original family crisis/stress response and subsequent adaptation. Family crisis/stress is at one end of the continuum of family adjustment over time, and family adaptation is the outcome at the other end of the continuum.

Boss (1988) cautions against the use of the term *adaptation* to refer to the optimal outcome of a stressful or crisis state. She contends that the family literature appears to assume that calm, serenity, orderliness, and stability are the desired ends for family life. Like Hoffman (1981), Boss maintains that systems naturally experience discontinuous change through the life cycle in the process of growth. If adaptation is valued over conflict and change, then families are limited to a perspective that promotes adjustment to the stressor event at the expense of individual or family change. Boss contends that sometimes dramatic change, including breaking family rules, changing boundaries, and revolution within the system, must occur for individual and family well-being. For example, an abused wife may need to leave or at least dramatically change her family system to achieve a sense of well-being for herself and perhaps for other family members. Boss prefers the use of the term *managing* to refer to the coping process that results from the family's reaction to stress or crisis.

Patterson (1988) has further revised the Double ABC-X Model to include the community system as well as the individual and family system. This complex form of analysis requires that the (a) stressors, (b) resources, and (c) meanings and definitions of the individual, family, and community systems, as well as their interactions, be considered. Patterson's extension of the Double ABC-X Model is consistent with biopsychosocial systems models that attempt to deal with the complex interplay and multiplicative interactions among biological, psychological, and social phenomena regarding health and illness (McDaniel, Hepworth, & Doherty, 1992). For example, research on domestic violence has noted the role of testosterone and alcohol use as it interacts with other variables in increasing the risk of men's abuse of a female intimate (Hillbrand & Pallone, 1994).

More recently, family scholars have begun to assess family stress outcomes from a family strengths perspective. On the basis of studies of children who thrive under adversity, family researchers have applied the concept of *resiliency* to family adaptation (Cowan et al., 1996; McCubbin et al., 1998). Resiliency refers to the coping strengths of those families that seem to benefit from the challenges of adversity; the ability to successfully deal with a stressor event actually results in outcomes as good as or better than those that would have been obtained in the absence of the adversity (Cicchetti & Garmezy, 1993; Rutter, 1987). These coping strengths are thought to be characteristics acquired through the repeated successful mastery of stressor events (Masten & Garmezy, 1985).

Conclusions

Families today are being challenged with numerous changes and problems that have the capacity to produce stress and crisis. After many years of focusing on individual stress responses, researchers have begun systematic assessments of whole-family responses. The major theoretical paradigm that has been used to study family responses to stressor events has been the social systems model. Developing from Hill's (1949) work on the effect of wartime separation, various characteristics of stressor events, as well as the moderating effects of perceptions and resources, have been studied, suggesting that there is nothing inherent in the event per se that is stressful or crisis producing.

More recently, family stress research has moved beyond the linear relationship of stressor, buffer/moderator, and response to look at coping and adaptation as processes that continue over time (i.e., how families actually manage stress and/or crisis). Coping is conceptualized as an ongoing process that facilitates family organization but also promotes individual growth. Increasingly, the outcome of interest is adaptation—that is, the ability of a family to make needed changes and ultimately recover from stress and crisis. However, adaptation, like coping, should not be perceived as a definitive end product because families are always growing and changing and the serenity and stability synonymous with adaptation are not always functional for family members. And for some families, the response to a stressor event may result in a higher level of functioning.

DISCUSSION QUESTIONS

1. Define family stress from both a positive and negative perspective. How would you distinguish between a positive and negative event?

2. What are some of the major stressors in your life? In your family life? How have these changed over the last few years?

3. How could the ABC-X Model be used to explain how your family dealt with a recent stressor event?

4. Review the debate about *adaptation* to, *managing,* and *coping* with stressor events. In your opinion, which is the best for families?

5. Using the Double ABC-X Model, how would you go about establishing an intervention strategy or strategies for families who have experienced a major natural disaster?

SUGGESTED READINGS

Boss, P. (1999). *Ambiguous loss.* Cambridge, MA: Harvard University Press.

Hill, R. (1949). *Families under stress.* Westport, CT: Greenwood.

Hill, R. (1999). *The strengths of African American families: Twenty-five years later.* New York: University Press of America.

McCubbin, H. I., Cauble, A. E., & Patterson, J. M. (1982). *Family stress, coping, and social support.* Springfield, IL: Charles C Thomas.

Olson, D. H., Russell, C. S., & Sprenkle, D. H. (1983). Circumplex Model of Marital and Family Systems: VI. Theoretical update. *Family Process, 22,* 69-83.

REFERENCES

Anderson, S. A., & Gavazzi, S. M. (1990). A test of the Olson Circumplex Model: Examining its curvilinear assumption and the presence of extreme types. *Family Process, 29,* 309-324.

Barnett, R. C. (1993). Multiple roles, gender, and psychological distress. In L. Goldberger & S. Breznitz (Eds.), *Handbook of stress: Theoretical and clinical aspects* (pp. 427-445). New York: Free Press.

Boss, P. G. (1988). *Family stress management.* Newbury Park, CA: Sage.

Buckley, W. (1967). *Sociology and modern systems theory.* Englewood Cliffs, NJ: Prentice Hall.

Burr, W. R. (1973). *Theory construction and the sociology of the family.* New York: John Wiley.

Burr, W. R. (1982). Families under stress. In H. I. McCubbin, A. E. Cauble, & J. M. Patterson (Eds.), *Family stress, coping, and social support* (pp. 5-25). Springfield, IL: Charles C Thomas.

Cannon, W. B. (1932). *The wisdom of the body.* New York: Norton.

Caplan, G. (1964). *Principles of preventive psychiatry.* New York: Basic Books.

Caplan, G. (1974). *Support systems and community mental health.* New York: Behavioral Publications.

Carter, B., & McGoldrick, M. (1989). Overview: The changing family life cycle: A framework for family therapy. In B. Carter & M. McGoldrick (Eds.), *The changing family life cycle: A framework for family therapy* (pp. 3-28). Boston: Allyn & Bacon.

Cherlin, A. J. (1996). *Public and private families.* New York: McGraw-Hill.

Cicchetti, D., & Garmezy, N. (1993). Prospects and promises in the study of resilience. *Developmental Psychopathology, 5,* 497-502.

Cobb, S. (1976). Social support as a moderator of life stress. *Psychosomatic Medicine, 38,* 300-314.

Coelho, G., Hamburg, D., & Adams, J. (1974). *Coping and adaptation.* New York: Basic Books.

Cowan, R. A., Cowan, C. P., & Schulz, M. S. (1996). Thinking about risk and resilience in families. In E. M. Hetherington & E. A. Blechman (Eds.), *Stress, coping, and resiliency in children and families* (pp. 1-38). Mahwah, NJ: Lawrence Erlbaum.

Derogatis, L. R., & Coons, H. L. (1993). Self-report measures of stress. In L. Goldberger & S. Breznitz (Eds.), *Handbook of stress: Theoretical and clinical aspects* (pp. 200-233). New York: Free Press.

Dohrenwend, B. S., & Dohrenwend, B. P. (1974). *Stressful life events: Their nature and effects.* New York: John Wiley.

Erikson, E. H. (1963). *Childhood and society.* New York: Norton.

Fisher, P. A., Fagot, B. I., & Leve, C. S. (1998). Assessment of family stress across low-, medium-, and high-risk samples using the Family Events Checklist. *Family Relations, 47,* 215-219.

Frankenhaeuser, M. (1994). A biopsychosocial approach to stress in women and men. In V. J. Adesso, D. M. Reddy, & R. Fleming (Eds.), *Psychological perspectives on women's health* (pp. 39-56). Philadelphia: Taylor & Francis.

Gore, S., & Colten, M. E. (1991). Gender, stress, and distress: Social-relational influences. In J. Eckenrode (Ed.), *The social context of coping.* New York: Plenum.

Gruen, R. J. (1993). Stress and depression: Toward the development of integrative models. In L. Goldberger & S. Breznitz (Eds.), *Handbook of stress: Theoretical and clinical aspects* (pp. 550-569). New York: Free Press.

Hall, A. D., & Fagan, R. E. (1968). Definition of system. In W. Buckley (Ed.), *Modern systems research for the behavioral scientist* (pp. 81-92). Chicago: Aldine.

Hansen, D. A. (1965). Personal and positional influence in formal groups: Propositions and theory for research on family vulnerability to stress. *Social Forces, 44,* 202-210.

Hansen, D. A., & Hill, R. (1964). Families under stress. In H. Christensen (Ed.), *Handbook of marriage and the family* (pp. 215-295). Chicago: Rand McNally.

Hill, R. (1949). *Families under stress.* Westport, CT: Greenwood.

Hill, R. (1999). *The strengths of African American families: Twenty-five years later.* New York: University Press of America.

Hillbrand, M., & Pallone, N. J. (1994). *The psychobiology of aggression: Engines, measurement, control.* New York: Haworth.

Hoffman, L. (1981). *Foundation of family therapy: A conceptual framework for systemic change.* New York: Basic Books.

Holmes, T. H., & Rahe, R. H. (1967). The social readjustment rating scale. *Journal of Psychosomatic Research, 11,* 213-218.

Lazarus, R. (1966). *Psychological stress and the coping process.* New York: McGraw-Hill.

Lazarus, R. (1976). *Patterns of adjustment.* New York: McGraw-Hill.

Lazarus, R. S., & Folkman, S. (1984). *Stress, appraisal, and coping.* New York: Springer.

Lazarus, R. S., & Launier, R. (1978). Stress-related transactions between person and environment. In L. A. Pervin & M. Lewis (Eds.), *Perspectives in interactional psychology* (pp. 360-392). New York: Plenum.

Lipman-Blumen, J. (1975). A crisis framework applied to macrosociological family changes: Marriage, divorce, and occupational trends associated with World War II. *Journal of Marriage and the Family, 27,* 889-902.

Lovallo, W. R. (1997). *Stress and health: Biological and psychological interaction.* Thousand Oaks, CA: Sage.

Masten, A. S., & Garmezy, N. (1985). Risk, vulnerability, and protective factors in developmental psychopathology. In B. B. Lahey & A. E. Kazdin (Eds.), *Advances in clinical child psychology* (Vol. 8, pp. 1-52). New York: Plenum.

May, R. (1950). *The meaning of anxiety.* New York: Ronald.

McCubbin, H. I. (1979). Integrating coping behavior in family stress theory. *Journal of Marriage and the Family, 41,* 237-244.

McCubbin, H. I., Cauble, A. E., & Patterson, J. M. (1982). *Family stress, coping, and social support.* Springfield, IL: Charles C Thomas.

McCubbin, H. I., Futrell, J. A., Thompson, E. A., & Thompson, A. I. (1998). Resilient families in an ethnic and cultural context. In H. I. McCubbin, E. A. Thompson, A. I. Thompson, & J. A. Futrell (Eds.), *Resiliency in African-American families* (pp. 329-351). Thousand Oaks, CA: Sage.

McCubbin, H. I., Joy, C. B., Cauble, A. E., Comeau, J. K., Patterson, J. M., & Needle, R. H. (1980). Family stress and coping: A decade review. *Journal of Marriage and the Family, 42,* 125-141.

McCubbin, H. I., & Patterson, J. M. (1982). Family adaptation to crisis. In H. I. McCubbin, A. E. Cauble, & J. M. Patterson (Eds.), *Family stress, coping, and social support* (pp. 26-47). Springfield, IL: Charles C Thomas.

McCubbin, H. I., & Patterson, J. M. (1985). Adolescent stress, coping, and adaptation: A normative family perspective. In G. K. Leigh & G. W. Peterson (Eds.), *Adolescents in families* (pp. 256-276). Cincinnati, OH: Southwestern.

McCubbin, H. I., Patterson, J. M., & Wilson, L. (1981). *Family Inventory of Life Events and Changes (FILE): Research instrument.* St. Paul: University of Minnesota, Family Social Science.

McDaniel, S. H., Hepworth, J., & Doherty, W. J. (1992). *Medical family therapy: A biopsychosocial approach to families with health problems.* New York: Basic Books.

Moos, R. H. (1976). *Human adaptation: Coping with life crisis.* Lexington, MA: D. C. Heath.

Moos, R. H. (1986). *Coping with life crises: An integrated approach.* New York: Plenum.

Naisbitt, J., & Aburdene, P. (1990). *Megatrends 2000: Ten new directions for the 1990s.* New York: William Morrow.

Olson, D. H., Russell, C. S., & Sprenkle, D. H. (1979). Circumplex Model of Marital and Family Systems cohesion and adaptability dimensions, family types, and clinical applications. *Family Process, 18,* 3-28.

Olson, D. H., Russell, C. S., & Sprenkle, D. H. (1980). Marital and family therapy: A decade review. *Journal of Marriage and the Family, 42,* 239-260.

Olson, D. H., Russell, C. S., & Sprenkle, D. H. (1983). Circumplex Model of Marital and Family Systems: VI. Theoretical update. *Family Process, 22,* 69-83.

Patterson, J. M. (1988). Families experiencing stress. *Family Systems Medicine, 6,* 202-237.

Pearlin, L. (1991). The study of coping: An overview of problems and directions. In J. Eckenrode (Ed.), *The social context of coping* (pp. 261-276). New York: Plenum.

Pearlin, L., & Schooler, C. (1978). The structure of coping. *Journal of Health and Social Behavior, 19,* 2-21.

Price, S. J., McKenry, P. C., & Murphy, M. (2000). *Families across time: A life course perspective.* Los Angeles: Roxbury.

Rees, H., & Smyer, M. (1983). The dimensionalization of life events. In E. Callahan & K. McCluskey (Eds.), *Life-span developmental psychology: Non-normative life events* (pp. 328-359). New York: Academic Press.

Roskies, E., & Lazarus, R. (1980). Coping theory and the teaching of coping skills. In D. Davidson & S. Davidson (Eds.), *Behavioral medicine: Changing health lifestyles* (pp. 38-69). New York: Brunner/Mazel.

Rutter, M. (1983). Stress, coping, and development: Some issues and questions. In N. Garmezy & M. Rutter (Eds.), *Stress, coping, and development* (pp. 1-41). New York: McGraw-Hill.

Rutter, M. (1987). Psychosocial resilience and protective mechanisms. *American Journal of Orthopsychiatry, 57,* 316-331.

Sarafino, E. P. (1990). *Health psychology: Biopsychosocial interactions.* New York: John Wiley.

Sarason, L., Johnson, J., & Siegel, J. (1978). Assessing the impact of life changes: Development of the life experiences survey. *Journal of Consulting and Clinical Psychology, 64,* 932-946.

Selye, H. (1978). *The stress of life.* New York: McGraw-Hill.

Settles, B. H. (1999). The future of families. In M. B. Sussman, S. K. Steinmetz, & G. W. Peterson (Eds.), *Handbook of marriage and the family* (pp. 143-175). New York: Plenum.

Spence, K. W. (1956). *Behavior therapy and conditioning.* New Haven, CT: Yale University Press.

Teachman, J. D., Polonko, K. A., & Scanzoni, J. (1999). Demography and families. In M. B. Sussman, S. K. Steinmetz, & G. W. Peterson (Eds.), *Handbook of marriage and the family* (pp. 39-76). New York: Plenum.

Thoits, P. A. (1991). On merging identity theory and stress research. *Social Psychology Quarterly, 54,* 101-112.

2

Marital Distress

From Complaints to Contempt

RONALD M. SABATELLI
JEANNE JOSEPH CHADWICK

According to a Spanish philosopher, "In human topography, no land is less explored than love" (Ortega y Gasset, 1957, p. 3). Individuals who enter into a lifetime partnership with another are in a metaphorical sense embarking on a journey through time. Couples start a lifetime journey firm in the conviction that their particular relationship is special. They believe that, because they have found the "right" person and are intensely in love, their relationship will be intimate and exclusive. And, while most couples probably expect that their lifetime journey will involve obstacles, they also expect their special relationship to endure the test of time.

However, the reality of many contemporary "marriage-like" relationships clearly paints a picture of distressed relationships dominated by the erosion of satisfaction, commitment, and stability. In this chapter, we explore the factors that contribute to the deconstruction of these special marriage-like relationships. We explore how couples fail to navigate the ordinary difficulties confronting lifetime partnerships to the point that they wind up believing that their formerly special relationship can no longer be salvaged. In other words, we explore the journey many couples make from intimacy and hope to hostility and despair.

Marital Distress Defined

Marriage-like relationships are metaphorically referred to throughout this chapter as special relationships—relationships dominated by the expectation that they will be intimate, exclusive, and enduring. The main objective of this chapter is to provide insight into the factors that contribute to the deconstruction of these special relationships—factors that lead to a buildup of distress within the relationship.

To accomplish this objective, we need to be clear about what we believe to be the defining features of the concept of "marital distress." Within this chapter, we use the term *distress* to mean those situations in which *one or both members of a marriage-like relationship have come to believe that their relationship suffers from serious problems of a long-standing nature that threaten the stability of the relationship.* While it is common for us to speak of distressed relationships, the term *distress,* as it is being used in this chapter, refers to an individual's experiences of and beliefs about his or her lifetime partnership. Extremes of distress are built on a legacy of unhappiness and dissatisfaction resulting from the mismanagement of the ordinary difficulties encountered by couples within lifetime partnerships. Distress, therefore, can be thought of as resulting from (a) a high level of complaints that lead to conflicts and (b) the inability to manage these conflicts in a way that promotes a sense of cohesion and ongoing intimacy within the relationship.

In other words, we believe that distress needs to be differentiated from relationship complaints and conflicts. We think of complaints and conflicts as the ordinary difficulties that need to be managed in all ongoing intimate relationships. While not meaning to minimize their significance, the presence of complaints and the presence of conflict do not necessarily mean that individuals are dissatisfied with their relationships. As long as complaints and conflicts are reasonably managed, these ordinary difficulties do not necessarily pose a major problem for a lifetime partnership. Distress is differentiated from complaints and from conflict in that it exists only when there is an ongoing history of complaints, a legacy of the mismanagement of conflicts, *and* the belief that the lifetime partnership is, in fact, dominated by problems that threaten the relationship's survival.

Current Trends

With this definition of distress in mind, is it possible for us to talk in a meaningful way about marital trends and how they relate to marital distress?

Without a doubt, divorce rates are high today, and they have risen considerably since the end of World War II. These high divorce rates may be used to support the conclusion that marriages may be worse off today than at any point in their history. Divorce rates alone, however, do not provide sufficient insight into the quality of contemporary marriages compared with those in the past. It is possible that divorce is more common today because distressed married couples have access to better alternatives than they did in the past, and because the costs of terminating a distressed marriage are fewer today than in the past. This is to suggest that, in the past, family and society dictated the reason people married (and divorced) more so than today. As such, in the past, marriage was designed to meet the needs or expectations of family and society, and the quality of the personal relationship between husband and wife was of secondary importance. Consequently, if a couple was distressed, community pressure would hold the marriage together; that is, contextual factors (the economy, cultural value orientations, family pressures, gender prescriptions, etc.) would combine to keep many couples together by making the psychological and social costs of terminating a distressed marriage untenable.

Today, the context of marriage has changed, perhaps making it easier than in the past to risk the costs of terminating an unhappy relationship. It could be argued that contemporary couples are increasingly removed from the community of extended family and widely shared values, and, as a result, there are fewer external reasons for a man and woman to spend their life together. The cultural environment that protected relationships in the past is today a global economy that uses information technology to create new options with rapid speed. Furthermore, women are taking advantage of these new options to become more and more self-reliant. As a result, women have more economic and lifestyle alternatives to marriage today than at any other time in recent history. Thus, they may be less likely to tolerate an unsatisfactory marital situation.

In addition, there is a nostalgic view of the past that possibly distorts the quality of marriage and family life in the past. Perhaps it makes us feel better, though we are not sure why, to say that relationships were better in the past. William Lederer and Don Jackson (1968), in *The Mirages of Marriage,* a profoundly original look at marital relationships in the 1960s, had this to say about the quality of relationships in the past:

> More often than spouses care to admit, marriage results in years of dislike and mutual destruction—rather than love and mutual growth. In interviews with hundreds of average marital pairs we learned that approximately 80 percent of the couples

had seriously considered divorce at one time or another, and many of them still think about it frequently. Often, only the existence of children, the restrictions of poverty, the edicts of religion, or a lack of courage blocks the decision to get divorced. (pp. 15-16)

In other words, the marriage process in the United States has been ailing for some time. Marriages in the past were perhaps as likely as marriages today to have a core of couples who would wish, if they could wave a magic wand and do it all over again, that they could marry someone else or choose not to marry (Lederer & Jackson, 1968). Our best guess at present is that contemporary couples are no more distressed with their lifetime partnerships than couples in the past were. What, no doubt, has changed, however, is the willingness or ability of contemporary couples to terminate these unhappy relationships.

The Epidemiology of Marital Distress

Why, then, be concerned about marital distress? Whether or not the rates of divorce reveal anything about the rates of marital distress, there are compelling reasons to be concerned about the impact that distress has on family members' physical and psychological well-being. Distressed married individuals who experience chronic sadness, pessimism, unremitting tension, hostility, or suspiciousness were found to have "double" the risk of disease—including asthma, arthritis, headaches, peptic ulcers, and heart disease. This has led some public health researchers to conclude that chronic marital distress is a more serious public health risk than smoking (Goleman, 1995).

There is also compelling evidence to suggest that marital distress and ongoing unresolved marital conflicts are associated with a wide range of deleterious effects on children (Cummings & Davies, 1994). These include depression, withdrawal, poor social competence, health problems, poor academic performance, and a variety of conduct-related difficulties (Cowan & Cowan, 1990). There is also evidence indicating that children of both genders who come from homes where the parents are unhappily married have greater quantities of stress-related hormones and greater physiological reactivity when expressing their own emotions (Gottman, Katz, & Hooven, 1997).

The Foundation of Distress:
A Focus on Relationship Complaints

At the heart of marital distress is the mismanagement of the ordinary difficulties confronting all couples in lifetime partnerships. Distress results when these ordinary difficulties consistently are mismanaged. This means that, to develop an understanding of the circumstances that fuel the experience of distress in lifetime relationships, we must develop an awareness of what couples complain about.

There are several "marital hot spots" or common issues that become the focus of complaints within lifetime partnerships. These include complaints about housework, child care, free time (how much and whether it is spent alone or together), how money is spent, sexual energy, and the need for intimacy versus independence (Hochschild, 1994; Tannen, 1990). Although knowing what couples commonly complain about is important, it should be clear that tremendous variability exists with respect to what individuals within a specific relationship might complain about. Furthermore, complaints differ in the impact they have on the overall experience of a relationship. Some complaints, even chronic ones, are not a source of distress within a relationship, whereas others are central to the experience of relationship distress.

For these reasons, we believe it is important to develop a theoretical understanding of the concept of complaints and the relationship between complaints and distress. We need to know (a) when and under what circumstances individuals are apt to complain about their partners and (b) why some complaints affect the overarching experience of the relationship more so than others. Finally, we need to develop a feel for why complaints generate the kinds of emotional reactions that they do within relationships. To accomplish these objectives, we turn our attention to the insights that the social exchange and symbolic interaction frameworks provide into how complaints originate and contribute to the potential undoing of a lifetime partnership.

A Social Exchange Perspective on
Relationship Complaints

The basic tenets of exchange theory suggest that people choose to participate in a particular relationship because of the relationship's ability to provide a satisfactory level of rewards or outcomes (Nye, 1979; Sabatelli, 1984, 1988; Sabatelli & Shehan, 1993; Thibaut & Kelley, 1959). Within this perspective, outcomes are defined as the rewards derived from the relationship minus the costs of participating in the relationship. The level of outcomes perceived to be available from a relationship is based primarily on a person's perception of his or her partner's attributes (e.g., sense of humor, physical appearance, etc.) and on the perception of the quality of the interaction between the partners (e.g., the affection expressed, the equity found in the relationship, etc.). Individuals are thought to be attracted to a particular relationship when the outcomes associated with a particular partner and relationship are sufficiently high and greater than those in competing alternatives.

According to the exchange framework, partners continuously evaluate their relationships by comparing their experiences to their expectations. These expectations are thought to constitute each participant's comparison level (CL) (Nye, 1979; Sabatelli, 1984; Thibaut & Kelley, 1959)—that is, the expectations for outcomes that a person feels are realistically obtainable from a relationship. When the outcomes available in a relationship tend to consistently fall above what is felt to be realistically obtainable, individuals are apt to be satisfied with their relationships. Conversely, when outcomes tend to fall consistently below this baseline of expectations, individuals then are likely to complain about that aspect of the relationship.

Complaints, therefore, occur within a relationship when individuals experience some aspect of their relationship as failing to measure up to what they feel is realistically obtainable and deserved (Sabatelli, 1984, 1988). For example, individuals complain about how often sexual relations occur only when the frequency consistently falls below some subjectively and individually constructed expectation level—whether this is once a night, once a week, or once a month.

Consequently, we need to view expectations as being shaped by a broad array of contextual factors, including both macro- and microlevel forces. As a result, there is considerable variability in terms of what people come to realistically expect and feel is deserving within an intimate, ongoing relationship. It thus becomes virtually impossible to predict with any degree of certainty what will generate complaints within a particular relationship, because complaints revolve around the subjectively held and individually constructed expectations of each partner within the relationship.

To further add to this complexity, exchange perspectives highlight the fact that individuals will differ with respect to the salience they attribute to different aspects of their relationships (Nye, 1979; Sabatelli & Shehan, 1993; Thibaut & Kelley, 1959). One individual might attribute a great deal of significance to whether his or her partner participates in household work. Another individual might attribute greater significance to the quality and frequency of sex. This means that not all complaints are equal in terms of the impact that they have on a relationship.

In addition, the exchange perspective highlights the fact that expectations are not fixed—they can and will change over the course of a relationship. Thibaut and Kelley (1959) suggest that when individuals change their investment in a relationship, they tend to expect more out of the relationship. This means that, over time, it is possible that partners' relationship expectations might "fluctuate upwards" when they perceive themselves to be investing more. This change in investments and the accompanying change in expectations can result in "new" complaints about the partner because patterns of behavior that were acceptable in the past now fail to measure up to these new, emergent expectations.

For example, when a wife becomes a mother, she may feel as if she is investing more in her family and marriage than she had in the past. As a result, she might expect her husband to do more housework than he has done in the past. This shifting of expectations can result in the wife having more complaints about what the husband does around the house, even though what he is doing was acceptable in the past.

In sum, the exchange framework provides several important insights into the concept of relationship complaints. First, complaints are conceived of as resulting when an aspect of a relationship fails to measure up to the expectations of a partner. To understand complaints, you have to examine the expectations of the person complaining. Second, it is important to understand that each individual has a unique point of comparison that is used to judge the qualities of the partner and the relationship. Because each of us has a different developmental history (including a history of relationships within and outside of the family), there is bound to be considerable variation among people regarding what is thought to be realistically obtainable from a relationship.

Third, the exchange perspective calls attention to the fact that not only do people differ in terms of what they feel is realistically expected from relationships, they differ in terms of the salience that they attribute to different aspects of the relationship. This means that it is possible for some individuals to have a lot of complaints about their relationship and still be relatively satisfied with the relationship if the complaints involve less salient issues. Conversely, complaints involving only one issue deemed of great importance can possibly flood the relationship with an overwhelming degree of negativity and conflict.

Last, the exchange perspective calls attention to the changing and fluid nature of expectations within relationships. When individuals shift expectations, they often expect their partners to shift their behaviors accordingly.

These shifts, however, require partners to negotiate new patterns of relating—negotiations that are apt to take time. This means that even the most reasonable shifts in expectations are likely to be accompanied by periods of heightened conflict and stress within an ongoing relationship.

Managing Complaints:
From Negotiations to Conflict

Not all complaints necessarily generate conflict. Complaints force couples to enter into a process of "negotiation" that involves, in essence, a discussion of the legitimacy of one partner's expectations and the other partner's behaviors (Sabatelli, 1988; Scanzoni, 1979). The "complaining partner" wades into this negotiation typically by calling attention to the manner in which the "offending partner" is acting inappropriately (i.e., the offending partner's behaviors are not consistent with the complaining partner's expectations). If the offending partner views the offense he or she is being accused of as being genuine and legitimate, then the negotiation process is a rather simple one. Not all complaints, in other words, involve protracted negotiations. When complaints are viewed as legitimate, the offending partner simply makes an efort to shift his or her behaviors to pull them in line with the partner's expectations.

For example, a wife who is balancing a career and parenthood might complain to her partner that he does not do enough housework. She justifies this complaint by calling attention to all the demands that are on her both at home and at work and by documenting how the work he does around the house does not measure up to the work that she is required to do. Implicit in her discussion of his behavior is the fact that she views his behaviors as failing to conform to what she expects is a reasonable amount of housework on his part. Although this complaint generates tension in their relationship, if her partner acknowledges the legitimacy of her complaint and makes an effort to adjust his behaviors to conform to her expectations, the basis for the complaint is neutralized, and harmony is restored in the relationship.

The so-called offending partner, however, may not concur with the complaining partner's construction of reality. An offending partner might view the partner's assessment of his or her behavior as being incorrect. Or an offending partner might view the partner's expectations as being unrealistic. When either of these occurs, the negotiations surrounding such complaints become more complex. Both partners hold to the view that their partner's construction of the reality of the relationship is distorted and wrong. Each partner stakes a claim for the legitimacy of his or her respective position (Gottman, 1994).

Simple negotiations, in other words, can turn ugly. They turn ugly when emotional reactivity and negativity dominate the "negotiation sessions." To this end, we feel it is important to develop an understanding of why some negotiations become dominated by emotional reactivity and negativity. Therefore, we turn our attention to the contribution that symbolic interaction perspectives make to our understanding of how emotion enters into the process of managing ordinary complaints.

Symbolic Interactionism and the Emotions Accompanying Complaints

Like the social exchange perspectives, symbolic interactionist (SI) perspectives focus on the relationship between expectations and the generation of complaints (Burr, Leigh, Day, & Constantine, 1979). Individuals in an intimate partnership occupy reciprocal and interdependent roles. Individuals carry into their relationships constructions of how they should enact their roles as partners. Because of the reciprocal nature of roles, each individual's construction of his or her role imposes a set of expectations on the individual who occupies the "counterrole" position as well (LaRossa & Reitzes, 1993). For example, if a wife believes that she should be responsible for only half of the housework, her construction of her role carries with it implications that her husband should be willing to be responsible for half of the housework.

But why do these complaints generate as much emotion as they do? We believe that the SI tradition provides an answer to this question by calling attention to the interdependent nature of role constructions and identity (see Stryker, 1968; Stryker & Serpe, 1982, 1994). Embedded within individuals' constructions of their roles are "statements" about how they see themselves and how they see their partner. This means that when a partner violates our role expectations, we can potentially feel as if our identity in some way has been discounted. A husband's failure to do his share of the housework, for example, discounts the part of his partner's identity that is invested in the view that she should do only half of the housework. If the role expectation that the partner violates is particularly salient or central to the identity of the individual, it would be expected that the felt injustice and sense of being discounted would be all the more extreme (Stryker, 1968).

Of course, not all complaints are so connected to our sense of self. Only certain role constructions are more central to our view of self than others.

This is why some issues are much more volatile within relationships than others. Those issues that evoke the greatest degree of emotional reactivity are those that are tied to our views of ourselves as individuals and partners. And it is these "identity-driven" negotiations that are most apt to turn ugly.

For example, my partner's "messiness" does not discount my sense of self as long as I do not take this violation of my expectations as a statement that my partner is making about me as a person. I might complain periodically about the messiness, but the messiness does not necessarily detract from my overall feelings of satisfaction with my partner and our relationship. If, however, I interpret this messiness to mean that my partner views me as "a second-class citizen whose only purpose in life is to pick up after him or her," then this violation of expectations generates considerably more emotional reactivity and interpersonal tension.

It is also interesting to note how complaints directed at the offending partner can disrupt his or her identity. For example, when a wife complains to her husband that he does not do enough housework, if this complaint discounts his view of himself as a caring and responsible spouse, and these identities are central to his view of himself, then he is likely to feel hurt and defensive in response to the complaint. Here again, the more the complaint is directed to aspects of role performance that are central to our core identity, the more we are likely to emotionally react to the complaint. Furthermore, the more the complaint is expressed as a criticism of us personally, which strikes at our image of ourselves and discounts our sense of self, the more likely simple complaints are to generate interpersonal tensions (Gottman, 1994).

It is, thus, possible to imagine situations arising in relationships in which complaints and counter-complaints occur that are accompanied by heightened degrees of emotional reactivity, increased negativity, and interpersonal tensions. These responses are understandable as long as we hold the view that the negotiation of some complaints revolves around each partner's constructions of the reality of the relationship *and* each partner's personal constructions of him- or herself as a person. Most of us find it difficult to legitimize our partner's behaviors that violate our expectations or to legitimize our partner's complaints about our behaviors if in the process we feel as if we are discounting our own identity. Our need to have our identity confirmed by our partner gets in the way of our abilities to negotiate our differences. Under these circumstances, the negotiation process breaks down into cascading patterns of negativity (Gottman, 1994) that undermine intimacy and heighten the experience of distress.

At the same time, it is important to emphasize that the negotiation of identity-driven complaints does not always result in a cascade of negativity

(Gottman, 1994). To this end, in the following section, we turn our attention to what the research literature tells us about the couples who effectively and ineffectively manage their personal "marital hot spots."

Conflict Management and the Deconstruction of Intimacy

Over the past two decades, a number of researchers have focused on issues related to the management of tensions in close personal relationships. Although there is no single coherent theory of marital distress that emerges from this research tradition, there seems to be some consensus that "distress" is assumed to be a function of couple interaction patterns. Inevitably, couples have conflicting needs and expectations. Distress results from couples' aversive and ineffectual responses to conflict (Koerner & Jacobson, 1994).

In our view, by far and away the most influential researchers represented by this research tradition are John Gottman and his colleagues (see Gottman, 1994; Gottman, Coan, Carrere, & Swanson, 1998; Gottman & Levenson, 1999a, 1999b). The main body of these empirical works explores the notion that there are styles of conflict management that differentiate distressed from nondistressed couples. Gottman's research identifies two types of marriages: nonregulated and regulated (Gottman, 1994). In nonregulated marriages, couples have a difficult time rebounding from disagreements and complaints. Ordinary difficulties tend to be managed in ways that build negativity and distress into the relationship. Regulated couples, in contrast, are better able to manage tensions in ways that promote closeness. This is to suggest that although there are disagreements (and often considerable disagreements), the processes and styles of interacting within the relationship manage to support the experience of intimacy.

Nonregulated Couples: Cascading Negativity and Marital Distress

The patterns of interaction within the nonregulated couples are characterized by processes that escalate tension and fuel distress. In addition, the general overall patterns of interaction found within the nonregulated couples are characterized by a low ratio of positive to negative interactions.

Within the nonregulated couples, four negativity processes, labeled the "four horsemen of the apocalypse" by Gottman, characterize the management of conflict. These include patterns of interaction characterized by criticisms, defensiveness, contempt, and withdrawal or stonewalling. According to Gottman, negativity and distancing often begin when complaints are expressed or viewed by partners as criticisms. These critical attacks, then, if not kept in check, lead to defensive patterns of interaction that erode the foundation of mutual respect within the relationship and replace it with a foundation of mutual contempt. High levels of contempt, then, increase the likelihood that partners will withdraw from one another.

Thus, in Gottman's work, criticisms form the foundation of marital distress. Distressed couples tend to have complaints that wind up being expressed or experienced as criticisms and can be thought of as complaints that turn personal. What apparently differentiates couples who manage conflict constructively from those who do not is the ability to minimize the degree to which discussions of violated expectations are directed at the core aspects of the partner's identity rather than at the lack of fit between expectations and behaviors. Nonregulated couples criticize their partners. These criticisms are directed at the partner's construction of him- or herself. Instead of saying "I am unhappy when you leave your clothes on the floor when you get home from work," nonregulated patterns of interaction involve statements that cut to the core of the partner's identity. The "complaining partner" personally attacks the other partner, saying things such as "You are so inconsiderate of me" or "You are such a slob." It is these identity-disrupting attacks that evoke emotionally reactive responses resulting in defensiveness, contempt, and, possibly, withdrawal.

In other words, criticisms and the defensive reactions and counter-criticisms that they evoke set in motion the cascade of negativity found within Gottman's nonregulated couples. These patterns of interaction are characterized by high levels of emotional reactivity because what is being discussed is each partner's construction of him- or herself. That is, we are more likely to criticize our partners when their behaviors disrupt our sense of who we are. Our criticisms, however, are directed at our partners' constructions of themselves, which then results in their getting defensive and countering our criticisms by being critical of us. Consequently, in a recursive way, criticism and defensiveness build on one another as patterns of interaction become increasingly more personal, attacking, and identity disrupting.

Furthermore, the work of Gottman and his colleagues makes it clear that when a certain threshold of negativity is reached, negativity becomes pervasive and affects the way couples view their partners and relationships. This reconstruction of the reality of the partner and the relationship begins when the negativity associated with the management of conflicts results in the development of contempt rather than positive regard for the partner. This evolving contempt for the partner represents an important turning point in the deconstruction of the relationship. Most of us can put up with our partners complaining about us to a certain degree. When these complaints cannot be negotiated and when the negotiations get personal, we begin to shift our views of our partners and the future of our relationships. We come to change the attributions that we make of our partners and of our relationships (Fincham & Bradbury, 1989). We increasingly focus on those aspects of our partner that bother us. That is, we view them as unreasonable and inflexible. This evolving contempt for the partner is of course directed at the core of the partner's identity. As this unfolds, it becomes increasingly more difficult for partners to believe that there is hope for the relationship.

A significant turning point in the relationship occurs when the first wave of negativity escalates to a more destructive level. This second wave of negativity overwhelms the relationship as cognitions about the relationship are coupled with negative, contemptuous thoughts of the partner and negative views of the future of the relationship. Distancing behaviors become the norm. In the final analysis, it is during these cascades of negativity and distancing that ultimately the relationship is deconstructed as an intimate relationship and reconstructed as one dominated by distress. Here is when individuals come to believe, consistent with our definition of marital distress, that the relationship is dominated by problems that cannot be resolved.

It is also at this point that Gottman (1994) finds that couples begin to revise the history of their relationship. Not only do distressed couples believe that their relationship does not have a future, but they also engage in a process of selectively attending to only negative aspects of the history of their relationship. In short, distressed couples recast the marital history in negative terms. They are unable to remember when the relationship was good. They recall only the times when their partners disappointed them. This reconstruction of the future and revision of the past increase the distinct possibility that couples will then be locked into patterns that ensure that they will experience years of dislike and mutual destruction rather than years of love and mutual growth.

Regulated Couples: Conflict and Happiness

Gottman's research makes it clear that more adaptive couples are not necessarily those with fewer complaints. Couples within "regulated relationships" have complaints and often do not deal with their complaints in ways that many professional therapists and family life educators would suggest are constructive. Gottman identifies three styles of marriage that fit into the regulated type: the *validating couple,* the *volatile couple,* and the *conflict-*

minimizing couple. These styles are based on the couple's predominant style of managing conflict (Gottman, 1994).

The *validating couple* style is generally the style that most professionals would agree represents a constructive style of conflict management. Within these couples, there is a low level of negative expressed emotion. These couples tend to listen respectively to one another and validate their partner's feelings. They tend to use metacommunication and feeling probes to take the emotional temperature of their partner (Gottman, 1994). And, while not necessarily passionate, validating couples are in fact quite happy with their life together and demonstrate a great deal of support and empathy for one another.

The *volatile couple* is characterized by intense emotion. They confront each other and argue persuasively in their efforts to get the "offending partner" to comply with the "complaining partner's" point of view. According to Gottman, high levels of passion, romance, and satisfaction characterize this volatile group. In a sense, these couples are passionate about their relationship, and this passion spills over into their conflicts. And despite the fact that they often have bitter disputes characterized by attacks, counterattacks, and fits of rage, they manage to maintain a sense of connection and genuine intimacy.

The *conflict-minimizing couple* tends to minimize or avoid conflict. They live with the pain of unsolved yet solvable problems. These are couples who, in Gottman's view, lack the skills necessary to work through conflict. Although their style of managing conflict may not be ideal, they still manage to avoid having their relationships dominated by pervasive levels of negativity and distancing. Hence, they can sustain a sense of cohesion and intimacy.

So the question arises, since there are couples who maintain high levels of satisfaction and yet do not typically manage conflicts in ways we would call constructive, why do we insist that it is the mismanagement of conflict that is the key to understanding marital distress? The answer to this question requires a consideration of the dynamic relationship between levels of conflict, the management of conflict, and the broader ecology of the lifetime partnership.

The Ecology of Lifetime Partnerships

Gottman's research suggests that successful couples are able to sustain a sense of intimacy and vitality even when conflicts are not managed in ways that experts think of as being effective. As a way of accounting for this,

Gottman (1994; Gottman & Levenson, 1999a, 1999b) explored the broader ecological niches of successful and distressed couples. He found that successful couples, compared with distressed couples, maintained a higher proportion of positive to negative interactions. He also found that successful couples, much more so than distressed couples, tended to have compatible styles of conflict resolution.

The Ratio of Positive to Negative Interactions

Gottman's research indicates that satisfied couples, no matter how their marriages stacked up against the ideal, were those who maintained a 5-to-1 ratio of positive to negative moments. Put another way, maintaining an appropriate ecological balance between positive and negative interactions enables relationships to overcome those occasional moments when the destructive forces of inappropriate conflict management threaten the overall health of the system.

It might be tempting to interpret this finding as meaning that the management of conflict is not related to the overall experience of distress. This would be misleading, in our view, because the ratio of positive to negative interactions clearly is influenced by the sheer amount of conflict that a couple has to manage and by how these conflicts are managed over the life course of the relationship. That is, if, over time, a sufficient proportion of the conflicts that inevitably occur within relationships are successfully negotiated, couples are apt to maintain a marital ecology dominated by a relatively high proportion of positive to negative interactions. Relationships turn ugly when conflicts, particularly identity-driven conflicts, are systematically mismanaged over time (i.e., over time, the proportion of negative to positive interactions escalates proportionately). Successful couples manage enough of these critical conflicts over the life course of their relationship, even if they do not always do this perfectly. In the process, they maintain a relationship ecology characterized by a sufficiently high ratio of positive to negative interactions.

Compatible Styles of Fighting

A second way in which the ecology of happy couples differs from the ecology of distressed couples has to do with the fit between or compatibility of their styles of fighting. Simply stated, successful couples have matching styles of fighting. They agree on the ways in which they will disagree with one another. In contrast, couples who fail to maintain a sufficiently high ratio of positive to negative interactions tend to have different styles of fighting.

One partner pursues, for example, while the other distances. One partner needs to "process" feelings and probe solutions; the other finds it difficult to talk about such issues.

Mismatched patterns of fighting are more likely than matched patterns to result in individuals feeling as though their identities and the importance of their relationships have been discounted by their partners' ways of dealing with complaints. An active effort to engage a partner who is prone to avoid conflict situations is obviously a source of frustration. But what fuels this frustration is the fact that the mismatch or lack of fit in styles results in individuals feeling as if they and their relationship are not respected or valued by their partners. For example, as I chase after you and try to engage you in a discussion of my complaints, I feel discounted by your distancing yourself from me. Furthermore, as I yell at you and you withdraw, I feel as if you do not value our relationship. You, in turn, feel discounted by my complaining about you and by my unwillingness to respect how you want to deal with our conflicts. You, too, feel as if I do not value our relationship (if I did, why would I insist on fighting?).

Gender, Conversational Styles, and the Management of Conflict

The discussion of compatibility in conflict-management styles and its relationship to distress calls our attention to the research that focuses on gender differences in the management of conflict. If it is the case that men and women generally differ in terms of how they manage conflict, then this gender-driven incompatibility must be examined in relation to overall satisfaction and distress levels noted in relationships.

This discussion of gender differences in conflict-management styles (see Gottman, 1994; Markman, Stanley, & Blumberg, 1994) and conversational styles (Tannen, 1986, 1990) is based on an analysis of the modal patterns of interaction and communication found within populations of men and women. As a result of this focus on central tendencies, we tend to talk as if all men communicate in certain ways and all women communicate in different ways. We want to caution against making the erroneous conclusion that all men differ from all women in terms of how they communicate.

We balance these concerns, however, against the "weight of the evidence" that suggests that there are, indeed, important differences in the conflict-management and conversational styles of men and women that affect the structure and experience of close personal relationships. Men and women often differ in terms of how they express intimacy and when dealing with conflicts often employ different strategies for the management of interpersonal tensions (Gottman, 1994; Markman et al., 1994). Because these stylistic differences often contribute to the escalation of tensions between men and women in lifetime partnerships, a discussion of the factors contributing to marital distress would be incomplete without some attention to gender issues.

Research suggests that men and women differ in terms of how they define intimacy and in terms of the critical indicators of it (see Bem, 1993; Markman et al., 1994; Tannen, 1990). Specifically, there is a tendency for women to define intimacy in terms of verbal communication; in other words, women express closeness by sharing feelings, talking about personal issues, and having in-depth conversations. Men, on the other hand, do not use conversation as a way to achieve closeness. Doing things together, participating in team sports, or working on a project makes connections for them. When men like someone, they express this through shared activities (Bem, 1993).

Thus, while men desire intimacy in their lifetime partnerships just as much as women do (Markman et al., 1994), men's and women's different preferences for how to express this connection can result in complaints and disaffection. When a wife asks her husband to spend some time talking about feelings, she is showing her preference for intimacy, as is a husband who asks his wife to take a walk with him or go fishing with him. A problem for the relationship exists if these different preferences result in husbands and wives feeling as if their partners fail to fulfill their expectations concerning the expressions of intimacy.

The negotiation of these complaints is made difficult by the fact that each partner's construction of how intimacy should be expressed is tied to his or her gender and, thus, personal identity. Men and women often are genuinely surprised when their partners have difficulty understanding "the right ways" to express closeness. If these differences are not constructively negotiated, the potential for an emotionally charged showdown exists.

Furthermore, the research on gender and conflict-management styles suggests that when conflicts arise, interpersonal tensions are often amplified by the fact that men and women differ with respect to (a) how they respond to potential or anticipated conflicts and (b) how they actually manage conflicts (Gottman, 1994; Markman et al., 1994; Tannen, 1990). When women go into a conflict-management mode, they pursue a dialogue around the issues (i.e., talking is the solution to the problem). When men go into a conflict-management mode, they limit their choices concerning intimacy because they are overly focused on preventing conflict from erupting. They tend to avoid or withdraw from it—sometimes at all costs.

As a result, a common mismatched pattern of conflict management fuels an amplification of negativity within many relationships. Women pursue; men distance. Women interpret the distancing as a lack of interest. Women voice concerns about withdrawn, avoidant husbands who will not open up or talk. These women feel shut out and begin to feel that their husbands do not care about the relationship. For these women, this lack of talking equals a lack of caring.

On the other hand, men complain that their wives get upset too much. They feel hassled by their partners chasing after them to get them to talk. Men want peace and harmony. They distance themselves from their partners during times of conflict in an effort to minimize the emotional tensions that seem to be at the heart of the crisis in the relationship. As a result of these different approaches to the management of conflict, each partner can come to view his or her spouse as being *the* problem. This sets in motion patterns of criticisms and negativity that can, ultimately, become a foundation for contempt and distress. However, it should be noted that the problem really lies in the relationship; it results from the lack of fit between the strategies that men and women use when dealing with interpersonal tensions.

With respect to these different modes of "solving" interpersonal tensions, it is interesting to note that both Gottman (1994) and Markman et al. (1994) have come to the conclusion that men tend to withdraw from conflictual situations simply because they are not equipped to handle conflict as well as women. Quoting Gottman (1994), "In a sea of conflict, women swim and men sink" (p. 140). To account for this assertion, Markman and Gottman focus attention on both cultural and biological factors.

Culturally, it is relatively easy to identify the ways in which socialization practices result in boys and girls growing up with different abilities to manage emotion-evoking situations. From early childhood, girls are encouraged to manage a complete range of emotions and to manage conflicts through talking about their feelings. Boys, in contrast, are socialized to suppress their emotions. Talking (particularly about feelings) is an activity that girls participate in. Boys grow up in a developmental niche that would ridicule them if they were to "act like a girl" (Kupers, 1993).

In addition, Gottman and Markman both offer physiological reasons for why men, more than women, are likely to withdraw from emotion-evoking situations (see Levenson & Gottman, 1983; Markman et al., 1994). Markman's work highlights the greater physiological vulnerability of males, as compared with females, and uses this vulnerability to argue that it may be more adaptive for men to avoid conflict situations. Gottman, in addition, suggests that the autonomic nervous system of males differs from that of females. Males, physiologically speaking, are more sensitive to emotion than women. They have stronger reactions to emotions and take longer to recover from emotional upset than women do. And men, once they are aroused, stay aroused longer than women and take longer to settle down. This means that they spend more time than women do being reactive.

Taken together, these cultural and biological factors are used to explain why men, in the final analysis, are much more likely than women to be what Gottman calls "stonewallers" when tensions build (Gottman, 1994). Women, while not invulnerable to stress, experience conflict less intensely than men do and typically have better skills for dealing with situations in which emotions "flood" or take over otherwise rational thinking. Men, in contrast, get flooded much more easily than women do by emotion-evoking situations. Their tendency is to shut down and withdraw. Unfortunately, their withdrawal often serves only to increase interpersonal tensions.

Implications for Application

What we have stated to this point is that marital distress evolves over time as the result of a failure on the part of couples to manage conflicts that inevitably occur within relationships. Research is clear in pointing out that programs that focus their attention on more constructive patterns of managing conflict (Markman & Hahlweg, 1993; Markman, Renick, Floyd, Stanley, & Clements, 1993; Markman, Stanley, & Blumberg, 1991) can help couples. Couples can often be helped by relearning how to respond to complaints using better communication and conflict-resolution skills (Margolin, 1988). Other researchers also recommend that, at the very least, couples greatly benefit by just agreeing about how to disagree (Cummings & Davies, 1994).

In other words, couples can benefit from programs that provide education, skills training, and insight into how to manage conflict to prevent cascading negativity from overwhelming their relationships. It is also fairly evident that, because distress evolves as a result of patterns of interaction over time, interventions should start early on in marriage or even before marriages occur. Waiting until couples are distressed to provide programs to prevent distress makes no sense. Distressed couples come into such programs with negative patterns of interaction already established. They have moved through a cycle of negativity that results in their being highly critical of their partners and highly suspicious of their partners' abilities to change. Such attributions, obviously, would make the reconstruction of the relationship more difficult.

How to get couples to use such programs is the critical remaining question. The future challenge for all professional educators and therapists involves coming up with strategies for engaging couples in educational interventions that prevent the deconstruction of "specialness" from occurring. We need to think strategically about how to break down the barriers to the use of existing programs, how to foster within couples an openness to the idea that conflict is inevitable and if mismanaged can overwhelm the relationship. We have moved beyond the need to justify these programs or to document the good they will do. Now it is time to "shift the discourse" to how to get couples to use the programs.

DISCUSSION QUESTIONS

1. Considering what we know about the rates at which couples divorce today, is it safe to conclude that today's marriages are more distressed than marriages in the past?

2. How does social exchange theory contribute to an understanding of relationship complaints? In what ways do changes that occur in relationships over time contribute to our understanding of how complaints form and evolve?

3. According to Gottman's research, what distinguishes distressed couples from nondistressed couples?

4. Discuss the various ways in which gender differences in conversational styles and approaches to conflict management might contribute to an escalation of marital conflicts.

5. In your view, what needs to happen in the United States to create an ecological context that is more supportive of lifetime partnerships?

SUGGESTED READINGS

Gottman, J. M. (1994). *Why marriages succeed or fail.* New York: Simon & Schuster.
Lederer, W. J., & Jackson, D. D. (1968). *The mirages of marriage.* New York: Norton.

Sabatelli, R. M. (1999). Marital commitment and family life transitions: A social exchange perspective on the construction and deconstruction of intimate relationships. In W. H. Jones & J. M. Adams (Eds.), *Handbook of interpersonal commitment and relationship stability.* New York: Plenum.

Tannen, D. (1990). *You just don't understand: Women and men in conversation.* New York: Ballantine.

Thibaut, J. W., & Kelley, H. H. (1959). *The social psychology of groups.* New York: John Wiley.

REFERENCES

Bem, S. (1993). *Lenses of gender.* New Haven, CT: Yale University Press.

Burr, W., Leigh, G. K., Day, R. D., & Constantine, J. (1979). Symbolic interaction and the family. In W. R. Burr, R. Hill, F. I. Nye, & I. L. Reiss (Eds.), *Contemporary theories about the family* (Vol. 2, pp. 42-111). New York: Free Press.

Cowan, P. A., & Cowan, C. P. (1990). Becoming a family: Research and intervention. In I. Sigel & A. Brody (Eds.), *Family research.* Hillsdale, NJ: Lawrence Erlbaum.

Cummings, E. M., & Davies, P. (1994). *Children and marital conflict: The impact of family dispute and resolution.* New York: Guilford.

Fincham, F. D., & Bradbury, T. N. (1989). Marital distress: Depression and attributions. *Journal of Consulting and Clinical Psychology, 57,* 768-771.

Goleman, D. (1995). *Emotional intelligence: Why it can matter more than I.Q.* New York: Bantam.

Gottman, J. M. (1994). *Why marriages succeed or fail.* New York: Simon & Schuster.

Gottman, J. M., Coan, J., Carrere, S., & Swanson, C. (1998). Predicting marital happiness and stability from newlywed interactions. *Journal of Marriage and the Family, 60,* 5-22.

Gottman, J. M., Katz, L. F., & Hooven, C. (1997). *Meta-emotion: How families communicate emotionally.* Mahwah, NJ: Lawrence Erlbaum.

Gottman, J. M., & Levenson, R. W. (1999a). How stable is marital interaction over time? *Family Process, 38,* 159-166.

Gottman, J. M., & Levenson, R. W. (1999b). What predicts change in marital interaction over time? A study of alternative models. *Family Process, 38,* 143-158.

Hochschild, A. (1994). *The second shift: Marriage in the stalled revolution.* New York: Academic Press.

Koerner, K., & Jacobson, N. S. (1994). Emotion and behavioral couple therapy. In S. M. Johnson & L. S. Greenberg (Eds.), *The heart of the matter: Perspectives on emotion in marital therapy* (pp. 207-226). New York: Brunner/Mazel.

Kupers, T. A. (1993). *Revisioning men's lives: Gender, intimacy, and power.* New York: Guilford.

LaRossa, R., & Reitzes, D. C. (1993). Symbolic interactionism and family studies. In P. Boss, W. Doherty, R. LaRossa, W. Schumm, & S. Steinmetz (Eds.), *Sourcebook of family theories and methods* (pp. 135-163). New York: Plenum.

Lederer, W. J., & Jackson, D. D. (1968). *The mirages of marriage*. New York: Norton.

Levenson, R. W., & Gottman, J. M. (1983). Marital interaction: Physiological linkage and affective exchange. *Journal of Personality and Social Psychology, 45*, 587-597.

Margolin, G. (1988). Marital conflict is not marital conflict is not marital conflict. In R. Peters & Z. McMahon (Eds.), *Social learning and systems approaches to marriage and the family* (pp. 193-216). New York: Brunner/Mazel.

Markman, H. J., & Hahlweg, K. (1993). The prediction and prevention of marital distress: An international perspective. *Clinical Psychology Review, 13*, 29-43.

Markman, H. J., Renick, M. J., Floyd, F. J., Stanley, S. M., & Clements, M. (1993). Preventing marital distress through communication and conflict management training: A 4- and 5-year follow up. *Journal of Consulting and Clinical Psychology, 61*, 1-18.

Markman, H. J., Stanley, S. M., & Blumberg, S. (1991). *Fighting for your marriage: The PREP approach* [Video and audiotape series]. Denver, CO: PREP Educational Videos.

Markman, H. J., Stanley, S. M., & Blumberg, S. (1994). *Fighting for your marriage: Positive steps for preventing divorce and preserving a lasting love*. San Francisco: Jossey-Bass.

Nye, F. I. (1979). Choice, exchange, and the family. In W. R. Burr, R. Hill, F. I. Nye, & I. L. Reiss (Eds.), *Contemporary theories about the family* (Vol. 2, pp. 1-41). New York: Free Press.

Ortega y Gasset, J. (1957). *On love: Aspects of a single theme* (T. Talbot, Trans.). New York: World Publishing.

Sabatelli, R. M. (1984). The marital comparison level index: A measure for assessing outcomes relative to expectations. *Journal of Marriage and the Family, 46*, 651-662.

Sabatelli, R. M. (1988). Exploring relationship satisfaction: A social exchange perspective on the interdependence between theory, research, and practice. *Family Relations, 37*, 217-222.

Sabatelli, R. M., & Shehan, C. (1993). Exchange and resource theories. In P. Boss, W. Doherty, R. LaRossa, W. Schumm, & S. Steinmetz (Eds.), *Sourcebook of family theories and methods* (pp. 385-412). New York: Plenum.

Scanzoni, J. (1979). Social exchange and behavioral interdependence. In R. Burgess & T. Huston (Eds.), *Social exchange in developing relationships* (pp. 61-98). New York: Academic Press.

Stryker, S. (1968). Identity salience and role performance: The relevance of symbolic interaction theory for family research. *Journal of Marriage and the Family, 30*, 558-564.

Stryker, S., & Serpe, R. T. (1982). Commitment, identity salience, and role behavior. In W. Ickes & E. Knowles (Eds.), *Personality, roles, and social behavior* (pp. 199-218). New York: Springer-Verlag.

Stryker, S., & Serpe, R. T. (1994). Identity salience and psychological centrality: Equivalent, overlapping, or complementary concepts? *Social Psychology Quarterly, 57*, 16-35.

Tannen, D. (1986). *That's not what I meant! How conversational style makes or breaks relationships*. New York: Ballantine.

Tannen, D. (1990). *You just don't understand: Women and men in conversation*. New York: Ballantine.

Thibaut, J. W., & Kelley, H. H. (1959). *The social psychology of groups*. New York: John Wiley.

3

The Challenges of Parenting Infants and Young Children

BARBARA M. NEWMAN

Families change through the birth or adoption and ongoing rearing of children. A family's ability to anticipate and respond to the changing demands and developmental capacities of young children is central to family adaptation. Therefore, this chapter focuses on the demands for coping and adaptation that are embedded in the process of parenting healthy, normal children. In discussing the ways families cope with the transition to parenthood and the parenting of infants and young children, we are addressing those ongoing, ever-changing, multidirectional, and intergenerational processes that foster individual growth and development while at the same time promoting a sense of family cohesiveness and adaptive self-regulation.

Infants and young children go through spurts of growth in the cognitive, emotional, and motor areas, often accompanied by periods of disorganization and regression (Bornstein, 1995). These are associated with changes in patterns of physical exploration, eating, sleeping, play behaviors, expressions of irritability and soothability, and requirements for social and cognitive stimulation. Thus, one of the significant challenges of parenting infants and young children involves the frequency with which family rhythms and patterns of daily functioning fall out of synchronization with children's needs.

As an example, consider the transition from crawling to walking. Sometime during the first 12 months of life, babies begin to pull themselves to a standing position. They may work their way around the crib, holding on to the side. They pull themselves up along a low table or the leg of a chair. Then, at some unexpected moment, they take a first step. The family is thrilled. The baby has attained a new, valued human capacity—walking upright. Yet this new accomplishment requires a major family adjustment. Some families begin to babyproof tabletops, place gates at the top of the stairs, put locks on cupboards and pantry doors, and put a fence around the yard. Most families begin a process of new vigilance and monitoring. "Don't touch" and "no" become more frequent aspects of a parent's vocabulary. Walking, a major developmental milestone, brings demands on the family to deal with the child in new ways. Throughout infancy and childhood, each element of a child's increased autonomy, self-expression, and mastery can be a stimulus for modifications to the family system. Efforts to remain responsive to infant cues, to be appropriately soothing in times of distress, and to provide a degree of predictability for the child during periods of rapid change require a capacity for flexible adaptation, emotional management, and creative problem solving.

This chapter begins with a discussion of parental role strain and parenting stress. These constructs, which are often used interchangeably in the family development literature, actually capture two different ways of thinking about the impact of children on families. *Parental role strain* reflects a social, interpersonal perspective; *parenting stress* suggests a psychological, intrapsychic perspective. The chapter then focuses on four themes of family life that illustrate how the presence of infants and young children serves as a source of stress: (a) transition to parenthood, (b) parental separation anxiety, (c) managing child care arrangements, and (d) coping with sibling conflicts. These stressors are examples of normative changes that can only be assessed effectively through the lens of the Double ABC-X Model (McCubbin & Patterson, 1983). The degree to which these changes result in growth or disorganization depends on the resources families have to cope with the events, the meaning or perception given to these events, and the feedback from earlier efforts at adaptation that lead to changes in resources and beliefs, as well as to positive or negative expectations about future change. The four topics raised in this chapter are likely to be faced by most families. (Other chapters in the book address issues of grave crisis and family dysfunction such as family violence, mental illness, and drug and alcohol abuse.) To understand the degree of stress they produce, one would need to understand the family context, especially poverty or underemployment, serious marital conflict, or chronic physical or mental health conditions. The four topics have been selected to clarify the meaningful challenges associated with parenting young children and the extent to which meeting these challenges can result in adaptive child and adult development and family growth.

Parental Role Strain

Parental role strain emphasizes the social nature of the parental role. Four dimensions are often considered when evaluating the impact of a role on personal development and interpersonal behavior: (a) the number of roles that a person occupies, (b) the intensity of role involvement or how deeply identified a person is with the role, (c) the amount of time the role demands, and (d) the flexibility or rigidity associated with role enactment (Newman & Newman, 1997). Parental role strain is defined as a sense of difficulty in complying with the expectations of a role or a set of competing roles and the perception that one is not fulfilling role-related obligations (Barnett & Baruch, 1985; Baruch & Barnett, 1986; Sabatelli & Waldron, 1995). Especially when trying to coordinate the demands of parent with those of worker and spouse, the new parent role may seem overwhelming. The parent role stimulates intense involvement for most people. This intensity carries over to the sense of involvement in all the behaviors associated with the role, and it provokes anxiety about failure to meet the expectations of the role. First-time parents may be especially worried about their ability to fulfill parental role expectations.

Parental role strain may result from the extraordinary time demands of parenting. The parent role is an ongoing, round-the-clock commitment. Many first-time parents underestimate how much time infants and toddlers require. When new parents, especially mothers, reflect on how much time they spend on the variety of their social roles, they typically single out the parent role as being more time-consuming than any other (Cowan & Cowan, 1988). Adding such a demanding time commitment to other ongoing roles may lead to sleep deprivation and exhaustion, especially if one lacks adequate social support.

Parental role strain may increase when partners disagree about how to enact the parent role, or if close family members or friends are critical of one's role enactment. By entering the parent role, one opens oneself up to new expressions of concern, criticism, and opinion from parents (now grandparents), siblings (now aunts and uncles), in-laws, friends and neighbors, pediatricians, and other "experts," which may raise doubts about how to parent. Although the parental role might be considered a flexible one, just about everyone has his or her own opinion about how to "do it right."

Although most of the literature focuses on difficulties in combining and balancing work and family roles, parental role strain can result from a variety of other social and interpersonal sources as well. Parental role strain occurs when one is trying to meet the needs of several children of different ages; when one's own expectations for the parent role are at odds with the views of significant family members such as one's spouse, mother, or mother-in-law; or when one's child is in a particularly demanding state (e.g., during a serious illness or a difficult developmental transition). Thus, parental role strain can occur as a result of competing external pressures or as a result of new or increasing demands of the parental role itself (Sabatelli & Waldron, 1995).

Parenting Stress

The parenting role is both rewarding and taxing. Bradley, Whiteside-Mansell, Brisby, and Caldwell (1997) suggest that a parent's psychological investment in his or her children can be summarized to include the following dimensions:

1. Joy or delight the parent experiences with a child
2. Expressions of affection toward the child
3. Sensitivity to the child's needs
4. Worry about the child's welfare
5. Acceptance of the child and the parenting role
6. Consistent efforts to act in the child's best interest

These dimensions provide the context for the definition of parenting stress: the balance of the positive aspects of enjoyment of one's children, satisfaction in enacting the parenting role, and emotional gratification of having a close, meaningful relationship with one's children with the negative aspects of worrying about one's children and how best to meet their needs, being frustrated with the amount of time involved in the parenting role, and finding that meeting the needs of one's children results in a loss of control over other important aspects of one's own life (Berry & Jones, 1995).

Parenting stress has been studied primarily under conditions involving some type of clinical condition, such as the child's physical or emotional disability, severe genetic disorder, or prolonged hospitalization (Anastopoulos, Guevremont, Shelton, & DuPaul, 1992; Quittner, Glueckauf, & Jackson, 1990). These studies tend to use the Parenting Stress Index (Abidin, 1983), which measures how the parent's perceptions of the child's conditions—especially the child's temperament, demandingness, and adaptability—are linked to parent conditions such as the sense of social isolation, competence in meeting the child's needs, and feelings of depression or unhappiness. However, recent work has applied the concept of parenting stress to more nor-

mative populations. For example, Jarvis and Creasey (1991) looked at the relationship between parenting stress and attachment among mothers, fathers,
and their 18-month-old infants. They found that infants were more likely to
have insecure attachments to both mothers and fathers who had high parenting stress. They suggest that high parenting stress results in psychological
distance or lack of psychological availability, which interferes with the formation of a secure attachment. In another study, Sanik (1993) considered the
relationship between the amount of time that parents allocated to child care,
household work, paid work, and leisure and the parenting stress of parents of
4- to 7-month-old infants. None of these time allocation factors predicted
stress; however, the age and gender of the infant were both significantly related to parenting stress, with parents of older infants and girls showing lower
stress scores.

Another approach to the concept of parenting stress has been the development of research on daily stressors associated with meeting the demands of
parenting. This view has been termed "parenting daily hassles" (Crnic &
Booth, 1991). The idea of hassles differs from stressful life events in that hassles are not perceived as major changes in family roles and relationships.
They are the common experiences of parenting such as picking up the toys,
doing the laundry, running out of diapers, or having a child whine and cry
while you are on the phone. They are also different from the Parenting Stress
Index measurement mentioned above, which addresses more general aspects
of the child's characteristics and parental responses (Crnic & Acevedo,
1995). The research on parenting hassles suggests that the more time a parent
spends with the children, the greater the experience and intensity of daily hassles. Crnic and Booth (1991) found that parenting hassles were reported to be
greater for parents of 2- and 3-year-olds than for parents of infants. They suggest that parents of infants interpret the many demands of infancy as necessary to meet the health, safety, and security needs of the young child. Parents
are likely to believe that infants cannot regulate their needs and therefore are
not being demanding "on purpose." However, as the child gets older, his or
her own autonomy and willfulness may produce conflict with the parent,
leading to parental perceptions that the child is being defiant or noncooper-
ative. Thus, perceptions of daily parenting hassles may become more intense
as the child's behavior conflicts with the parent's socialization goals or with
the parent's own timetable and agenda.

These studies suggest an important direction for family development research. They acknowledge the potentially stressful nature of meeting daily
developmental needs of infants and young children and provide information
about the coping strategies and dynamics of family life that help reduce

parenting stress. The two concepts of parental role strain and parenting stress suggest that difficulties in coping with parenting may begin with feelings of incompetence, overload, social isolation, and confusion about whether one will be a "good parent" and, over time, shift to feelings of stress about managing the ongoing, day-to-day requirements of parenting.

The Transition to Parenthood

One of the most widely used approaches to assessing exposure to stress is Holmes and Rahe's (1967) Social Readjustment Rating Scale. In the development of this scale, Holmes and Rahe presented participants with a list of life events. Raters were asked to judge the stressful impact of each event. They arbitrarily gave marriage a value of 50 and asked participants to rate all the other events on a scale from 1 to 100. On the basis of the data from more than 6,000 raters across several countries, Holmes and Rahe found that pregnancy was given the 12th highest rating among 43 life events, with an average of 40 points. This was followed closely by "gain of a family member," with an average of 39 points. Thus, according to this method of assessing stressors, even when pregnancy is viewed as highly desirable and planned, it is associated with many new demands and worries, as well as changes in roles and role relationships. The birth of a child introduces disequilibrium into a family system, requiring role adjustments, reorganization, redistribution of resources, and the formation of new relationships within the family. Disequilibrium introduces new opportunities for learning, coping, and adapting. It may also bring about maladaptation if the parent(s) lack the ego strengths to respond to these new demands or if the relationship between the partners is already distressed.

Within the Double ABC-X Model, perceptions of the stressor play a central role. People enter the parent role with varying values and beliefs about the importance of this role and its centrality to their overall sense of self. The more salient the parental role, the greater importance one will attach to meeting one's child's needs. Thus, stress is likely to be greater for those parents who are more deeply invested in parenting as a central aspect of identity. Simon (1992) found that, in general, parental salience is greater for mothers than for fathers. However, for both men and women, when parental salience was high, so was their vulnerability to the role strains associated with parenting. Thus, the more one cares about parenting and the more devoted one is to enacting the parental role with a high degree of responsiveness and caring, the more one is likely to experience it as stressful.

On average, the presence of children in the family is associated with lower marital satisfaction and less marital happiness, although ratings of marital satisfaction do not usually drop dramatically from before to after childbirth (Belsky & Pensky, 1988; Cowan & Cowan, 1995). Belsky and Rovine (1990) found evidence of individual differences among couples regarding this pattern. In a longitudinal study, they observed four patterns of change in the assessment of marital quality. Some couples showed rapid decline in marital quality after the baby was born. Some showed a slow, steady decline. A third group showed no significant change, and the fourth group showed slight increases in marital quality.

Generally, the quality of marital adjustment over the transition to parenthood is closely related to marital quality before the child was born (Heinicke, 1995). Couples who are in close, confiding, satisfying marriages before their children are born tend to show higher levels of marital adjustment 3 months after childbirth than couples in conflictual marriages do (Cox, Owen, Lewis, & Henderson, 1989; Wallace & Gotleib, 1990). However, many studies find that couples experience more frequent conflicts after the birth of a child than before. The idea that having a baby will bring a couple closer does not seem to be supported by the research literature. If the partners have high levels of conflict and are disappointed in the quality of their relationship before a baby is born, these difficulties are likely to increase after childbirth (Crohan, 1996).

The decline in marital satisfaction that often accompanies the transition to parenthood can be accounted for in several ways. In the first few months after a child is born, both parents are exhausted from lack of sleep. They have new responsibilities and a new schedule. Thus, they are experiencing new levels of role strain. Many parents feel inadequate to care for their babies, and they turn to their parents, friends, other parents, pediatricians, and books for expert advice. This lack of self-confidence may create tension between the marriage partners.

Potential conflicts may arise about child-rearing philosophies or child care practices. Feelings of jealousy, competition, and abandonment may arise between partners in the first months after the child is born. The exclusiveness that the partners experienced in meeting one another's needs is disrupted as they attend to the child's demands. Although couples with and without children show about the same drop in marital satisfaction, the amount of time that couples with children have to spend alone in leisure and adult companionship is substantially reduced in comparison with couples without children (MacDermid, Huston, & McHale, 1990). In comparison with childless couples, new parents find themselves making more traditional, gender-specific assignments of family and household roles, which may cause increased dissatisfaction, especially when a couple's sex-role attitudes conflict with their new role assignments. For example, Sanchez and Thomson (1997) analyzed the effect of parenthood on the division of labor among married couples using two waves of the National Survey of Families and Households. Becoming a father had little impact on men's hours of employment or hours of housework. However, becoming a mother typically modified the women's daily routine by increasing housework time and reducing time in the labor market. The greater the wife's initial economic dependency on her husband, the more her time in housework and her husband's time in employment increased, thus elaborating the traditional nature of gendered family roles.

In many families, with the birth of the first child, the majority of child care and household responsibilities fall to the mother. If the mother withdraws from the labor force, her partner may need to spend more time at work in order to compensate for the loss of income. In some families, women try to compensate for their loss of involvement in areas outside the home, such as work, community service, and friendships, by investing more energy in their mother role. Consequently, fathers may actually be discouraged from spending as much time with their babies as they may wish (Cowan & Cowan, 1988). In other families, the father does not have the confidence or personal qualities that orient him toward an active role in his infant's care, so more child care responsibilities are left by default to the mother (Volling & Belsky, 1991). When one partner is disappointed in the amount of time and involvement that the other is giving to household tasks and child care, the outcome is often an increase in marital dissatisfaction, as well as perceived stress surrounding the parental role.

A variety of contextual factors play a part in parents' ability to promote their children's optimal development while preserving a sense of companionship and closeness in their own adult relationship. Parents must rely heavily on their own psychosocial maturity and on the loving support of caring friends and family to sustain their ego strengths, creative energy, and the emotional resources necessary for the task of parenting. The ways that parents conceive their roles have major implications for their child's development. Adults who themselves have had difficult experiences with a caregiver come to the parent role with special challenges. They may not have experienced the comfort, responsiveness, or appropriate stimulation that is essential for effective parenting. Adults who have experienced early loss or the disruption of an attachment relationship have more difficulty providing a secure base for their offspring and experience greater anxiety in meeting the challenges of the parent role (Ainsworth, 1989; Fonagy, Steele, & Steele, 1991; Ricks, 1985).

The quality of the partners' relationship and the functional as well as emotional support they give each other are crucial in sustaining positive parent-child relationships (Cox et al., 1989; Dickstein & Parke, 1988; Egeland, Jacobvitz, & Sroufe, 1988). Parents who experience higher levels of partner support and closeness provide a more optimal environment for their child's development. Especially for men, the quality of the relationship they have with their partner is a strong predictor of the quality of their relationship with their infant. The more engaged and satisfied a man is with his partner, the more likely he is to be actively involved in the care of his child and to express satisfaction with the father role (Parke, 1995).

Additional support from the child's grandparents and other family members, health and mental health professionals, and friends is helpful in reducing parental role strain (Jayakody, Chatters, & Taylor, 1993; Levitt, Weber, & Clark, 1986; Stevens, 1988). The effective use of a social support network ensures that other adults are available to help the parent identify and solve child-rearing problems. Often, the help is very direct, such as providing child care, clothes, playthings, furniture, or household help. Support may also come through providing companionship, emotional reassurance, and validation about the importance of the parental role.

Parental Separation Anxiety

John Bowlby (1969) proposed the construct of the attachment behavior system to describe the organized pattern of infant signals and adult responses that promotes a relationship characterized by infant trust and adult protection. The primary adaptive function of the attachment system is to maintain an appropriate degree of infant-caregiver proximity that will protect the vulnerable infant from dangers and, at the same time, promote the infant's confidence in the caregiver's ability to comfort and protect. The formation of a secure attachment is the result of a synchronous interaction between infant signals and parental responses. As such, it requires the investment of a responsive caregiver who will be concerned about the infant's welfare and willing to modify his or her behavior to respond to the infant's signals.

One of the major threats to infant safety is separation from the caregiver. In fact, from an evolutionary perspective, separation from the caregiver may be considered a basic threat to infant survival. Although most of the research on the attachment system has focused on the infant's response to separation and reunion with the caregiver, a growing interest focuses on the caregiver's response to separation. If the attachment paradigm is accurate, the caregiver must be highly motivated to maintain proximity in order to monitor and respond to the infant's needs.

It is reasonable to expect that separation from the infant would be a source of distress for the caregiver as well as for the infant (Hock & Lutz, 1998). In fact, family systems theorists suggest that distance regulation is one of the major challenges facing families across the life span (Bomar & Sabatelli, 1996). Parents must constantly balance their desires for their child to be safe, protected, and emotionally close with their desires for their child to become autonomous and self-reliant. In this light, parental separation anxiety can be interpreted as a product of conflicts about distance regulation. Some parents are very reluctant to leave their babies during the first few months of the child's life. They resist suggestions to call a baby-sitter or have a relative take the baby for a while so that they can go out with their partner or enjoy some time alone. One sees evidence of separation anxiety as a parent lingers at the door of the day care center, not wanting to leave the baby, or calls the baby-sitter every half hour to make sure everything is all right. As the child matures, parental separation anxiety takes on new forms as parents send their children off to kindergarten, respond to a child's request to spend the night at a friend's house, and allow their child to drive the car or go on a road trip with friends in adolescence. Perhaps parental separation anxiety comes to a crescendo as parents watch their son or daughter walk down the aisle at their wedding!

Although both fathers and mothers can be expected to experience parental separation anxiety, research on this construct began with a focus on mothers, since mothers seem to be implicated so centrally in the attachment literature. Maternal separation anxiety was defined as a mother's feelings of sadness, guilt, or worry about leaving her child or about anticipating leaving her child. It also refers to the mother's perceptions of how effectively her child can cope with separation. This would include perceptions of how distressed the child is likely to be, how well the child can manage in her absence, and how appropriate or even developmentally advantageous it is for her child to be away from her for a while (Hock, McBride, & Gnezda, 1989). Maternal separation anxiety can be thought of as a dispositional characteristic. Even though maternal anxiety shows evidence of stability, it is neither a trait nor a state; rather, it is a reaction that is likely to be stimulated by a combination of the mother's personality and attachment history, characteristics of the infant, and the situation that requires the separation (Hock et al., 1989; McBride & Belsky, 1988). For example, studies have shown that mothers who view their babies as having a more negative or unadaptable temperament have more anxiety about separation than do mothers of "easy" babies (Fein, Gariboldi, & Boni, 1993;

McBride & Belsky, 1988). Women who recall their own childhood as rejecting and controlling and those who are highly self-critical and dependent are
likely to have higher levels of separation anxiety (Hock & Lutz, 1998; Lutz &
Hock, 1995).

Some attention has been given to the interaction of maternal separation
anxiety and maternal employment. Studies suggest that mothers who experience higher levels of separation anxiety are likely to return to work later in the
first year of their child's life and work fewer hours per week than those with
lower levels of separation anxiety (McBride, 1990). Although moderate levels of maternal separation anxiety are associated with a secure mother-infant
attachment, high levels of maternal separation anxiety are viewed as potentially dysfunctional for the mother-infant attachment. This may be explained
by the association between maternal separation anxiety and maternal depression (Hock, Schirtzinger, & Lutz, 1992) or by the fact that mothers who experience high levels of maternal separation anxiety have a more negative attachment history on which to draw as they engage in their own parenting role
(Lutz & Hock, 1995).

Managing Child Care Arrangements

Selecting, monitoring, and modifying child care arrangements make up one
of the major family stressors of contemporary life. In the United States, it is
normative for mothers of infants and young children to be involved in the paid
labor force. As a result, whether in a single-parent or a dual-earner family,
families with young children have to make child care arrangements during
the hours that the adults are away from home. Data from the U.S. Bureau of
the Census from 1995 found that 60% of children under the age of 6 were in
nonparental care, including care with relatives, nonrelatives, and center-
based programs. Perhaps somewhat more surprising, more than 50% of
young children spend some time in nonparental child care (other than periodic baby-sitting) before 12 months of age.

The following factors are associated with the stressors of managing child
care arrangements:

1. Many women believe that they are best suited to take care of their child
and would prefer to care for them at home if they did not have to work. Many
men believe that if they had their choice, their wives would be home with the
children rather than in the paid labor force. In general, parents who work
seem to prefer having another family member care for their child in their own

home, particularly during infancy. In a survey of child care satisfaction among 1,600 families, Erdwins, Casper, and Buffardi (1998) found that those families whose children were being cared for by a relative or an au pair in the infant's own home were more satisfied than those families whose child was in a center or with a home-based provider. Satisfaction with the child care arrangement, no matter the type, was a significant predictor of a parent's ability to balance the demands of work and family life.

Another study carried out among members of an international organization of infant mental health professionals found that the majority of the members recommended maternal care as the optimal arrangement during the first 36 months. In addition, care by a family member was preferred over any form of purchased care (Leach, 1997). With these values pervading the public's outlook, many couples who are not able to care for their child at home or able to have someone else care for their child at their home are making child care arrangements that are in conflict with their basic beliefs about what would be ideal. As a result, they experience more role strain and greater evidence of depression, marital conflict, or both (Hock & DeMeis, 1990; Hoffman, 1989).

2. At present, high-quality, affordable child care is very difficult to find, particularly for infants, for children who are ill, for evening and late-night shifts, and for children who need special medical attention (Donson, 1999). Thus, some families place children in settings that are viewed as adding to their financial strain. Others place children in arrangements that they know do not adequately meet their child's needs, such as under the supervision of older children or elderly relatives (National Commission on Children, 1993).

3. Roughly 13% of toddlers are in multiple care arrangements, including family members or neighbors, group care, and baby-sitters (National Commission on Children, 1993). Strain arises from the time and energy required to coordinate these various arrangements, from the frequency with which one of the components of the system does not work, and from efforts to compensate when something goes wrong.

4. Because there is no comprehensive network of child care services in each community and the quality of these services is largely unregulated, parents have to make judgments about quality and evaluate services based on limited experience and information (Honig, 1995). There is growing concern about safety in day care centers. Both licensed centers and family day care homes are loosely regulated, licensing standards vary widely from state to state, and few states maintain systematic records of inspections or complaints

(Pope, 1997). Thus, decisions about child care arrangements are often made within a context of uncertainty, which heightens anxiety.

The decision to place a child in early child care is a result of family characteristics, infant characteristics, and the availability of child care resources of various types within the community. Singer, Fuller, Keiley, and Wolf (1998) examined the factors influencing the placement of children under age 6 in nonparental care in a national sample of over 2,500 participating families. During the first 6 months of life, children in the South and the Midwest are much more likely to be placed in care than children in the West or the Northeast. Especially in the South, there is a tendency to place children in nonparental care earlier and for a longer time, thus bringing the median age at first care to 20 months, as compared with 43 months in the West and Northeast. These differences are explained in part by the high proportion of centers in the South relative to the population of children and the high proportion of African American mothers in the South who work full-time. These conditions support cultural norms that emphasize a more communal view of child care responsibilities.

Aside from geographic differences, the most significant predictor of early entry into nonparental care was whether a mother was working before her pregnancy. This effect was greater than single-parent status or mother's education, race, or age at her first child's birth. For every subcategory examined, infants were in alternative care before 12 months if the mother was working during the pregnancy. This was equally true if the child was the first or second born. However, the pattern shifted dramatically if the child was third or later born. At this point, even if the mother was working during pregnancy, she was likely to delay the child's entry into alternative care. In contrast, children born to women who were not in the labor force during pregnancy showed a much later entry into alternative care, and if they were second born, they were likely never to be placed in nonparental care. The children least likely to enter nonparental care were those born to women who delayed parenting to an older age and were not working during their pregnancy. However, women with a college education were more likely to place their children in nonparental care at an earlier age than were those with only a high school degree, regardless of employment status or single-parent status. One can see here the converging expression of values and beliefs about the benefit of nonparental care as they interact with economic needs and market resources to influence a child care decision.

The potential for compounded stressors influencing the child care decision emerges from this profile of family factors. Economic factors, such as the cost of child care and employer deadlines for returning to work, plus the need to find a stable arrangement that will not have to be renegotiated tend to lead to child care decisions based on availability, cost, and convenience (in terms of location and hours of operation). For employed women who intend to continue their employment, the arrangement must be available to cover the hours and days of their work schedules. Families that are most stressed, whether as a result of poverty, limited flexibility in the employment setting, or the sudden loss of previous child care services, are also most likely to settle for poor-quality care. These settings are more likely to expose children to more staff turnover and fewer positive interactions with adults. As a result, the children themselves become more distressed and less sociable and cooperative, leading to fewer positive exchanges at home or more reluctance to leave home and attend the center. This scenario suggests that a poor child care arrangement, arrived at as a result of family stress, may actually increase stress as the child brings the frustrations of a nonsupportive, unstimulating environment back into the family (Goelman & Pence, 1990; Honig, 1995).

The stressors associated with finding and managing child care arrangements are a product of the larger cultural system that places substantial responsibility on families to identify, monitor, evaluate, and pay for care. In contrast, many European countries provide a more fully integrated child care support system, including periods of financial support during maternity or paternity leave that, in some countries, last up to 2 years; state-regulated and subsidized child care regardless of family income; and guaranteed health care coverage for children and families. As a result, many of the strains that are experienced by families in the United States are eliminated through a well-integrated program of early childhood services and care (Donson, 1999; Honig, 1995).

Just as with other aspects of parenting, the process of managing child care arrangements can bring satisfactions as well as worries. By establishing links with nonfamily child care, the family opens itself to possible influences from these caregivers or centers. Studies of the impact of child care typically focus on the social and intellectual advantages for young children and the possible long-term consequences for academic success and social relationships. However, it is important to consider the potential benefits to parents as well. For example, Head Start has an active parent-focused program that includes helping families with links to other social services, recruiting parents as volunteers and paid classroom assistants, involving parents in the program planning and governance of the centers, and providing parenting education (Zigler, 1999).

In a positive parent-caregiver relationship, a sense of trust and mutual respect emerges. Parents are willing to discuss concerns they have about their child and look to the caregiver as a source of support and advice. Caregivers are able to share with parents observations about their child that the parent can integrate to reach a more complex understanding of the child's temperament, abilities, and social skills. Programs that have an active parent-involvement component typically introduce new educational strategies to parents and convey new information about developmentally appropriate expectations. Especially for parents who have had little formal education, positive child outcomes can be explained in part by the ability of the program to modify parent-child interactions outside the child care setting (Christian, Morrison, & Bryant, 1998; Woolfson, 1999). Parents learn to value the child's emerging separateness, to become more sensitive play companions and language partners, and to extend the benefits of the day care setting as a learning environment into the home. Thus, a parent can appreciate the optimally effective day care setting as one that supports the easy flow of influence between family and school. As the children become increasingly competent, parents change their expectations and perceptions of their child and find new ways to enjoy their child's emerging abilities.

Coping With Sibling Conflicts

Although the study of the effects of sibling order has a relatively long history, few studies focus on the specific ways that families change with the birth or adoption of additional children (Furman, 1995). This is an especially interesting aspect of the family development process. Parents typically choose to have a second child; that is, the change is usually voluntary, expected, and desired. Yet this change dramatically modifies the family environment and calls for a multitude of adaptive responses. Parents and the first child are older when the second and subsequent children join the family. The complexity of interacting personalities and developmental processes introduces new challenges in trying to respond appropriately to the demands of caregiving. In particular, the siblings create a new family subsystem, the sibling dyad, which eventually takes on a dynamic life of its own. One model of family change associated with the birth of a second child was proposed by Kreppner, Paulsen, and Schuetze (1982).

1. In the first 8 months, the challenge is to restructure home-management tasks to respond to the needs of an infant and an older child.
2. In the period from 9 to 16 months, the challenge is to monitor and manage sibling interactions as the younger infant becomes more autonomous and the older child may resent the younger child's incursions into his or her territory.

3. In the period from 17 to 24 months, the family tries to find ways to function in a more integrated way. Rather than viewing themselves as a family with an older child and an infant, they shift to finding activities and patterns that are suitable for two older children.

In the process of incorporating a new family member, some important changes are observed. The presence of a sibling may reduce the intimacy parents have with the firstborn. Mothers and their firstborns interact less frequently after the birth of the sibling, and the interactions are likely to be more confrontational (Dunn & Kendrick, 1980). As parents observe familiar patterns of development in the second child, they begin to appreciate some of the regularities of development and can learn to anticipate future changes. With a second child, parents may recognize certain temperamental differences, thus helping them to accept some of their children's "natural" qualities. This may help parents realize that they are not responsible for every aspect of their child's personality. The siblings begin to have interactions of their own, which may require parental monitoring but, over time, also take on an independent life that cannot be totally monitored; this also relieves parents of being their child's sole play companion. Thus, the addition of a sibling can result in both increased role demands and a new sense of parental confidence.

One of the characteristics of sibling relationships that has received attention in child development theory and practice is sibling rivalry. It is important to note that this is not the only important feature of sibling relationships. Sibling play, conversation, friendship, modeling, teaching, and emotional support are all developmentally important elements of sibling relationships and the sibling subsystem (Garner, Jones, & Palmer, 1994; Howe, 1991). In fact, sometimes parents become so preoccupied with sibling rivalry that they forget to observe the many ways that siblings have developed their own supportive subsystem within the family. However, because parents have made a commitment to the growth and development of all their children, it can be especially stressful for parents to observe conflict, competition, and rivalry among them. At times, siblings may become so angry with each other that their fighting threatens their safety and disrupts ongoing family functioning. Conflict is generally perceived as stressful. To the extent that children increase the amount of conflict that occurs in the home by arguing and fighting with their siblings, they heighten the levels of stress for parents as well as for themselves.

Although sibling rivalry is related in part to the age and temperaments of the siblings, some research suggests that the severity of sibling rivalry is related to parental behaviors. If parents spend considerably less time with an older child once a new baby is born or if a parent persistently praises one child and criticizes another, children are likely to identify these behaviors as evidence of parental preference. At first, the older child's reaction to his or her mother spending so much time with the new baby is likely to be small acts of naughtiness, increased anxiety, and ritualistic behaviors. Usually, these behaviors have the desired result of shifting the mother's attention back to the older child (Dunn, 1985). However, if parental behavior continues to be preferential, sibling conflicts are likely to ensue (Brody, Stoneman, & Burke, 1987; Stocker, Dunn, & Plomin, 1989).

Preferential treatment by parents seems to be associated with higher levels of sibling conflict. Most of the studies that address this issue are correlational; that is, they report on data collected at one period in the family's history and do not lend themselves to a causal interpretation. The findings suggest that high levels of negative interaction between siblings and low levels of sibling warmth are associated with differences in the way that mothers interact with their children (Furman, 1995). For example, in some families, mothers consistently respond to one child's needs more than the other's or punish one child more than the other even when both siblings were involved in some misbehavior. This could be called the Smothers Brothers effect!

Fathers play a particularly important role in promoting sibling harmony. When fathers have a close, loving relationship with the first child, that child seems to have an easier time accepting the new sibling, and the sibling interactions tend to be more positive. It is important for fathers to provide parental closeness to the older child, especially when the mother's attention is distracted by caring for an infant. In addition, fathers who treat both children equally and emphasize family harmony when sibling conflicts arise appear to contribute in a positive way to the relationships that develop between siblings. In families in which there are frequent disagreements between parents or fathers are unavailable, sibling conflicts tend to be greater (Brody, Stoneman, & McCoy, 1992; Brody, Stoneman, McCoy, & Forehand, 1992; Volling & Belsky, 1992).

Recent research suggests that mothers and fathers differ in their perceptions of sibling conflict and the best approaches for managing it. Fathers tend to view a control-oriented or power-assertive approach as more effective in managing conflict, whereas mothers tend to see negotiation or inductions (child-centered explanations) as better strategies. In a study that compared parents' beliefs about what was effective with their actual behavior during sibling conflict, both mothers and fathers viewed passive nonintervention (e.g., ignoring the conflict or letting the children settle it themselves) as the least effective strategy for managing sibling conflicts (Perozynski & Kramer,

1999). Interestingly, however, nonintervention was the most common strategy actually employed when parents were observed at home. Some fathers believed that child-centered strategies (e.g., working with the children to help them find a satisfactory solution) were most effective, but when the fathers were observed at home, they used control strategies because they were not confident in their ability to use child-centered strategies effectively. Mothers, who were more likely to use child-centered strategies, did so in large part because they believed control strategies to be ineffective. Thus, the actual parental response to sibling conflict appears to be linked loosely to beliefs and values and somewhat more closely to what one thinks will actually work in the situation. Overall, results from this study suggest that parents learn to pick their battles about when to intervene in sibling conflicts. By using the method of nonintervention, they transfer power to the sibling subsystem and, whether deliberately or inadvertently, allow that subsystem to establish its own process for conflict resolution and the management of grievances.

Conclusions and Implications

Parenting infants and young children brings a wealth of new challenges to adults and to the family system. These challenges are often the result of role strain and parenting stress. These concepts are not interchangeable. Each refers to distinct processes, and each deserves further clarification through research and in practice. Role strain emphasizes the social nature of the parental role, the expectations that are held for role enactment, and how the parental role is linked with other roles. Changing cultural expectations for mothers and fathers results in new uncertainty and conflict about how well modern parents are enacting their roles. Conflicts between work and family are often the target of much research about role strain, but other potential conflicts, especially between mother and father or across generations, can intensify role strain as well. Parenting stress is stress that occurs as one attempts to meet the daily demands and responsibilities of parenting. Relevant questions about parenting stress include the following: How often does a parent feel frustrated, annoyed, and out of control in the parenting role? How successful has the parent been in finding creative strategies to meet the continuous, changing demands of parenting? Psychological variables such as worry, unhappiness, and feelings of incompetence may increase parental stress.

Family life educators need to develop different interventions depending on the source of stress. To reduce role strain, adults may need assistance in identifying the range of expectations they hold for their parenting role, the nature and source of competing expectations, and the possibility of meeting these expectations. Through a process of articulating key values and beliefs about the satisfactions and goals of parenting, adults can begin to focus on a small number of expectations that they accept as central to their successful parental role enactment. They may also need support in examining the degree to which they allow adjoining systems (e.g., work, extended family, or neighborhood) to define their parental role. When adults are embedded in a supportive relationship with a partner and an enthusiastic network of family and friends, they may be able to combine resources so that they are not the only ones who can meet the full range of parenting demands.

When thinking about reducing parenting stress, the focus should be at a more behavioral level. Here we are looking for how to get more moments of joy and satisfaction and fewer moments of drudgery or tension out of interactions with one's children. This may require new solutions to meeting daily tasks. Parents discover creative ways of anticipating hassles or making fun out of routine. They get exercise while taking their children out for a walk by wearing roller blades or jogging behind the stroller. They put toys in see-through bins so that children can get what they want without having to ask for help. They wait for nap time to make important phone calls. They remember to have a snack and a box of handy wipes in the car in case there is a traffic jam and the baby gets hungry or spills the juice. Parenting requires a willingness to change one's timeframe and pace and to be patient with transitions. The more parents can communicate with affectionate, positive interactions, the more socially cooperative their children will become over time.

Turning to the four issues addressed in the chapter, each one has implications for adult development and growth. The transition to parenthood can be especially challenging to the sense of intimacy and companionship that adults have before the child is born. The best chances for a positive transition occur when the couple has established a loving relationship with effective, open communication before the child is born and when they have shared expectations for how each partner will enact the parenting role. Once the baby arrives, time for communication is reduced, and new demands bring new potential conflicts. Good quality communication is the best defense against lowered marital satisfaction. The transition to parenthood is likely to bring out new aspects of the partners that have not been seen before. When both partners are actively engaged in parenting, they are likely to reveal capacities for nurturance, playfulness, reassurance, and resourcefulness. This can be a very endearing process in which the partners admire one another's parental competencies and come to love and trust each other as the parents of their child. On the other hand, perceptions that one's partner lacks an investment or competence in the parent role can introduce new disappointments that may pull the partners further apart.

The topic of maternal separation anxiety highlights the emotional side of the parenting process and the investment that most parents have in protecting their children from harm. Cultures differ in the timing and degree to which they expect parents to encourage autonomy in their children. For example, in the United States, we have very early expectations for infants to sleep in their own bed in a separate room. In research on the attachment process, Hispanic, in comparison with Anglo, mothers are more tolerant of clinging behavior in the *Strange Situation* (Harwood, 1992). In many cultures, mothers carry their children on their side or their back much longer than is true in the United States. One might hypothesize that it is our culture's early expectations for infant/toddler autonomy that result in many parents' experiences of separation anxiety.

Most parents experience some conflict in trying to support new levels of autonomy for their children while doing their best to avoid exposing them to dangers. This is a growth process for the parent as well as the child. In the extreme, parental separation anxiety may be a signal of more serious psychological dysfunction. In everyday parenting, however, it is evidence of the struggle to have optimism that your child will be safe and will be able to cope without you. As a child moves out into widening spheres of independence and physical distance from home, a parent must develop a growing confidence about the child's ability to make good decisions and avoid harm. One can see these concerns expressed in parents' efforts to seek a home in a safe community, to support laws against drunk driving, and, increasingly, to support efforts at gun control.

Parents' efforts to manage child care arrangements are one example of the many ways that parents have to identify services and function as advocates for their child within the larger community. Many studies find that parents express satisfaction with their child care arrangements, even when the arrangements do not match what experts would say are the key indicators of quality. For parents, the most important factors appear to be affordability, convenience, and a sense of rapport with the caregiver. For experts, the cornerstones of quality have been identified as group size, caregiver/child ratio, and caregiver qualifications. Following this, parents should look for stability in the staff (low turnover) and a developmentally appropriate curriculum (Honig, 1995). It is not necessarily the case that more expensive care is better. However, parents are generally uninformed about the characteristics of quality care and their links to child outcomes. Beginning in high school, we need to talk with young people about the importance of making sound child care decisions and help them have the confidence to reject mediocre arrangements.

The theme of sibling conflicts raises the issue that by adding children parents create a more complex family system. As a parent, you begin to see the family as being made up of relationships over which you have little control. Siblings add variety, companionship, and new forms of playfulness to the family environment. While the demands of parenting increase during the early years when siblings are infants and toddlers, they may decrease somewhat as siblings begin to enjoy each other as playmates. In large families, older siblings often become parent surrogates for younger siblings, taking over some of the responsibilities from parents. The more positive, affectionate, and nonpreferential one can be as a parent, the greater the likelihood that the children will enjoy each other's company and feel a close bond to their family of origin.

In closing, the study of the impact of infants and young children on the family is an opportunity to consider how children provide a stimulus for adult development. This process is the reciprocal of Vygotsky's (1978) concept of the zone of proximal development. Vygotsky emphasized the natural process through which children learn and develop by interacting with more skilled partners. For adults who are enacting the parent role with energy and commitment, interacting with infants and young children brings new opportunities for problem solving and self-insight. The affection that children express toward their parents can be a tremendous incentive for parents to want to optimize the relationship and promote the child's well-being. The concerns and worries that accompany parenting often lead to reaching out to family members, friends, and experts, thus expanding their own knowledge and understanding of their role. The more complex the family dynamics, the greater the need to invent unique strategies that are appropriate for the needs of family members. As partners collaborate in parenting, they find that their talents, their love, and their commitment to their children form a new synthesis. With each phase of the child's development, new adult capacities are uncovered and new definitions of family life are forged.

DISCUSSION QUESTIONS

1. What is the difference between parental role strain and parenting stress? What steps might be taken to reduce these two different types of stress?

2. How might parental beliefs and values increase or decrease the stresses of parenting?

3. How might the presence of children alter a couple's relationship in the transition to parenthood? What factors might determine whether the level of satisfaction in the relationship increases or decreases after having children?

4. What are the most important factors influencing a decision to place a child in nonparental care? How are age of the child, mother's employment status, and market factors related to this decision? What might be the most stressful aspects of managing nonparental care?

5. Describe some ways that the birth or adoption of a second child changes the family. What might be some new stressors for the family that are associated with having additional children? In what ways might the sibling subsystem reduce parental stress?

SUGGESTED READINGS

Cowan, C. P., & Cowan, P. A. (1995). Interventions to ease the transition to parenthood: Why they are needed and what they can do. *Family Relations, 44* [Special issue: *Helping contemporary families*], 412-423.

Crnic, K. A., & Acevedo, M. (1995). Everyday stresses and parenting. In M. H. Bornstein (Ed.), *Handbook of parenting: Vol. 4. Applied and practical parenting* (pp. 277-297). Mahwah, NJ: Lawrence Erlbaum.

Crohan, S. E. (1996). Marital quality and conflict across the transition to parenthood in African American and white couples. *Journal of Marriage and the Family, 58,* 933-944.

Hock, E., & Lutz, W. (1998). Psychological meaning of separation anxiety in mothers and fathers. *Journal of Family Psychology, 12,* 41-55.

Lewis, E. A. (1988). Role strengths and strains of African-American mothers. *Journal of Primary Prevention, 9*(1-2) [Special issue: *Prevention strategies in the problems of women*], 77-91.

Volling, B. L., & Belsky, J. (1992). The contribution of mother-child and father-child relationships to the quality of sibling interactions: A longitudinal study. *Child Development, 63,* 1209-1222.

REFERENCES

Abidin, R. R. (1983). *Parenting stress/index manual.* Charlottesville, VA: Pediatric Psychology Press.

Ainsworth, M. D. S. (1989). Attachments beyond infancy. *American Psychologist, 44,* 709-716.

Anastopoulos, A. D., Guevremont, D. C., Shelton, T. L., & DuPaul, G. J. (1992). Parenting stress among families of children with attention deficit hyperactivity disorder. *Journal of Abnormal Child Psychology, 20,* 503-520.

Barnett, R. C., & Baruch, G. K. (1985). Women's involvement in multiple roles and psychological distress. *Journal of Personality and Social Psychology, 49,* 135-145.

Baruch, G. K., & Barnett, R. C. (1986). Consequences of fathers' participation in family work: Parents' role strain and well-being. *Journal of Personality and Social Psychology, 51,* 983-992.

Belsky, J., & Pensky, E. (1988). Marital change across the transition to parenthood. *Marriage and the Family Review, 12,* 133-156.

Belsky, J., & Rovine, M. (1990). Patterns of marital change across the transition to parenthood. *Journal of Marriage and the Family, 52,* 5-20.

Berry, J. O., & Jones, W. H. (1995). The parental stress scale: Initial psychometric evidence. *Journal of Social and Personal Relationships, 12,* 463-472.

Bomar, J. A., & Sabatelli, R. M. (1996). Family system dynamics, gender, and psychosocial maturity in late adolescence. *Journal of Adolescent Research, 11,* 421-439.

Bornstein, M. H. (1995). Parenting infants. In M. H. Bornstein (Ed.), *Handbook of parenting: Vol. 1. Children and parenting* (pp. 3-39). Mahwah, NJ: Lawrence Erlbaum.

Bowlby, J. (1969). *Attachment and loss: Vol. 1. Attachment.* London: Hogarth.

Bradley, R. H., Whiteside-Mansell, L., Brisby, J. A., & Caldwell, B. M. (1997). Parents' socioemotional investment in children. *Journal of Marriage and the Family, 59,* 77-90.

Brody, G. H., Stoneman, Z., & Burke, M. (1987). Child temperaments, maternal differential behavior, and sibling relationships. *Developmental Psychology, 23,* 354-362.

Brody, G. H., Stoneman, Z., & McCoy, J. K. (1992). Associations of maternal and paternal direct and differential behavior with sibling relationships: Contemporaneous and longitudinal analyses. *Child Development, 63,* 82-92.

Brody, G. H., Stoneman, Z., McCoy, J. K., & Forehand, R. (1992). Contemporaneous and longitudinal associations of sibling conflict with family relationship assessments and family discussions about sibling problems. *Child Development, 63,* 391-400.

Christian, K., Morrison, F. J., & Bryant, F. B. (1998). Predicting kindergarten academic skills: Interactions among child care, maternal education, and family literacy environments. *Early Childhood Research Quarterly, 13,* 501-521.

Cowan, C. P., & Cowan, P. A. (1988). Who does what when partners become parents: Implications for men, women, and marriage. In R. Palkovitz & M. B. Sussman (Eds.), *Transitions to parenthood* (pp. 105-132). New York: Hawthorn Press.

Cowan, C. P., & Cowan, P. A. (1995). Interventions to ease the transition to parenthood: Why they are needed and what they can do. *Family Relations, 44,* 412-423.

Cox, M. J., Owen, M. T., Lewis, J. M., & Henderson, V. K. (1989). Marriage, adult adjustment, and early parenting. *Child Development, 60,* 1015-1024.

Crnic, K. A., & Acevedo, M. (1995). Everyday stresses and parenting. In M. H. Bornstein (Ed.), *Handbook of parenting: Vol. 4. Applied and practical parenting* (pp. 277-297). Mahwah, NJ: Lawrence Erlbaum.

Crnic, K. A., & Booth, C. L. (1991). Mothers' and fathers' perceptions of daily hassles across early childhood. *Journal of Marriage and the Family, 53,* 1042-1050.

Crohan, S. E. (1996). Marital quality and conflict across the transition to parenthood in African American and white couples. *Journal of Marriage and the Family, 58,* 933-944.

Dickstein, S., & Parke, R. D. (1988). Social referencing in infancy: A glance at fathers and marriage. *Child Development, 59,* 506-511.

Donson, N. (1999). Caring for day care: Models for early intervention and primary prevention. In T. B. Cohen & M. H. Etezady (Eds.), *The vulnerable child* (Vol. 3, pp. 181-212). Madison, CT: International Universities Press.

Dunn, J. (1985). *Sisters and brothers.* Cambridge, MA: Harvard University Press.

Dunn, J., & Kendrick, C. (1980). The arrival of a sibling: Changes in patterns of interaction between mother and firstborn child. *Journal of Child Psychology and Psychiatry, 21,* 119-132.

Egeland, B., Jacobvitz, D., & Sroufe, L. A. (1988). Breaking the cycle of abuse. *Child Development, 59,* 1080-1088.

Erdwins, C. J., Casper, W. J., & Buffardi, L. C. (1998). Child care satisfaction: The effects of parental gender and type of child care used. *Child & Youth Care Forum, 27,* 111-123.

Fein, G., Gariboldi, A., & Boni, R. (1993). Antecedents of maternal separation anxiety. *Merrill-Palmer Quarterly, 39,* 481-495.

Fonagy, P., Steele, H., & Steele, M. (1991). Maternal representations of attachment during pregnancy predict the organization of infant-mother attachment at one year of age. *Child Development, 62,* 891-905.

Furman, W. (1995). Parenting siblings. In M. H. Bornstein (Ed.), *Handbook of parenting: Vol. 1. Children and parenting* (pp.143-162). Mahwah, NJ: Lawrence Erlbaum.

Garner, P. W., Jones, D. C., & Palmer, D. J. (1994). Social cognitive correlates of preschool children's sibling caregiving behavior. *Developmental Psychology, 30,* 905-911.

Goelman, H., & Pence, A. R. (1990). Children in three types of daycare: Daily experiences, quality of care, and developmental outcomes. In A. S. Honig (Ed.), *Optimizing early child care and education* (pp. 67-76). London: Gordon & Breach.

Harwood, R. (1992). The influence of culturally derived values on Anglo and Puerto Rican mothers' perceptions of attachment behavior. *Child Development, 63,* 822-839.

Heinicke, C. M. (1995). Determinants of the transition to parenting. In M. H. Bornstein (Ed.), *Handbook of parenting: Vol. 3. Status and social conditions of parenting* (pp. 277-303). Mahwah, NJ: Lawrence Erlbaum.

Hock, E., & DeMeis, D. (1990). Depression in mothers of infants: The role of maternal employment. *Developmental Psychology, 26,* 285-291.

Hock, E., & Lutz, W. (1998). Psychological meaning of separation anxiety in mothers and fathers. *Journal of Family Psychology, 12,* 41-55.

Hock, E., McBride, S., & Gnezda, M. T. (1989). Maternal separation anxiety: Mother-infant separation from the maternal perspective. *Child Development, 60,* 793-802.

Hock, E., Schirtzing, E., & Lutz, W. (1992). Dimensions of family relationships associated with depressive symptomatology in mothers of young children. *Psychology of Women Quarterly, 16,* 229-241.

Hoffman, L. W. (1989). Effects of maternal employment in the two-parent family. *American Psychologist, 44,* 283-292.

Holmes, T. H., & Rahe, R. H. (1967). The Social Readjustment Rating Scale. *Journal of Psychosomatic Research, 11,* 213-218.

Honig, A. S. (1995). Choosing child care for young children. In M. H. Bornstein (Ed.), *Handbook of parenting: Vol. 4. Applied and practical parenting* (pp. 411-435). Mahwah, NJ: Lawrence Erlbaum.

Howe, N. (1991). Sibling-directed internal state language, perspective taking, and affective behavior. *Child Development, 62,* 1503-1512.

Jarvis, P. A., & Creasey, G. L. (1991). Parental stress, coping, and attachment in families with an 18-month-old infant. *Infant Behavior and Development, 14,* 383-395.

Jayakody, R., Chatters, L. M., & Taylor, R. J. (1993). Family support to single and married African-American mothers: The provision of financial, emotional, and child care assistance. *Journal of Marriage and the Family, 55,* 261-276.

Kreppner, K., Paulsen, S., & Schuetze, Y. (1982). Infant and family development: From triads to tetrads. *Human Development, 25,* 373-391.

Leach, P. (1997). Infant care from infants' viewpoint: The views of some professionals. *Early Development and Parenting, 6,* 47-58.

Levitt, M. J., Weber, R. A., & Clark, M. C. (1986). Social network relationships as sources of maternal support and well-being. *Developmental Psychology, 22,* 310-316.

Lutz, W., & Hock, E. (1995). Maternal separation anxiety: Relations to adult attachment representations in mothers of infants. *Journal of Genetic Psychology, 156,* 57-72.

MacDermid, S. M., Huston, T. L., & McHale, S. M. (1990). Changes in marriage associated with transition to parenthood. *Journal of Marriage and the Family, 52,* 475-486.

McBride, S. (1990). Maternal moderators of child care: The role of maternal separation anxiety. *New Directions for Child Development, 49,* 53-70.

McBride, S., & Belsky, J. (1988). Characteristics, determinants, and consequences of maternal separation anxiety. *Developmental Psychology, 24,* 407-414.

McCubbin, H. I., & Patterson, J. M. (1983). The family stress process: The Double ABC-X Model of adjustment and adaptation. *Marriage and Family Review, 6,* 7-37.

National Commission on Children. (1993). *Just the facts: A summary of recent information on America's children and their families.* Washington, DC: Author.

Newman, P. R., & Newman, B. M. (1997). *Childhood and adolescence.* Pacific Grove, CA: Brooks/Cole.

Parke, R. D. (1995). Fathers and families. In M. H. Bornstein (Ed.), *Handbook of parenting: Vol. 3. Status and social conditions of parenting* (pp. 27-63). Mahwah, NJ: Lawrence Erlbaum.

Perozynski, L., & Kramer, L. (1999). Parental beliefs about managing sibling conflict. *Developmental Psychology, 35,* 489-499.

Pope, V. (1997). Day-care dangers. *U.S. News & World Report, 23,* 31-37.

Quittner, A. L., Glueckauf, R. L., & Jackson, R. L. (1990). Chronic parenting stress: Moderating versus mediating effects of social support. *Journal of Personality and Social Psychology, 59,* 1266-1278.

Ricks, M. H. (1985). The social transmission of parental behavior: Attachment across generations. *Monographs of the Society for Research in Child Development, 50*(1-2, Serial No. 209), 211-227.

Sabatelli, R. M., & Waldron, R. J. (1995). Measurement issues in the assessment of the experiences of parenthood. *Journal of Marriage and the Family, 57,* 969-980.

Sanchez, L., & Thomson, E. (1997). Becoming mothers and fathers: Parenthood, gender, and the division of labor. *Gender & Society, 11,* 747-772.

Sanik, M. M. (1993). The effects of time allocations on parental stress. *Social Indicators Research, 30,* 175-184.

Simon, R. W. (1992). Parental role strains, salience of parental identity, and gender differences in psychological distress. *Journal of Health and Social Behavior, 33,* 25-35.

Singer, J. D., Fuller, B., Keiley, M. K., & Wolf, A. (1998). Early child-care selection: Variation by geographic location, maternal characteristics, and family structure. *Developmental Psychology, 34,* 1129-1144.

Stevens, J. H., Jr. (1988). Social support, locus of control, and parenting in three low-income groups of mothers: Black teenagers, black adults, and white adults. *Child Development, 59,* 635-642.

Stocker, C., Dunn, J., & Plomin, R. (1989). Sibling relationships: Links with child temperament, maternal behavior, and family structure. *Child Development, 60,* 715-727.

Volling, B. L., & Belsky, J. (1991). Multiple determinants of fathering during early infancy in dual-career and single-earner families. *Journal of Marriage and the Family, 53,* 461-474.

Volling, B. L., & Belsky, J. (1992). The contribution of mother-child and father-child relationships to the quality of sibling interaction: A longitudinal study. *Child Development, 63,* 1209-1222.

Vygotsky, L. S. (1978). *Mind in society.* Cambridge, MA: Harvard University Press.

Wallace, P. M., & Gotleib, I. H. (1990). Marital adjustment during the transition to parenthood: Stability and predictors of change. *Journal of Marriage and the Family, 52,* 21-29.

Woolfson, L. H. (1999). Using a model of transactional developmental regulation to evaluate the effectiveness of an early intervention programme for pre-school children with motor impairments. *Child: Care, Health, & Development, 25,* 579.

Zigler, E. (1999). Head Start is not child care. *American Psychologist, 54,* 142.

4

● ● ● ● ● ● ●

Understanding Parental Stress

A Family Perspective

GARY W. PETERSON
KATHLEEN MATHIESON

Research on adolescents and adults often identifies the "desire to become a parent" as an attitude shared by the vast majority of those who respond. That is, the common expectation is for satisfactions with parenting to outweigh any sense of dissatisfaction with this important life endeavor (Calvert & Stanton, 1992). Anyone who has been a mother or father, however, understands what is meant, at a visceral level, by the concept "parental stress." Experiences of stress occur regularly for parents—during the intense hours of childbirth as well as the subsequent periods of child and adolescent development. Moreover, stress occurs even during the positive accomplishments of children. For example, a father's stress becomes evident as he fidgets nervously waiting for his 10-year-old daughter's gymnastic performance, hoping that she will execute her recently learned back flip without a hitch.

Most parents of adolescents will feel acute stress (perhaps experienced as a crisis) when their 16-year-old daughter tearfully informs them she is pregnant or when their 17-year-old son must be bailed out of jail for possession of marijuana. Parents of children who are victims of autistic or attention deficit disorders often experience high levels of stress in their efforts to cope with the relentlessly difficult behavior demonstrated by these youngsters. Other mothers and fathers are simply "stressed" from having to compromise their time as parents because of demanding job circumstances or having to assist their own elderly parents whose failing health requires attention. The major point here is that some degree of parental stress is probably a universal experience. All parents, regardless of class, ethnicity, or other "social memberships," experience stress from their roles as caregivers and socializers of children. This reality that parental stress is an extremely common experience in no way minimizes the importance of this topic. Instead, the universality of parental stress underscores the importance of understanding how wide variations of this concept may contribute to the effective or ineffective functioning of mothers and fathers (Creasey & Reese, 1996; Deater-Deckard & Scarr, 1996).

The purpose of this chapter, therefore, is to integrate the existing research on parental stress with concepts that are central to family stress theory (Boss, 1988; Hill, 1949; McKenry & Price, 1994) and to address the following issues: (a) why the experience of parental stress may be universal, (b) why parental stress varies widely within the larger population of mothers and fathers, (c) why parents vary in their capacities to cope with and adapt to stress, and (d) what linkages exist between parental stress and the adjustment (or maladjustment) of children. The primary focus of this integrative effort includes several concepts from family stress theory: (a) stress and crisis, (b) stressor events (or stressors), (c) resources, (d) definition of the stressor (or perception), (e) coping, and (f) adaptation. Rethinking parental stress literature in terms of family stress theory will provide a more *systemic view* of this research, consistent with basic concepts from family stress theory. Most of the current research on parental stress is largely an outgrowth of psychological theory (Crnic & Acevedo, 1995; Dohrenwend & Dohrenwend, 1974; Holmes & Rahe, 1967), much of which deals with constructs emphasizing the experience of individuals at the expense of "relationship" or "systemic perspectives."

Family Stress Theory and Parental Stress: The X Factor

The foundation of family stress theory, of course, is the classic work by Reuben Hill (1949) on the ABC-X Model, in which a family crisis (the X factor) was conceptualized as the product of a complex three-way interaction among (a) the stressor event (the A factor), (b) the resources that families bring to bear on a stressor (the B factor), and (c) the definition or meaning assigned to a stressor by families (the C factor). Thus, stress or crisis was not viewed simply as the direct result of the event itself (although this cannot be completely discounted) but also as a product of how families define demanding circumstances and the extent to which they have resources available for coping.

Family stress theory was originally developed to examine the circumstances of "crisis" when a sudden, dramatic event (e.g., a hurricane or a young child's cancer diagnosis) occurs that immobilizes or incapacitates the family system (Hill, 1949). Subsequent research using family stress theory, however, has increasingly dealt with ordinary, normative, cumulative, and long-term changes within the steady state of families, rather than focusing solely on dysfunction in response to dramatic events (Boss, 1988; Crnic & Acevedo, 1995; McKenry & Price, 1994). Greater attention has been focused on both normative transitions in the life course (e.g., adolescents negotiating greater autonomy from parents) and the accumulation of demanding circumstances (e.g., work stress adding to parental stress) that impair effective parental functioning and influence the daily experiences of mothers, fathers, and children. Increased attention is now being devoted to understanding how families (and parents) cope with stress and how they are resilient in the face of demanding circumstances.

Neither family nor parental stress is viewed as inherently bad or good. They become problematic only when family members experience dissatisfaction as change becomes disruptive and impairs effective functioning. Change is viewed as an almost inevitable source of stress, often experienced as tension within either the parent-child or the larger family system (Boss, 1988). Various life transitions and events (e.g., the transition to parenthood) are viewed as providing the essential ingredients for normal psychosocial development, but they often do so by evoking significant disturbances and pressures for change (i.e., stress). Thus, because family members (e.g., parents) and family systems develop and change over time, stress is viewed as an inevitable consequence of everyday life within both families and parent-child relationships (Crnic & Greenberg, 1990).

A major contribution of family stress theory, therefore, is to move the construct "stress" from applications only at psychological levels of analysis to those at both relationship and family-system levels of analysis (Boss, 1988; McKenry & Price, 1994). At the psychological level, parental stress is defined as an aversive internal reaction to the demands of occupying parental roles (Deater-Deckard, 1998); at the relationship or family-systems level, stress is defined as pressure or tension within a relationship system that is synonymous with change (Boss, 1988). Such pressures for change, depending on how they are viewed by parents, may contribute to psychological stress at the individual level of experience. Thus, both family and parental stress involve changes that result from responding to the demands of either a crisis event, a stressor, or the accumulation of stressors at both the individual and relationship levels of experience (Boss, 1988).

Parental stress is both a *product* of connections with other systemic elements and an *activator* of parental behavior that has important consequences for other members of the system (e.g., children) (Deater-Deckard, 1998). Thus, parental stress results, in part, from a great variety of mothers' and fathers' systemic connections, including sudden job loss, the quality of marriage, and support from extended family members. Moreover, parental stress has consequences within the parent-child relationship by activating or fostering changes in both the psychological experience of parents and their child-rearing behavior (i.e., relationship-level behavior) (Abdin, 1992; Belsky, 1984). These responses by parents, in turn, may have consequences for the social, emotional, and cognitive development of children (Parke & Buriel, 1998; Peterson & Hann, 1999). Specifically, highly stressed parents are more inclined to be emotionally reactive, more preoccupied with adult-centered goals, and less likely to maintain child-centered objectives and behavior. Subsequently, these parents also tend to be less responsive, more punitive (authoritarian), and possibly neglectful or abusive in reference to children. Such declines in parenting may lead to several negative outcomes in the young, such as a reduced willingness to be responsive to parents' expectations, lower social competence, feelings of rejection, aggressive behaviors, and stressful experiences (Deater-Deckard, 1998; Peterson & Hann, 1999). Correspondingly, lower-stress parents tend to be more responsive, warm, rational, and moderate in the kinds of control (e.g., firm control, consistent rule enforcement, monitoring) that are used with the young. The most frequent child characteristics associated with these parental behaviors are higher self-esteem, higher school achievement, better social skills, and a balance between conforming to parents' expectations and making progress toward autonomy (Peterson & Hann, 1999; Peterson, Madden-Derdich, & Leonard, 2000).

As with other systemic relationships, the "connections" between parental stress and child characteristics are not limited to conceptions in which social influence flows in only one direction from parent to child. In fact, children and their perceived attributes often have considerable influence on the degree of stress that parents experience (see the next section) (Ambert, 1992; Peterson & Hann, 1999; Peterson & Rollins, 1987; Stafford & Bayer, 1993). Clearly, the parent-child relationship is characterized by reciprocal consequences (a basic characteristic of systems); parental stress is both an "instigator" and a product of change within the family system.

Stressors or Stressor Events:
The A Factor

Stressors or stressor events (i.e., the A factor) are those occurrences that may be of sufficient magnitude to bring about feelings of tension for parents as well as change within the parent-child and larger family relationships. Because many stressful circumstances for parents do not occur as discrete events, the general concept *stressor* is the preferred term for this chapter, encompassing both short-term and more long-term occurrences (sometimes composed of many stressors). Although stressors or stressor events carry the *potential* for evoking change and specific psychological responses, these occurrences that impinge on the parent-child relationship are not synonymous with the onset of stress. Stressors threaten the status quo of families and parent-child relationships, but they are *not solely capable* of fostering stress and imposing demands on individuals and relationships. The reason for this limitation is that, by themselves, stressors (a) do not have all the necessary ingredients (i.e., B factor *resources* and C factor *definitions*) for creating parental stress (Boss, 1988; Deater-Deckard, 1998); (b) do not have any inherent positive or negative attributions; and (c) may never produce a crisis that immobilizes the parent-child relationship. Instead, stressors are best described as inherently neutral phenomena involving pressures that may either develop quickly or unfold over a long period of time. Rather than being sudden disruptions, many are of moderate strength and accumulate as demanding circumstances "pile up" over time (McCubbin & Patterson, 1986).

Despite the fact that stressors have no inherent meaning, methods of classification have been developed to identify the most common ways that parents and families respond to each of these circumstances. A variety of classification systems have been developed (Boss, 1988; McKenry & Price, 1994), with the most common categories being described as *chronic, normative,* and *nonnormative stressors.* Moreover, because specific stressors can sometimes be viewed as fitting more than one category, such classification systems often fail to be mutually exclusive.

Chronic Stressors

The first of these categories, chronic stressors, refers to *atypical circumstances that occur over extended periods of time, are difficult to amend, and may have debilitating effects* for both parents and the parent-child relationship. The concept *chronic stressor* is exemplified by the time, energy, and financial and emotional demands faced by parents of children with long-term illnesses or abnormal qualities (e.g., heart disease, congenital birth defects), as well as by the multiple stressors associated with poverty.

Poverty

The condition of poverty is a general construct composed of several chronic stressors that are pervasive in the daily lives of many parents. Chronic stressors that are components of poverty include poor housing, lack of food, cold in the winter, heat in the summer, untreated illnesses, crime-infested neighborhoods, inabilities to provide material possessions (i.e., clothing, toys), and poor-quality schooling (McLoyd, 1990). Such stressors often evoke such experiences as general irritability, the loss of control over one's life, the inability to plan ahead, and a sense of relative deprivation (Ambert, 1997). Parents who face the multiple stressors of poverty on a daily basis must try to adjust to these circumstances. A common outcome, however, is that aversive experiences from the stressors of poverty tend to "spill over" into the parental domain; the result is that parents' child-rearing approaches become more harsh, inconsistent, conflictual, and distant, and less sensitive (Brooks-Gunn & Duncan, 1997; Conger et al., 1992; McLoyd, Jayaratne, Ceballo, & Borquez, 1994). Such problematic child rearing may result, in part, from poverty-based stressors that are added to the normative, everyday demands of parenting. The experience of poverty, therefore, is a composite experience involving multiple chronic stressors that spill over and *pile up* in the lives of parents.

Child Effects:
Long-Term Demands

A large number of chronic stressors for parents appear to have their basis in specific child characteristics (i.e., child effects). This is especially true in those cases in which the shock of an initial diagnosis of serious illness or disability has passed and *the realities of long-term responsibility have set in for parents.* Commonly referred to as "child effects," such a conception underscores the fundamental impact of children on the social-emotional lives of mothers and fathers (Ambert, 1992; Peterson & Hann, 1999; Peterson & Rollins, 1987). For example, children who have either long-term illnesses or physical discrepancies from the norm such as asthma, heart disease, congenital birth defects, and physical handicaps confront parents with substantial demands for investments of time, energy, and emotion.

Of particular interest to social scientists are children with identified social-emotional problems whose attributes serve as potential sources of chronic demands that parents find particularly challenging. Examples of such persistent, child-based stressors include youngsters who are diagnosed as demonstrating conduct disorders, attention deficit disorders, autism, or schizophrenia (Anastopoulos, Guevremont, Shelton, & DuPaul, 1992; Baker & McCal, 1995; Cook & Cohler, 1986; Donenberg & Baker, 1993; Dumas, Wolf, Fisman, & Culligan, 1991). Especially when disturbed children reside with parents, these circumstances can exert highly negative influences, even throughout the parents' later years of life (Greenberg, Siltzer, & Greenlay, 1993). Accumulating stressors from these relationships include such things as demanding supervision requirements, the constant need for care, and treatment costs, as well as great potential for feelings of anger, embarrassment, guilt, and despair. Moreover, many youngsters with social-emotional problems never truly become emancipated (or launched) as more adjusted children do, and they have great potential to continuously function as chronic stressors for parents (Ambert, 1992).

Normative Stressors

The second of these categories, *normative stressors,* refers to events that are endemic to everyday life (i.e., daily hassles) or to longer-term developmental transitions that are inherent components of the typical family life cycle (Carter & McGoldrick, 1989; McKenry & Price, 1994).

Daily Hassles

Some normative stressors that occur on an everyday basis, or *daily hassles,* consist of the constant caregiving demands and pressures that arise in relationships with developing children. Many everyday child-rearing experiences are sources of self-defined competence for parents as challenges are engaged, perceived as positive, and solved. In contrast, other experiences involve dealing with children's whining behavior, annoying conduct, endless cleaning-up activities, constant interruptions (and a resulting lack of privacy), and time-consuming errands. By themselves, of course, such daily hassles may have little consequence, but the cumulative impact of many normative stressors over time may result in substantial amounts of stress for parents. Compared with the circumstances of two-parent families, for example, single-parent families are not inherently pathological environments but may be more vulnerable to stress resulting from the multitude of daily hassles. Specifically, single parents may be more susceptible because "backup" or supportive partners are not available to share everyday hassles and buffer some of the stress from these challenges (Weinraub & Gringlas, 1995).

Many hassles, in fact, may reoccur simply because individuals remain in the same contexts that have consistent, predictable demands that structure their relationships (Crnic & Acevedo, 1995; Crnic & Greenberg, 1990; Lazarus, 1984). Consequently, the cumulative daily hassles associated with parenting may, over time, change the nature of parent-child relationships. As parents increasingly experience frequent and problematic daily hassles with children, relationships that were once competent may gradually become redirected down dysfunctional and stressful pathways. Such constantly evolving circular processes eventually may produce less competent, less satisfied, and unresponsive parents, as well as children who demonstrate problematic behavior (Crnic & Acevedo, 1995).

Developmental Transitions

Another source of normative stress is not limited to daily situations but is more a function of major developmental transitions that are integral to the life cycle of families and parent-child relationships. That is, at different periods of time, the developing characteristics of children and the changing social meanings associated with these transitions serve to challenge parents and initiate necessary changes within the parent-child relationship. Developmental transitions of this kind provide the potential for an accumulation of stressors over time that may be perceived collectively as disruptive change that contributes to psychological distress.

One of these pivotal periods of developmental transition occurs during the time period in which the young are experiencing the adolescent years. A key issue that evokes stress for parents during this period is the process of granting increased autonomy to the young. Normally, parents who grant autonomy to adolescents engage in a gradual process of allowing greater adolescent choice and independence as relationship rules concerning power and control are renegotiated (Peterson, 1995; Peterson, Bush, & Supple, 1999). This process of gradually "letting go," if conducted competently, is not a sudden transition for parents of adolescents (Grotevant, 1998). Instead, mothers and fathers of teenagers must engage in a gradual process that originates in childhood and accelerates during adolescence until the eventual transition to adulthood is accomplished.

This "letting go" process presents parents with many potential stressors, especially when mothers and fathers are very reluctant to grant autonomy. Some parents have considerable difficulty accommodating these changes and resist recognizing that an important stage in their own lives is coming to a gradual end. Consequently, the adolescent's desire for autonomy may evoke feelings of distress for parents as they confront demands for unwanted relationship changes that lead to loss of control (Small, Eastman, & Cornelius, 1988). Parental stress and parent-adolescent conflict may be normative results of the letting go process as mothers, fathers, and teenagers renegotiate family rules. Moreover, in ethnic-minority families who are experiencing immigration (e.g., Asian Americans or Hispanic Americans), a process referred to as *generational dissonance* may further exacerbate the normal levels of parental stress and conflict with adolescents. Specifically, the typical pattern for this process becomes evident when members of the younger generation adjust to the new culture faster than their immigrant parents do (and may be perceived by parents as betraying their culture of origin); the result is that parents experience increased stress as a product of differential acculturation rates across generations. This *acculturative stress* often magnifies the normal levels of stress experienced by parents of adolescents, which, in turn, fosters greater *relationship distance* between the generations (Portes & Rumbaut, 1996).

Through such processes, relationships that were once clearly dominated by parents are transformed gradually, either in the direction of greater equality or toward leadership roles for the young. An important developmental challenge for parents is to manage their stress and provide a base of security (i.e., a base of connectedness) from which the young can expand into the social environment and progress toward adulthood (Grotevant, 1998; Peterson, 1995; Peterson, Bodman, Bush, & Madden-Derdich, 2000).

Nonnormative Stressors

Parents also face stressor events that are nonnormative—unpredictable occurrences that are substantially disruptive to the everyday pattern of parent-child relationships (McKenry & Price, 1994). Consistent with the earliest interests of family crisis theorists (Hill, 1949), nonnormative stressor events are often sudden, dramatic occurrences that have considerable potential to disrupt the lives of parents. Usually, these stressor events are a product of unique situations that are unlikely to be repeated. Examples of nonnormative stressors include natural disasters, the sudden death of a child from drowning, severe injuries from automobile accidents, unexpected job promotions, or "big gambling wins in Vegas." Although the first three are widely regarded as negative developments and the second two commonly viewed as positive events, all five are unexpected and have the potential for evoking substantial disruptions in the daily rhythms of parent-child and family relationships. Moreover, the disruptive family relationship and the structural changes that are evoked by such events have the potential to increase the psychological stress of parents (McKenry & Price, 1994). None of these events, however, is inherently stressful in exactly the same way for all parents; they also depend on such factors as each parent's subjective interpretations and the available resources (or vulnerabilities).

Off-Time Developments

Virtually all parents anticipate that certain stressful circumstances, such as retirement, a family member's death, or the advent of grandparenthood, will occur as part of normal family transitions. However, when such "normal" events occur at unanticipated times, these off-time developments can become significant sources of disruptive stress. For example, during a child's school-age years, the death of a parent often is extremely traumatic due, in part, to the "off-time" nature of this event. In a similar fashion, parents may experience considerable upheaval when learning from their teenage daughter that they will become grandparents much earlier than they had anticipated. By causing families to mobilize resources for coping, such off-schedule, unanticipated events can greatly obstruct the functioning of family systems and disrupt the individual experiences of family members (Figley & McCubbin, 1983).

Initial Awareness or Diagnosis

Another type of nonnormative stressor for parents may result from acute situations involving the *initial awareness* of unexpected circumstances and deviant or abnormal child characteristics. Examples of nonnormative stressors that are based in initial awareness include delinquency, conduct disorders, attention deficit behavior (Ambert, 1992), physical illness, poor mental health, and birth defects (Cronin, 1995; Rimmerman & Duvdevani, 1996). Specifically, the *initial awareness or diagnosis* of these attributes or conditions often becomes an acute stressor event for parents. For example, the initial diagnosis that a child has leukemia or some other form of cancer is likely to be defined as an acute stressor that disrupts the lives and psychological well-being of parents. The experience of acute stress or crisis is also likely to result for parents when a phone call suddenly informs them that their son has just been arrested for selling drugs. Recent research indicates that parents who are initially confronted with their child's delinquency often experience distress, worry, edginess, devastation, and crying spells (Ambert, 1997, 1999). Moreover, subsequent experience with severe, nonnormative stressors may be converted, over time, into chronic stressors as parents become more accustomed (or adapted) to the issues at hand.

Parental Resources: The B Factor

The level of disruptive change within parent-child relationships and the psychological stress experienced by parents may be partially determined (or mediated) by *positive resources* (i.e., the B factor), which vary in their availability to parents. The concept *positive resources* refers to traits, characteristics, or abilities of parents, parent-child relationships, family systems, and the larger social context that can help address the demands of stressor events that parents face (McCubbin & Patterson, 1986). Such individual and relationship resources (or potential "regenerative power") have the latent capability to buffer stress by decreasing the negative effects of stressful events. The concept *resources* also encompasses *negative resources,* or the potential vulnerabilities of parents and parent-child relationships to stressors and crisis events. It is important to emphasize that resources refer largely to *potential* sources of support or vulnerability rather than to *actual* or guaranteed access to assistance. (Actual efforts to use or orchestrate resources, referred to as "coping," are described in the section titled "Parental Coping.")

Individual Resources

Individual or personal resources of parents include economic well-being (e.g., finances), knowledge (e.g., of child development), health (physical and emotional well-being), and psychological qualities (e.g., self-efficacy). Illustrative of such individually based resources are the psychological and emotional qualities that are commonly identified as being components of parental competence (Peterson & Hann, 1999). Consequently, linkages exist between parents' psychological functioning, their abilities to manage stress, and the competence needed to retain appropriate levels of authority and create close, caring relationships. Parental competence, an individual resource, is composed of such desirable personal qualities as psychological maturity, empathy, warmth, a secure self-image, self-efficacy, and the ability to exercise firm control (Peterson & Hann, 1999). Such personal competencies appear to be potential resources because parents who feel personally capable also tend to marshal their resources for managing stressful circumstances (e.g., an infant's distress or an adolescent's combativeness).

The inverse circumstances, or negative resources, also apply to the psychological and relationship experiences of parents. Specifically, adults who have psychological or emotional problems (e.g., extensive depression, anger, or anxiety) often bring personal issues into the parent-child relationship and become more vulnerable to the adverse consequences of stress that result from parenting (Brook, Whiteman, Balka, & Cohen, 1995; Vondra & Belsky, 1993). Parents who are self-preoccupied, depressed, highly anxious, or abusers of substances will be less able to deal effectively with stressors or crisis events (Forgays, 1992; Gelfand, Teti, & Fox, 1992; Kelley, 1992) and less able to demonstrate the patience, sensitivity, and responsiveness necessary to raise children (Vondra & Belsky, 1993).

Familial and Social Resources

Parents also draw on resources and experience vulnerabilities that are located within the family system and the larger social-ecological context (Luster & Okagaki, 1993). Under certain circumstances, assistance from social networks, often referred to as *social support,* has been associated with a variety of positive mental health outcomes for parents, including lower psychological stress (Pierce, Sarason, & Sarason, 1996) and better capacities to deal with stressful events (Koeske & Koeske, 1990). Supportive adult partners, extended kin, and aspects of larger social networks have the potential to assist parents by providing advice, emotional support, material assistance, and encouragement to deal with stressors and crisis events.

Scholars differ in the types of social support they have identified. Most, however, distinguish between *emotional support,* or behavior that communicates caring and love (Pierce et al., 1996), and *instrumental support,* or concrete assistance that reduces the tasks and responsibilities of parents (Cochran & Niego, 1995). Although conceptualized as separate dimensions for the purposes of clarification, emotional and instrumental support are by no means mutually exclusive in reality. Such an overlap is illustrated by a grandfather who quickly cancels his afternoon golf plans (i.e., a longtime plan with his buddies) so that he can assist his single-parent daughter by baby-sitting his grandson. This unselfish act allows his daughter to help with an emergency situation at work during a time when her son's day care is temporarily closed. Consequently, the tangible child care represents instrumental support, whereas the selfless quality of the grandfather's actions displays emotional support.

The marital relationship is another aspect of the immediate social network that may function as a potential source of support for parents or increase their vulnerability (Belsky, 1984; Peterson & Hann, 1999). Scholars have frequently concluded that the role of potential social support beyond family boundaries is secondary to the role of marital relationships (Belsky, 1984; Belsky & Rovine, 1990). A key factor in preventing stress is the extent to which parents support each other (i.e., usually studied as fathers either supporting or not supporting mothers) in a variety of ways. Current research indicates that parental (usually maternal) stress is reduced when humor is used by the spouse to lighten difficult moments, frustrations are listened to, caregiving responsibilities are shared, marital satisfaction is high, marital conflict is low, and housework is shared. Providing support to one's marital partner may be particularly important because research clearly indicates that mothers, compared with fathers, are more responsible for, more involved in, and experience greater parental stress from child rearing (Parke, 1995). Likewise, the opposite marital circumstances (i.e., a lack of shared caregiving, low paternal support, marital dissatisfaction, and high marital conflict) provide family emotional climates that have considerable potential to function as negative resources and foster parental stress (Cochran & Niego, 1995; Deater-Deckard & Scarr, 1996; Roggman, Moe, Hart, & Forthun, 1994; Webster-Stratton, 1990).

Social support from family or nonfamily sources has the potential to diminish feelings of parental depression (Kessler, Price, & Wortman, 1985) and increase coping abilities during times of stress (Koeske & Koeske, 1990). Support from outside family boundaries becomes especially important when a person is not married, a partner's involvement is inadequate, or alternative significant others (e.g., siblings) are not available within one's family. Moreover, social support has the potential to indirectly affect the quality of parenting by enhancing, maintaining, or impairing the emotional well-being of mothers and fathers (Pierce et al., 1996). Support from social networks that reduces parental stress appears to encourage parents to be more nurturant, more rational, and to use more moderate forms of control, while avoiding harsh or rejecting forms of child rearing (Belsky, 1984; Belsky & Vondra, 1989).

Consistent with conceptions of both resources and vulnerabilities, an important recognition is that social networks are not inherently supportive but are only potentially so. This is illustrated by the stress, conflict, frustration, and disappointment that often characterize families of unmarried teenage mothers (Kurtz & Derevensky, 1994). Under these circumstances, the social support conveyed may be judgmental and restrictive in a manner that actually increases the stress of young parents. Instead, effective social support involves providing assistance but also fostering autonomy in a manner that acknowledges another person's viewpoints, accepts their feelings, and refrains from efforts to excessively control another's experiences and behaviors (Pierce et al., 1996). Such an approach reduces the stress of young parents, provides short-term assistance for the daily demands of parenting, and provides encouragement for the long-term psychosocial maturity of youthful parents.

The Definitions Assigned by Parents: The C Factor

As previously indicated, events or phenomena (e.g., stressors or crisis events) by themselves do not create the experience of stress and crisis. Instead, parents and other family members construct their own realities or impose subjective "definitions" on their physical and social circumstances. Consequently, the *meaning or perception of phenomena* (i.e., the C factor) *helps to determine whether stressors or crisis events are experienced as something positive, negative, or neutral.* Such active, subjective qualities of parents and other family members mean that virtually identical stressors or crisis events may evoke varied responses from distinct individuals. Substantial variability in definitions is rooted in many sources, including differences in individual life experiences, diversity in ethnic and cultural norms, and distinctive family traditions and rule systems.

The subjective quality of these appraisals means that some parents may view stressors as challenges to be met "head-on," whereas other parents may view the same circumstances as debilitating. At least in a theoretical sense, parents who redefine stressors in a positive manner tend to make these experiences more manageable through the clarification of the issues, hardships, and tasks that must be addressed. Such constructed appraisals can give positive meaning to events, help to decrease the emotional burdens associated with a given stressor (McCubbin & Patterson, 1986), and provide a sense of hopelessness, denial of reality, or simply the acceptance of fate in the face of unpredictable circumstances (Boss, 1988).

These general ideas from family stress theory are reinforced by more specific research on the subjective experiences of parents. Of special importance is the idea that parental beliefs, values, attitudes, expectations, and "developmental scenarios" define the meaning of their relationships with children and help to determine how they will respond to the young. Specifically, parents make attributions about children's moods, motives, intentions, conscious responsibilities, and competencies that, in turn, help to shape mothers' and fathers' emotional responses (e.g., stress) as well as their subsequent child-rearing approaches (McGillicuddy-Delisi & Sigel, 1995). That is, mothers and fathers tend to hold their young accountable for negative behavior when attributions are made that children both "intend" to misbehave and could choose to restrain themselves if so inclined. These parents, in turn, are more likely to be distressed and to use punitive behavior, partly because their children are perceived as being sufficiently competent to "know better." In contrast, parents who believe that children are not fully competent, intentional, or responsible for their actions would be less distressed and less inclined to respond with punitive (or rejecting) behavior. Instead, these parents are more likely to be more nurturant and moderate in their control attempts (e.g., more likely to use reasoning, monitoring, and consistent rule enforcement) (Dix, Ruble, & Zambarano, 1989; Peterson & Hann, 1999).

A closely related means of conceptualizing how subjective interpretations may lead to parental stress involves the extent to which children's characteristics are viewed as deviating from parents' expectations about what is normative (Ambert, 1992; Goodnow, 1995). According to this conception, parents may define the young as deviating from their expectations in either positive or negative directions, with greater deviations from the subjectively accepted "norm" producing greater stress for parents. A negative deviation is an adverse view of a characteristic that is perceived as being deficient compared with contemporary social norms or cultural values (Goodnow, 1995). The most frequent parental responses to such negative deviations (e.g., aggressive or conduct disorder behavior) are (a) adverse subjective experiences (i.e., psychological stress) and (b) feedback to children that reflects the parent's negative feelings (e.g., punitive or rejecting behavior). In contrast, positive deviations are those characteristics that are assigned favorable definitions, in part because parents have come to view these attributes (e.g., successful school achievement) as either meeting or surpassing existing social norms. Some parents, in fact, may experience satisfaction or positive stress from specific developmental changes (e.g., growing autonomy during adolescence) that are viewed as affirming the growing competence of the young. Common responses to positive definitions include supportive behavior and moderate control strategies such as reasoning and rule-based supervision. Consequently, the specific responses of parents to children tend to be shaped not simply in terms of their children's actual characteristics but also in terms of subjective attributions and expectations of the young that may or may not reflect reality (Goodnow, 1995; McGillicuddy-Delisi & Sigel, 1995).

Parental Coping

The current emphasis of family stress theory on coping underscores how this perspective has grown to include not only the experiences of crisis and dysfunction but also how family members manage, endure, and recover from stressor events. Coping by parents and other family members involves *taking direct actions* (e.g., acquiring resources, learning new skills, and asking for assistance), *altering one's interpretations* (e.g., reframing one's circumstances), and *managing one's emotions* (e.g., through social support or substance use) that are generated by stressors (Boss, 1988; McKenry & Price, 1994). These coping strategies can be used individually, successively, or, more often, in various combinations to meet the demands of stressors and crisis events. Specific coping strategies are neither inherently adaptive nor maladaptive; rather, they depend extensively on the precise nature of the particular circumstances at hand (McKenry & Price, 1994).

Although the process of coping interacts with both the available resources and the perceptions of parents, this does not mean that each of these concepts is indistinguishable from the other. That is, instead of being simply a potential ability (i.e., a resource), *the process of coping often involves specific efforts that parents expend to manage a stressor or crisis event.* Although active coping may seek to either maintain the status quo or achieve new levels of organization, this concept involves *making actual responses to or redefining* the circumstances at hand (Boss, 1988; Lazarus & Folkman, 1984; McKenry & Price, 1994). Moreover, the kind of coping responses used may vary with the parents' ethnic or cultural background. Asian American parents, for example, are less inclined than European American parents to use mental health agencies as a means of coping with stress. From the standpoint of Asian American parents, revealing one's personal stress to a professional clinician tends to be culturally stigmatized as immaturity, weakness, and poor self-discipline (Fong, 1998).

Several examples of coping with parental stress can be found in the current literature on parent-child relationships. Cognitive coping strategies used by parents include passive approaches such as denial or avoidance as well as active approaches involving positive reappraisal and problem-focused strategies (Jarvis & Creasey, 1991; Miller, Gordon, Daniele, & Diller, 1992). Current research indicates that active approaches, which reframe stressors in a positive manner (i.e., as challenges or problems to be mastered), are more successful in reducing stress and restoring constructive parental behavior than passive approaches (i.e., accepting what is happening as the hand of uncontrollable "fate").

Other strategies involve actually drawing on or orchestrating resources (i.e., social support) from the social-ecological context to deal with parental stress. One approach, for example, is to seek increased parent education as a means of learning more about quality parenting and child development. The logic here is that parents who understand children better and are more informed about how to parent will be more likely to develop realistic expectations for children during each stage of development. Subsequently, these parents would tend to be more capable of accessing resources and developing the necessary social support networks to buffer stress levels and enhance parenting skills (Cochran & Niego, 1995). Critical attributes for coping are parents' willingness and ability (i.e., the necessary social skills) to take advantage of existing sources of social support that are only potentially available (Pierce et al., 1996). For example, a single mother who is struggling to supervise and control a delinquent teenage son may actually have a potential social network to rely on for assistance consisting of parents (i.e., grandparents), siblings, or friends. However, the actual use of this network may be problematic when pride, embarrassment, or feelings of personal responsibility (i.e., a lack of social skills) prevent the effective use of this support.

Parental Adaptation

A final concept used by family stress theorists is *adaptation, or the ability of parents and other family members to recover from stress and crisis.* Recovery from stress and crisis may occur either by eliminating disruptions in parents' relationships and returning to preexisting patterns (i.e., homeostasis) or by moving to novel levels of relationship organization and stability (i.e., morphostasis) (McCubbin & Patterson, 1986).

In reference to parental adaptation, the most prominent example of related research is the work on the experience of custodial mothers following marital separation or divorce (Hetherington & Stanley-Hagen, 1995). According to existing scholarship, stress is a frequent part of custodial mothers' lives, as role transitions are forced on them with the loss of their marital partners and the withdrawal of fathers from parental roles. Subsequently, custodial mothers must shoulder new responsibilities as providers, build new support networks, and incorporate aspects of the father's role (e.g., disciplining children) into their parenting repertoires. Such circumstances often involve income declines that contribute to stress, anxiety, and depression, which in turn place them at risk for psychological problems and declines in the quality of their performance as parents. Custodial mothers who experience increased irritability and stress often become (a) less capable of monitoring children, (b) more permissive, (c) more punitive, and (d) more inclined to engage in coercive exchanges with children (especially boys). Fortunately, in the majority of cases, maternal stress tends to subside and mother-child relationships often restabilize or recover, either at the same or new levels of functioning, approximately 1 to 2 years following the onset of marital crisis (Hetherington & Stanley-Hagen, 1995). The most frequent outcome is that parents eventually adapt to new circumstances, manage their stress, and restore the quality of their child-rearing behavior.

Conclusions

The scholarship on parental stress, therefore, is a special case of more general concepts from family stress theory that apply both to the individual and relationship levels of family systems. The experience of parental stress or crisis is a complex result of several factors, consisting of (a) the nature of the stressor or crisis event, (b) the potential resources available to parents, (c) the subjective definitions assigned by parents, (d) the particular coping styles used, and (e) the relative abilities of parents and the parent-child relationship to recover from stress and crisis (i.e., adaptation).

The application of family stress concepts to the existing research on parental stress helps us to understand a wide range of circumstances varying from a highly disruptive (nonnormative) crisis, to chronic stress, to more normative challenges. A major contribution of family stress theory is to increase our understanding about how parental stress applies to both the individual and relationship levels of families. Parental stress is a universal phenomenon, but one that varies widely in the intensity experienced by parents. Applying family stress theory to the literature on parental stress helps us understand more clearly (a) how parental stress is such a ubiquitous experience, (b) why parental stress varies widely from parent to parent, (c) why parents cope with and adapt to stress differently, and (d) how parental stress influences the psychosocial well-being of the young by affecting the child-rearing strategies (i.e., parental behavior) that parents use. Parental stress may function to devastate, inhibit, or even energize mothers and fathers, depending on numerous individual and social-environmental factors.

DISCUSSION QUESTIONS

1. Describe why stressors or stressor events do not inherently have qualities that cause parental stress or crises to occur.

2. Describe why the study of normative or everyday events is increasingly a part of the study of parental stress.

3. How does the stress experienced by parents have effects on child-rearing behavior? What consequences can parental behavior have for children's development?

4. What are some examples of coping strategies that parents may use to deal with stress?

5. During your own childhood and adolescence, which period of development was the most stressful for your parents? Find out by asking your parents and have them explain why.

SUGGESTED READINGS

Ambert, A. (1992). *The effects of children on parents.* Binghamton, NY: Haworth.
Ambert, A. (1997). *Parents, children, and adolescents: Interactive relationships and development in context.* Binghamton, NY: Haworth.
Crnic, K., & Acevedo, M. (1995). Everyday stresses and parenting. In M. H. Bornstein (Ed.), *Handbook of parenting: Vol. 4. Applied and practical parenting* (pp. 277-298). Mahwah, NJ: Lawrence Erlbaum.
Deater-Deckard, K. (1998). Parenting stress and child adjustment: Some old hypotheses and new questions. *Clinical Psychology: Science and Practice, 5*(3), 314-333.
Koeske, G. F., & Koeske, R. D. (1990). The buffering effect of social support on parental stress. *American Journal of Orthopsychiatry, 60,* 440-451.

REFERENCES

Abdin, R. R. (1992). The determinants of parenting behavior. *Journal of Clinical Child Psychology, 21,* 407-412.
Ambert, A. (1992). *The effects of children on parents.* Binghamton, NY: Haworth.

Ambert, A. (1997). *Parents, children, and adolescents: Interactive relationships and development in context.* Binghamton, NY: Haworth.

Ambert, A. (1999). The effect of male delinquency on mothers and fathers: A heuristic study. *Sociological Inquiry, 69*(4), 368-384.

Anastopoulos, A. D., Guevremont, D. C., Shelton, T. L., & DuPaul, G. J. (1992). Parenting stress among families of children with attention deficit hyperactivity disorder. *Journal of Abnormal Child Psychology, 20*(3), 503-520.

Baker, D. B., & McCal, K. (1995). Parenting stress in children with attention-deficit hyperactivity disorder and parents of children with learning disabilities. *Journal of Child and Family Studies, 4,* 57-68.

Belsky, J. (1984). The determinants of parenting. *Child Development, 55,* 83-96.

Belsky, J., & Rovine, M. (1990). Patterns of marital change across the transition to parenthood: Pregnancy to three years postpartum. *Journal of Marriage and the Family, 53,* 1083-1110.

Belsky, J., & Vondra, J. (1989). Lessons from child abuse: The determinants of parenting. In D. Cicchetti & V. Carlson (Eds.), *Child maltreatment: Theory and research on the causes and consequences of child abuse and neglect* (pp. 153-202). New York: Cambridge University Press.

Boss, P. G. (1988). *Family stress management.* Newbury Park, CA: Sage.

Brook, J. S., Whiteman, M., Balka, E. B., & Cohen, P. (1995). Parent drug use, parent personality, and parenting. *Journal of Genetic Psychology, 156,* 137-151.

Brooks-Gunn, J., & Duncan, G. J. (1997). The effects of poverty on children. *Children and Poverty, 7*(2), 55-71.

Calvert, B., & Stanton, W. (1992). Perceptions of parenthood: Similarities and differences between 15-year-old girls and boys. *Adolescence, 27,* 315-329.

Carter, B., & McGoldrick, M. (1989). Overview: The changing family life cycle: A framework for family therapy. In B. Carter & M. McGoldrick (Eds.), *The changing family life cycle: A framework for family therapy* (2nd ed., pp. 3-28). Boston: Allyn & Bacon.

Cochran, M., & Niego, S. (1995). Parenting and social networks. In M. H. Bornstein (Ed.), *Handbook of parenting: Vol. 3. Status and social conditions of parenting* (pp. 393-418). Mahwah, NJ: Lawrence Erlbaum.

Conger, R. D., Conger, K. J., Elder, G. H., Jr., Lorenz, F. O., Simons, R. L., & Whitbeck, L. B. (1992). A family process model of economic hardship and adjustment of early adolescent boys. *Child Development, 63,* 526-554.

Cook, J., & Cohler, B. J. (1986). Reciprocal socialization and the care of offspring with cancer and with schizophrenia. In N. Datan, A. Greene, & H. Reese (Eds.), *Life-span developmental psychology: Intergenerational relations* (pp. 223-243). Hillsdale, NJ: Lawrence Erlbaum.

Creasey, G., & Reese, M. (1996). Mothers' and fathers' perceptions of parenting hassles: Associations with psychological symptoms, nonparenting hassles, and child behavior problems. *Journal of Applied Developmental Psychology, 17,* 393-406.

Crnic, K., & Acevedo, M. (1995). Everyday stresses and parenting. In M. H. Bornstein (Ed.), *Handbook of parenting: Vol. 4. Applied and practical parenting* (pp. 277-298). Mahwah, NJ: Lawrence Erlbaum.

Crnic, K. A., & Greenberg, M. T. (1990). Minor parenting stresses with young children. *Child Development, 61,* 1628-1637.

Cronin, A. F. (1995). *The influence of attention deficit disorder on mother's perception of family stress: Or "lady, why can't you control your child?"* Unpublished doctoral dissertation, University of Florida, Gainesville.

Deater-Deckard, K. (1998). Parenting stress and child adjustment: Some old hypotheses and new questions. *Clinical Psychology: Science and Practice, 5,* 314-333.

Deater-Deckard, K., & Scarr, S. (1996). Parenting stress among dual-earner mothers and fathers: Are there gender differences? *Journal of Family Psychology, 10,* 45-59.

Dix, T., Ruble, D. N., & Zambarano, R. J. (1989). Mothers' implicit theories of discipline: Child effects, parent effects, and the attribution process. *Child Development, 60,* 1373-1391.

Dohrenwend, B. S., & Dohrenwend, B. P. (1974). *Stressful life events: Their nature and effects.* New York: John Wiley.

Donenberg, G., & Baker, B. L. (1993). The impact of young children with externalizing behaviors on their families. *Journal of Abnormal Child Psychology, 21,* 179-198.

Dumas, J. E., Wolf, L. C., Fisman, S. N., & Culligan, A. (1991). Parenting stress, child behavior problems, and dysphoria in parents of children with autism, Downs syndrome, behavior disorders, and normal development. *Exceptionality, 2,* 97-110.

Figley, C. R., & McCubbin, H. I. (1983). *Stress and the family: Vol. 2. Coping with catastrophe.* New York: Brunner/Mazel.

Fong, T. P. (1998). *The contemporary Asian American experience: Beyond the model minority.* Upper Saddle River, NJ: Prentice Hall.

Forgays, D. K. (1992). Type A behavior and parenting stress in mothers with young children. *Current Psychology Research and Reviews, 11,* 3-19.

Gelfand, D. M., Teti, D. M., & Fox, C. R. (1992). Sources of parenting stress for depressed and nondepressed mothers of infants. *Journal of Clinical Child Psychology, 21,* 262-272.

Goodnow, J. J. (1995). Parents' knowledge and expectations. In M. H. Bornstein (Ed.), *Handbook of parenting: Vol. 3. Status and social conditions of parenting* (pp. 305-332). Mahwah, NJ: Lawrence Erlbaum.

Greenberg, J. S., Siltzer, M. M., & Greenlay, J. R. (1993). Aging parents of adults with disabilities: The gratifications and frustrations of later-life caregiving. *Gerontologist, 33,* 542-549.

Grotevant, H. D. (1998). Adolescent development in family contexts. In W. Damon & N. Eisenberg (Eds.), *Handbook of child psychology* (5th ed., pp. 1097-1149). New York: John Wiley.

Hetherington, M. E., & Stanley-Hagen, M. (1995). Parenting in divorced and remarried families. In M. H. Bornstein (Ed.), *Handbook of parenting: Vol. 3. Status and social conditions of parenting* (pp. 233-254). Mahwah, NJ: Lawrence Erlbaum.

Hill, R. (1949). *Families under stress.* Westport, CT: Greenwood.

Holmes, T. H., & Rahe, R. H. (1967). The Social Readjustment Rating Scale. *Journal of Psychosomatic Research, 11,* 213-218.

Jarvis, P. A., & Creasey, G. L. (1991). Parental stress, coping, and attachment in families with an 18-month-old infant. *Infant Behavior and Development, 14,* 383-395.

Kelley, S. J. (1992). Parenting stress and child maltreatment in drug-exposed children. *Child Abuse and Neglect, 16,* 317-328.

Kessler, R. C., Price, R. H., & Wortman, C. B. (1985). Social factors in psychopathology: Stress, social support, and coping processes. *Annual Review of Psychology, 36,* 531-572.

Koeske, G. F., & Koeske, R. D. (1990). The buffering effect of social support on parental stress. *American Journal of Orthopsychiatry, 60,* 440-451.

Kurtz, L., & Derevensky, J. (1994). Adolescent motherhood: An application of the stress and coping model to child-rearing attitudes and practices. *Canadian Journal of Community Mental Health, 13,* 5-24.

Lazarus, R. S. (1984). Puzzles in the study of daily hassles. *Journal of Behavioral Medicine, 7,* 375-389.

Lazarus, R. S., & Folkman, S. (1984). *Stress, appraisal, and coping.* New York: Springer.

Luster, T., & Okagaki, L. (1993). Multiple influences on parenting: Ecological and life-course perspectives. In T. Luster & L. Okagaki (Eds.), *Parenting: An ecological perspective* (pp. 227-250). Hillsdale, NJ: Lawrence Erlbaum.

McCubbin, H. I., & Patterson, J. M. (1986). Adolescent stress, coping, and adaptation: A normative family perspective. In G. K. Leigh & G. W. Peterson (Eds.), *Adolescents in families* (pp. 256-276). Cincinnati, OH: Southwestern.

McGillicuddy-Delisi, A. V., & Sigel, I. E. (1995). Parental beliefs. In M. H. Bornstein (Ed.), *Handbook of parenting: Vol. 3. Status and social conditions of parenting* (pp. 333-359). Mahwah, NJ: Lawrence Erlbaum.

McKenry, P.C., & Price, S. J. (1994). Families coping with problems and change. In P. C. McKenry & S. J. Price (Eds.), *Families and change* (pp. 1-18). Thousand Oaks, CA: Sage.

McLoyd, V. C. (1990). The impact of economic hardship on black families and children: Psychological distress, parenting, and socioemotional development. *Child Development, 61,* 311-346.

McLoyd, V. C., Jayaratne, T. E., Ceballo, R., & Borquez, J. (1994). Unemployment and work interruption among African American single mothers: Effects on parenting and adolescent socioemotional functioning. *Child Development, 65,* 562-589.

Miller, A. C., Gordon, R. M., Daniele, R. J., & Diller, L. (1992). Stress, appraisal, and coping in mothers of disabled and nondisabled children. *Journal of Pediatric Psychology, 17,* 587-605.

Parke, R. D. (1995). Fathers and families. In M. H. Bornstein (Ed.), *Handbook of parenting: Vol. 3. Status and social conditions of parenting* (pp. 27-63). Hillsdale, NJ: Lawrence Erlbaum.

Parke, R., & Buriel, R. (1998). Socialization in the family: Ethnic and ecological perspectives. In W. Damon & N. Eisenberg (Eds.), *Handbook of child psychology: Vol. 3. Social, emotional, and personality development* (pp. 463-552). New York: John Wiley.

Peterson, G. W. (1995). Autonomy and connectedness in families. In R. D. Day, K. R. Gilbert, B. H. Settles, & W. R. Burr (Eds.), *Research and theory in family science* (pp. 20-41). Pacific Grove, CA: Brooks/Cole.

Peterson, G. W., Bodman, D. A., Bush, K. R., & Madden-Derdich, D. (2000). Gender and parent-child relationships. In D. H. Demo, K. R. Allen, & M. A. Fine (Eds.), *The handbook of family diversity* (pp. 82-104). New York: Oxford University Press.

Peterson, G. W., Bush, K. R., & Supple, A. (1999). Predicting adolescent autonomy from parents: Relationship connectedness and restrictiveness. *Sociological Inquiry, 69*(3), 431-457.

Peterson, G. W., & Hann, D. (1999). Socializing children and parents in families. In M. B. Sussman, S. K. Steinmetz, & G. W. Peterson (Eds.), *Handbook of marriage and the family* (2nd ed., pp. 327-370). New York: Plenum.

Peterson, G. W., Madden-Derdich, D., & Leonard, S. (2000). Parent-child relationships: A life-course perspective. In S. Price & P. McKenry (Eds.), *Families across time* (pp. 187-203). Los Angeles: Roxbury.

Peterson, G. W., & Rollins, B. C. (1987). Parent-child socialization. In M. B. Sussman & S. K. Steinmetz (Eds.), *Handbook of marriage and the family.* New York: Plenum.

Pierce, G. R., Sarason, B. R., & Sarason, I. G. (Eds.). (1996). *Handbook of social support and the family.* New York: Plenum.

Portes, A., & Rumbaut, R. G. (1996). *Immigrant America: A portrait* (2nd ed.). Berkeley: University of California Press.

Rimmerman, A., & Duvdevani, I. (1996). Parents of children and adolescents with severe mental retardation: Stress, family resources, normalization, and their application for out-of-home placement. *Research in Developmental Disabilities, 17,* 487-494.

Roggman, L. A., Moe, S. T., Hart, A. D., & Forthun, L. F. (1994). Family leisure and social support: Relations with parenting stress and psychological well-being in Head Start parents. *Early Childhood Research Quarterly, 9,* 463-480.

Small, S., Eastman, G., & Cornelius, S. (1988). Adolescent autonomy and parental stress. *Journal of Youth and Adolescence, 17,* 377-391.

Stafford, L., & Bayer, C. L. (1993). *Interaction between parents and children.* Newbury Park, CA: Sage.

Vondra, J., & Belsky, J. (1993). Developmental origins of parenting: Personality and relationship factors. In T. Luster & L. Okagaki (Eds.), *Parenting: An ecological perspective* (pp. 1-33) Hillsdale, NJ: Lawrence Erlbaum.

Webster-Stratton, C. (1990). Stress: A potential disruptor of parent perceptions and family interactions. *Journal of Clinical Child Psychology, 19,* 302-312.

Weinraub, M., & Gringlas, M. B. (1995). Single parenthood. In M. H. Bornstein (Ed.), *Handbook of parenting: Vol. 3. Status and social conditions of parenting* (pp. 65-87). Mahwah, NJ: Lawrence Erlbaum.

5

Aging and Adaptation

How Families Cope

ADAM DAVEY

Take a moment to make a partial list of all the experiences that typically accompany the first 20 years of life and how they might shape development. Now, make a second list for the last 20 years of life. How much do you know about the changes that accompany the first 20 years of life compared with the last 20 years of life? Although aging is one of life's great universals, the process of aging has not always been of interest to developmental and family researchers. However, as interest in this topic began to emerge, it became clear that many of the concepts we have taken for granted in looking at the first part of life needed to be elaborated and extended to consider development across the life span.

This chapter begins by describing (a) some of the many and considerable changes in the aging of our population, (b) the enormous changes that families have faced in post–World War II United States, and (c) the intersection of aging and family relationships. From there, several theoretical perspectives are presented that help us to understand the family context of aging and adaptation. The chapter concludes by presenting some examples of how these principles apply to some of the most important issues related to aging in a family context. Wherever possible, this chapter also presents what we know

AUTHOR'S NOTE: Preparation of this chapter was partially supported by a grant from the National Institutes of Health (R03-AG17243).

about how adaptation to aging in the family context varies across ethno-cultural groups and different family forms.

Changes in Aging and Family Structure

Toward a Definition of Late-Life Families

What is the scope of a chapter on aging and the family? For example, should we confine consideration only to nuclear family units that include at least one older family member or only to older couples, or should our emphasis lie with the effects of individual aging within a family context? Clearly, the scope of a chapter such as this one could easily fill a book the length of this entire volume. For our purposes, we consider the effects of individual and family development on individuals, and relationships within and between generations. In other words, studying the intersection between aging and the family necessitates a dynamic and intergenerational approach. The circumstances and decisions (e.g., depression, functional limitations, divorce, or remarriage) made by members of one generation within the family necessarily have implications for the development of members within the same generation and for members of other generations.

Defining late-life families requires taking a dynamic and intergenerational approach. As we shall see, there have been tremendous changes both in the experience of individual aging and in family form and function that warrant careful consideration. In addition, it is important to appreciate the balance between the "typical" intersections of aging and the family as they occur in the population as a whole and the specific circumstances that may lead individuals to the therapeutic context. This is an important distinction because often the portraits of aging and the family painted from each perspective differ in ways that have important implications for determining what kinds of problems need to be addressed and resolved.

Aging and the Family:
Past, Present, and Future

During the 20th century, the Western industrialized world has seen a profound increase in the proportion of the population age 65 and older. A recent estimate (Rowe & Kahn, 1998) suggests that roughly half of all individuals who have ever lived to be 65 years of age or older are alive today. In the United States, we have seen life expectancy at birth increase from 47 years to 76 years between 1900 and today. Population aging is likely to continue until well into the 21st century as the baby boom cohorts approach old age. By the year 2025, our best estimates suggest that more than 59 million individuals (or 20% of the population) will be at least 65 years old (Myers, 1990). This dramatic increase in the older population has resulted from the combination of several changes. Medical breakthroughs have greatly reduced premature deaths from infectious diseases and poor nutrition and death during childbirth, thus greatly extending the expected life span. At the same time, decreases in fertility rates across the 20th century (except for the baby boom cohorts born between 1946 and 1964) are responsible for much of the increase in the proportion of the population age 65 and over, and rates of disability and mortality have also decreased among older age groups, extending life expectancy in old age as well.

The aging population often has been described as the most heterogeneous segment of the population. That is, with increasing age, the utility of "age" as a marker for development becomes less and less useful. Thus, knowing that an individual is 75 years old tells us little more than the year that he or she was born. We cannot do more than speculate about other characteristics such as cognitive abilities, health status, marital status, employment status, or a host of other variables that might be important. For this reason, it is important to consider each individual's situation, rather than making generalizations. Older adults are the most diverse segment of the population.

Demographic changes have also resulted in considerable changes in the older population. There are long-standing and widening differences between the life expectancies of men and women. Life expectancy for women currently stands at 79 years, whereas for men it is only 72 years (Kinsella, 1995). The added years at the end of the life span have resulted in a dramatic increase in the number and percentage of the oldest old, those age 85 and over, who currently make up 12% of the older population and are projected to account for nearly one quarter of all older adults by the year 2050 (Hobbs & Damon, 1996). These individuals are also those who are most likely to experience functional limitations and cognitive impairment and most likely to reside in nursing homes. In fact, it has been estimated that 49.5% of those age 85 and over have one or more physical limitations (Hobbs & Damon, 1996). Our best estimates of the prevalence of cognitive impairment in this age group rest between 23.8% and 28.5% (Ebly, Parhad, Hogan, & Fung, 1994; Gatz, Kasl-Godley, & Karel, 1996; Jette, 1996), and 24.5% reside in an institutional setting (Pynoos & Golant, 1996). In contrast, less than 3% of those ages 65 to 74 have dementia, less than 12% have a functional limitation, and just 1.4% live in institutions. Despite the dramatic increase in the prevalence of dementia with age, it should still not be considered a part of normal aging.

There are also important differences in the experiences of different ethnocultural groups. Until approximately age 85, life expectancy of non-Hispanic whites exceeds that of African Americans. Beyond this age, however, mortality rates for African Americans are lower than for whites. Although immigration patterns complicate estimates of life expectancy, Asian Americans appear to have slightly greater life expectancies than whites; those for Hispanics are mixed but generally comparable to those for whites. Native Americans have the lowest life expectancies of any ethnocultural group, although there is encouraging evidence that differences in mortality rates have decreased in recent years. One important implication of ethnocultural differences in longevity, however, is that there are more older members of minority groups today than at any point in the past—a trend that is certain to continue into the foreseeable future. This aspect of the changing compositions of the elderly population is only now beginning to receive the full attention it deserves, with researchers focusing on differences in family structure, intergenerational assistance, and access to formal services, to name but a few topics.

Finally, increases in the older population are no longer limited to Western industrialized nations. While fertility rates remain high in most developing nations, the numbers of older adults are also growing rapidly. Although population aging is truly a transnational phenomenon, the experience of aging in developing nations is a topic that has only recently begun to receive attention (e.g., Kinsella, 1995; Kinsella & Taeuber, 1993).

Changes in the population structure of the United States clearly have been considerable over the course of the 20th century. Equally profound, however, are the changes in the family structure in the United States, particularly subsequent to World War II. We have seen changes in family structure and development, patterns of living arrangements, divorce, remarriage, fertility, and women's labor force participation. Each of these has the potential to affect the experience of aging in a family context.

On the one hand, a longer time spent pursuing education has resulted in the delay of both marriage and fertility for many individuals. In addition, increases in rates of cohabitation largely account for the observed decrease in marriage rates. Starting a family later, coupled with decreased fertility, means that families are smaller today, with the typical family having fewer children, spaced more closely together in age, than in previous generations. This pattern has resulted in what Bengtson, Rosenthal, and Burton (1990) refer to as the "beanpole family," in which each generation is smaller but

there are more generations alive at any one time, and with more years between each generation. Offsetting this trend to some extent is the rise in rates
of teen pregnancy and out-of-wedlock births, which Bengtson et al. (1990)
refer to as "age-compressed families." It is unclear how the nature of intergenerational ties may be affected by these changing family structures and
whether fewer and more enduring ties might lead to increased closeness
between generations or serve instead to accentuate conflict between generations (Bengtson, Rosenthal, & Burton, 1996).

The changing structure of intergenerational relationships is further complicated by the large increase in rates of divorce and remarriage. Divorce
rates roughly doubled between the 1970s and 1990s, where they have since
remained consistently high, now hovering at around 51% for first-time marriages (e.g., Cherlin, 1992; Martin & Bumpass, 1989). It is well-known that
most individuals who divorce will eventually remarry and that divorce rates
among subsequent marriages are even higher than those of first-time marriages. Marital dissolution and reconstitution affect intergenerational ties in
ways that we are only now beginning to appreciate. For example, as we consider the cumulative effects of families being formed, dissolved, and reconstituted, an older adult may find himself or herself embedded in a complex
web of ties with biological children and stepchildren, as well as children-in-
law. Given that a majority of baby boomers can expect to find themselves in
one of these complex family forms, it will be important to learn more pre-
cisely how these marital transitions affect the availability of support for
future generations of older adults.

One final noteworthy trend in families is the great increase in women's labor force participation. Women work outside of the home in the vast majority
of households. Their careers have implications for the individual's or couple's wealth upon retirement, the timing of retirement, parent-child relationships, and the availability of family caregivers for frail older adults (e.g.,
Zarit & Eggebeen, 1995). Rather than relieving women of care responsibilities, it appears to add the potential of stressors secondary to provision of
family care (Aneshensel, Pearlin, Mullan, Zarit, & Whitlach, 1995). Cross-
national work on the relationship between family and professional systems of
care also suggests that families will likely continue to provide high levels of
assistance to older adults despite changes in family structures (Davey et al.,
1999; Davey & Patsios, 1999).

To date, we still know little about long-term gay male and lesbian relationships in old age. However, what little research does exist points to both similarities and differences compared with heterosexual couples. Factors such as
relationship satisfaction, love felt, and mental health are comparable to het-

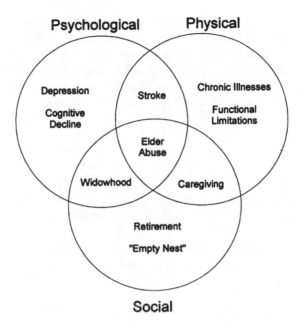

Figure 5.1. Domains of Age-Graded Stressors and Their Intersections

erosexual couples (Huyck, 1995; Kimmel & Sang, 1995). Likewise, many of the longitudinal changes in relationships and predictors of relationship success are the same for both heterosexual and same-sex couples (Kurdek, 1995). At the same time, gay male and lesbian couples face unique difficulties as a result of social barriers that emerge in later life. Consider, for example, access to inheritances, pension benefits, the ability to participate in health care decisions, or social support following the death of one's partner (Huyck, 1995). Clearly, aging in the context of a same-sex relationship is an important topic we need to learn much more about.

Domains of Aging and Adaptation

Before moving on to consider theoretical perspectives on aging and adaptations within a family context, we briefly need to examine some of the domains that will prove important. In this chapter, we will consider three sets of influences and their interactions, as shown in Figure 5.1. On the one hand, aging may be accompanied by any number of *physical changes* to which an individual might need to adapt. First, we might be interested in adaptation to common *age-related chronic illnesses,* such as heart disease, arthritis, or cancer. These illnesses have the potential to affect one's ability to perform everyday *activities of daily living* (ADLs). Typical instrumental activities (i.e., to get things done) might include using a telephone, preparing a meal, transportation, shopping, and managing finances. Another set of activities of daily living is more personal in nature and reflects even more fundamental levels of impairment; this includes tasks such as eating, dressing, bathing, or using the toilet. The likelihood of having difficulty with one or more of these tasks increases with age, particularly very late in life (after 85 years of age). Because they affect what an individual can do, or at least how an individual needs to accomplish a task, physical changes almost certainly require adaptation on the part of an individual.

A second set of influences relates to the *social* domain. Common social changes requiring adaptation might include *retirement* from full-time employment or the *"empty nest"* stage, when the last child has left the parent's home. Although neither of these changes typically has negative consequences for older adults, they both require adaptation on the part of the individual. *Family caregiving* reflects changes in the intersection of the physical and social domains. Adaptation to this transition for both the person providing care and the person receiving it will be considered in much greater depth later in this chapter.

The third set of influences we might consider is largely *psychological* in nature. Examples might include *depression* and *cognitive decline.* Contrary to popular conceptions, major depressive episodes (characterized by fairly severe symptoms and a duration of at least 2 weeks) are actually considerably less common among older adults than younger adults (e.g., Gatz et al., 1996). However, older adults tend to report more depressive symptoms (e.g., changes in appetite or sleeping patterns and lack of energy), a syndrome that has been referred to as "dysthymia." Many of the symptoms of depression are affected by the aging process itself and so in some cases may reflect underlying physical changes rather than psychological ones. Although generally considered to reflect diseases such as Alzheimer's disease, rather than being a part of normal aging (i.e., they do not appear to be an inevitable part of aging, no matter how long an individual lives), cognitive changes related to dementia are most common in later life (e.g., Zarit, Davey, Edwards, Femia, & Jarrott, 1998). Psychological changes may intersect with physical changes. For example, a stroke can cause both psychological and physical impairments. Likewise, social and psychological changes can interact, resulting in a greater likelihood of depression, for example, following the loss of a spouse in *widowhood*. Finally, social, psychological, and physical domains may all interact in the case of *elder abuse*. To organize and better understand the full range of adaptation and aging in a family context, we will need to make good use of existing theory, the topic to which we now turn.

Theoretical Perspectives on Aging and Adaptation in a Family Context

It has often been remarked that the field of gerontology is "data rich and theory poor" (e.g., George, 1995). Sadly, the reality appears to be much the opposite. Although a multitude of biological, psychological, and social "theories of aging" have been proposed (e.g., Marshall, 1987, 1996), they typically attempt to explain only a small component of the aging process such as well-being or else have received very little research support. As a result, a great deal of gerontological research, particularly on aging and the family, tends to be scattered and even atheoretical.

Pearlin's Stress Process Model

Research on psychosocial stress has a long history in the social sciences. Only recently, however, have researchers begun to study stress as a dynamic *process* over time. Pearlin's stress process model (e.g., Pearlin, Mullan, Semple, & Skaff, 1990) exemplifies the kind of contextual and developmental perspective necessary to understand aging and adaptation. Aneshensel and colleagues (1995) applied the stress process model to longitudinal data from 555 spouse and adult-child caregivers to a relative with dementia, recognizing that care had an *onset* (role acquisition), a *duration* (role enactment), and a *conclusion* (role disengagement).

The stress process model, shown in Figure 5.2, consists of several components. *Primary stressors* arise directly from providing care and include both objective and subjective components. *Primary objective stressors* include variables such as the level of cognitive impairment of the care recipient, behavior problems, and the extent of functional limitations. *Primary subjective stressors* are the caregiver's perceptions of stress as a direct result of providing care, typically indexed by role overload, role captivity, and loss of intimate exchange. Most intriguing, two caregivers faced with the same primary objective stressors can have widely different experiences of primary subjective stress. That is, the same caregiving circumstances that are experienced as

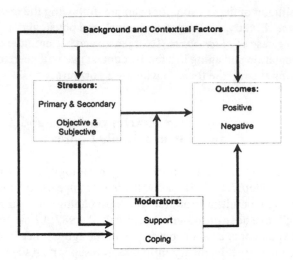

Figure 5.2. Multidimensional Representation of Pearlin's Stress Process Model

highly stressful by one caregiver may be experienced as deeply rewarding by
another. We still know very little about what links objective and subjective
stressors of care (Aneshensel et al., 1995).

Equally important, *secondary stressors* result from the spillover of the
caregiving role into other domains such as work and other family relationships. *Secondary role strains* include family conflict, work strain, work reduction, and financial strains from the added costs of providing care. *Secondary intrapsychic strains* include a sense of lack of self, lack of feelings of
competence, and guilt.

The process of providing care to a relative can lead to both positive and
negative consequences. Negative outcomes typically include depression, anger, or anxiety. However, physical health and immune function can also be affected by prolonged stress. Although not often studied, many caregivers find
providing care to be immensely rewarding, feeling that their relative is receiving the best care possible or that the support they give now is a natural
outgrowth of a positive relationship history.

A second key component to the stress process model is that stress does not
inevitably lead to negative outcomes. Additional processes of social support,
a sense of mastery over one's environment, and coping strategies can help to
ameliorate the potential negative consequences of providing care. Finally,
background characteristics of the caregiving context, such as caregiver and

care recipient age, sex, ethnocultural background, and economic resources, are also important for the caregiving experience.

Contingent Exchange Theory

The contingent exchange perspective (Davey & Eggebeen, 1998; Davey & Norris, 1998) ties the motivations for flows of assistance between generations to the functions of these relationships themselves. In particular, flows of assistance in family relationships may not operate according to the same "rules" as those between strangers (the groups typically studied by social psychologists) or less intimate but established relationships. According to Deutsch (1975), when the function of a relationship is to foster development or it is seen as irreplaceable, assistance will be given on the basis of need. All else being equal, more assistance will be given to the child (or parent) with the greatest need. Likewise, because available resources may constrain the limits of what can be given, individuals with the greatest resources may be the most likely to provide assistance. Support that is received on the basis of need will be psychologically beneficial, whereas provision of noncontingent assistance (i.e., which taxes available resources) may be psychologically detrimental. Because both needs and resources are age graded, this model has implications for generational flows of assistance over time.

For example, hypothetical trajectories of the resources and needs of parents and children across adulthood are shown in Figure 5.3. Parents initially have more resources than their children from a lifetime of work and experience; however, these resources may diminish over time as a result of events such as the transition to retirement, the loss of a spouse, and declining physical health (Panel A). Over the same period of time, adult children's needs are likely to diminish as they make the transition to marriage, begin their families, and build their careers. By the time parents are in very old age, however, children's own needs may begin to increase somewhat, perhaps even related to care for an elderly parent (Panel B). Children's own resources will generally increase from early adulthood through late midlife but will begin to diminish as the adult child makes the transition into old age (Panel C). Parents' needs can be expected to show a gradual increase in later life, with an accelerated increase in very old age (Panel D).

What is the expected net effect of these four interrelated trajectories for flows of support between generations? One hypothetical situation is depicted in Figure 5.4. Support from parents to adult children is generally expected to decrease over time (Line A). However, support from children to parents increases with the age of the parent, particularly when the parent is very old

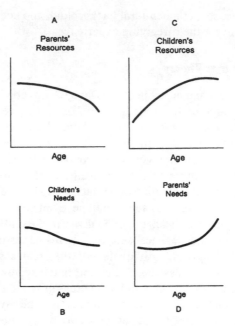

Figure 5.3. Hypothetical Trajectories of Needs and Resources of Two
Generations Over Time

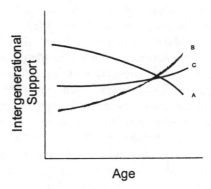

Figure 5.4. Predicted Patterns of Support Balance in Intergenerational
Exchanges

(Line B). The net effect of these two patterns of support is that parents will
generally provide more support to their children than the reverse until very
late in life (Line C).

Research Examples of Aging and
Adaptation in a Family Context

By now it should be clear that aging brings with it a great many opportunities requiring adaptation. In this chapter, we will focus on two that have the most potential to draw together the role of family context in individual adaptation: *family caregiving* and *intergenerational relationships*.

Family Caregiving

Perhaps no issue within the literature on aging and the family has received as much attention as family caregiving. This topic is complex from both a research and a clinical standpoint. Within this topic, the most attention has been devoted to investigating the stress and burden often associated with providing care to a frail older relative, particularly in the context of Alzheimer's disease or other dementias. One of the most striking features of this topic is that faced with objectively identical circumstances, two caregivers can have dramatically different responses. Understanding the sources of these individual differences is thus one important task for researchers and clinicians alike.

One theoretical perspective that has proven to be extremely useful in understanding the process of family caregiving is the stress process model (e.g., Aneshensel et al., 1995; Gaugler, Davey, Pearlin, & Zarit, in press; Pearlin et al., 1990). According to the model, primary stressors originate from the context of providing care itself and include both objective (e.g., the level of cognitive impairment, the number of functional limitations, and problematic behaviors) and subjective (e.g., a sense of role overload, role captivity, and loss of intimate exchanges) components. Aneshensel et al. (1995), within the context of a longitudinal study with 555 caregivers to a relative with dementia, reported that all forms of primary objective stressors appeared to contribute to loss of intimate exchanges but problematic behaviors were most important in determining feelings of role overload and role captivity.

Primary stressors, which stem directly from the caregiving context, may proliferate into other roles occupied by the caregiver and may lead to conflict in other family relationships, problems in the workplace, or financial strain. These stressors are secondary to the care situation but are no less important in terms of their effects on caregivers. The role strains and intrapsychic strains caregivers experience as a result of stress in the caregiving context can be very detrimental to their well-being. For example, common outcomes of the prolonged stress of providing care to an older relative include depression, poor physical health, and impaired immune function (for a review, see Zarit et al., 1998).

Fortunately, these detrimental outcomes are not a necessary part of the caregiving career. The stress process model emphasizes the role of family relationships (including history, quality, type, support, and conflict) and caregiver resources (including coping strategies and assistance) in moderating stress proliferation and negative outcomes of providing care.

Family Context of Caregiving

Research on family caregiving has identified a great number of structural variables associated with who is most likely to become a caregiver. By any estimation, gender is the single strongest predictor of who will become a caregiver, with women making up approximately 70% of all caregivers (Aneshensel et al., 1995; Stone, Cafferata, & Sangl, 1987). Most research has suggested that caregivers assume their role hierarchically within the family structure. Married individuals will first turn to a spouse for assistance in times of need. In the absence of a spouse, adult children are the next choice, followed by siblings, more distant relatives, and, finally, neighbors and friends (e.g., Penning, 1990).

Demographic and social trends make wives and daughters, and daughters-in-law, the most common female caregivers and husbands the most common male caregivers, followed distantly by sons (Aneshensel et al., 1995), who are likely to assume the caregiving role only in the absence of a female sibling (Horowitz, 1985).

Chappell (1990) and Tennstedt, Crawford, and McKinlay (1993) investigated whether living arrangement was more important than relationship to the care recipient. With regard to receipt of instrumental ADL assistance, that the care recipient lives with at least one other person matters more than his or her marital or parental status. However, because so few spouse caregivers do not reside with the care recipient, it is difficult to design a formal test of their hypothesis. Nevertheless, the findings do underscore the importance of living arrangement in caregiving.

Marital status of parents and their children has emerged as an important predictor of caregiving and exchange. Specifically, parental divorce has been shown to affect the quality of relationships, the frequency of contact with fathers, and the frequency of contact with mothers (Webster & Herzog, 1995). In general, these authors found that the effects were much greater for fathers than for mothers, which has been confirmed in research adopting the older parents' reports (e.g., Cooney & Uhlenberg, 1990; White, 1992).

Disruption in adult children's marital status has also been found to relate to lower levels of help given to elderly parents, perceptions that parents need less assistance, and a lower sense of filial obligation to provide assistance (Cicirelli, 1983). A study by Brody, Litvin, Albert, and Hoffman (1994) elaborates on these findings, suggesting that daughters' marital status can have considerable effects on the amount of care they provide to an older parent. In particular, never-married and widowed daughters were found to provide the greatest proportion of care needed by a frail older parent. Never-married daughters, in particular, were most likely to be sole caregivers for their elderly parents. Conversely, married daughters were more likely to receive assistance with care tasks from informal sources, and divorced daughters were more likely to report using formal services.

Caregiver–Care Recipient Relationships

Providing care to an elderly relative with dementia presents stressors that differ in fundamentally important ways from situations in which cognition is spared or recovery is possible. In a comparison of caregivers of relatives with dementia and of relatives with cancer, Clipp and George (1993) found that dementia caregivers reported poorer self-rated health, greater substance use, poorer emotional health, reduced social functioning, and poorer financial status, even when the effects of employment status, age, and duration of illness were controlled. These findings offer support to the idea that there is something uniquely debilitating about losing a relative to dementia as compared with another terminal illness in which cognitive functioning is typically spared. Surprisingly, however, we are only now beginning to gain insights into the ways in which caregiving alters the relationship between caregivers and care recipients.

Wright (1993) compared a small, nonrepresentative sample of Alzheimer's disease caregiving couples with well couples across a variety of dimensions. Although the generalizability of her findings is likely quite limited, the study is unique in that she considered the perspective of both members of the couples in each group, having each report on specific aspects of their marriage. Briefly, she found that Alzheimer's caregivers reported decreased companionship and difficulty dealing with changes in sexual intimacy. She also found that ratings of past marital happiness were associated with current valuing of the afflicted spouse as a unique individual but were not associated with future commitment, which was lowest among caregiving spouses.

Majerovitz (1995) examined the moderating relationship between family adaptability, as measured retrospectively using the Family Adaptability and Cohesion Scale. In her study of 54 caregivers to a spouse with dementia, she found that for spouses reporting low levels of family adaptability, memory problems that spouses experienced and hours of care provided were both related to higher levels of depression; however, there was no such relationship for spouses reporting high levels of family adaptability. More interesting, her follow-up analyses of low-adaptability spouses indicated that these individuals were more likely to cling to an unrealistic role for their dementing spouse, expecting their partner to continue to meet former expectations. Although these data are cross-sectional, they do suggest that caregivers who have more realistic expectations of their dementing spouse are likely to experience fewer negative consequences as a result of the care they provide.

In spousal relationships, the quality of the relationship between the caregiver and care recipient may also play a role in the decision to institutionalize. Pruchno, Michaels, and Potashnik (1990) found that spouses who perceived a better-quality relationship with the care recipient reported less desire to institutionalize, but this finding did not extend to actual decisions regarding institutionalization. By the same token, however, desire to institutionalize was a strong predictor of actual institutionalization, suggesting that an indirect link may exist. In other words, relationship quality leads to desire to institutionalize, and desire leads to the decision to place a relative in an institution, but not all caregivers who want to place a relative in an institution actually do so.

Dementia caregiving also has important consequences for adult children's relationship with their parents. Feelings of attachment and obligation have both been found to predict the amount of help that daughters provide to their older parents (Cicirelli, 1993). Those who reported stronger attachment experienced lower levels of burden, whereas those who reported higher levels of obligation experienced higher levels of burden. Thus, children providing care out of a sense of obligation rather than affection may experience greater negative consequences.

There are other important implications of prior relationship quality for the caregiving experience. Caregivers who have a poor relationship with the care recipient are less likely to assume the caregiving role and if they do, experience more stress (Whitlach & Noelker, 1996). In a study by Uchino, Kiecolt-

Glaser, and Cacciopo (1994), higher ratings of affection for the care recipient were associated with lower heart rate reactivity, a physiological indicator of stress, measured 2 years later.

Walker, Martin, and Jones (1992) examined the role of intimacy in predicting adult daughters' and mothers' perceived costs and benefits of caregiving. Adult daughters' feelings of intimacy were associated with fewer feelings of having insufficient time for extra caregiving activities, less frustration with caregiving, and less anxiety about providing care. For mothers receiving care, intimacy was related only to less anger and resentment about the care they received. Other research has found conflict in the caregiver–care recipient relationship to be associated with greater caregiver strain and negative affect (Sheehan & Nuttall, 1988).

Townsend and Franks (1995) found that adult children's perceptions of the quality of the relationship with their parent were an important moderator of the relationship between the parent's cognitive impairment and the adult child's well-being. In their study of 90 adult-child caregivers, perceived closeness was associated with lower levels of reported caregiver burden and a greater sense of caregiving efficacy. Their study also underscores the importance of conflict in the relationship, which was associated with higher levels of stress, efficacy, and depression.

Even after institutionalization, families typically retain a high level of involvement in their relative's care (Aneshensel et al., 1995). Pruchno, Peters, Kleban, and Burant (1994) found that children's perceptions of their parent's affective state are predictive of feelings of attachment toward their institutionalized parent.

One extreme outcome of a poor relationship between caregiver and care recipient is violence directed toward the elderly care recipient. In a study of 236 caregivers to a relative with dementia, Pillemer and Suitor (1992) examined predictors of violence and violent feelings toward the care recipient. With regard to care recipient characteristics, they found that both violent behaviors and disruptive behaviors were associated with caregivers' greater risk of becoming violent with their relative. Violent behaviors by the care recipient were also associated with a greater likelihood of actual violence on the part of the caregiver. Caregivers who lived with their relative were more likely to report being afraid of acting violently toward their relative, and spouse caregivers were more likely to have acted violently toward their relative than adult children were.

Thus, there is evidence to suggest that the quality of the past and present relationship between caregivers and care recipients plays an important role in the caregiving experience, and these characteristics have an effect, for both spouses and adult children, on the caregiving burden.

Because dementia has such profound effects on all aspects of an older adult's functioning, it can be expected to alter the nature of interaction dramatically. For this reason, new patterns of interaction can be a source of stress for caregivers. Pruchno and Resch (1989) examined the effects of care recipient behaviors on the mental health of caregivers. They found that asocial and disoriented behaviors on the part of the care recipient were associated with greater burden, decreased social participation, and less satisfaction with caregiving. The consequences of care recipients' forgetful behaviors for caregiver mental health increase at first and again diminish as the severity of behavior problems increases, suggesting a curvilinear relationship between the two. Disruptive behaviors and disruptive social functioning resulting from cognitive impairment have also been shown to predict poorer relationships between caregivers and care recipients, more restricted caregiver social activities, and poorer caregiver health (Deimling & Bass, 1986; Poulshock & Deimling, 1984).

In a study of depression in dementia caregivers, Redinbaugh, MacCallum, and Kiecolt-Glaser (1995) found that caregivers who experienced chronic depression over a 3-year period reported experiencing their relative's behavior as more problematic and experiencing higher levels of upsetting social support than had nondepressed caregivers or caregivers who had experienced a transient depressive episode during the course of the study.

Vitaliano, Young, Russo, Romano, and Magana-Amato (1993) were interested in examining the possibility that caregiver behaviors, specifically in the form of expressed emotion, were predictive of subsequent care recipient behaviors a year and a half later. Controlling for initial levels of negative care recipient behaviors, those individuals cared for by a caregiver with high levels of expressed emotion displayed significantly more negative behaviors at follow-up. These findings are significant because caregiver expressed emotion is correlated with higher levels of depression, suppressed anger, and lower life satisfaction (Bledin, MacCarthy, Kuipers, & Woods, 1990; Vitaliano et al., 1993).

To this point, we know very little about caregiving processes in African American families, Hispanic families, and Asian American families. Several key points from other areas of research, however, can suggest what we are likely to be overlooking in current research. For example, "fictive kin" relationships (non-blood ties that are functionally and emotionally equivalent to family relationships) are much more common among African American families than white families (e.g., Bengtson et al., 1990). Traditional survey methodologies that ask only about "family" relationships are unlikely to tap these vital sources of support. Related to this, Burton has found skip-generation patterns of support, in which grandparents care for grandchildren early in life and grandchildren provide care for grandparents later in life, to be quite common among African American families. A study such as that by Aneshensel et al. (1995), which focuses only on spouse and adult-child care-givers, is likely to provide only a partial picture of the family context of care.

Among Hispanic families, a different set of issues might arise. Older generations are more likely to be immigrants to the United States than are younger generations, resulting in differences in language, culture, and expectations for support that might be a source of conflict or consensus among Hispanic families. Hispanic families in many geographic regions also are more likely to have several generations living in close proximity within a particular neighborhood. These different cultural expectations and living arrangements have the potential to create a very different dynamic of care. Similarly, cultural norms for filial piety are relevant for many Asian American families, where there are strong expectations for who will have primary responsibility for elder care. Very few studies have focused on the unique contributions of these expectations to the caregiving career. Variability within and between different ethnocultural groups is an area in need of substantially greater attention.

Intergenerational Relationships

What can we say about the nature of intergenerational relationships over time? Several studies examine expectations, motives, and behaviors related to intergenerational support. Davey and Norris (1998) studied younger and older adults' perceptions of the availability of support from specific members of their social support network, along with the perceived costs of seeking support from those individuals. Within close relationships, individuals reported expecting to receive support contingent on needs. Likewise, expectations for short-term reciprocity, considered as the costs of seeking assistance, were very low. Findings also indicated that expectations for support and reciprocity differed between very close relationships and those that were not so close. There was also evidence, consistent with socioemotional selectivity theory (e.g., Carstensen, 1992; Lang & Carstensen, 1994), that older adults make distinctions along these dimensions in close relationships to a greater extent than younger adults do. Because individuals' social resources may decline with age, it has been suggested that they will place greater importance on their closest relationships, compared with those that are not so central in their social networks (Lang & Carstensen, 1994).

Understanding individuals' perceptions of support in close relationships is certainly important, but is there any evidence to support the notion that, in times of need, adult children *do* in fact provide assistance in a manner consistent with the contingent exchange perspective? A study by Eggebeen and Davey (1998) elaborated on this idea by bringing longitudinal data to bear on the issue. Beyond midlife, experiencing transitions such as loss of spouse, decreases in health status, increases in functional limitations, and substantial drops (i.e., > 50%) in income are all quite common. In the National Survey of Families and Households (Sweet, Bumpass, & Call, 1998), for example, nearly two thirds of individuals over age 50 experienced one or more such events over a 5-year period. In addition, each transition (27% of the total sample experienced more than one) was associated with an increased probability that parents would receive assistance from at least one adult child. This was true for receipt of any form of assistance (i.e., help with shopping, help with ADLs, and the hours of help received). Only receipt of help around the house and advice were not associated with the number of transitions. What makes these results surprising is that they control for previous levels of support to parents, previous levels of health and functioning, parents' expectations that children would provide assistance in times of need, and beliefs that children had an obligation to support aging parents. These results speak clearly to the power of social norms for the intergenerational provision of support contingent on need. In addition, these norms seem more powerful than either beliefs or expectations regarding intergenerational support.

A further implication of the contingent exchange perspective is that the way in which support is given and received may have consequences for the mental health and well-being of older adults—over and above the effects of the events that elicit such support. In a longitudinal study, Davey and Eggebeen (1998) examined the psychological implications for older adults of giving and receiving support according to perspectives derived from social exchange theory, equity theory, and the contingent exchange perspective. Longitudinal data were necessary to address these issues because the same factors that have been shown to elicit intergenerational flows of assistance (i.e., loss of spouse, increase in ADL limitations, etc.) may also be expected to have implications for the psychological functioning of older adults. Failure to employ longitudinal data, then, would artificially induce a negative correlation between receipt of assistance and psychological functioning. Net of past patterns of intergenerational flows of assistance and prior levels of psychological functioning, Davey and Eggebeen (1998) found that older adults who were overbenefited in relationships with an adult child reported greater depression than would be expected based on their previous levels of functioning. This is in direct contrast to the predictions of social exchange theory and only partially consonant with the predictions of equity theory (which suggests that both underbenefit and overbenefit will be psychologically detrimental). In striking contrast, however, Davey and Eggebeen (1998) found substantial evidence for the importance of contingent exchange. Controlling for prior levels of psychological functioning and intergenerational support, individuals who receive greater than expected (based on previous levels) support contingent on the experiences of decline in health status, decline in income, and birth of a grandchild have lower levels of depression and greater life satisfaction than those who do not. Likewise, individuals who provided greater than predicted assistance around the loss of a spouse, retirement, and birth of a grandchild had higher levels of depression and lower life satisfaction than would be predicted from their previous levels. Thus, although receipt of contingent assistance is beneficial, there may be negative psychological consequences of providing assistance around one's own needs.

Finally, it must be acknowledged that families are complex systems. Understanding what is occurring within a single specific relationship, in fact, represents only one component of parent-child relationships within the family. Davey (1999) examined multiple relationships within the same family and four outcomes of emotional support and instrumental support given and received by older parents. Results indicated that the youngest unmarried daughter who lives closest and with whom the parent reports the closest relationship is most likely to be providing instrumental assistance to the parent. Furthermore, consistent with our previous research, we also see strong evidence for the contingent exchange perspective in that a decrease in self-rated health, an increase in ADL limitations, and the loss of a spouse are all associated with parents' greater receipt of instrumental assistance. In addition, children also appear to respond to the emotional needs of parents by providing greater emotional assistance as disability increases. We do not see a concomitant increase in emotional support around the loss of a spouse; however, this event may have occurred as long as 5 years prior to the follow-up interview, which may be too long a time period to consider.

Research Needs in the Family Context of Aging and Adaptation

From the brief overview provided in this chapter, it is clear that much remains to be examined regarding aging and adaptation in a family context. Several topics seem particularly underdeveloped. In the context of family relationships, we still know almost nothing about the process by which families decide who will become a primary caregiver and the implications of this decision process for the caregiver's ultimate experience. Similarly, most research on caregiving to date does not consider how past relationship quality affects the adjustment to caregiving, even though there is evidence to suggest that it is likely to be quite important (e.g., Aneshensel et al., 1995; Davey, Murphy, & Price, in press; Eggebeen & Davey, 1998). More fundamentally, very few studies have yet considered how older adults adjust to the role of care recipient. Although the results from Davey and Eggebeen (1998) suggest that receiving assistance may buffer some of the negative consequences of declines in physical functioning, less research has considered more intensive forms of support. Wright (1993) examined couples in which one member had Alzheimer's disease and found that changes in intimacy were commonplace. However, she was not able to take the next step, which is to examine how the loss of intimacy affects caregiver and care recipient adjustment; we also cannot extend her findings to couples in which the individual receiving care does not have cognitive impairment. Clearly, this is one of the most fruitful avenues for future research on aging and the family.

Another related area with great promise is identifying sources of individual differences in adaptation to the caregiving role to learn why the same set of objective stressors may lead to vastly different experiences of subjective stress. Better understanding of these processes might lead to more effective interventions for family caregivers. Another key research need is to consider the effects of marital histories throughout life on patterns of familial assistance and intergenerational support in later life. One of the next, and sorely needed, major research efforts should be an investigation of the range of variability within and between ethnocultural groups in the family context of aging and adaptation, if we are to have anything to say about a large and rapidly growing segment of the population.

Conclusions

It is clear that age-related physical, social, and psychological changes all require adaptation on the part of the aging individual and his or her family. A lifespan framework was used to organize these changes, as applied to family caregiving and intergenerational relationships using the stress process model and contingent exchange theory. These perspectives shed light on some of the incredible variability in the experience of aging and on how the effects of individual and family development can cascade through generations with positive and negative repercussions. Considering the range of what we know about aging and adaptation serves the equally valuable purpose of highlighting the areas in which there is the most pressing need to learn more about the resiliency of individual and family development.

DISCUSSION QUESTIONS

1. How has the age structure of the population changed over the course of the past century? How is it projected to change in the future?

2. Select a specific family form that is different from your own. Try to identify all of the intersections of aging and the family as you trace the family over time. What are some of the unique circumstances faced by this family?

3. What is the difference between primary objective stressors, primary subjective stressors, and secondary stressors? What are some examples of each?

4. Consider your relationship with your parent(s). Looking ahead, how do you expect the nature of support you give and receive to change from now until old age?

5. The beginning of this chapter asked you to think about the past 20 years of life. Based on what you have learned, how do you think your experience of old age will differ from that of today's older adults?

SUGGESTED READINGS

Aneshensel, C. S., Pearlin, L. I., Mullan, J. T., Zarit, S. H., & Whitlach, C. J. (1995). *Profiles in caregiving: The unexpected career.* New York: Academic Press.

Baltes, P. B. (1987). Theoretical propositions of life-span developmental psychology: On the dynamics between growth and decline. *Developmental Psychology, 23,* 611-626.

Blieszner, R., & Bedford, V. H. (1995). *Handbook of aging and the family.* Westport, CT: Greenwood.

Elder, G. H., Jr. (1997). The life course and human development. In W. Damon (Series Ed.) & R. M. Lerner (Vol. Ed.), *Handbook of child psychology: Vol. 1. Theoretical models of human development* (pp. 929-991). New York: John Wiley.

Shanks, L. K. (1997). *Your name is Hughes Hannibal Shanks.* New York: Penguin Putnam.

Wright, L. K. (1993). *Alzheimer's disease and marriage: An intimate account.* Newbury Park, CA: Sage.

REFERENCES

Aneshensel, C. S., Pearlin, L. I., Mullan, J. T., Zarit, S. H., & Whitlach, C. J. (1995). *Profiles in caregiving: The unexpected career.* New York: Academic Press.

Bengtson, V., Rosenthal, C. J., & Burton, L. (1990). Families and aging: Diversity and heterogeneity. In R. H. Binstock & L. K. George (Eds.), *Handbook of aging and the social sciences* (3rd ed., pp. 263-287). New York: Academic Press.

Bengtson, V., Rosenthal, C. J., & Burton, L. (1996). Paradoxes of families and aging. In R. H. Binstock & L. K. George (Eds.), *Handbook of aging and the social sciences* (4th ed., pp. 254-282). New York: Academic Press.

Bledin, K. D., MacCarthy, B., Kuipers, L., & Woods, R. T. (1990). Daughters of people with dementia: Expressed emotion, strain, and coping. *British Journal of Psychiatry, 157,* 221-227.

Brody, E. M., Litvin, S. J., Albert, S. M., & Hoffman, C. J. (1994). Marital status of daughters and patterns of parent care. *Journals of Gerontology, 49,* S95-S103.

Carstensen, L. L. (1992). Social and emotional patterns in adulthood: Support for socioemotional selectivity theory. *Psychology and Aging, 7,* 331-338.

Chappell, N. L. (1990). Living arrangements and sources of caregiving. *Journals of Gerontology, 46,* S1-S8.

Cherlin, A. J. (1992). *Marriage, divorce, and remarriage.* Cambridge, MA: Harvard University Press.

Cicirelli, V. G. (1983). A comparison of helping behavior to elderly parents of adult children with intact and disrupted marriages. *Gerontologist, 23,* 619-625.

Cicirelli, V. G. (1993). Attachment and obligation as daughters' motives for caregiving behavior and subsequent effect on subjective burden. *Psychology and Aging, 8,* 144-155.

Clipp, E. C., & George, L. K. (1993). Dementia and cancer: A comparison of spouse caregivers. *Gerontologist, 33,* 534-541.

Cooney, T. M., & Uhlenberg, P. (1990). The role of divorce in men's relations with their adult children after mid-life. *Journal of Marriage and the Family, 52,* 677-688.

Davey, A. (1999). *Longitudinal predictors of emotional and instrumental support between older parents and their adult children.* Manuscript submitted for publication.

Davey, A., & Eggebeen, D. J. (1998). Patterns of intergenerational exchange and mental health. *Journals of Gerontology: Psychological Sciences, 53,* P86-P95.

Davey, A., Femia, E. E., Shea, D. G., Zarit, S. H., Sundstrom, G., Berg, S., & Smyer, M. A. (1999). How much do families help? A cross-national comparison. *Journal of Aging and Health, 11,* 199-221.

Davey, A., Murphy, M., & Price, S. J. (2000). Aging and the family: Dynamics and therapeutic interventions. In W. C. Nichols, M. A. Pace-Nichols, D. S. Becvar, & A. Y. Napier (Eds.), *Handbook of family development: Dynamics and therapeutic interventions* (pp. 235-252). New York: John Wiley.

Davey, A., & Norris, J. E. (1998). Social networks and exchange norms across the adult life-span. *Canadian Journal on Aging, 17,* 212-233.

Davey, A., & Patsios, D. (1999). Formal and informal care to older citizens: Comparative analysis of the United States and Great Britain. *Journal of Family and Economic Issues, 20,* 271-300.

Deimling, G. T., & Bass, D. M. (1986). Symptoms of mental impairment among elderly adults and their effects on family caregivers. *Journal of Gerontology, 41,* 778-784.

Deutsch, M. (1975). Equity, equality, and need: What determines which value will be used as the basis of distributive justice. *Journal of Social Issues, 31,* 137-149.

Ebly, E. M., Parhad, I. M., Hogan, D. B., & Fung, T. S. (1994). Prevalence and types of dementia in the very old: Results from the Canadian study of health and aging. *Neurology, 44,* 1593-1600.

Eggebeen, D. J., & Davey, A. (1998). Do safety nets work? The role of anticipated support in times of need. *Journal of Marriage and the Family, 60,* 939-950.

Gatz, M., Kasl-Godley, J. E., & Karel, M. J. (1996). Aging and mental disorders. In J. E. Birren & K. W. Schaie (Eds.), *Handbook of the psychology of aging* (4th ed., pp. 365-382). New York: Academic Press.

Gaugler, J. E., Davey, A., Pearlin, L. I., & Zarit, S. H. (in press). Interrelationship of objective and subjective primary stressors over time: A growth curve modeling approach. *Psychology and Aging.*

George, L. K. (1995). The last half-century of aging research—and thoughts for the future. *Journals of Gerontology: Social Sciences, 50B,* S1-S3.

Hobbs, F. B., & Damon, B. L. (1996). *65+ in the United States* (U.S. Bureau of the Census International Population Rep. No. P23-190). Washington, DC: Government Printing Office.

Horowitz, A. (1985). Sons and daughters as caregivers to older parents: Differences in role performance and consequences. *Gerontologist, 25,* 612-617.

Huyck, M. H. (1995). Marriage and close relationships of the marital kind. In R. Blieszner & V. H. Bedford (Eds.), *Handbook of aging and the family* (pp. 181-200). Westport, CT: Greenwood.

Jette, A. M. (1996). Disability trends and transitions. In R. H. Binstock & L. K. George (Eds.), *Handbook of aging and the social sciences* (4th ed., pp. 94-116). New York: Academic Press.

Kimmel, D. C., & Sang, B. E. (1995). Lesbians and gay men in midlife. In A. R. D'Augelli & C. J. Patterson (Eds.), *Lesbian, gay, and bisexual identities over the lifespan: Psychological perspectives* (pp. 190-214). New York: Oxford University Press.

Kinsella, K. (1995). Aging and the family: Present and future demographic issues. In R. Blieszner & V. H. Bedford (Eds.), *Aging and the family: Theory and research* (pp. 32-56). Westport, CT: Praeger.

Kinsella, K., & Taeuber, C. (1993). *An aging world II* (U.S. Bureau of the Census International Population Rep. No. P95/92-3). Washington, DC: Government Printing Office.

Kurdek, L. A. (1995). Developmental changes in relationship quality in gay and lesbian cohabiting couples. *Developmental Psychology, 31,* 86-94.

Lang, F. R., & Carstensen, L. L. (1994). Close emotional relationships in late life: Further support for proactive aging in the social domain. *Psychology and Aging, 9,* 315-324.

Majerovitz, S. D. (1995). Role of family adaptability in the psychological adjustment of spouse caregivers to patients with dementia. *Psychology and Aging, 10,* 447-457.

Marshall, V. W. (1987). Social perspectives on aging: Theoretical notes. In V. W. Marshall (Ed.), *Aging in Canada: Social perspectives* (pp. 39-59). Toronto, Canada: Fitzhenry & Whiteside.

Marshall, V. W. (1996). The state of theory in aging and the social sciences. In R. H. Binstock & L. K. George (Eds.), *Handbook of aging and the social sciences* (4th ed., pp. 12-30). New York: Academic Press.

Martin, T. C., & Bumpass, L. L. (1989). Recent trends in marital disruption. *Demography, 26,* 37-51.

Myers, G. C. (1990). Demography of aging. In R. H. Binstock & L. K. George (Eds.), *Handbook of aging and the social sciences* (3rd ed., pp. 19-44). New York: Academic Press.

Pearlin, L. I., Mullan, J. T., Semple, S. J., & Skaff, M. M. (1990). Caregiving and the stress process: An overview of concepts and their measures. *Gerontologist, 30,* 583-594.

Penning, M. J. (1990). Receipt of assistance by elderly people: Hierarchical selection and task specificity. *Gerontologist, 30,* 220-227.

Pillemer, K., & Suitor, J. J. (1992). Violence and violent feelings: What causes them among family caregivers? *Journals of Gerontology, 47,* S165-S172.

Poulshock, S. W., & Deimling, G. T. (1984). Families caring for elders in residence: Issues in the measurement of burden. *Journal of Gerontology, 39,* 230-239.

Pruchno, R. A., Michaels, J. E., & Potashnik, S. L. (1990). Predictors of institutionalization among Alzheimer disease victims with caregiving spouses. *Journals of Gerontology, 45,* S259-S266.

Pruchno, R. A., Peters, N. D., Kleban, M. H., & Burant, C. J. (1994). Attachment among adult children and their institutionalized parents. *Journals of Gerontology, 49,* S209-S218.

Pruchno, R. A., & Resch, N. L. (1989). Aberrant behaviors and Alzheimer's disease: Mental health effects on spouse caregivers. *Journals of Gerontology, 44,* S177-S182.

Pynoos, J., & Golant, S. (1996). Housing and living arrangements for the elderly. In R. H. Binstock & L. K. George (Eds.), *Handbook of aging and the social sciences* (4th ed., pp. 303-325). New York: Academic Press.

Redinbaugh, E. M., MacCallum, R. C., & Kiecolt-Glaser, J. K. (1995). Recurrent syndromal depression in caregivers. *Psychology and Aging, 10,* 358-368.

Rowe, J. W., & Kahn, R. L. (1998). *Successful aging.* New York: Pantheon.

Sheehan, N. W., & Nuttall, P. (1988). Conflict, emotion, and personal strain among family caregivers. *Family Relations, 37,* 92-98.

Stone, R., Cafferata, G. L., & Sangl, J. (1987). Caregivers of the frail elderly: A national profile. *Gerontologist, 27,* 616-626.

Sweet, J., Bumpass, L., & Call, V. (1998). *The design and content of the National Survey of Families and Households* (Working Paper No. 1). Madison: University of Wisconsin.

Tennstedt, S. L., Crawford, S., & McKinlay, J. B. (1993). Determining the pattern of community care: Is coresidence more important than caregiver relationship? *Journals of Gerontology, 48,* S74-S83.

Townsend, A. L., & Franks, M. M. (1995). Binding ties: Closeness and conflict in adult children's caregiving relationship. *Psychology and Aging, 10,* 343-351.

Uchino, B. N., Kiecolt-Glaser, J. K., & Cacciopo, J. T. (1994). Construals of preillness relationship quality predict cardiovascular response in family caregivers of Alzheimer's disease victims. *Psychology and Aging, 9,* 113-120.

Vitaliano, P. P., Young, H. M., Russo, J., Romano, J., & Magana-Amato, A. (1993). Does expressed emotion in spouses predict subsequent problems among care recipients with Alzheimer's disease? *Journals of Gerontology, 48,* P202-P209.

Walker, A. J., Martin, S. S. K., & Jones, L. L. (1992). The benefits and costs of caregiving and care receiving for daughters and mothers. *Journals of Gerontology, 47,* S130-S139.

Webster, P. S., & Herzog, A. R. (1995). Effects of parental divorce and memories of family problems on relationships between adult children and their parents. *Journals of Gerontology, 50B,* S24-S34.

White, L. (1992). The effect of parental divorce and remarriage on parental support for adult children. *Journal of Family Issues, 13,* 234-250.

Whitlach, C. J., & Noelker, L. S. (1996). Caregiving and caring. In J. E. Birren (Ed.), *Encyclopedia of gerontology* (pp. 258-264). New York: Academic Press.

Wright, L. K. (1993). *Alzheimer's disease and marriage: An intimate account.* Newbury Park, CA: Sage.

Zarit, S. H., Davey, A., Edwards, A. B., Femia, E. E., & Jarrott, S. E. (1998). Family caregiving: Research findings and clinical implications. In A. S. Bellack & M. Hersen (Series Eds.) & B. A. Edelstein (Vol. Ed.), *Comprehensive clinical psychology: Vol. 7. Clinical geropsychology* (pp. 499-523). Oxford, UK: Elsevier Science.

Zarit, S. H., & Eggebeen, D. J. (1995). Parent-child relationships in adulthood and old age. In M. H. Bornstein (Ed.), *Handbook of parenting: Vol. 1. Children and parenting* (pp. 119-140). Mahwah, NJ: Lawrence Erlbaum.

6

Coping With Death, Dying, and Grief in Families

COLLEEN I. MURRAY

Death has been viewed as something that we make invisible and deny, yet as something to which we have become desensitized. How, then, can death be the experience that "poses the most painful adaptational challenges for families" (Walsh & McGoldrick, 1991, p. 25)? The inconsistencies seem related to the extent that we personally are affected by the death—whether it is one of "us" or one of "them." Annually, there are more than 2.3 million deaths in the United States, affecting 8 to 10 million surviving immediate family members (Ventura, Anderson, Martin, & Smith, 1998). The death of an immediate family member is a crisis that *all* families will encounter, and it is recognized as *the* most stressful life event that families face (Dohrenwend & Dohrenwend, 1974; Holmes & Rahe, 1967). However, only recently has death been given visibility in the family science and family therapy literature (e.g., Shapiro, 1994; Walsh & McGoldrick, 1991).

Etiology of "Invisible Death" and
Its Consequences

Since the Middle Ages, and for more than a thousand years, death was viewed as natural and inevitable (Aries, 1974). A movement to deny the realities of death occurred during the 18th and early 19th centuries; by the 20th century, a lack of firsthand familiarity with death fostered an era in which death has been sequestered, privatized, and invisible (Aries, 1985; Mellor & Shilling, 1993).

Factors contributing to our lack of familiarity with death include increased life expectancy; changes in the leading causes of death from communicable diseases to chronic and degenerative diseases; the redistribution of death from the young to old; decreased mortality rates; and lengthier chronic illnesses (Doka, 1997; U.S. Bureau of the Census, 1975; Ventura et al., 1998). Geographic mobility and the social reorganization of families also result in reduced intergenerational contact and less opportunity to participate in death-related experiences of family members (Rando, 1993). In addition, the use of life-extending technologies has (a) confined dying to an institution rather than one's home (Lerner, 1980), (b) resulted in care dominated by efforts to delay death by all means available, (c) questioned our definitions of what constitutes life and death, and (d) confronted families with decisions of prolonging dying or terminating life.

Although families have been distanced from the intimacies of death, they are bombarded with its public presentation via the media (Cummock, 1996; Kates, 1996; Murray & Gilbert, 1997, 1998). Children and adults are flooded with a media-fostered awareness of death (Walter, Littlewood, & Pickering, 1995). The violent, frequent, and sensationalized portrayals present death as unnatural and contribute to desensitization, repression, and personal traumatization, particularly for the bereaved (Rando, 1993; Redmond, 1996).

The media-orchestrated emotional invigilation (Walter et al., 1995) in reporting recent deaths of famous individuals (e.g., John F. Kennedy Jr. and Princess Diana) and mass tragedies (e.g., the shootings at Columbine High School) has left consumers with an illusion of intimacy, and a related illusion of grieving. Individuals who did not personally know the deceased can go through rituals of mourning and "virtually" attend the funeral through television or the Internet without feeling the depth of pain and depression of actual grief. Viewers may confuse their emotional response (i.e., "virtual grief") with the actual grief experienced by loved ones (Cose, 1999). Because recovery from virtual grief is quick, individuals may become less sensitive to the extent of time required by friends or coworkers to "return to normal" when actual grief occurs.

The overall effect of these many changes has been to increase the potential stress that families experience when coping with death. Death, dying, and bereavement are not viewed as normal experiences throughout the life span, and death has become compartmentalized, with children frequently excluded from family experiences (Hurd, 1999; Walsh & McGoldrick, 1991). Adapting to loss has been hampered by a lack of cultural supports that could assist families in "integrating the fact of death with ongoing life" (Walsh & McGoldrick, 1991, p. 2). For many Americans, there is a minimum of rituals surrounding death, the roles of the chronically ill or bereaved are not clearly defined, and geographic distance hinders the completion of "unfinished business" (Shapiro, 1994).

Although the death of a family member is a normal experience and grieving is a normal family process (Gilbert, 1995; Paul & Paul, 1982), there can be physical, psychological, and social consequences for surviving family members that can be viewed as stressor experiences (Burnell & Burnell, 1989; Murphy, 1996). Bereavement can result in negative consequences for physical health (Frank, Prigerson, Shear, & Reynolds, 1997; Prigerson et al., 1997; Summers et al., 1995), including physical illness, aggravation of existing medical conditions, increased use of medical facilities, and presence of new symptoms and complaints (Burnell & Burnell, 1989; Parkes, 1988). Immune system functioning also may be impaired during bereavement (Carman, 1997; Lindstrom, 1997). Intrusive thoughts and avoidance behaviors are correlated with sleep disturbances, which appear to intensify the effects of grief, resulting in a drop in number and function of natural killer cells (Hall et al., 1998; Ironson et al., 1997). Bereavement also appears related to increased adrenocortical activity, long-lasting brain changes, and possible long-term changes in gene expression (Biondi & Picardi, 1996).

A limitation of epidemiologic bereavement studies is that they cannot assess a direct causal relationship but can only present bereavement as an antecedent of disease (Rando, 1993). Many conditions leading to increased morbidity and mortality rates may result from self-damaging or neglectful behaviors that can occur during bereavement (Jacobs & Osfeld, 1977; Zisook & Shuchter, 1986). In addition, most studies on morbidity and mortality rates are limited to bereaved spouses (e.g., Bowling & Windsor, 1995; Lichtenstein, Gatz, & Berg, 1998), with some attention to bereaved parents (Huygen, van den Hoogen, van Eijk, & Smits, 1989).

The consequences of bereavement as a stressor for mental health also are difficult to measure (Parkes, 1988). Many of the characteristics typically associated with the emotion of grief are ones that would evoke concern in other circumstances. High rates of depression, insomnia, suicide, and anorexia reported by the bereaved may exist in conjunction with consumption of drugs, alcohol, and tobacco (Clayton, 1974). Individuals with personality disorders are more likely to exhibit complications (Rando, 1993). The lack of differentiation between grief and depression (Devan, 1993; Pessagno, 1999), as well as the failure to separately examine traumatic or complicated grief reactions and "normal" grief, adds to the confusion (Frank et al., 1997; Prigerson et al., 1999).

Individuals identify bereavement as a social stressor (Burnell & Burnell, 1989) and report a lack of role clarity and social or familial support (Rando, 1993). Factors that may accompany the death, such as change in the survivor's social status, loss of roles or conflicts in identity (Lopata, 1973), conflict over family inheritance, and loss of income or retirement funds, can contribute to a sense of social isolation. Common problems include changes in family communication patterns and changes in relationships with people outside the family (Moos, 1995).

In addition to the focus on problems manifest in grief, a new body of literature is emerging emphasizing growth as an outcome. Posttraumatic growth is both a process and outcome in which, following a trauma, growth occurs *beyond* the previous level of functioning (Tedeschi, Park, & Calhoun, 1998). Types of growth outcomes include those related to *perception of self* (i.e., as a survivor rather than a victim, and self-reliant yet with heightened vulnerability), *interpersonal relationships* (i.e., the increased ability to be compassionate, to self-disclose important information, and to express emotions), and *philosophy of life* (i.e., reorganizing priorities, gaining a greater appreciation of life, grappling with the meaning and purpose of life, going through a spiritual change, and gaining a sense of wisdom; Schaefer & Moos, 1998; Tedeschi & Calhoun, 1995). In a unique study using the Swedish Twin Registry, psychological growth after bereavement has been identified as the major factor in the decreased risk of death 4 years or more after spousal death for bereaved older adults as compared with their married twins (Lichtenstein et al., 1998).

Theories of Grieving

Theories of grieving include those focused on the individual's experience as a family member and those based on the family system.

Individual-Based Theories

Scholars have proposed and used a variety of developmental theories focusing on stages or trajectories for the dying person (e.g., Andershed & Ternestedt, 1998; Kubler-Ross, 1969; Pattison, 1977) and survivors (e.g., Rando, 1988; Raphael, 1983; Worden, 1982). Such theories generally are derived from the works of Freud (1917) or Bowlby (1969, 1980). These theories differ in the number of stages proposed, but each assumes that grieving follows three basic phases: (a) shock, denial, and disorganization; (b) a period of extremes with intense separation pain, volatile emotions, and active grief work; and (c) resolution, acceptance, and (for the bereaved) withdrawal of energy from the deceased and reinvestment into the world of the living.

Critics of individual theories question the definition of "normal" grief and many of the assumptions about how people should respond to death, including the following: (a) Intense emotional distress or depression is inevitable; (b) failure to experience distress is indicative of pathology; (c) it is important to work through loss (intense distress will not last forever, and there will be recovery); and (d) by working through loss, individuals can achieve a state of resolution, including intellectual acceptance (Stroebe, 1997; Stroebe, Stroebe, Abakoumkin, & Schut, 1996; Wortman & Silver, 1989).

Stage theories have been criticized for being population specific and for presenting the image that progress toward adjustment is linear (Corr, 1993; Doka, 1995-1996). Critics contend that progress is unsteady, that it is not always forward, and that there may be no definite ending to the process of grieving (Glick, Weiss, & Parkes, 1974; Rosenblatt, 1983; Wortman & Silver, 1989). Recently, authors have suggested that the grief process does not end but, rather, undergoes adaptation and change. Therefore, the emphasis should not be on recovery or closure but on issues such as renegotiating the meaning of loss over time (Klass, Silverman, & Nickman, 1996). A longitudinal study of coping suggests that two types of meaning—making sense of the event and finding benefits in the experience—independently play roles in the adjustment process (Davis, Nolen-Hoeksema, & Larson, 1998).

Another concern deals with viewing grief as passive, with "little choice of paths through the process" (Attig, 1991, p. 386). Critics contend that grieving is active, presenting challenges, choices, and opportunities. Also questioned is the necessity of "grief work"—traditionally viewed as a cognitive process of confronting loss that is essential for adjustment (Bowlby, 1969, 1980; Freud, 1917; Lindemann, 1944; Parkes, 1988). Pathological grief is seen as the failure to undergo or complete grief work. Recently, Stroebe (1992, 1997) suggested that grief work is not a universal concept, that its definitions and operationalizations are problematic, that few studies have yielded substantial conclusions, and that research findings were intended for understanding processes rather than as prescriptions for recovery.

In response to these criticisms, new models are emerging, many based on varied tasks of grieving (e.g., Doka, 1995-1996). Worden (1991) moved away from the view of grief as illness and delineated a model based on four tasks: (a) acknowledging the reality of the loss, (b) working through emotional turmoil, (c) adjusting to the environment where the deceased is absent, and (d) loosening ties to the deceased. Horacek's (1995) heuristic model identifies tasks related to high-grief deaths and views the grief response as both reactive and proactive. Attig (1996) presented a model of grief as active, in which the task is a relearning of the world in terms of our new place in physical surroundings, relationships, and who we are.

Among the individually centered process-based models is Rando's (1993) "6 R Model," which delineates processes of mourning assumed necessary for accommodating a loss. The processes include recognizing the loss, reacting to separation, recollecting and reexperiencing the deceased and the relationship, relinquishing old attachments and the old assumptive world, readjusting to move into a new world without forgetting the old, and reinvesting (p. 45). In contrast, the Dual Process Model of Coping (Stroebe & Schut, 1995) suggests that active confrontation with loss is not a necessary condition for a positive outcome. There may be circumstances when denial, avoidance of reminders, and repressive strategies are essential. Most individuals will experience flexibility and ongoing oscillation between a *loss orientation* (coping with the loss through grief work, dealing with denial, and avoiding changes) and a *restoration orientation* (adjusting to the many life changes triggered by the death, changing routines, transitioning to a new equilibrium, and avoiding or taking time off from grief). There is movement between coping with loss and moving forward, but the need for each orientation may differ by individual, type of loss, culture, and gender.

Family Theories of Coping With Death

Much of what has been written about coping with loss focuses on dying or bereaved individuals or occasionally on the dyadic relationship between the bereaved and the deceased (e.g., Schiff, 1977; Viorst, 1986). Yet individuals do not deal with death and dying in isolation (Pattison, 1977). Certainly, the process models previously discussed could be broadened for use at the family level. Family stress theory, family systems theory, and recent integrative approaches can facilitate understanding of the complex issues occurring in relation to the death of a family member.

Family Stress Theory

Family stress theory (see Chapter 1) conceptualizes the family's response to the dynamic processes of dying and bereavement through an examination of the nature of the event, meanings that families give to loss, available resources, and coping strategies. One version, the Typology Model of Family Adjustment and Adaptation (McCubbin & McCubbin, 1989), can be used to understand differing amounts of crisis and disorganization that families experience in relation to loss by isolating characteristics of the individual, family unit, and community/society (Boss, 1987; Hill, 1949). The three basic *adjustment* coping strategies (i.e., avoidance, elimination, and assimilation) (McCubbin & Patterson, 1983) are often inadequate as long-term responses in cases of chronic illness or bereavement (McCubbin & McCubbin, 1989).

Recent elaboration, resulting in the Resiliency Model of Family Adjustment and Adaptation (McCubbin, Thompson, Thompson, Elver, & McCubbin, 1998), further delineates the interaction of issues of meaning (family schema, paradigms, coherence, and culture), making the model more effective for understanding and working with family grief.

Family Systems Theory

Systems theory focuses on dynamics and provides concepts for describing relationships (e.g., Bertalanffy, 1968; Jackson, 1965; Kantor & Lehr, 1975). The following premises of systems theory can be useful in examining families' adaptation to death:

1. A family reacts to loss as a system. Although we grieve as individuals, the family system has qualities beyond those of the individual members (Jackson, 1965), and all members participate in mutually reinforcing interactions (Walsh & McGoldrick, 1991).
2. The reactions of one family member affect the others.
3. The death of a family member disrupts a family system's equilibrium, modifies the structure, and requires reorganization of the system's feedback processes, distribution of roles, and functions (Bowen, 1976; Buckley, 1967; Jackson, 1965).
4. Death may produce an emotional shock wave—that is, a series of serious life events that can occur anywhere in the extended family in the years following a

death (Bowen, 1976). Shock waves exist in an environment of denied emotional dependence and may seem unrelated to the death.

5. There is no single outcome from the death of a family member that characterizes all family systems. Various family characteristics, such as feedback processes (Jackson, 1965), family schema, and family paradigm (McCubbin et al., 1998), influence the outcome.

Although family systems theory appears well suited for examining families' adaptation to death (Worden, 1991), it has not been frequently applied. Instead, loss has traditionally been identified as a historical, individual, or content issue and inappropriate for systems work (which tends to focus on process, current interaction, and the present) (Madanes & Haley, 1977; Walsh & McGoldrick, 1991).

Integrative Models

Models particularly useful in understanding and working with illness, dying, and grief are those that simultaneously consider individual, family, and cultural dimensions. Rolland's (1994) Family Systems-Illness Model examines the interface of the individual, family, illness, and health care team. Rather than focusing on the ill individual as the central unit of care, it focuses on the family or caregiving system as a resource affected by and influencing the course of illness. It can be used in understanding the experiences of the individual and family during the terminal phase of a chronic illness, as they exist in multiple contexts and across time.

Moos' (1995) model shows the interrelationship of processes involving the grief tasks of individuals and those of the family. It highlights the interdependence of family processes and individual perceptions, addressing the relationships between individual and family grief symptoms, the influence of each family member on the family system's coping strategies and grief reactions, and mediating roles of family history, cultural constraints, feedback, and nuclear-family functioning.

Shapiro (1994) applied a systemic developmental approach in examining grief as a family process. This clinical model views grief as a developmental crisis influenced by family history, sociocultural context, and family and individual life-cycle stages. A crisis of identity and attachment, grief disrupts family equilibrium but makes possible the development of a new "growth-enhancing stability" (p. 17).

Factors Related to
Family Adaptation to Death

Characteristics of the Loss

Various factors have been identified as being related to death itself and to how society's interpretation of the loss influences family adaptation. These include the following.

Timing of Illness or Death

When the duration of time before the actual death is far longer (Doka, 1997; Rando, 1997) or shorter than expected, or the sequence of death differs from the expected order, problems may occur. The elderly are assumed to experience "timely" deaths. Early parental loss, the death of a young spouse, and the death of a child or grandchild of any age are considered tragic (Ponzetti & Johnson, 1991) and evoke rage and a search for an explanation (Counts & Counts, 1991; Ramsden, 1991).

Nature of Death

The initial grief reaction to a sudden or unexpected death has been viewed as more intense (Bowlby, 1980), with survivors experiencing a shattering of their normal world, a series of concurrent stressors, and secondary losses (Doka, 1996). In these cases, unfinished business is more likely to remain (Lindemann, 1944). Factors existing along a continuum that can affect how one copes with the loss include one's perceptions of (a) whether the loss was natural or human made; (b) the degree of intentionality or premeditation; (c) the degree of preventability; (d) the amount of suffering, anxiety, or physical pain experienced in relation to the death experience; (e) the number of people killed or affected; (f) the degree of expectedness (Doka, 1996, pp. 12-13); and (g) senselessness (Walsh & McGoldrick, 1991). Whether the survivor witnessed the death or its aftermath (Williams, 1998) or found out through the media (Redmond, 1996) also can affect how an individual copes with the loss. In addition, violence such as homicide and suicide often occurs with a sudden death (Murphy et al., 1999; Stone, 1999).

Deaths following protracted illness can also be particularly stressful. In the case of such illness, family members have experienced a series of stressors before the death. These can include increased time commitments for caring, a loss of financial well-being as a result of the costs of care and lost employ-ment, emotional exhaustion, the interruption of career and family routines, a sense of social isolation, and a lack of time for self or other family members (McCubbin & McCubbin, 1989; Rolland, 1994). Although research findings on the existence, role, and multidimensionality of anticipatory grief are in-consistent, protracted illness appears associated with trauma and secondary morbidity (i.e., the difficulties in physical, emotional, cognitive, and social functioning of those closely involved with the terminally ill person) (Rando, 1993, 1997). In addition, deaths following chronic illness may still be per-ceived as sudden or unexpected by surviving adults who are not yet "ready," by children whose developmental stage inhibits their understanding that the death is inevitable, and following multiple cycles of relapse and improve-ment (Rolland, 1994; Saldinger, Cain, Kalter, & Lohnes, 1999). Overall, re-cent work suggests that trauma and certain deaths have much in common (Figley, 1999). For example, families experiencing prolonged or compli-cated grief, those experiencing multiple deaths simultaneously or a series of deaths in close proximity, and those with members who witnessed or expe-rienced violence may display signs of posttraumatic stress disorder, with family caregivers experiencing secondary traumatic stress (Barnes, 1998; Rando, 1993, 1997; Shellenberger & Phelps, 1997; Sprang & McNeil, 1998).

Losses Unacknowledged by Society

Recently, attention has been devoted to unrecognized and unsanctioned grief (Pine et al., 1990) or disenfranchised grief (Doka, 1989)—that is, grief that exists although society does not recognize one's "need, right, role, or capacity to grieve" (Doka, 1989, p. 3). Examples of unrecognized family relationships and unacknowledged losses (i.e., ones not recognized as sig-nificant) include grief over (a) former spouses, lovers, cohabitors, and extra-marital lovers; (b) foster children and foster parents; (c) stepparents or stepchildren; (d) coworkers; (e) partners in gay or lesbian relationships; (f) companion animals; (g) professional caretakers; or (h) deaths related to pregnancy (i.e., miscarriage, elective abortion, stillbirth, or neonatal death). Bereaved grandparents, men in general (Gilbert, 1995), and families of de-ceased addicts may also be disenfranchised. In addition, some people are seen as incapable of, or without a need for, grief (Doka, 1989; Kauffman, 1993); these include young children, older adults, and mentally disabled per-sons. Recently, Corr (1998-1999) suggested that the concept of unsanctioned grief be expanded to examine what aspects of grief and mourning are them-selves disenfranchised.

Stigmatized Losses

Many people who are grieving report that they believe their grief has been stigmatized (Froman, 1992; Schiff, 1977). They feel the discomfort of others who distance themselves from the griever, and they experience direct or indirect social pressure to become "invisible mourners" (Rosaldo, 1989). Disenfranchised grief often results from stigmatized losses, particularly when there is the assumption that the death was caused by an individual's disturbed or immoral behavior (Shapiro, 1994), or a fear of contagion, such as with AIDS or cancer-related deaths (Sontag, 1988). AIDS-related deaths also are stigmatized in U.S. society because of their concentration in the homosexual community and, more recently, in poor inner-city Latino or African American neighborhoods (Demmer, 1998). In both groups, survivors are experiencing multiple losses among family and friends (Froman, 1992; Nord, 1998). Surviving companions of gay relationships frequently deal with a lack of legal standing, a denial of death benefits, and isolation. In some inner-city neighborhoods, 50% of those infected with HIV may be women, some with children who also are infected and many who have already lost companions, siblings, children, and friends.

Suicide has been identified as the most painful death for families (Dunne, McIntosh, & Dunne-Maxim, 1988; Stone, 1999). It is both violent and stigmatizing, in addition to provoking feelings of anger and guilt (Miles & Demi, 1994). The resulting secrecy and blame can distort family communication, isolate family members, and diminish social support (Walsh & McGoldrick, 1991). One issue that has not been well addressed has been the grief of families in which a member has killed others, been portrayed as evil, and then took his or her own life or was subject to the death penalty.

Factors Affecting Family Vulnerability

Timing and Concurrent Stressors in the Family Life Cycle

Families may have more difficulty adapting to loss if other stressors are present. When normative events associated with the stages of the family life cycle (e.g., a new marriage, the birth of a child, or an adolescent's move toward increased independence) are concurrent with illness or death, they may pose incompatible tasks (Brown, 1989; Hopmeyer & Werk, 1994; Shapiro, 1994; Walsh & McGoldrick, 1991).

Function and Position of Person Prior to His or Her Death

The centrality of the individual's functional role and the degree of the family's emotional dependence on the individual influence adaptation (Brown, 1989; Shapiro, 1994). Shock waves rarely follow the deaths of well-liked people who played peripheral roles or the deaths of dysfunctional members, unless the dysfunction played a central role in maintaining family equilibrium (Bowen, 1976).

Conflicted Relationship With the Deceased

Although conflict exists in all family relationships, when there is ambivalence, estrangement, or conflict that is intense and continuous, there is potential for complications in adaptation (Gamino, Sewell, & Easterling, 1998; Walsh & McGoldrick, 1991). In the case of life-threatening illnesses, there may be time to repair estranged relationships. However, family members may hesitate, fearing that confrontations may increase the risk of death.

Family Resources, Capabilities, and Strengths

Resources that assist in meeting demands may be tangible (e.g., money or health) or intangible (e.g., friendship, self-esteem, or a sense of mastery) (McCubbin & McCubbin, 1989). For example, young and middle-aged women's participation in the labor force, regardless of marital status, is consistently related to lower suicide rates, suggesting that role accumulation may provide protective resources (Stack, 1996, 1996-1997). The amount of disruption a bereaved family experiences also is related to its degree of openness (Brown, 1989) and is mediated by the intensity and chronicity of family stress. Although all family systems are open to some degree, adaptation is facilitated by "the ability of each family member to stay nonreactive to the emotional intensity in the system and to communicate his or her feelings to the others without expecting the others to act on them" (Brown, 1989, p. 472). Within-family resources that are identified as being related to favorable bereavement experiences include open and honest communication with children (Hurd, 1999), family cohesion and adaptability (Payne & Range, 1996a, 1996b), and marital intimacy (Lang, Gottlieb, & Amsel, 1996).

Social support appears to be one of the best buffers for dealing with stress (Eckenrode, 1991; Reed, 1998; Vierthaler, LeMay, Macey, & Wayment, 1998), but it does not mediate sex differences in loneliness and depression (Stroebe, Stroebe, & Abakoumkin, 1999). In addition, the availability of formal or informal networks does not guarantee support, especially in a society in which the expression of emotions surrounding loss is expected to be confined. In response, some bereaved family members turn to self-help groups composed of persons who have experienced a similar type of loss (Klass, 1984). However, the rules of some family systems discourage sharing intimate information and feelings with persons outside the family.

Family Belief System, Definition, and Appraisal

Family Paradigm

To fully understand how a family perceives a death or the coping strategies it uses, it is necessary to determine the family's view of the world (Boss, 1987). One common paradigm (Lerner, 1971; Lerner & Simmons, 1966) is the "belief in a just world." This perspective values control and mastery and assumes that there is a fit between one's efforts and outcomes; underlying this view is the belief that one gets what one deserves. Such a view is functional only when something can be done to change a situation. For example, it can lead to chronically ill persons being blamed for their conditions and lack of recovery or to linking adolescent deaths to drug use or reckless behavior as a way of affirming "it can't happen to my child."

Death's Legacy

Family history and experiences with death provide a legacy (a way of looking at loss that has been received from ancestors) that is related to how the family will adapt to subsequent loss (McGoldrick, 1991). Particularly in relation to several traumatic untimely deaths, there can be a legacy of empowerment (in which family members see themselves as survivors who can be hurt but not defeated) or a legacy of trauma (with a feeling of being "cursed" and unable to rise above the losses), both of which can inhibit openness of the system. Families may not recognize transgenerational anniversary patterns or the concurrence of a death with other life events, and members may have a lack of memory or discrepant memories regarding a death (Brown, 1989).

Family Appraisal and Meaning

Families appear to use several factors when appraising their crisis situation within a broader set of values, including family schema, coherence, paradigms, and situational and stressor appraisals (McCubbin et al., 1998). In addition, individual and family grief may be facilitated when the members view coping as a "communal process" (Lyons, Mickelson, Sullivan, & Coyne, 1998), looking at the stressor as *our* issue and addressing it with underlying notions of interdependence. Recent research places increased importance on meaning, whether it is in finding a sense of meaning and control (Thompson, 1996), flexibility in the family's belief system (Rolland, 1994), cross-cultural traditions that give meaning (Gersie, 1991; Korte, 1995-1996), the multiple meanings of a child's death (Gilbert & Smart, 1992; Hagemeister & Rosenblatt, 1997; Rosenblatt, 1996), or using life themes to understand terminal illness (Zlatin, 1995).

Boundary Ambiguity

Boundary ambiguity refers to the confusion a family experiences when it is not clear who is in and who is out of the system (Boss, 1987, 1999). Ambiguity rises when (a) facts surrounding a death are unclear, (b) a person is missing but it is unclear if death has occurred, or (c) the family denies the loss. The degree of boundary ambiguity, rather than specific coping skills or resources, may better explain adaptation and coping. Both denial and boundary ambiguity initially may be functional because they give a family time to deny the loss and then cognitively accept the fact that it is real. If a high degree of ambiguity exists over time, however, the family is at risk for maladaptation.

Factors of Diversity

Gender

Despite cultural expectations, most couples experience incongruent grieving, often with one adult whose grief could be called *cognitive and solitary* and the other whose grief is more *social and emotional* (Gilbert, 1996; Gilbert & Smart, 1992). Perhaps such discrepancy can be attributed to a family-system-level manifestation of Stroebe and Schut's Dual Process Model (1995). That is, for the system to function, both the *loss orientation* and *restoration orientation* need to be addressed.

Societal expectations claim that women should be responsible for the social and emotional tasks related to bereavement, including caregiving for the chronically ill and surviving family members (Walsh & McGoldrick, 1991). Women display more sorrow, guilt, and depression than men do (DeFrain,

Ernst, Jakub, & Taylor, 1991; Schwab, 1996), and support outside of the marriage is primarily directed toward women (Gilbert, 1989; Stroebe et al., 1999). Men are socialized to manage instrumental tasks, such as those related to the funeral, burial, finances, and property (Bach-Hughes & Page-Lieberman, 1989). Whether such distributions are influenced by biology is under debate (cf. Moir & Jessel, 1991). However, gender-related differences are influenced by expectations and socialization patterns (Gilbert, 1996; Stroebe, 1998) and may be a result of diverse activities performed in relation to illness and death (Littlewood, 1992).

It has been thought that men have unrecognized problems because their socialization interferes with active grief work (Staudacher, 1991, p. 9). Their response to grief typically includes coping styles that mask fear and insecurity, including remaining silent; taking physical or legal action in order to express anger and exert control; immersing themselves in work, domestic, recreational, or sexual activity; engaging in solitary or secret mourning; and exhibiting addictive behavior, such as alcoholism. Over time, elderly widowers appear to become increasingly bitter, as compared with widows (Bierhals et al., 1995-1996). Cook (1988) identified a double bind that bereaved fathers experience: Societal expectations are that they will contain their emotions in order to protect and comfort their wives, but they cannot heal their own grief without sharing their feelings.

Much of what appears to be a problem may not be in men's grieving but in our understanding of the mourning process (Cook, 1988), which largely has been formulated through the study of women. As such, understanding meaning making (i.e., attributing meaning to the loss, as well as reconstructing a sense of what a new "normal" life entails for the bereaved) (Gilbert, 1996, p. 271) and the Dual Process Model (Stroebe & Schut, 1995) may be more relevant for men than Lindemann's (1944) concept of grief work.

Cultural, Religious, and Ethnic Factors

As a result of immigration and contact between different groups, mourning patterns of groups in the United States continue to change (Braun & Nichols, 1997; McGoldrick et al., 1991). Yet group differences in values and practices continue to exist and present a wide range of normal responses to death. General areas in which differences exist include (a) the extent of ritual (e.g., the importance of attending funerals, types of acceptable emotional displays, and the degree to which these affairs should be costly); (b) the need to see the dying relative; (c) openness and the type of display of emotion; (d) the emphasis on verbal expression of feelings, and public versus private (namely, solitary or family) expression of grief; (e) the appropriate length of mourning; (f) the importance of anniversary events; (g) the roles of men and women; (h) the role of the extended family; (i) beliefs about what happens after death, particularly related to the ideas of suffering, fate, and destiny; (j) the value of autonomy or dependence in relation to bonds after death; (k) coping strategies; (l) social support for hospice patients; and (m) whether certain deaths are stigmatized (Biddle & Walter, 1998; Ita, 1995-1996; Klass, 1996; McGoldrick et al., 1991; Parkes, Laungani, & Young, 1997; Salahu-Din, 1996).

Specific Losses

Death of a Child

The death of one's child is viewed as the most difficult loss to experience, for it is contrary to the expected developmental progression and thrusts one into a marginal social role that has unclear role expectations (Klass & Marwit, 1988; Middleton, Raphael, Burnett, & Martinek, 1998). From an Eriksonian perspective, young adult parents grapple with death-related issues of identity as a parent and intimacy with the spouse; middle-aged parents deal with loss of generativity with a child's death (Kalish, 1989); and elderly parents deal with loss in terms of ego integrity versus despair. Attachment and psychoanalytic models appear to be inadequate in addressing parents' experiences. Newer models focus on integrating the deceased child into the parent's psychic and social worlds (Klass, 1997).

Society expects spouses to provide support and comfort during times of stress; however, this may not be possible for bereaved parents who are both experiencing intense grief as a result of the death of a child. They grieve as individuals, with unique timetables, and may not be "in sync" (Rando, 1993). Sexual expression can serve as a reminder of the child and elicit additional distress (Gottlieb, Lang, & Amsel, 1996; Hagemeister & Rosenblatt, 1997). However, previously reported high divorce rates of bereaved parents appear to be erroneous, lacking longitudinal value and confusing marital distress and divorce (Schwab, 1998).

Recent work on the meaning of a child's death has examined the importance of cultural context with regard to meaning ascribed to perinatal death (Hebert, 1998), cognitive coping strategies for finding meaning in the life and death of children with developmental disabilities (Milo, 1997), and the loss of both the child and parenting role following the death of a single child

(Talbot, 1996-1997). The death of an adult child also may be very disturbing even though there is likely to be a degree of separation between the child and parent (Raphael, 1983). This untimely death can provoke survivor guilt for the older parent and mean the loss of a major caregiver.

Death of a Sibling

Most research on sibling death is recent and tends to focus on children and adolescents (cf. Balk, 1990, 1991; Donnelly, 1988). Prior examination of sibling loss generally was confined to clinical studies. Sibling grief reactions are not uniform, and they are not the same as those experienced by bereaved parents (Hankoff, 1975; Rando, 1988). Such reactions can be best understood in relation to individual characteristics (e.g., sex, developmental stage, and relationship to the sibling). Recent work suggests no behavioral or at-risk differences in school-age children who experienced either parental death or sibling death; however, gender differences existed, with boys more affected by the loss of a parent and girls more affected by the death of a sibling, especially a sister (Worden, Davies, & McCown, 1999; Worden & Silverman, 1996).

Common reactions of siblings of all ages include (a) fear and insecurity from seeing the family foundation shaken (Schiff, 1977), (b) a sense that parents are unreachable, and (c) a frightening sense of abandonment (Hare-Mustin, 1979). Guilt as a result of sibling interactions and rivalry prior to the death is common and persists even when siblings can recognize the irrationality of such beliefs (Cain, Fast, & Erickson, 1964; Murray, 1982). Survivor guilt and anger also are common (Rando, 1988), and siblings report more family conflict than do their parents (Nelson & Frantz, 1996). However, rarely is anger directed toward a parent; parents are perceived to be vulnerable and hence need protection from any additional pain.

Deceased siblings still have an identity function. For example, surviving siblings in a triangulated position may feel a need to fulfill the roles the deceased child played for the parents, or they may act in an opposite manner from the sibling in an attempt to show that they are different (Bank & Kahn, 1975). Overall, more conceptual clarity is needed in the study of sibling bereavement, as are studies that extend beyond adolescence (Robinson & Mahon, 1997).

Death of a Parent

Each year, an estimated 5% of Americans experience the death of a parent (Perlin & Lieberman, 1979). Children's reactions vary and are influenced by emotional and cognitive development, closeness to the deceased parent, and the responses of or interactions with the surviving parent (Kubler-Ross, 1983, 1999; Rando, 1988). Comparisons of retrospective data from adults who experienced a parent's death during adolescence and those who experienced parental divorce suggest that both groups received comfort-intended communication, but the bereaved adolescents were more accepting of comments that highlighted the parent's positive attributes (Marwit & Carusa, 1998).

The death of a parent is the most common form of loss in middle age (Moss & Moss, 1989). Adult response to the death of a parent is influenced by the meaning of the relationship and the roles the parent played at the time of death (Rando, 1988). Adults with mental disabilities experience some aspects of grief in common with others but have some unique concerns (Luchterhand & Murphy, 1998). Adults whose parents lived in a nursing home prior to death exhibit multidimensional responses to the death, including sadness, grief, relief, persistence of memories about the parent, and a sense that the protection against death provided by the parent has vanished (Pruchno, Moss, Burant, & Schinfeld, 1995). The death of a parent also may create a "developmental push," a realization of new responsibilities as the surviving adult children become the oldest generation in the family (Osterweis, Solomon, & Green, 1984).

Death of a Spouse

Death of a spouse has been the most intensively studied adulthood loss (e.g., Clayton, 1974; Glick et al., 1974; Lopata, 1973). However, little attention has been given to (a) the death of a spouse in early or middle adulthood, (b) widowed parents with dependent children (Demi, 1989), (c) committed homosexual couples, or (d) the experiences of widowers (Clark, Siviski, & Weiner, 1986; Stroebe, 1998).

Loneliness and emotional adjustment to the loss of a primary relationship are major concerns of spouses who lose a companion—and a source of emotional support (Clark et al., 1986). The couple orientation of middle-class America contributes to a feeling of isolation (Osterweis et al., 1984; Rando, 1988). Conjugal bereavement can be especially difficult for individuals whose relationships assumed a sharp division of traditional sex roles (Lindstrom, 1999; Lopata, 1973; Rando, 1988), leaving them unprepared to assume the range of tasks required to maintain a household; it can also be particularly difficult when the spouse had an integral role in one's self-concept or when the cultural status of the widow(er) is low (Lopata, 1993). The death of one's spouse brings up issues of self-definition and prompts the need for developing a new identity. Despite these problems, many bereaved spouses adjust very well. Some even derive pleasure and independence from their new lifestyle, feeling more competent than when their spouse was alive (Rando, 1988).

Interventions

Clinical

Before family clinicians successfully intervene, they need to come to terms with the experiences of loss in their own lives. This may include examining the fears, reactions, and beliefs they hold that are influenced by their gender-related experiences and ethnic and religious backgrounds, as well as exploring what "healthy mourning" entails.

McGoldrick (1991) has identified several goals to facilitate the adaptation of bereaved family members. These goals include shared acknowledgment of the reality of death, shared experience, putting the death in context, reorganization of the family system, and reinvestment in other relationships or interests (pp. 54-55). Several suggestions follow.

1. Use a multigenerational perspective to attend to the legacies of past losses. Genograms can provide insight into family experiences with death, loss, and ambiguity (Brown, 1989; Rolland, 1994); coping; the family's belief system; and its hardiness (McGoldrick, 1991; Rolland, 1991). Attend to the impact of anticipated losses as well as to those that have occurred in the past few years to help families establish functional patterns before a loss (Rolland, 1991, 1994).

2. Increase your understanding of the relationship between trauma, posttraumatic stress, and complicated grief. Although there may be some common symptoms, the treatment and underlying issues can differ.

3. Develop an awareness of the beliefs, rituals, and roles related to death and bereavement for the ethnic, religious, or socioeconomic groups your practice serves. Differences also exist in the time required to create trust in a therapeutic relationship (McGoldrick & Giordano, 1996). Encourage families to form a healing theory (i.e., a theory to explain the loss) through

discussion of their own personal theories (Figley, 1998). Introduce families to personal narrative exercises to assist in their taking perspective of losses and in recognizing the significance of those losses for their ongoing lives (Neimeyer, 1999).

4. Explore with families their use of rituals (i.e., presence, changes in rigidity, or absence) and plans for subsequent rituals as potential indicators of family functioning (McGoldrick et al., 1991). When appropriate, therapists may assist in designing rituals to facilitate healing but not serve as the sole creator (Imber-Black, 1991; Shapiro, 1994). Rituals include the development of virtual memorial Internet sites.

5. When warranted, suggest self-help group participation and individual psychotherapy *in conjunction with* family therapy (Videka-Sherman & Lieberman, 1985). The bereaved persons most likely to find groups useful may be those who have experienced a sudden death and feel a need to share their grief beyond preexisting support networks (Schwab, 1995-1996).

6. Identify the overall circumstances and demands on family members regarding specific types of loss. For example, caregivers of persons with AIDS may be simultaneously dealing with their own illness and that of a number of friends or family members who are at various stages of HIV/AIDS, thus concurrently experiencing different stages of anticipatory loss (Demmer, 1998; Rolland, 1991).

7. Consider the therapeutic implications of viewing the bereaved from a victim paradigm (e.g., victims movement, vicarious victimization), as well as recognizing when it is disguised under our belief that *we* can foster their empowerment.

8. Question a managed care approach, solution-focused brief therapy, and a focus on recovery from grief to prior homeostasis (Wolfert, 1998a, 1998b). This approach is in contrast to what we know about grief and may actually be contributing to the "epidemic of 'complicated mourning' in North America" (Wolfert, 1997, p. 5).

9. Encourage the use of Internet resources (a) for social support from those in similar situations (through sites such as GriefNet) and (b) for obtaining information. Provide simple guidelines for evaluating the quality of Internet sites (e.g., DeSpelder, 1998).

10. Openly deal with questions related to loss to avoid reinforcement of the "invisible community of the bereaved" (Rosaldo, 1989). Acknowledge spiritual aspects of loss that may be part of an appropriate need for continuing bonds and finding meaning.

Public Policy/Education

Education regarding various aspects of death, dying, and bereavement is necessary before public policy can be instituted to facilitate individuals and their families in dealing with loss. Topics may include the following.

1. Death, dying, and bereavement as normal and natural experiences throughout the life span. Issues covered would include varying reactions related to type of loss, cultural factors, and characteristics of the family or survivor, with no single appropriate response or timeline. This information would sensitize policy makers and practitioners to (a) the normality of grief, (b) individual differences in grief, and (c) the needs of individuals and families as they cope with grief.

2. Planning for loss, including preparation of advance directives and discussion of living wills. Family members are increasingly confronted with the dilemma over whether (and how long) to maintain life-support efforts for a person with a protracted illness or injury when there is virtually no hope of recovery. They are caught in the controversy that involves the patient's right to die, family rights and expenses, medical ethics, religious beliefs, and criminal prosecution. Preplanning can encourage individuals to pursue efforts to encourage the courts, hospitals, and politicians to rethink policies in light of technological advances.

3. Rethinking the current approach to dealing with difficulty, which suggests that personal responsibility and effort are the way to improve health and postpone death (cf. Siegel, 1986; Simonton, Mathews-Simonton, & Creighton, 1978). This approach may be interpreted as placing blame on the individual, resulting in a sense of shame and failure. Such an experience can alter a family's paradigm for several generations (Rolland, 1991). This is not to say that it is unimportant for families to believe that they have some control over their circumstances but that control can be perceived in various nuances of the situation—not limited to controlling health and death.

4. Grief is not compartmentalized and can influence the workplace for a lengthy period of time. Granting a 3- to 5-day leave at the time of a death and expecting the employee to "return to normal" is not in the best interest of the employee or the workplace (Eyetsemitan, 1998; National Public Radio, 1999). Policies need to allow allotted grief days to be taken when needed; similar to sick leave, these days off do not appear costly to employers and improve employee attitude.

5. An examination of future terminal care options needs to take place in the context of the health care/reform movement. Federal policy related to hospice care needs reexamination in light of meeting the actual needs of individuals and their families, particularly for those in rural areas.

6. Developing a community-based plan for responding to tragedy. This coordinated effort needs to provide a continuum of services over time, not just an implosion early on of those in helping professions (Lattanzi-Licht, Mahoney, Miller, & Maloney, 1998).

Future Directions

There are many directions that research and intervention strategies dealing with death, dying, and grief can take. There continues to be a need for longitudinal work that gives attention to selective attrition as it relates to type of bereavement (Hayslip, McCoy-Roberts, & Pavur, 1998-1999). In addition, a shift from examining bereavement as an individual experience to viewing it within a developmental systemic or ecological context could yield much needed information. From this perspective, instruments need to be developed that address the coexistence of loss orientations and restoration orientations at the individual, couple, family, and societal levels. This work may be particularly useful in examining the paradigms of families with children living in inner cities, in which child development occurs amid chronic community violence, terror, and death (Garbarino, Dubrow, Kostelny, & Pardo, 1992), or the grief of the family and community following natural or human-made disasters.

Our research needs to examine the role that media reporting of violence plays in influencing societal and family attitudes toward death, grief, trust, and violence. What is printed or photographed has the potential to create additional problems for grieving family members. Cross-cultural studies that examine governing practices and the reporting of tragedy may provide other models.

We have come to view bereavement as a form of pathology (Rosen, 1986; Wolfert, 1998a). As such, we know more about the problems of coping than about the process of coping, and we know more about factors that inhibit grieving than about those that facilitate it. In their examination of coping and adaptation related to loss, both researchers and clinicians could benefit from structuring work around the premise that bereavement is natural and functional.

Conclusions and Summary

Dealing with death involves a process, not an event. It is an experience that all families *will* encounter. "Bereavement is complex, for it reaches to the heart of what it means to be human and what it means to have a relationship" (Klass, 1987, p. 31). Despite its importance in the experiences of individuals and families, death still appears to be a taboo subject. Research and theory have focused on the experiences of the dying individual or on the dyadic relationship of the bereaved and deceased. A multigenerational approach to family systems theory is well suited to address issues of loss and needs further application to research and clinical practice. Families' adaptation to death varies; factors that influence the process include characteristics of the death, family vulnerability, the history of past losses, incompatible life-cycle demands, resources, and belief systems.

Although loss is a normal experience, it has been treated by theorists and researchers as a problem. At this point, more work needs to focus on processes, such as the process of coping (rather than problems), and strengths, such as factors that facilitate growth from loss (rather than those that inhibit growth). The emergence of an examination of posttraumatic growth is a first step but warrants application beyond the individual to assess its applicability to families.

DISCUSSION QUESTIONS

1. Individual-based theories have been a popular approach to understanding the grief process, whether it is through stage models or task-based ones. Why might they be preferred to the family-based models? What are the strengths of family-based models?

2. What was once called abnormal or dysfunctional grief is now referred to as "complicated grief." On the basis of the factors that relate to family adaptation to loss, would you expect the percentage of the bereaved who experience complicated grief to be increasing or decreasing? Explain your position.

3. What would be the positive ramifications of enfranchising all grievers? What would be the potential negative ramifications of enfranchising all grievers?

4. What are some examples of posttraumatic growth? Does it always occur after grieving a death? Under what conditions would it be most likely to occur?

5. Describe the Dual Process Model of Coping. Give examples of areas of bereavement research and practice where its application might be helpful.

SUGGESTED READINGS

Doka, K. J. (Ed.). (1996). *Living with grief after sudden loss: Suicide, homicide, accident, heart attack, stroke.* Bristol, PA: Taylor & Francis.

Gilbert, K. R. (1996). "We've had the same loss, why don't we have the same grief?" Loss and differential grief in families. *Death Studies, 20,* 269-283.

Gilbert, K. R. (1999). *Grief in a family context* [On-line course]. Available: http://www.indiana.edu/~famlygrf

Shapiro, E. R. (1994). *Grief as a family process: A developmental approach to clinical practice.* New York: Guilford.

Webb, N. B. (Ed.). (1993). *Helping bereaved children: A handbook for practitioners.* New York: Guilford.

REFERENCES

Andershed, B., & Ternestedt, B. M. (1998). The illness trajectory—for patients with cancer who died in two different cultures of care. *Omega, 37,* 251-272.

Aries, P. (1974). *Western attitudes toward death: From the Middle Ages to the present.* Baltimore, MD: Johns Hopkins University Press.

Aries, P. (1985). *Images of man and death.* Cambridge, MA: Harvard University Press.

Attig, T. (1991). The importance of conceiving of grief as an active process. *Death Studies, 15,* 385-393.

Attig, T. (1996). *How we grieve: Relearning the world.* New York: Oxford University Press.

Bach-Hughes, C., & Page-Lieberman, J. (1989). Fathers experiencing a perinatal loss. *Death Studies, 13,* 537-556.

Balk, D. E. (1990). The self-concepts of bereaved adolescents: Sibling death and its aftermath. *Journal of Adolescent Research, 5,* 112-132.

Balk, D. E. (1991). Sibling death, adolescent bereavement, and religion. *Death Studies, 15,* 1-20.

Bank, S., & Kahn, M. D. (1975). Sisterhood-brotherhood is powerful: Sibling sub-systems and family therapy. *Family Process, 14,* 311-337.

Barnes, M. F. (1998). Understanding the secondary traumatic stress of parents. In C. R. Figley (Ed.), *Burnout in families: The systemic costs of caring* (pp. 75-90). Boca Raton, FL: CRC Press.

Bertalanffy, L. von. (1968). *General systems theory* (Rev. ed.). New York: George Braziller.

Biddle, L., & Walter, T. (1998). The emotional English and their queen of hearts. *Forum Newsletter, 24,* 1, 13-15.

Bierhals, A. J., Prigerson, H. G., Fasicza, A., Frank, E., Miller, M., & Reynolds, C. F., III. (1995-1996). Gender differences in complicated grief among the elderly. *Omega, 32,* 303-317.

Biondi, M., & Picardi, A. (1996). Clinical and biological aspects of bereavement and loss-induced depression: A reappraisal. *Psychotherapy and Psychosomatics, 65,* 229-245.

Boss, P. (1987). Family stress. In M. B. Sussman & S. K. Steinmetz (Eds.), *Handbook of marriage and the family* (pp. 695-723).

Boss, P. (1999). *Ambiguous loss: Learning to live with unresolved grief.* Cambridge, MA: Harvard University Press.

Bowen, M. (1976). Family reaction to death. In P. J. Guerin (Ed.), *Family therapy: Theory and practice.* New York: Gardner.

Bowlby, J. (1969). *Attachment and loss: Vol. 1. Attachment.* New York: Basic Books.

Bowlby, J. (1980). *Attachment and loss: Vol. 3. Loss: Sadness and depression.* New York: Basic Books.

Bowling, A., & Windsor, J. (1995). Death after widow(er)hood: An analysis of mortality rates up to 13 years after bereavement. *Omega, 31,* 35-49.

Braun, K. L., & Nichols, R. (1997). Death and dying in four Asian American cultures: A descriptive study. *Death Studies, 21,* 327-359.

Brown, F. H. (1989). The impact of death and serious illness on the family life cycle. In B. Carter & M. McGoldrick (Eds.), *The changing family life cycle* (2nd ed.). Needham Heights, MA: Allyn & Bacon.

Buckley, W. (1967). *Sociology and modern systems theory.* Englewood Cliffs, NJ: Prentice Hall.

Burnell, G. M., & Burnell, A. L. (1989). *Clinical management of bereavement: A handbook for healthcare professionals.* New York: Human Sciences.

Cain, A. C., Fast, I., & Erickson, M. E. (1964). Children's disturbed reactions to the death of a sibling. *American Journal of Orthopsychiatry, 34,* 741-752.

Carman, M. B. (1997). The psychology of normal aging. *Psychiatric Clinics of North America, 20,* 15-24.

Clark, P. G., Siviski, R. W., & Weiner, R. (1986). Coping strategies of widowers in the first year. *Family Relations, 35,* 425-430.

Clayton, P. (1974). Mortality and morbidity in the first year of widowhood. *Archives of General Psychiatry, 125,* 747-750.

Cook, J. A. (1988). Dad's double binds: Rethinking fathers' bereavement from a men's studies perspective. *Journal of Contemporary Ethnography, 17,* 285-308.

Corr, C. A. (1993). Coping with dying: Lessons that we should and should not learn from the work of Elisabeth Kubler-Ross. *Death Studies, 17,* 69-83.

Corr, C. A. (1998-1999). Enhancing the concept of disenfranchised grief. *Omega, 38,* 1-20.

Cose, E. (1999, August 2). The trouble with virtual grief: The pain that so many people feel for JFK, Jr. should not be confused with the actual suffering of family and friends. *Newsweek* [On-line]. Available: http://web5.searchbank.com/itw/session/601/680/35911852w3/sig!1

Counts, D. R., & Counts, D. A. (1991). Conclusions: Coping with the final tragedy. In D. R. Counts & D. A. Counts (Eds.), *Coping with the final tragedy: Cultural variation in dying and grieving* (pp. 277-291). Amityville, NY: Baywood.

Cummock, V. (1996). Journey of a young widow. In K. J. Doka (Ed.), *Living with grief after sudden loss: Suicide, homicide, accident, heart attack, stroke* (pp. 1-9). Bristol, PA: Taylor & Francis.

Davis, C. G., Nolen-Hoeksema, S., & Larson, J. (1998). Making sense of loss and benefitting from the experience: Two construals of meaning. *Journal of Personal and Social Psychology, 75,* 561-574.

DeFrain, J., Ernst, L., Jakub, D., & Taylor, J. (1991). *Sudden infant death: Enduring the loss.* Lexington, MA: Lexington Books.

Demi, A. S. (1989). Death of a spouse. In R. A. Kalish (Ed.), *Midlife loss* (pp. 218-248). Newbury Park, CA: Sage.

Demmer, C. (1998). AIDS in the inner city: Coping with life and death. *Forum Newsletter, 24,* 9, 12.

DeSpelder, L. (1998). Internet resources. *Forum Newsletter, 24*(6), 1, 13-14.

Devan, G. S. (1993). Management of grief. *Singapore Medical Journal, 34,* 445-448.

Dohrenwend, B. S., & Dohrenwend, B. P. (Eds.). (1974). *Stressful life events: Their nature and effects.* New York: John Wiley.

Doka, K. J. (Ed.). (1989). *Disenfranchised grief.* Lexington, MA: Lexington Books.

Doka, K. J. (1995-1996). Coping with life-threatening illness: A task model. *Omega, 32,* 111-122.

Doka, K. J. (1996). Commentary. In K. J. Doka (Ed.), *Living with grief after sudden loss: Suicide, homicide, accident, heart attack, stroke* (pp. 11-15). Bristol, PA: Taylor & Francis.

Doka, K. J. (1997). When illness is prolonged: Implications for grief. In K. J. Doka (Ed.), *Living with grief: When illness is prolonged* (pp. 5-16). Bristol, PA: Taylor & Francis.

Donnelly, K. F. (1988). *Recovering from the loss of a sibling.* New York: Dodd, Mead.

Dunne, E., McIntosh, J., & Dunne-Maxim, K. (1988). *Suicide and its aftermath.* New York: Norton.

Eckenrode, J. (Ed.). (1991). *The social context of coping.* New York: Plenum.

Eyetsemitan, F. (1998). Stifled grief in the workplace. *Death Studies, 22,* 469-479.

Figley, C. R. (1998). Burnout as systemic traumatic stress: A model for helping traumatized family members. In C. R. Figley (Ed.), *Burnout in families: The systemic costs of caring* (pp. 15-28). Boca Raton, FL: CRC Press.

Figley, C. R. (1999). Introduction. In C. R. Figley (Ed.), *Traumatology of grieving: Conceptual, theoretical, and treatment foundations* (pp. xv-xxi). Philadelphia: Brunner/ Mazel.

Frank, E., Prigerson, H. G., Shear, M. K., & Reynolds, C. F., III. (1997). Phenomenology and treatment of bereavement-related distress in the elderly. *International Clinical Psychopharmacology, 12* [Suppl. 7], S25-S29.

Freud, S. (1917). Mourning and melancholies. In J. Strachey (Ed. and Trans.), *The standard edition of the complete psychological works of Sigmund Freud* (Vol. 14, pp. 243-258). London: Hogarth.

Froman, P. K. (1992). *After you say goodbye: When someone you love dies of AIDS.* San Francisco: Chronicle Books.

Gamino, L. A., Sewell, K. W., & Easterling, L. W. (1998). Scott and White Grief Study: An empirical test of predictors of intensified mourning. *Death Studies, 22,* 333-355.

Garbarino, J., Dubrow, N., Kostelny, K., & Pardo, C. (1992). *Children in danger: Coping with the consequences of community violence.* San Francisco: Jossey-Bass.

Gersie, A. (1991). *Storymaking in bereavement: Dragons fight in the meadow.* London: Jessica Kingsley.

Gilbert, K. R. (1989). Interactive grief and coping in the marital dyad. *Death Studies, 13,* 605-626.

Gilbert, K. R. (1995). Family loss and grief. In R. D. Day, K. R. Gilbert, B. Settles, & W. R. Burr (Eds.), *Advanced family science* (pp. 304-318). Pacific Grove, CA: Brooks/ Cole.

Gilbert, K. R. (1996). "We've had the same loss, why don't we have the same grief?" Loss and differential grief in families. *Death Studies, 20,* 269-283.

Gilbert, K. R., & Smart, L. S. (1992). *Coping with infant or fetal loss: The couple's healing process.* New York: Brunner/Mazel.

Glick, I., Weiss, R., & Parkes, C. (1974). *The first year of bereavement.* New York: John Wiley.

Gottlieb, L. N., Lang, A., & Amsel, R. (1996). The long-term effects of grief on marital intimacy following an infant's death. *Omega, 33,* 1-19.

Hagemeister, A. K., & Rosenblatt, P. C. (1997). Grief and the sexual relationship of couples who have experienced a child's death. *Death Studies, 21,* 231-252.

Hall, M., Baum, A., Buysse, D. J., Prigerson, H. G., Kupfer, D. J., & Reynolds, C. F., III. (1998). Sleep as mediator of the stress-immune relationship. *Psychosomatic Medicine, 60,* 48-51.

Hankoff, L. D. (1975). Adolescence and the crisis of dying. *Adolescence, 10,* 373-387.

Hare-Mustin, R. T. (1979). Family therapy following the death of a child. *Journal of Marital and Family Therapy, 5,* 51-59.

Hayslip, B., McCoy-Roberts, L., & Pavur, R. (1998-1999). Selective attrition effects in bereavement research: A three-year longitudinal analysis. *Omega, 38,* 21-35.

Hebert, M. P. (1998). Perinatal bereavement in its cultural context. *Death Studies, 22,* 61-78.

Hill, R. (1949). *Families under stress.* New York: Harper & Row.

Holmes, T. H., & Rahe, R. H. (1967). The Social Readjustment Rating Scale. *Journal of Psychosomatic Research, 11,* 213-218.

Hopmeyer, E., & Werk, A. (1994). A comparative study of family bereavement groups. *Death Studies, 18,* 243-256.

Horacek, B. J. (1995). A heuristic model of grieving after high-grief deaths. *Death Studies, 19,* 21-31.

Hurd, R. C. (1999). Adults view their childhood bereavement experiences. *Death Studies, 23,* 17-41.

Huygen, F. J. A., van den Hoogen, H. J. M., van Eijk, J. Y. M., & Smits, A. J. A. (1989). Death and dying: A longitudinal study of their medical impact on the family. *Family Systems Medicine, 7,* 374-384.

Imber-Black, E. (1991). Rituals and healing process. In F. Walsh & M. McGoldrick (Eds.), *Living beyond loss* (pp. 207-224). New York: Norton.

Ironson, G., Wynings, C., Schneiderman, N., Baum, A., Rodriguez, M., Greenwood, D., Benight, C., Antoni, M., LaPerriere, A., Huang, H. S., Klimas, N., & Fletcher, M. A. (1997). Posttraumatic stress symptoms, intrusive thoughts, loss, and immune function after Hurricane Andrew. *Psychosomatic Medicine, 59,* 128-141.

Ita, D. J. (1995-1996). Testing of a causal model: Acceptance of death in hospice patients. *Omega, 32,* 81-92.

Jackson, D. (1965). The study of the family. *Family Process, 4,* 1-20.

Jacobs, S., & Osfeld, A. (1977). An epidemiological review of the mortality of bereavement. *Psychosomatic Medicine, 39,* 344-357.

Kalish, R. A. (Ed.). (1989). *Midlife loss: Coping strategies.* Newbury Park, CA: Sage.

Kantor, D., & Lehr, W. (1975). *Inside the family.* San Francisco: Jossey-Bass.

Kates, B. (1996). Sudden death: How the media can help. In K. J. Doka (Ed.), *Living with grief after sudden loss: Suicide, homicide, accident, heart attack, stroke* (pp. 191-199). Bristol, PA: Taylor & Francis.

Kauffman, J. (1993). Mourning and retardation. *Forum, 18*(2), 1, 12-13.

Klass, D. (1984). Bereaved parents and the compassionate friends: Affiliation and healing. *Omega, 15,* 353-373.

Klass, D. (1987). John Bowlby's model of grief and the problems of identification. *Omega, 18,* 13-21.

Klass, D. (1996). Ancestor worship in Japan: Dependence and the resolution of grief. *Omega, 33,* 279-302.

Klass, D. (1997). The deceased child in the psychic and social worlds of bereaved parents during the resolution of grief. *Death Studies, 21,* 147-175.

Klass, D., & Marwit, S. J. (1988). Toward a model of parental grief. *Omega, 19,* 31-50.

Klass, D., Silverman, P. R., & Nickman, S. L. (Eds.). (1996). *Continuing bonds: New understandings of grief.* Bristol, PA: Taylor & Francis.

Korte, A. O. (1995-1996). Despedidas as reflections of death in Hispanic New Mexico. *Omega, 32,* 245-267.

Kubler-Ross, E. (1969). *On death and dying.* New York: Macmillan.

Kubler-Ross, E. (1983). *On children and death.* New York: Collier.

Kubler-Ross, E. (1999). *The tunnel and the light.* New York: Marlowe.

Lang, A., Gottlieb, L. N., & Amsel, R. (1996). Predictors of husbands' and wives' grief reactions following infant death: The role of marital intimacy. *Death Studies, 20,* 33-57.

Lattanzi-Licht, M., Mahoney, J. J., Miller, G., & Maloney, J. J. (1998). *The hospice choice: In pursuit of a peaceful death.* New York: Simon & Schuster.

Lerner, M. (1971). Justice, guilt, and veridical perception. *Journal of Personality and Social Psychology, 20,* 127-135.

Lerner, M. (1980). When, why, and where people die. In E. S. Schneidman (Ed.), *Death: Current perspectives* (pp. 87-106). Palo Alto, CA: Mayfield.

Lerner, M., & Simmons, C. (1966). Observers' reactions to the innocent victim: Compassion or rejection? *Journal of Personality and Social Psychology, 14,* 203-210.

Lichtenstein, P., Gatz, M., & Berg, S. (1998). A twin study of mortality after spousal bereavement. *Psychological Medicine, 28,* 635-643.

Lindemann, E. (1944). Symptomology and management of acute grief. *American Journal of Psychiatry, 101,* 141-148.

Lindstrom, T. C. (1997). Immunity and somatic health in bereavement: A prospective study of Norwegian widows. *Omega: Journal of Death and Dying, 35,* 231-241.

Lindstrom, T. C. (1999). Coping with bereavement in relation to different feminine gender roles. *Scandinavian Journal of Psychology, 40,* 33-41.

Littlewood, J. (1992). *Aspects of grief: Bereavement in adult life.* London: Tavistock/Routledge.

Lopata, H. (1973). Self-identity in marriage and widowhood. *Sociological Quarterly, 14,* 407-418.

Lopata, H. Z. (1993). Widowhood and husband sanctification. In L. A. Bugen (Ed.), *Death and dying: Theory/research/practice* (pp. 205-211). Dubuque, IA: William C. Brown.

Luchterhand, C., & Murphy, M. N. (1998). *Helping adults with mental retardation grieve a death loss.* Philadelphia: Accelerated Development.

Lyons, R. F., Mickelson, K. D., Sullivan, M. J. L., & Coyne, J. C. (1998). Coping as a communal process. *Journal of Social and Personal Relationships, 15,* 579-605.

Madanes, C., & Haley, J. (1977). Dimensions of family therapy. *Journal of Nervous and Mental Disease, 165,* 88-98.

Marwit, S. J., & Carusa, S. S. (1998). Communicated support following loss: Examining the experiences of parental death and parental divorce in adolescence. *Death Studies, 22,* 237-255.

McCubbin, H. I., & Patterson, J. (1983). Family transitions: Adaptation to stress. In H. I. McCubbin & C. R. Figley (Eds.), *Stress and the family: Vol. 1. Coping with normative transitions.* New York: Brunner/Mazel.

McCubbin, H. I., Thompson, A. I., Thompson, E. A., Elver, K. M., & McCubbin, M. A. (1998). Ethnicity, schema, and coherence: Appraisal processes for families in crisis. In H. I. McCubbin, E. A. Thompson, A. I. Thompson, & J. E. Fromer (Eds.), *Stress, coping, and health in families: Sense of coherence and resiliency* (pp. 41-67). Thousand Oaks, CA: Sage.

McCubbin, M. A., & McCubbin, H. I. (1989). Theoretical orientations to family stress and coping. In C. R. Figley (Ed.), *Treating stress in families* (pp. 3-43). New York: Brunner/Mazel.

McGoldrick, M. (1991). Echoes from the past: Helping families mourn their losses. In F. Walsh & M. McGoldrick (Eds.), *Living beyond loss* (pp. 50-78). New York: Norton.

McGoldrick, M., Almeida, R., Hines, P. M., Garcia-Preto, N., Rosen, E., & Lee, E. (1991). Mourning in different cultures. In F. Walsh & M. McGoldrick (Eds.), *Living beyond loss* (pp. 176-206). New York: Norton.

McGoldrick, M., & Giordano, J. (1996). Overview: Ethnicity and family therapy. In M. McGoldrick, J. Giordano, & J. K. Pearce (Eds.), *Ethnicity and family therapy* (2nd ed.). New York: Guilford.

Mellor, P., & Shilling, C. (1993). Modernity, self-identity, and the sequestration of death. *Sociology, 27,* 411-432.

Middleton, W., Raphael, B., Burnett, P., & Martinek, N. (1998). A longitudinal study comparing bereavement phenomena in recently bereaved spouses, adult children, and parents. *Australian and New Zealand Journal of Psychiatry, 32,* 235-241.

Miles, M. S., & Demi, A. S. (1994). Toward the development of a theory of bereavement guilt. *Omega, 14,* 299-314.

Milo, E. M. (1997). Maternal responses to the life and death of a child with a developmental disability: A story of hope. *Death Studies, 21,* 443-476.

Moir, A., & Jessel, D. (1991). *Brain sex.* New York: Carol.

Moos, N. L. (1995). An interactive model of grief. *Death Studies, 19,* 337-364.

Moss, M. S., & Moss, S. Z. (1989). The death of a parent. In R. Kalish (Ed.), *Midlife loss* (pp. 89-114). Newbury Park, CA: Sage.

Murphy, S. A. (1996). Parent bereavement stress and preventive intervention following the violent deaths of adolescent or young adult children. *Death Studies, 20,* 441-452.

Murphy, S. A., Das Gupta, A., Cain, K. C., Johnson, L. C., Lohan, J., Wu, L., & Mekwa, J. (1999). Changes in parents' mental distress after the violent death of an adolescent or young adult child: A longitudinal prospective analysis. *Death Studies, 23,* 129-159.

Murray, C. I. (1982). Bereaved parent-adolescent interaction: A need for understanding. *Proceedings of the 1982 Ohio Council on Family Relations Annual Meeting* (pp. 33-44). Ohio Council on Family Relations.

Murray, C. I., & Gilbert, K. R. (1997, June). *British and U.S. reporting of the Dunblane school massacre.* Paper presented at the meeting of the 5th International Conference on Grief and Bereavement in Contemporary Society/Association for Death Education and Counseling, Washington, DC.

Murray, C. I., & Gilbert, K. R. (1998, November). *U.S. freedom of information or British code of practice: Grief and the media response to two massacres of children.* Paper presented at the annual meeting of the National Council on Family Relations, Milwaukee, WI.

National Public Radio. (1999). Grief at work [On-line transcript]. *The end of life: Exploring death in America.* Available: http://www.npr.org/programs/death/990217.death.html

Neimeyer, R. A. (1999). Meaning reconstruction and the experience of loss. *Forum Newsletter, 25*(1), 1, 13-14.

Nelson, B. J., & Frantz, T. T. (1996). Family interactions of suicide survivors and survivors of non-suicidal death. *Omega, 33,* 131-146.

Nord, D. (1998). Traumatization in survivors of multiple AIDS-related loss. *Omega, 37,* 215-240.

Osterweis, M., Solomon, F., & Green, M. (Eds.). (1984). *Bereavement: Reactions, consequences, and care.* Washington, DC: National Academy Press.

Parkes, C. M. (1988). Research: Bereavement. *Omega, 18,* 365-377.

Parkes, C. M., Laungani, P., & Young, B. (Eds.). (1997). *Culture and bereavement across cultures.* New York: Routledge.

Pattison, E. M. (1977). *The experience of dying.* Englewood Cliffs, NJ: Prentice Hall.

Paul, N., & Paul, B. (1982). Death and changes in sexual behavior. In F. Walsh (Ed.), *Normal family processes* (pp. 325-410). New York: Guilford.

Payne, B. J., & Range, L. M. (1996a). Family environment, attitudes toward life and death, depression, and suicidality in elementary-school children. *Death Studies, 20,* 481-494.

Payne, B. J., & Range, L. M. (1996b). Family environment, depression, attitudes toward life and death, and suicidality in young adults. *Death Studies, 20,* 237-246.

Perlin, L., & Lieberman, M. (1979). Social sources of distress. In R. Simons (Ed.), *Research in community health.* Greenwich, CT: JAI.

Pessagno, R. A. (1999). Differentiating between grief and depression. *Clinical Journal of Oncologic Nursing, 3,* 31-33.

Pine, V. R., Margolis, O. S., Doka, K., Kutscher, A. H., Schaefer, D. J., Siegel, M., & Cherico, D. J. (Eds.). (1990). *Unrecognized and unsanctioned grief: The nature and counseling of unacknowledged loss.* Springfield, IL: Charles C Thomas.

Ponzetti, J. J., & Johnson, M. A. (1991). The forgotten grievers: Grandparents' reactions to the death of grandchildren. *Death Studies, 15,* 157-167.

Prigerson, H. G., Bierhals, A. J., Kasl, S. V., Reynolds, C. F., III, Shear, M. K., Day, N., Beery, L. C., Newson, J. T., & Jacobs, S. (1997). Traumatic grief as a risk factor for mental and physical morbidity. *American Journal of Psychiatry, 154,* 616-623.

Prigerson, H. G., Shear, M. K., Jacobs, S. C., Reynolds, C. F., III, Maciejewski, P. K., Davidson, J. R., Rosenheck, R., Pilkonis, P. A., Wortman, C. B., Williams, J. B., Widiger, T. A., Frank, E., Kupfer, D. J., & Zisook, S. (1999). Consensus criteria for traumatic grief: A preliminary empirical test. *British Journal of Psychiatry, 174,* 67-73.

Pruchno, R. A., Moss, M. S., Burant, C. J., & Schinfeld, S. (1995). Death of an institutionalized parent: Predictors of bereavement. *Omega, 31,* 99-119.

Ramsden, P. G. (1991). Alice in the afterlife: A glimpse in the mirror. In D. R. Counts & D. A. Counts (Eds.), *Coping with the final tragedy: Cultural variation in dying and grieving* (pp. 27-41). Amityville, NY: Baywood.

Rando, T. A. (1988). *Grieving: How to go on living when someone you love dies.* Lexington, MA: Lexington Books.

Rando, T. A. (1993). *Treatment of complicated mourning.* Champaign, IL: Research Press.

Rando, T. A. (1997). Living and learning the reality of a loved one's dying: Traumatic stress and cognitive processing in anticipatory grief. In K. J. Doka (Ed.), *Living with grief: When illness is prolonged* (pp. 33-50). Bristol, PA: Taylor & Francis.

Raphael, B. (1983). *The anatomy of bereavement.* New York: Basic Books.

Redmond, L. M. (1996). Sudden violent death. In K. J. Doka (Ed.), *Living with grief after sudden loss: Suicide, homicide, accident, heart attack, stroke* (pp. 53-71). Bristol, PA: Taylor & Francis.

Reed, M. D. (1998). Predicting grief symptomatology among the suddenly bereaved. *Suicide and Life Threatening Behavior, 28,* 285-301.

Robinson, L., & Mahon, M. M. (1997). Sibling bereavement: A concept analysis. *Death Studies, 21,* 477-499.

Rolland, J. S. (1991). Helping families with anticipatory loss. In F. Walsh & M. McGoldrick (Eds.), *Living beyond loss* (pp. 144-163). New York: Norton.

Rolland, J. S. (1994). *Families, illness, and disability: An integrative treatment model.* New York: Basic Books.

Rosaldo, R. (1989). *Culture and truth: The remaking of social analysis.* Boston: Beacon.

Rosen, H. (1986). *Unspoken grief.* Lexington, MA: Lexington Books.

Rosenblatt, P. (1983). *Bitter, bitter tears: Nineteenth century diarists and twentieth century grief theorists.* Minneapolis: University of Minnesota Press.

Rosenblatt, P. (1996). Grief that does not end. In D. Klass, P. Silverman, & S. Nickman (Eds.), *Continuing bonds: New understanding of grief* (pp. 45-58). Bristol, PA: Taylor & Francis.

Salahu-Din, S. N. (1996). A comparison of coping strategies of African American and Caucasian widows. *Omega, 33,* 103-120.

Saldinger, A., Cain, A., Kalter, N., & Lohnes, K. (1999). Anticipating parental death in families with young children. *American Journal of Orthopsychiatry, 69,* 39-48.

Schaefer, J. A., & Moos, R. H. (1998). The context of posttraumatic growth: Life crises, individual and social resources, and coping. In R. G. Tedeschi, C. L. Park, & L. G. Calhoun (Eds.), *Posttraumatic growth: Positive changes in the aftermath of crisis* (pp. 99-125). Mahwah, NJ: Lawrence Erlbaum.

Schiff, H. (1977). *The bereaved parent.* New York: Crown.

Schwab, R. (1995-1996). Bereaved parents and support group participation. *Omega, 32,* 49-61.

Schwab, R. (1996). Gender differences in parental grief. *Death Studies, 20,* 103-113.

Schwab, R. (1998). A child's death and divorce: Dispelling the myth. *Death Studies, 22,* 445-468.

Shapiro, E. R. (1994). *Grief as a family process: A developmental approach to clinical practice.* New York: Guilford.

Shellenberger, S., & Phelps, G. L. (1997). When it never stops hurting: A case of chronic pain. In S. H. McDaniel, J. Hepworth, & W. J. Doherty (Eds.), *The shared experience of illness* (pp. 231-241). New York: Basic Books.

Siegel, B. S. (1986). *Love, medicine, and miracles.* New York: Harper & Row.

Simonton, C., Mathews-Simonton, S., & Creighton, J. (1978). *Getting well again.* Los Angeles: J. P. Tarcher.

Sontag, S. (1988). *AIDS and its metaphors.* New York: Farrar, Straus, & Giroux.

Sprang, G., & McNeil, J. (1998). Post-homicide reactions: Grief, mourning, and post-traumatic stress disorder following a drunk driving fatality. *Omega, 37,* 41-58.

Stack, S. (1996). Effect of female labor force participation on female suicide attitudes. *Death Studies, 20,* 285-291.

Stack, S. (1996-1997). Effect of labor force participation on female suicide rates: An analysis of individual data from 16 states. *Omega, 34,* 163-169.

Staudacher, C. (1991). *Men and grief.* Oakland, CA: New Harbinger.

Stone, G. (1999). *Suicide and attempted suicide.* New York: Carroll & Graf.

Stroebe, M. (1992). Coping with bereavement: A review of the grief work hypothesis. *Omega, 26,* 19-42.

Stroebe, M. (1997, June). *Coping with bereavement: The sense and nonsense of science.* Paper presented at the meeting of the 5th International Conference on Grief and Bereavement in Contemporary Society/Association for Death Education and Counseling, Washington, DC.

Stroebe, M. S. (1998). New directions in bereavement research: Exploration of gender differences. *Palliative Medicine, 12,* 5-12.

Stroebe, M. S., & Schut, H. (1995, June). *The dual process model of coping with loss.* Paper presented at the meeting of the International Work Group on Death, Dying, and Bereavement, Oxford, UK.

Stroebe, W., Stroebe, M., & Abakoumkin, G. (1999). Does differential social support cause sex differences in bereavement outcome? *Journal of Community and Applied Social Psychology, 9,* 1-12.

Stroebe, W., Stroebe, M., Abakoumkin, G., & Schut, H. (1996). Social and emotional loneliness: A comparison of attachment and stress theory explanations. *Journal of Personality and Social Psychology, 70,* 1241-1249.

Summers, J., Zisook, S., Atkinson, J. H., Sciolla, A., Whitehall, W., Brown, S., Patterson, T., & Grant, I. (1995). Psychiatric morbidity associated with Acquired Immune Deficiency Syndrome-related grief resolution. *Journal of Nervous and Mental Disease, 183,* 384-389.

Talbot, K. (1996-1997). Mothers now childless: Survival after the death of an only child. *Omega, 34,* 177-189.

Tedeschi, R. G., & Calhoun, L. G. (1995). *Trauma and transformation: Growing in the aftermath of suffering.* Thousand Oaks, CA: Sage.

Tedeschi, R. G., Park, C. L., & Calhoun, L. G. (1998). Posttraumatic growth: Conceptual issues. In R. G. Tedeschi, C. L. Park, & L. G. Calhoun (Eds.), *Posttraumatic growth: Positive changes in the aftermath of crisis* (pp. 1-22). Mahwah, NJ: Lawrence Erlbaum.

Thompson, S. C. (1996). Barriers to maintaining a sense of meaning and control in the face of loss. *Journal of Personal and Interpersonal Loss, 1,* 333-358.

U.S. Bureau of the Census. (1975). *Historical statistics: Colonial times to 1970.* Washington, DC: Government Printing Office.

Ventura, S. J., Anderson, R. N., Martin, J. A., & Smith, B. L. (1998). Births and deaths: Preliminary data for 1997. *National Vital Statistics Report, 47*(4) [On-line]. Available: http://www.cdc.gov/nchs/data/nvsr47_4.pdf

Videka-Sherman, L., & Lieberman, M. (1985). The effects of self-help and psychotherapy intervention on child loss: The limits of recovery. *American Journal of Orthopsychiatry, 55,* 70-82.

Vierthaler, J. S., LeMay, S. F., Macey, H. L., & Wayment, H. A. (1998, April). *The impact of social support and strain on bereavement outcomes.* Paper presented at the annual meeting of the Western Psychology/Rocky Mountain Psychological Association, Albuquerque, NM.

Viorst, J. (1986). *Necessary losses.* New York: Simon & Schuster.

Walsh, F., & McGoldrick, M. (1991). Loss and the family: A systems perspective. In F. Walsh & M. McGoldrick (Eds.), *Living beyond loss* (pp.1-29). New York: Norton.

Walter, T., Littlewood, J., & Pickering, M. (1995). Death in the news: The public invigilation of private emotion. *Sociology, 29,* 579-596.

Williams, M. B. (1998). Treating STSD in children. In C. R. Figley (Ed.), *Burnout in families: The systemic costs of caring* (pp. 91-138). Boca Raton, FL: CRC Press.

Wolfert, A. D. (1997). Blessed are those who mourn quickly: Managed care and the rapid "resolution" of grief. *Forum Newsletter, 23*(3), 5, 11.

Wolfert, A. D. (1998a). Companioning vs. treating: Beyond the medical model of bereavement: Part 1. *Forum Newsletter, 24*(4), 1, 10.

Wolfert, A. D. (1998b). Companioning vs. treating: Beyond the medical model of bereavement: Part 3. *Forum Newsletter, 24*(6), 3, 15.

Worden, J. W., Davies, B., & McCown, D. (1999). Comparing parent loss with sibling loss. *Death Studies, 23,* 1-15.

Worden, J. W., & Silverman, P. R. (1996). Parental death and the adjustment of school-age children. *Omega, 33,* 91-102.

Worden, W. (1982). *Grief counseling and grief therapy.* New York: Springer.

Worden, W. (1991). *Grief counseling and grief therapy: A handbook for the mental health practitioner* (2nd ed.). New York: Springer.

Wortman, C. B., & Silver, R. C. (1989). The myths of coping with loss. *Journal of Consulting and Clinical Psychology, 57,* 349-357.

Zisook, S., & Shuchter, S. R. (1986). The first four years of widowhood. *Psychiatric Annals, 16,* 288-298.

Zlatin, D. M. (1995). Life themes: A method to understand terminal illness. *Omega, 31,* 189-206.

7

Physical Illness

Challenges to Families

THOMAS L. CAMPBELL

Until recently, family therapists and family researchers have largely ignored physical illness and its relationship to the family. This is partially a result of the academic community's split between mind and body and biology and psychology, as well as the tendency of family scientists to avoid the biological aspects of family life. Exceptions to this trend have been the pioneering work of Bowen (1978), Minuchin (Minuchin et al., 1975; described below), Weakland (1977), and Wynne (Wynne, Cromwell, & Matthysse, 1978).

More recently, there has been a growing interest in the role of family therapists working in medical settings, caring for patients with physical illnesses, and collaborating with medical providers (Blount, 1998; Cummings, Cummings, & Johnson, 1997; Seaburn, Gunn, Mauksch, Gawinski, & Lorenz, 1996). In 1983, Donald Bloch (1983) began the journal *Family Systems Medicine,* which addresses the interface of family therapy and medicine. In 1992, McDaniel, Hepworth, and Doherty (1992) coined the term *medical family therapy* to refer to a "biopsychosocial treatment of individuals and families who are dealing with medical problems" (p. 2). In addition, family therapists, family nurses, family physicians, and others have come together to form the Collaborative Family Health Care Coalition to help promote a more family-centered and collaborative model of health care delivery (Bloch, 1994).

The U.S. health care system is in the midst of enormous changes—unlike any that have been seen since the early part of the 20th century—and crisis.

Under tremendous pressures to control rising health care costs, most health care services are being reorganized into large, vertically integrated managed care systems in which providers must demonstrate that they are offering the most cost-effective services available. Although this new health care system will provide many challenges to family therapists, it does offer new opportunities to demonstrate how collaborative health care (integrating traditional medical care with psychosocial services) can provide the most effective and cost-efficient services. With such health care changes rapidly spreading across the United States, it is an important time to review the research on families and health, as well as the evidence that family interventions can lead to better health outcomes in the treatment of physical illness.

In the past two decades, a substantial body of research has been published exploring the relationships between family factors and health; this has been accompanied by the increasing recognition of the importance of the family in all aspects of health care (Campbell, 1986; Doherty & Campbell, 1988; Turk & Kerns, 1985). This family and health research clearly has demonstrated that families have a powerful impact on family members' physical health. Despite these advances in our understanding of the relationships between family factors and health, research on family interventions in health care remains in its infancy. There are very few randomized controlled trials of family therapy in health care. Most of the studies are case reports or uncontrolled trials of family interventions. Part of the reason for this lack of research is that we are just beginning to understand what family variables are important in physical health and how they exert their influence, as well as the role of health-related stressors on a family's ability to cope. This chapter will review the research on families and health—studies that examine (a) the impact of family factors on physical illness and (b) the effects of physical illness on families. Particular attention will be paid to clinical trials of family interventions in physical disorders, as they provide the best support for a family-oriented approach to health care. Finally, the implications of this research for family professionals will be discussed.

The Family Health and Illness Cycle

Clinical experience holds that families influence and are influenced by the health of their members, and family-oriented health care can lead to improved health for both the individual and the whole family. However, assumptions and experiences that point toward a new approach to medical care should be scientifically validated through empirical research (i.e., they

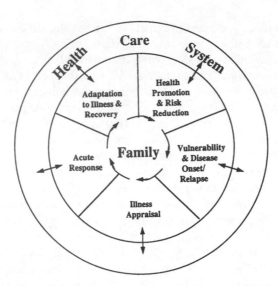

Figure 7.1. Family Health and Illness Cycle
SOURCE: Doherty and Campbell (1988, p. 23). Reprinted by permission of authors.

should be evidence based). The family health and illness cycle (see Figure 7.1) developed by Doherty and Campbell (1988) can help organize research on families and health because it provides a sequence of families' experiences with health and illness. The two-way arrows between the family and health care system emphasize the importance of families' ongoing interactions with health care professionals. Starting at the top of the cycle with health promotion and risk reduction, research in each of the five categories will be reviewed.

Family Health Promotion and Risk Reduction

Much of the current suffering and mortality from physical illness now results from chronic, degenerative diseases that follow from our own unhealthy behaviors. In a recent review of causes of mortality in the United States, it was estimated that 37% of all deaths are directly attributable to four unhealthy behaviors: smoking (18%), poor diet and lack of exercise (14%), and alcohol abuse (5%) (McGinnis & Foege, 1993). As a result, the federal government initiated a major program titled "Healthy People 2000" to help promote health and reduce health risks (Public Health Service, 1990).

The World Health Organization (1976) has characterized the family as the "primary social agent in the promotion of health and well being" (p. 17). A healthy lifestyle is usually developed, maintained, or changed within the family setting. Behavioral health risk factors cluster within families, because family members tend to share similar diets, physical activities, and use of substances (e.g., tobacco, alcohol, and illicit drugs) (Doherty & Campbell, 1988). Parents' health-related behaviors strongly influence whether a child or adolescent will adopt a healthy behavior, and family support is an important determinant of an individual's ability to change an unhealthy lifestyle.

Almost every important health behavior is a family activity or is strongly influenced by the family. An emphasis on physical activity and fitness is usually a shared family value. Parents' exercise habits and attitudes have a strong influence on their children's level of physical activity (Sallis & Nader, 1988). Individuals with or at high risk of cardiac disease are more likely to participate in a cardiac rehabilitation or exercise program if their spouses are supportive or attend with them (Heinzelmann & Bagley, 1970).

Cigarette Smoking

Cigarette smoking remains the number one health problem in the United States today, with more than 350,000 deaths each year directly attributable to smoking. The initiation, maintenance, and cessation of smoking are strongly influenced by other family members. An adolescent who has a parent and an older sibling who smoke is 5 times more likely to smoke than an adolescent from a nonsmoking family (Bewley & Bland, 1977). Smokers are more likely to marry smokers, to smoke the same number of cigarettes as their spouse, and to quit at the same time (Venters, Jacobs, Luepker, Maiman, & Gillum, 1984). Smokers who are married to nonsmokers or ex-smokers are more likely to quit and remain abstinent (Price, Chen, & Cavallii, 1981). Several studies have demonstrated that support from the spouse is highly predictive of successful smoking cessation (Graham & Gibson, 1971). In particular, supportive behaviors involving cooperative behaviors (e.g., talking the smoker out of smoking the cigarette) and reinforcement (e.g., expressing pleasure at the smoker's efforts to quit) predict successful quitting (Coppotelli & Orleans, 1985; Mermelstein, Lichtenstein, & McIntyre, 1983). Negative behaviors, such as nagging the smoker and complaining about smoking, are predictive of relapse.

Based on this research, a number of smoking-cessation studies have attempted to use partner support as an adjunct to their programs. These studies have tried to combine or integrate a social support intervention with standard cognitive-behavioral programs to increase abstinence from smoking. Four different studies involving a total of more than 150 subjects have tested a partner support program in randomized trials (Glasgow & Lichtenstein, 1987; Lichtenstein, Glasgow, & Abrams, 1986; Malott, Glasgow, O'Neill, & Klesges, 1984; McIntyre-Kingsolver, Lichtenstein, & Mermelstein, 1986). Most of these programs were centered around an individual smoking-cessation program, involving nicotine replacement, self-management training, and relapse prevention. In the partner support groups, the partner, usually the spouse, participated in all the treatment sessions, and the couples were given suggestions and feedback on helpful and unhelpful behaviors. Couples were encouraged to problem solve about how to encourage smoking cessation and were given homework assignments in some programs.

The results of these trials were quite consistent and discouraging. The smoking-cessation rates in the partner support groups were not significantly different from the standard individually treated subjects—either at the end of the trials or at the 6- and 12-month follow-ups. The results of only one study favored the partner support group, but the results were not statistically significant (McIntyre-Kingsolver et al., 1986). In each of the studies, the amount of spousal or partner support reported by the smokers was predictive of the successful cessation, and the absence of negative or unsupportive behaviors was generally more important than the presence of supportive behaviors. However, these interventions failed to significantly increase the amount of support provided by the spouse. Thus, these studies confirm the hypothesis that spousal support and the absence of spousal criticisms are important for smoking cessation, but they also indicate that these behaviors are not easily changed through education and problem solving.

The failure of these interventions to increase smoking cessation may result partially from their lack of systemic orientation. Smoking is a complex behavior that is influenced by biological factors (nicotine addiction), individual psychological issues, extrafamilial social relationships and pressures, and the marital relationship. Supportive behaviors by the spouse are part of a complex marital relationship and are probably related to overall marital quality and satisfaction. Unfortunately, none of these observational or experimental studies of smoking cessation have measured any marital variables (other than spousal support) such as marital communication or satisfaction. Some of these studies do support the general finding in marital research that negative spousal interactions have a greater impact on outcomes than positive interactions do (Coppotelli & Orleans, 1985; Mermelstein et al., 1983).

Obesity

Obesity is a major public health problem; more than 30% of the adult population weighs more than 20% above their ideal body weight. Obesity contributes to higher rates of hypertension, diabetes, arthritis, coronary heart disease, and numerous other disorders. Studies have shown how eating behaviors and obesity can play important homeostatic functions within families (Stuart & Davis, 1972). Twenty-five percent of mothers report that they use food as a reward for their children, and 10% use it as punishment (Bryan & Lowenberg, 1958). Parents of obese children are more likely to encourage their children to eat (Klesges et al., 1983) and less likely to encourage exercise (Waxman & Stunkard, 1980). The family also plays an important role in the development and treatment of major eating disorders such as anorexia nervosa and bulimia.

The research on family involvement in weight-reduction programs for adults parallels that of smoking cessation. Observational studies have shown that spousal support predicts successful weight loss (Mahoney & Mahoney, 1976), and criticism and nagging (including high levels of expressed emotion) from the spouse are associated with poor outcomes (Fischman-Havstad & Marston, 1984). A number of randomized controlled trials have examined the effect of spousal involvement in weight-reduction programs (Brownell & Stunkard, 1981; O'Neill et al., 1979; Weisz & Bucher, 1980; Zitter & Fremouw, 1978). Similar to the smoking studies, these trials have been based on a cognitive-behavioral model in which the spouse is seen as a reinforcer of the desired behavior. In general, spouses attend all training sessions (varying from 6 to 18 sessions) and are instructed in basic behavior-modification techniques. Spouses are trained to give positive reinforcement and instructed not to criticize their partner's weight or eating behaviors.

The results of these studies have been mixed; approximately one half of the studies demonstrated a positive effect of spouse involvement, particularly on the maintenance of weight loss after the end of the intervention. The most successful programs (Brownell, Heckerman, Westlake, Hayes, & Monti, 1978) have reported two to three times greater weight loss in the spouse-involved groups at 3-month and 3-year follow-ups. Pearce, LeBow, and Orchard (1981) demonstrated that the greatest weight loss occurred in the group in which the spouses were asked not to nag or otherwise participate in their partners' weight loss efforts. Their study emphasizes the importance of spousal criticism in weight reduction and suggests that blocking negative marital interactions may be more important than promoting supportive behaviors.

Because several well-designed studies have failed to demonstrate any effect of spouse involvement, it is difficult to draw any overall conclusions from this research. Black, Gleser, and Kooyers (1990) conducted a meta-analysis of couples' weight loss programs and found that, based on effect sizes, the couples' programs were slightly, but significantly, superior to subject-alone programs at posttreatment. At 2- to 3-month follow-ups, the couples' programs maintained a nearly significant ($p = .06$) improvement, which disappeared at lengthier follow-up.

Several studies have looked at family variables that may help explain these findings. One study found that higher marital adjustment scores correlated with more weight loss in the spouse involvement group (Dubbert & Wilson, 1984). Another found that spousal support in weight reduction was more important in highly cohesive than in disengaged families (Barbarin & Tirado, 1984). Women have been found to be more supportive of their husbands' losing weight than vice versa. Similar to the smoking studies, several intervention studies that measured supportive behaviors pre- and postintervention showed no significant increase in these behaviors.

Nutrition is an obvious family activity. Despite changes in traditional family roles, women still do most of the meal preparation and planning for the entire family. Family members consume similar amounts of salt, calories, cholesterol, and saturated fats (Baranowski & Nader, 1985). A number of studies have shown that interventions directed at individuals within a family have a "spin-off" effect on other family members, resulting in improvement in their health as well. For example, in the cardiovascular Multiple Risk Factor Intervention Trial (MR FITT), the wives of the men who were involved in the intervention made significant improvements in their diets and other risk factors even though they were not directly involved in the study (Sexton et al., 1987). Some studies of school-based child nutrition programs have resulted in improvements in the parents' diets (Perry, Crockett, & Pirie, 1987). Because diet is a family activity, several dietary intervention programs have focused on families rather than individuals. Most of these family heart studies have dealt with cardiovascular risk reduction and have focused on either high-risk families or the general population. A number have developed from child-focused, school-based programs in which a family component has been added.

A number of intervention studies have demonstrated that a family intervention to improve nutrition is effective and results in better outcomes than no intervention. The largest and most ambitious trial, the British Family Heart Trial (Family Heart Study Group, 1994), included more than 12,000 middle-aged couples recruited from 26 general practices in Britain. Couples were screened for cardiovascular risk factors (smoking, elevated blood pressure, cholesterol and glucose, and obesity) and received "family-centered" counseling about healthy lifestyles and cardiac risk reduction by a trained nurse. Families received variable amounts of follow-up depending on the level of cardiac risk. After 1 year, the men and women in the intervention group had a 16% overall reduction in their cardiac risk score, mostly resulting from reduced smoking, blood pressure, and cholesterol levels. The authors estimate that such a level of risk reduction would reduce heart attacks and cardiac deaths in Britain by approximately 8%.

Several smaller scale studies have compared the effectiveness of family approaches with more traditional individual approaches to cardiovascular risk reduction. Researchers from the University of Minnesota's School of Public Health compared the effectiveness of a school-based nutritional program to reduce diet fat and sodium with a home-based program that included the parents (Perry et al., 1989). More than 1,000 families of third graders participated in a 5-week course in which parents and children engaged in family games that used a baseball motif and rewarded healthy nutrition activities. Students who participated in the family-based intervention reported more behavioral changes and greater reduction in fat consumption than did the students in the similar school-based program. Unfortunately, these differences disappeared at a 1-year follow-up.

In the Tromso Family Intervention Study (Knutsen & Knutsen, 1991), 1,373 men with elevated cholesterol levels and their families were randomly assigned to a family counseling or control group. Seven years after the family intervention, the men and their wives whose families received counseling about diet, exercise, and smoking had significantly lower risk-factor levels than the controls. The differences in the children's risk factors were not significant.

These studies demonstrate that a family approach to cardiovascular risk reduction, especially nutritional changes, is more effective than individual approaches. This remains a promising area for future research.

Vulnerability and Disease Onset/Relapse

There is now ample evidence that psychosocial factors can affect an individual's susceptibility to disease, whether it is the common cold or cancer. Studies of stress and social support have shown the most convincing evidence that families are often the most important source of stress or support and that families have a potent influence on health.

One successful method for studying stress and its impact on health has been to examine the relationship between stressful life events and illness. Many retrospective and prospective studies have used the Holmes and Rahe scale to demonstrate that stressful life events precede the development of a wide range of different diseases (Holmes & Rahe, 1967).

Most of the events on the Holmes and Rahe scale occur within the family, and 10 of the 15 most stressful events are family events. Because children are likely to be affected by family stress, a number of studies have looked at the relationship between family life events and child health. In an early study, Meyer and Haggerty (1962) found that chronic stress was associated with higher rates of streptococcal pharyngitis and that 30% of the strep infections were preceded by a stressful family event. Children in a day care setting who experienced more stressful life events had longer but not more frequent episodes of respiratory illness (Boyce & Chesterman, 1990). A prospective study of more than 1,000 preschoolers found that family life events were strongly correlated with subsequent visits to the physician and hospital admissions for a wide range of conditions. Children from families with more than 12 life events during the 4-year study period were six times more likely to be hospitalized (Beautrais, Fergusson, & Shannon, 1982).

The death of a spouse is the most stressful common life event, and the health consequences of bereavement have been extensively studied. Large, well-controlled, epidemiologic studies have confirmed that the death of a spouse is associated with an increased mortality in the surviving spouse, especially within the first 6 months (Martikainen & Valkonen, 1996). The effect of a death of a spouse is greater on surviving men than women, probably because women usually have better social networks and supports.

Divorce or marital separation is also an extremely stressful event, and it is ranked second on the Holmes and Rahe scale. Cross-sectional studies reveal that divorcées have a higher death rate from all diseases than single, widowed, or married persons (Burman & Margolin, 1992). However, chronic physical illness can have an adverse effect on marital satisfaction and may eventually lead to divorce. Prospective studies of divorce and health suggest that both processes are occurring: Physical illness can lead to marital disruption, and divorce can influence health.

Research in psychoimmunology has demonstrated that stress can lead to immunosuppression and an increase in illness (Calabrese, Kling, & Gold, 1987). Two well-controlled studies demonstrated a decrease in cellular immunity (T-lymphocyte stimulation) during bereavement (Bartrop,

Luckhurst, Lazarus, Kiloh, & Penny, 1977; Schleifer, Keller, Bond, Cohen, & Stein, 1989). Divorced or separated women have significantly poorer immune function than sociodemographically matched married women (Kiecolt-Glaser et al., 1987). Among the married women, poor marital quality correlated with both depression and decreased immunity. Immune function is also impaired in major depression, and researchers have suggested that changes occurring in the central nervous system during depression may be a common pathway.

Whereas family stress can have harmful effects on health, family support can be beneficial. An extensive body of research has demonstrated that social networks and supports can directly improve health, as well as buffer the adverse effects of stress. Furthermore, the family has been found to be the most important source of social support.

Several large epidemiologic studies have demonstrated that social isolation is highly predictive of mortality and that family support (particularly marriage and contact with relatives) is protective. In an article in the journal *Science,* sociologist James House (House, Landis, & Umberson, 1988) reviewed the research on social support and health and concluded,

> The evidence regarding social relationships and health increasingly approximates the evidence in the 1964 Surgeon General's report that established cigarette smoking as a cause or risk factor for mortality and morbidity from a range of diseases. The age-adjusted relative risk ratios are stronger than the relative risks for all cause mortality reported for cigarette smoking. (p. 543)

The relative importance of different aspects of family support may change over the life span. Elderly persons with impaired social supports have two to three times the death rate of those with good supports (Blazer, Burchett, Service, & George, 1991; Zuckerman, Kasl, & Osterfeld, 1984), but widowhood is not associated with mortality. The presence and number of living children are the most powerful predictors of survival in the elderly. This finding suggests that adult children become the most important source of social support in older populations.

Family support and family stress, especially bereavement, can have a powerful influence on health and mortality. An understanding of the family and potential sources of stress and support can provide health care professionals with ways to reduce family stress, bolster family supports, and improve health. There is a need for randomized clinical trials to examine how interventions to reduce family stress and increase family support affect health outcomes.

Family Illness Appraisal

Most individuals who experience physical symptoms never consult health professionals; instead, they handle these problems at home with family and friends. It is estimated that only 10% to 30% of all health problems are brought to professional attention. Little is known about what factors influence whether an individual consults a physician or other health professional under these circumstances. Most research in this area has focused exclusively on individual factors such as the severity of the symptoms, individual health beliefs, and access to health care services. However, there is considerable evidence that health care utilization and health appraisal are influenced by family factors, and there are distinct family patterns of health care utilization.

When an individual develops symptoms, he or she usually discusses the problem with those closest to him or her—usually other family members. The decision-making process may involve the entire family and be affected by the family's history with other health problems. One study of middle-age couples found that when a decision was made to consult a physician about a symptom, it was usually initiated by the spouse. If the decision made was to wait or delay medical consultation, it was usually the symptomatic person who made the decision, sometimes against the spouse's advice or wishes. Prior experiences with similar symptoms often influenced the decision making (Dowds & Bibace, 1996).

Older couples are often more dependent on each other and seem to have different patterns of decision making. One study found that elderly couples made their health care decisions jointly, but the wife usually had a more influential voice in the final decision. This is consistent with the concept that many families have a "family health expert" (Doherty & Baird, 1983) who has been assigned and assumes the role as the expert in health matters. Traditionally, this role is played by a woman, often the wife or mother, but it can also be assumed by family members who are health professionals.

The appraisal of a child's symptoms and the decision to consult a physician are strongly influenced by the parents' health beliefs and levels of stress. A child may serve as a surrogate patient who directly or indirectly expresses the stress and dysfunction within the family. A study of 500 families (Roghmann & Haggerty, 1973) found that family stress dramatically increased the use of health services and that in one third of the visits, there was no evidence of any physical symptoms. Others have found that a family history of a similar symptom or problem was the strongest predictor of health care treatment for children's symptoms.

Families often have distinct patterns of health care behavior and utilization. Several studies have shown a strong association among family members regarding their use of medication and health care services. For example, the mother's health care utilization is a better predictor of the number of medical visits by the child than is the child's own health status (Newacheck & Halfon, 1986). An individual's use of medications is more strongly related to other family members' medication use than to the individual's severity of symptoms or illness. Because many of the barriers to health care access (e.g., lack of health insurance, money, transportation, or identified source of health care) are usually shared by family members, efforts to improve access to health care are likely to be more effective and cost-efficient if they are directed at families rather than individuals.

This research documents the important role of the family in health care decision making and the need for the clinician to inquire about other family members' concerns or opinions about the presenting symptoms. Learning more about the family decision-making process will help the clinician to better understand the reason for the patient's visit and the underlying fears or concerns of the patient and family.

Family's Response to Acute Illness

The diagnosis of a serious or life-threatening illness is one of the most feared threats to family life. Illness in the family ranks near the top of the Holmes and Rahe Stressful Life Events Scale (Holmes & Rahe, 1967). Many family members can remember the moment that they learned of a serious illness in their family.

A family's initial response to the diagnosis of a serious illness often follows a predictable course. There may be a period of denial or disbelief about the diagnosis, followed by a rapid mobilization of resources and support within the family. During this crisis phase, most families pull together and rally around the patient even when there is a history of major conflicts, separation, or disengagement.

Most research on the spouses of acutely ill patients has shown that they experience levels of stress and anxiety as high as or higher than that of the patients themselves (Oberst & James, 1985). This effect is strongest for the wives of male patients. Some men recovering from a myocardial infarction (MI) may seem relatively unconcerned, whereas their wives are extremely anxious. Many male cardiac patients report feeling overprotected by their wives, and some studies suggest that this interaction predicts poor functional outcomes. A large body of research, largely from the nursing field, has demonstrated that the family's greatest need during this acute period is for information about the patient's health problems. Family members often report feeling left out and uninformed. Providing information to family members helps to reduce their anxiety and feelings of helplessness, which can be beneficial to the patient's health. One study of post-MI couples found that the best predictor of the patient's recovery was whether the wife was provided with information at the time of discharge (Fiske, Coyne, & Smith, 1991).

Many hospitals still allow only limited family contact with seriously ill patients, often for 5 to 10 minutes every hour in intensive care units. These policies are based on the unproven belief that family members will either interfere with ongoing medical treatments or tire the patient. Studies have shown that even the presence of a loved one can have beneficial physiologic effects, especially in the intensive care unit (Lynch, 1977). There is some evidence that more collaborative, family-centered inpatient programs speed up the patient's recovery, reduce hospital stays, and improve patient and family satisfaction. Some hospitals, such as the New York University Cooperative Care Program, have developed innovative programs that allow family members to remain with the patient throughout the hospitalization and provide physical care and emotional support (Grieco, Garnett, Glassman, Valoon, & McClure, 1990).

Research on the family's response to the acute phase of illness suggests that providing medical information to the family may be the most beneficial level of involvement by health care providers. If the illness progresses to a chronic phase, families may experience more difficulties and need more intensive involvement.

Family Adaptation to Illness and Recovery

Families, not health care providers, are the primary caretakers of patients with chronic illness. They are the ones who help most with the physical demands of an illness, including preparing special meals, administering medication, and helping with bathing and dressing. In addition, families are usually the major source of emotional and social support, someone with whom they can share the frustrations, discouragements, and despair of living with chronic illness.

Over the past decade, a substantial amount of research has addressed family caregiving and the impact of chronic disease on the family. Chronic illness affects all aspects of family life. Old and familiar patterns of family life are changed forever, shared activities are given up, and family roles and responsibilities must often change. Most patients and their families cope well with the stresses and demands of chronic illness and tend to pull together and become closer. Some families may become too close or enmeshed; by assuming too much responsibility and care for the ill member, they may inhibit his or her autonomy and independence. Other families may come apart under the stress of chronic illness and separate or divorce.

The quality of family life and functioning has a strong impact on how well the patient copes with the illness and on long-term health outcomes. The impact of the family on chronic illness is very clear in the studies of children's reaction to illness. Adequate control of diabetes and asthma is strongly correlated with healthy family functioning (Doherty & Campbell, 1988). Chronic family conflict, parental indifference, and low cohesion have all been associated with poor metabolic control in diabetes, whereas clear family organization and high parental self-esteem correlate with good control (Campbell & Patterson, 1995).

In a series of seminal studies, Salvador Minuchin and his colleagues at the Philadelphia Child Guidance Clinic (Minuchin et al., 1975; Minuchin, Rosman, & Baker, 1978) studied poorly controlled diabetic children and their families. These children had recurrent episodes of diabetic ketoacidosis, but when hospitalized, their diabetes was easily managed. It appeared that stress and emotional arousal within the family directly affected the child's blood sugar. In these families, Minuchin discovered a specific pattern of interaction, characterized by enmeshment (high cohesion), overprotectiveness, rigidity, and conflict avoidance. He called these families "psychosomatic families."

To determine how these family patterns can affect diabetes, Minuchin (Minuchin et al., 1978) studied the diabetic children's physiologic responses to a stressful family interview. During the family interview, the children from psychosomatic families had a rapid rise in free fatty acids (FFA; a precursor to diabetic ketoacidosis), which persisted beyond the interview. The parents of these children exhibited an initial rise in FFA levels, which fell to normal when the diabetic child entered the room. Minuchin hypothesized that, in psychosomatic families, parental conflict is detoured or defused through the chronically ill child, and the resulting stress leads to exacerbations of the illness. Minuchin was the first investigator to demonstrate a link between family and physiologic processes.

In general, the family can influence a disease process by one of two pathways. As Minuchin demonstrated, the family can have direct psychophysiologic effects, or the family can influence health-related behaviors, such as compliance with medical treatments. In diabetes, it appears that both pathways are important. In emotionally distant or disengaged families, inadequate supervision and parental support can lead to noncompliance with treatment and poor diabetic control. In enmeshed families, family conflict may lead to emotional arousal and hormonal changes that disrupt diabetic control.

Several different family interventions have been shown to have a beneficial effect on childhood illness outcomes. Minuchin and his colleagues (1975) successfully treated psychosomatic families using structural family therapy to help disengage the diabetic and establish more appropriate family boundaries. In 15 cases, the pattern of recurrent ketoacidosis ceased and insulin doses were reduced. Minuchin reported similar success with cases of asthma and anorexia nervosa occurring in psychosomatic families.

Two randomized controlled trials of therapy with families of children with severe asthma have reported improved health outcomes (Gustafsson, Kjellman, & Cederblad, 1986; Lask & Matthew, 1979). The therapy was designed to change the family's strong emotional response to the child's symptoms. The children who received family therapy had reduced symptoms, reduced medication use, and fewer school absences. Their lung function improved as well.

The most successful and widely used family interventions for childhood illnesses have been family psychoeducation programs. Family psychoeducation provides information, support, and problem-solving skills to help families cope with a chronic illness. Unlike with traditional family therapy, the focus of family psychoeducation is on the illness rather than on the family. Family dysfunction is generally viewed as inadequate to coping with the illness. Family psychoeducation has been shown to improve outcomes in childhood diabetes, asthma, recurrent abdominal pain, and developmental disabilities (Campbell & Patterson, 1995), and it is one of the most promising areas for family interventions.

Two different types of family interventions have been effective in the treatment of hypertension. Couples communication training can lower blood pressure in couples in which one member has hypertension (Ewart, Burnett, & Taylor, 1983). In one large study, providing family support to assist with compliance with blood pressure medication resulted in improved compliance, reduced blood pressure, and 50% reduction in cardiac mortality (Morisky et al., 1983). On the basis of this and similar compliance research, the National Heart, Lung, and Blood Institute (1982) recommends that all physicians use the following as one of three basic strategies for increasing compliance with antihypertensive regimens:

Enhance support from family members—identifying and involving one influential person, preferably someone living with the patient, who can provide encouragement, help support the behavior change and, if necessary, remind the patient about the specifics of the regimen. (p. 422)

With the aging of the population, an increasing number of elderly must rely on family members for care. Most elderly people with Alzheimer's disease or other incapacitating illnesses are cared for at home by adult children and are never institutionalized. Family caregivers experience tremendous burdens and strain in caring for their impaired elders. These caregivers, usually spouses or children, suffer poorer physical and emotional health and have high rates of anxiety and depression (Biegel, Sales, & Schulz, 1991). Several family psychoeducational programs for caregivers have reduced caregivers' distress and depression, improved caregivers' physical health, and reduced or delayed nursing home admissions (Campbell & Patterson, 1995).

Mittelman and colleagues' clinical trial (Mittelman, Ferris, Shulman, Steinberg, & Levin, 1996) deserves special attention because it can serve as a model for other intervention studies. They provided a comprehensive family intervention for the caregivers of patients with moderately advanced Alzheimer's disease. The intervention included six individual and six group family psychoeducational sessions, an ongoing family support group, and crisis counseling for behavioral problems that arose. The intervention improved the caregivers' physical and mental health and postponed nursing home admission for the patient by almost a year. The cost of the intervention was less than a tenth of the cost of a year's care in most nursing homes. This kind of family program should become the standard of care for all patients with Alzheimer's disease and their families. Similar programs should be developed and tested for other disabling conditions such as strokes and Parkinson's disease.

Conclusion

Several conclusions can be made from this review of the research on families and health. First, family relationships have a powerful influence on health, at least as strong an influence as that of most recognized biological risk factors (e.g., smoking, elevated cholesterol, and lack of exercise). Despite the evidence for this conclusion, medical providers rarely pay adequate attention to family issues. Second, family functioning, especially emotional support or intimacy, is more important than family structure for physical health. The social support literature seems to have established that emotional support has a stronger influence than structural or instrumental support. In addition, for most adults, the quality of the marriage has the most influence on health. It appears that marital distress and conflict can have direct physiologic effects (Levenson & Gottman, 1983) and influence health behaviors. Also, negative family interactions ("being nasty") are more powerful than positive family interactions ("being nice"). Family criticism and expressed emotion play an important role in physical as well as mental health (see below). Furthermore, the family's influence on health behaviors is at least as important as psychophysiological effects, and it is more accessible to interventions. Because health behaviors play such an important role in overall morbidity and mortality, utilizing the family to help change unhealthy behaviors may be the most cost-effective family intervention. Finally, family psychoeducation is the most effective family intervention for chronic physical illness.

Although there is solid evidence that the family has a powerful impact on health across different age groups and illnesses, the results of family intervention studies are promising but not conclusive. This research demonstrates that family interventions are more effective than individual approaches for some chronic childhood diseases, especially asthma and diabetes. Family therapy improves the medical outcome in dysfunctional families who have an asthmatic child.

Examining outcomes from family interventions across age groups and disorders, it is evident that family psychoeducation is the most commonly studied and, consistently, the most effective type of family intervention (Campbell & Patterson, 1995). It has been demonstrated to be more effective than either family support groups or the direct provision of services to families. There is insufficient research to compare family therapy with family psychoeducation, and these approaches tend to be directed toward different populations (dysfunctional vs. distressed but functional families).

There are many parallels between this literature and the research on family psychoeducation in schizophrenia and other chronic illnesses. Negative family interactions, including spousal criticism, conflict, marital dissatisfaction, and family-expressed emotion, seem to play a more important role than positive interactions in these physical disorders, similar to findings in studies of chronic mental illness (Rook, 1984) and marital outcomes (Gottman, 1994). In some physical disorders, such as Alzheimer's disease, family criticism (and high expressed emotion) may result from the misinterpretation of disease symptoms (forgetfulness, incontinence, etc.) as willful, similar to what has been described in schizophrenia and depression. Family psychoeducation seems to be effective in educating the family about the physical illness, providing specific problem-solving skills, and decreasing isolation through improved social supports. One significant difference between physical and mental disorders is that family group psychoeducation appears to be less effective than individual family psychoeducation for dementia caregivers. It may be that families with chronic physical illness suffer less isolation and stigma but need more specific problem-solving skills that may be better provided in individual family sessions.

Implications for Family Professionals

The most important implication of the research on families and health is the need for health professionals and health care planners to recognize that families are essential partners in the delivery of health care. When one accepts the importance of families in health and illness and the need to involve families in health care, it becomes apparent that most health care clinicians, educators, planners, and researchers are not experts in understanding and caring for families and need help from family professionals. There are four areas where family professionals can play major roles in health care.

Clinical Practice

Many physicians, nurses, and other clinicians have a basic understanding of families and can work effectively with them in different settings, providing education, support, and, occasionally, counseling. However, families often present problems that are beyond the expertise of the average clinician. These problems may be directly related to a health problem, such as the abuse or neglect of a handicapped child, depression resulting from a stroke or other disabling condition, a pathological grief reaction, or alcoholism. In addition, many patients consult their physician about common family problems, such as marital conflicts, infidelity, parenting difficulties, substance abuse, or family violence. Most of these problems, whether or not they are intimately related to a health problem, are beyond the expertise of medical providers and require referral to a family therapist or other mental health professional.

To effectively treat these families and their psychosocial problems, there must be close collaboration between the medical professionals and family therapists (McDaniel, Campbell, & Seaburn, 1990). Family professionals and health care providers can work together as a team to provide a comprehensive biopsychosocial approach and avoid a split between the physical and mental health care of the patient and family. This requires ongoing communication, which begins at the time of the referral. Physicians often complain that therapists do not keep them informed of their patients' treatment and progress, and therapists say the same things about medical providers. For example, the therapist may suggest that the patient see a medical specialist about a health problem without speaking with the referring physician, or the physician may prescribe an antidepressant or other psychotropic without consulting the family therapist. Just as the health professional must form a partnership with the family to provide the best care of the patient, so must the family professional develop a partnership with the health professional to provide comprehensive care for the patient and family.

Education for Family and Health Professionals

As recognition of the importance of the family in health care grows, there is an increasing need to train physicians, nurses, and other health professionals to work effectively with families. Training medical providers about families is best done by family professionals teaching in conjunction with health professionals. A large number of family professionals, including family therapists and family social scientists, currently teach in family practice residency programs and have helped bring a family systems approach into family medicine. Many family professionals teach in medical schools, and a few work in pediatric and internal medicine residencies. Teaching about families is most effective when family professionals work closely with physicians or other health professionals. Medicine has a unique culture with its own customs, rituals, and language, which usually takes several years for family professionals to learn. Family professionals who use teaching methods they learned in graduate school to teach medical students or physicians in training are doomed to failure. It is impossible for the family professional alone to know what areas of family science are relevant to health care professionals.

Many resources are available to family professionals who are interested in teaching in medical settings. Numerous books written on family-oriented health care and family systems medicine provide basic curricula for teaching about families to health professionals (Christie-Seely, 1984; Doherty & Baird, 1983, 1987; McDaniel et al., 1990; Sawa, 1985). In addition, the Society of Teachers of Family Medicine (STFM) has a working group devoted to teaching about families. This Group on the Family has published a monograph on curricula currently being taught in family medicine and has a yearly conference devoted to the family in family medicine (STFM, 1989).

Just as health professionals need more training in family systems, family professionals need more education in medical and health care issues and how to collaborate with health care providers. To work effectively in health care settings, family therapists and other family professionals need to have a basic understanding of how the health care system works and of the culture and language of medicine. As part of their training, family professionals should have some coursework in medicine, health care, and basic psychopharmacology. Ideally, family professionals should be trained alongside health professionals in multidisciplinary teams or at least trained in multidisciplinary settings (Gawinski, Edwards, & Speice, 1999). Several training programs or internships in marriage and family therapy are located in health care settings (Hepworth, Gavazzi, Adlin, & Miller, 1988; Muchnick, Davis, Getzinger, Rosenberg, & Weiss, 1993; Patterson, Bischoff, Scherger, & Grauf-Grounds, 1996). These programs train family therapists to work with medical patients and to effectively collaborate with medical providers.

Health Care Policy

The U.S. health care system is in a state of crisis and will go through enormous changes over the next decade. This situation offers an opportunity for family professionals to become involved in the reform of the health care system to make it more receptive to the needs of families. The current health care system is individually focused and does not address the needs of the entire family. Under managed care, less money is available for health care, and the care of many patients with chronic illness is being shifted from paid professional health care providers to unpaid family members. When a patient returns home from the hospital, the family is expected to provide most of the patient's care, and home services are often inadequate. In particular, the family caregivers of patients with chronic illnesses such as Alzheimer's disease often receive meager services and support in the home. However, there is a risk that, as hospital and other expensive health care services are reduced to save money, an increasing burden will be placed on family members to provide these services in the home without adequate assistance. Family professionals must make the needs of families known to the health care policy makers.

Family and Health Research

Although a great deal of research on families and physical health has been conducted over the past two decades, many more studies are needed to understand the relationships between family factors and physical health and the effectiveness of family interventions for medical problems. By the very nature of this topic, this research should be interdisciplinary and involve health and family professionals. Neither field has an adequate understanding of the other to conduct the needed research in this area. For example, research conducted solely by family social scientists tends to have an oversimplified view of health and often uses crude and unvalidated measures of health status. The same is true for health professionals who are trying to study families.

Family professionals can be particularly helpful in developing theories about how family interactions influence health. Much of the current research on families and health is atheoretical and tends to be driven by either disease outcomes or a particular family assessment instrument. For example, there are many studies looking at the relationship between cohesion and adaptability as measured by the Family Adaptability and Cohesion Scale (FACES) and a health outcome such as blood sugar levels in diabetes. These studies are relatively easy to conduct and often show relationships between family and health variables. However, they lack an underlying theory of how families influence health and provide little rationale for choosing the family variables or any mechanisms for how this process takes place. Careful attention should be given to conceptually defining those aspects of family functioning that are related to illness. These studies rarely control for potential confounding variables (e.g., socioeconomic status) or examine possible intervening variables such as individual psychological states (e.g., depression or anxiety) or health-related behaviors.

Some of the research on families and health has tended to pathologize families and inadvertently blame them for causing health problems. For example, cross-sectional studies showing that some families with chronic illness, such as diabetes, tend to be overly close or enmeshed have been interpreted as demonstrating that enmeshment causes or can worsen chronic illness. It is equally plausible that families become closer in response to the illness and that this response may be quite functional. More recently, family social scientists have emphasized the strengths and resiliency of families. Family professionals can help bring this perspective to family and health research with research examining the health-promoting and -enhancing functions of the family.

Family interventions need to be designed and studied in a wider range of physical disorders, especially common disorders that have enormous impact on families. These include cancer of all types, adulthood diabetes, chronic lung disease, end-stage renal disease, and HIV. Family psychoeducational programs should be developed for each of these disorders using an approach similar to Mittelman's (Mittelman et al., 1996) highly effective program for caregivers of patients with Alzheimer's disease.

The cost-effectiveness of these family interventions should be evaluated and should include health care costs for the whole family, as well as social and opportunity costs to the family. In the current health care environment, there is a constant demand to demonstrate that interventions not only are effective but also reduce overall health costs. Research on family-based cardiovascular risk reduction and family caregiving offers the most promise for showing the cost savings.

Future Directions and Opportunities

Many of the advances in medical technology and changes in health care delivery have major implications for families and family professionals. Four areas represent the cutting edge of the field of families and health: genetics, reproductive technology, family caregiving, and "end of life" decisions. The genetic revolution is beginning to have profound effects on the ways in which we consider health and illness. Within a few years, we will have the ability to screen or test for hundreds of genetic disorders. However, the impact of this technology on families is just beginning to be examined. For example, consider a woman found to carry one of the BRAC genes that puts her at much higher risk of breast and ovarian cancer. Should she tell her family members? What is the impact of testing on the other family members? Should they be consulted about whether genetic testing should be done? Genetic counseling needs to be informed by family systems principles to address many of these issues.

Advances in reproductive technology have changed the way that we think about parenting. A child may be the product of donated egg or sperm or be born to a surrogate mother. What are the effects of these methods of reproduction on subsequent family relationships? What should children be told about how they were conceived or about biological or surrogate parents? These are controversial issues that need further exploration as these technologies are more widely used.

The aging of the population and changes in our health care delivery system have resulted in a dramatic increase in family caregiving. Unfortunately, adequate services have not been provided to families to manage these increased demands, and it has become more challenging for families to cope with chronic illness. Family caregiving has led to (a) increasing physical and psychological burdens on family members and (b) physical and psychological problems for many caregivers. Only recently has family caregiving been recognized as a major public health issue. Several national organizations and government agencies are beginning to address these family issues. Much more research is needed on family caregiving.

As medical advances allow us to prolong life, more attention has been paid to end-of-life decision making. Only recently has the role of the family in these decisions been addressed. The development of health care proxy laws has allowed patients to identify an individual, usually a close family member, to make medical decisions on their behalf if the patient is unable to. Very little research has been done on how patients make these choices, what they discuss with their designated health care agent, and whether family members follow the wishes of the patient. Consider the children of an elderly woman with severe dementia who must decide how much medical care their mother should receive when they know that her nursing home care is consuming all of her financial savings that they had hoped to inherit. What is the impact of end-of-life decision making on family relationships? This is another priority area for research.

The Chinese character for crisis includes two symbols: one representing danger and the other, opportunity. The current health care system, with its emphasis on biomedical reductionism, overspecialization, high technology, and high costs, is in a state of crisis. This crisis offers many new opportunities for family professionals to become involved in the health care field. Additional research is needed to demonstrate to clinicians, medical educators, and policy makers that the family plays a crucial role in all aspects of health and illness. This research must be methodologically sound and sophisticated with regard to health and family measures. Family professionals are needed to advocate for families at all levels of government so that new health care policies are "family friendly." Medical professionals need basic education and training about families at all levels, from medical and nursing school to continuing education for practicing providers, and across all specialties. Physicians' education about families is primarily limited to family medicine, with some family teaching occurring in pediatrics and general internal medicine. Oncologists, surgeons, cardiologists, and other specialists also need to have a basic understanding of how to work effectively with the families of their patients.

Perhaps most important, family professionals can use their own skills and knowledge gained from research on families and health to work collaboratively with health professionals to help families who are struggling with health problems. It is at the clinical level, working with families and medical providers, that this new family-centered approach to health care will grow and prosper, where its success is more widely recognized and implemented.

DISCUSSION QUESTIONS

1. Describe how the family can be an agent for health promotion and the intervention studies that support this concept.

2. Discuss the evidence that family support is beneficial for physical health.

3. What are the pathways by which the family can influence health? Give examples of each.

4. Describe a situation from your personal life in which an illness has affected your entire family. How were family roles changed?

5. Choose a chronic illness and discuss how the family may influence the course of the illness.

SUGGESTED READINGS

Biegel, D. E., Sales, E., & Schulz, R. (1991). *Family caregiving in chronic illness.* Newbury Park, CA: Sage.

Campbell, T. L., & Patterson, J. M. (1995). The effectiveness of family interventions in the treatment of physical illness. *Journal of Marital and Family Therapy, 21,* 545-584.

Doherty, W. J., & Campbell, T. L. (1988). *Families and health.* Newbury Park, CA: Sage.

McDaniel, S. H., Hepworth, J., & Doherty, W. (1992). *Medical family therapy.* New York: Basic Books.

Seaburn, D., Gunn, W., Mauksch, L., Gawinski, B., & Lorenz, A. (1996). *Models of collaborative family health care.* New York: Basic Books.

REFERENCES

Baranowski, T., & Nader, P. R. (1985). Family health behavior. In D. C. Turk & R. D. Kerns (Eds.), *Health, illness, and families: A life-span perspective* (pp. 51-80). New York: John Wiley.

Barbarin, O. A., & Tirado, M. (1984). Family involvement and successful treatment of obesity: A review. *Family Systems Medicine, 2,* 37-45.

Bartrop, R. W., Luckhurst, E., Lazarus, L., Kiloh, L. G., & Penny, R. (1977). Depressed lymphocyte function after bereavement. *Lancet, 1,* 834-836.

Beautrais, A. L., Fergusson, D. M., & Shannon, F. T. (1982). Life events and childhood morbidity: A prospective study. *Pediatrics, 70,* 935-940.

Bewley, B. R., & Bland, J. M. (1977). Academic performance and social factors relating to cigarette smoking by school children. *British Journal of Preventive and Social Medicine, 31,* 8-24.

Biegel, D. E., Sales, E., & Schulz, R. (1991). *Family caregiving in chronic illness.* Newbury Park, CA: Sage.

Black, D. R., Gleser, L. J., & Kooyers, K. J. (1990). A meta-analytic evaluation of couples weight-loss programs. *Health Psychology, 9,* 330-347.

Blazer, D., Burchett, B., Service, C., & George, L. K. (1991). The association of age and depression among the elderly: An epidemiologic exploration. *Journal of Gerontology, 46,* M210-M215.

Bloch, D. (1983). Family systems medicine: The field and the journal. *Family Systems Medicine, 1,* 3-11.

Bloch, D. (1994). Staying alive while staying alive. *Family Systems Medicine, 12,* 103-105.

Blount, A. (Ed.). (1998). *Integrated primary care.* New York: Norton.

Bowen, M. (1978). *Family therapy in clinical practice.* New York: Jason Aaronson.

Boyce, W. T., & Chesterman, E. (1990). Life events, social support, and cardiovascular reactivity in adolescence. *Journal of Developmental and Behavioral Pediatrics, 11,* 105-111.

Brownell, K. D., Heckerman, C. L., Westlake, R. J., Hayes, S. C., & Monti, P. M. (1978). The effect of couples training and partner co-operativeness in the behavioral treatment of obesity. *Behavior Research and Therapy, 16,* 323-333.

Brownell, K. D., & Stunkard, A. J. (1981). Couples training, pharmacotherapy, and behavior therapy in the treatment of obesity. *Archives of General Psychiatry, 38,* 1224-1229.

Bryan, M. S., & Lowenberg, M. E. (1958). The father's influence on young children's food preferences. *Journal of American Dietetic Association, 34,* 30-35.

Burman, B., & Margolin, G. (1992). Analysis of the association between marital relationships and health problems: An interactional perspective. *Psychological Bulletin, 112,* 39-63.

Calabrese, J. R., Kling, M. A., & Gold, P. W. (1987). Alterations in immunocompetence during stress, bereavement, and depression: Focus on neuroendocrine regulation. *American Journal of Psychiatry, 144,* 1123-1134.

Campbell, T. L. (1986). *Family's impact on health: A critical review and annotated bibliography* (NIMH Series DN, No. 6; DHHS Publication No. ADM 86-1461). Washington, DC: U.S. Government Printing Office. (Also published in *Family Systems Medicine, 4*(2+3), 1986, 135-328.)

Campbell, T. L., & Patterson, J. M. (1995). The effectiveness of family interventions in the treatment of physical illness. *Journal of Marital and Family Therapy, 21,* 545-584.

Christie-Seely, J. (Ed.). (1984). *Working with the family in primary care: A systems approach to health and illness.* New York: Praeger.

Coppotelli, H. C., & Orleans, C. T. (1985). Partner support and other determinants of smoking cessation among women. *Journal of Consulting and Clinical Psychology, 53,* 455-460.

Cummings, N. A., Cummings, J. L., & Johnson, J. N. (1997). *Behavioral health in primary care: A guide for clinical integration.* Madison, CT: Psychosocial Press.

Doherty, W. J., & Baird, M. A. (1983). *Family therapy and family medicine: Toward the primary care of families.* New York: Guilford.

Doherty, W. J., & Baird, M. A. (Eds.). (1987). *Family-centered medical care: A clinical casebook.* New York: Guilford.

Doherty, W. J., & Campbell, T. L. (1988). *Families and health.* Newbury Park, CA: Sage.

Dowds, B. N., & Bibace, R. (1996). Entry into the health care system: The family's decision-making process. *Family Medicine, 28,* 114-118.

Dubbert, P. M., & Wilson, G. T. (1984). Goal setting and spouse involvement in the treatment of obesity. *Behavior Research and Therapy, 22,* 227-242.

Ewart, C. K., Burnett, K. F., & Taylor, C. B. (1983). Communication behaviors that affect blood pressure: An A-B-A-B analysis of marital interaction. *Behavior Modification, 7,* 331-344.

Family Heart Study Group. (1994). Randomized controlled trial evaluating cardiovascular screening and intervention in general practice: Principal results of British family heart study. *British Medical Journal, 308,* 313-319.

Fischman-Havstad, L., & Marston, A. R. (1984). Weight loss management as aspect of family emotion and process. *British Journal of Clinical Psychology, 23,* 265-271.

Fiske, V., Coyne, J., & Smith, D. (1991). Couples coping with myocardial infarction: An empirical reconsideration of the role of overprotectiveness. *Journal of Family Psychology, 5,* 4-20.

Gawinski, B. A., Edwards, T. M., & Speice, J. (1999). A family therapy internship in a multidisciplinary healthcare setting: Trainees' and supervisor's reflections. *Journal of Marital and Family Therapy, 25,* 469-484.

Glasgow, R. E., & Lichtenstein, E. (1987). Long-term effects of behavioral smoking cessation interventions. *Behavior Therapy, 18,* 297-324.

Gottman, J. (1994). *What predicts divorce? The relationship between marital processes and marital outcomes.* Hillsdale, NJ: Lawrence Erlbaum.

Graham, S., & Gibson, R. W. (1971). Cessation of patterned behavior: Withdrawal from smoking. *Social Science and Medicine, 5,* 319-337.

Grieco, A. J., Garnett, S. A., Glassman, K. S., Valoon, P. L., & McClure, M. L. (1990). New York University Medical Center's Cooperative Care Unit: Patient education and family participation during hospitalization: The first ten years. *Patient Education & Counseling, 15,* 3-15.

Gustafsson, P. A., Kjellman, N. I., & Cederblad, M. (1986). Family therapy in the treatment of severe childhood asthma. *Journal of Psychosomatic Research, 30,* 369-374.

Heinzelmann, F., & Bagley, R. W. (1970). Response to physical activity programs and their effects on health behavior. *Public Health Reports, 85,* 905-911.

Hepworth, J., Gavazzi, S., Adlin, M., & Miller, W. (1988). Training for collaboration: Internships for family therapy students in a medical setting. *Family Systems Medicine, 161,* 69-79.

Holmes, T. H., & Rahe, R. H. (1967). The Social Readjustment Rating Scale. *Journal of Psychosomatic Research, 39,* 413-431.

House, J. S., Landis, K. R., & Umberson, D. (1988). Social relationships and health. *Science, 241,* 540-545.

Kiecolt-Glaser, J. K., Fisher, L. D., Ogrockl, P., Stout, J. C., Spelcher, C. E., & Glaser, R. (1987). Marital quality, marital disruption, and immune function. *Psychosomatic Medicine, 49,* 13-32.

Klesges, R. C., Coates, T. J., Brown, G., Sturgeon-Tillisch, J., Moldenhauer, L. M., Holzer, B., Woolfrey, J., & Vollmer, J. (1983). Parental influences on children's eating behavior and relative weight. *Journal of Applied Behavioral Analysis, 16,* 371-378.

Knutsen, S. F., & Knutsen, R. (1991). The Tromso Survey: The Family Intervention Study: The effect of intervention on some coronary risk factors and dietary habits, a 6-year follow-up. *Preventive Medicine, 20,* 197-212.

Lask, B., & Matthew, D. (1979). Childhood asthma: A controlled trial of family psychotherapy. *Archives of Diseases in Children, 54,* 116-119.

Levenson, R. W., & Gottman, J. M. (1983). Marital interaction: Physiological linkage and affective exchange. *Journal of Personality and Social Psychology, 3,* 587-597.

Lichtenstein, E., Glasgow, R. E., & Abrams, D. B. (1986). Social support in smoking cessation: In search of effective interventions. *Behavior Therapy, 17,* 606-619.

Lynch, J. (1977). *The broken heart: The medical consequences of loneliness.* New York: Basic Books.

Mahoney, M. J., & Mahoney, K. (1976). Treatment of obesity: A clinical exploration. In B. J. Williams, S. Martin, & J. P. Foreyt (Eds.), *Obesity: Behavioral approaches to dietary management* (pp. 30-39). New York: Brunner/Mazel.

Malott, J. M., Glasgow, R. E., O'Neill, H. K., & Klesges, R. C. (1984). Coworker social support in a worksite smoking control program. *Journal of Applied Behavior Analysis, 17,* 485-495.

Martikainen, P., & Valkonen, T. (1996). Mortality after death of spouse in relation to duration of bereavement in Finland. *Journal of Epidemiology & Community Health, 50,* 264-268.

McDaniel, S., Campbell, T., & Seaburn, D. (1990). *Family-oriented primary care: A manual for medical providers.* New York: Springer-Verlag.

McDaniel, S. H., Hepworth, J., & Doherty, W. (1992). *Medical family therapy.* New York: Basic Books.

McGinnis, J. M., & Foege, W. H. (1993). Actual causes of death in the United States. *Journal of the American Medical Association, 270,* 2207-2212.

McIntyre-Kingsolver, K., Lichtenstein, E., & Mermelstein, R. J. (1986). Spouse training in a multicomponent smoking-cessation program. *Behavior Therapy, 17,* 67-74.

Mermelstein, R., Lichtenstein, E., & McIntyre, K. (1983). Partner support and relapse in smoking cessation programs. *Journal of Consulting and Clinical Psychology, 51,* 465-466.

Meyer, R. J., & Haggerty, R. J. (1962). Streptococcal infections in families: Factors altering individual susceptibility. *Pediatrics, 29,* 539-549.

Minuchin, S., Baker, L., Rosman, B. L., Liebman, R., Milman, L., & Todd, T. C. (1975). A conceptual model of psychosomatic illness in children: Family organization and family therapy. *Archives of General Psychiatry, 32,* 1031-1038.

Minuchin, S., Rosman, B. L., & Baker, L. (1978). *Psychosomatic families.* Cambridge, MA: Harvard University Press.

Mittelman, M. S., Ferris, S. H., Shulman, E., Steinberg, G., & Levin, B. (1996). A family intervention to delay nursing home placement of patients with Alzheimer disease: A randomized controlled trial. *Journal of the American Medical Association, 276,* 1725-1731.

Morisky, D. E., Levine, D. M., Green, L. W., Shapiro, S., Russell, R. P., & Smith, C. R. (1983). Five- year blood pressure control and mortality following health education for hypertensive patients. *American Journal of Public Health, 73,* 153-162.

Muchnick, S., Davis, B., Getzinger, A., Rosenberg, A., & Weiss, M. (1993). Collaborations between family therapy and health care: An internship experience. *Family Systems Medicine, 11,* 271-279.

National Heart, Lung, and Blood Institute. (1982). Management of patient compliance in the treatment of hypertension. *Hypertension, 4,* 415-423.

Newacheck, P. W., & Halfon, N. (1986). The association between mother's and children's use of physician services. *Medical Care, 24,* 30-38.

Oberst, M. T., & James, R. H. (1985). Going home: Patient and spouse adjustment following cancer surgery. *Topics in Clinical Nursing, 7,* 46-57.

O'Neill, P. M., Curey, H. S., Hirsch, A. A., Riddle, F. E., Taylor, C. I., Malcolm, R. J., & Sexauer, J. D. (1979). Effects of sex of subject and spouse involvement on weight loss in a behavioral treatment program: A retrospective investigation. *Addictive Behaviors, 4,* 167-177.

Patterson, J., Bischoff, R., Scherger, J., & Grauf-Grounds, C. (1996). University family therapy training and a family medicine residency in a managed care setting. *Families, Systems, & Health, 14,* 5-19.

Pearce, J. W., LeBow, M. D., & Orchard, J. (1981). Role of spouse involvement in the behavioral treatment of overweight women. *Journal of Consulting and Clinical Psychology, 49,* 236-244.

Perry, C. L., Crockett, S. L., & Pirie, P. (1987). Influencing parental health behaviors: Implications for community assessments. *Health Education, 18,* 68-77.

Perry, C. L., Luepker, R. V., Murry, D. M., Hearn, M. D., Halper, A., Dudvitz, B., Maile, M. C., & Smyth, M. (1989). Parent involvement with children's health promotion: A one-year follow-up of the Minnesota Home Team. *Health Education Quarterly, 16,* 171-180.

Price, R. A., Chen, K. H., & Cavallii, S. L. (1981). Models of spouse influence and their applications to smoking behavior. *Social Biology, 28,* 14-29.

Public Health Service. (1990). *Healthy People 2000: National health promotion and disease prevention objective.* Washington, DC: Department of Health and Human Services.

Roghmann, K. J., & Haggerty, R. J. (1973). Daily stress, illness, and the use of health services in young families. *Pediatric Research, 7,* 520-526.

Rook, K. S. (1984). The negative side of social interaction: Impact on psychological well-being. *Journal of Personality and Social Psychology, 46,* 1097-1108.

Sallis, J. F., & Nader, P. R. (1988). Family determinants of health behaviors. In D. S. Gochman (Ed.), *Health behavior* (pp. 107-124). New York: Plenum.

Sawa, R. J. (1985). *Family dynamics for physicians: Guidelines to assessment and treatment.* Lewiston, NY/Queenstown, Ontario: Edwin Mellon Press.

Schleifer, S. J., Keller, S. E., Bond, R. N., Cohen, J., & Stein, M. (1989). Major depressive disorder and immunity: Role of age, sex, severity, and hospitalizations. *Archives of General Psychiatry, 46,* 81-87.

Seaburn, D., Gunn, W., Mauksch, L., Gawinski, B., & Lorenz, A. (1996). *Models of collaborative family health care.* New York: Basic Books.

Sexton, M., Bross, D., Hebel, J. R., Schumann, B. C., Gerace, T. A., Lasser, N., & Wright, N. (1987). Risk-factor changes in wives with husbands at high risk of coronary heart disease (CHD): The spin-off effect. *Journal of Behavioral Medicine, 10,* 251-261.

STFM Family in Family Medicine Task Force. (1989). *The family in family medicine: Graduate curriculum and teaching strategies* (2nd ed.). Kansas City, MO: STFM.

Stuart, R. B., & Davis, B. (1972). *Slim chance in a fat world: Behavioral control obesity.* Champaign, IL: Research Press.

Turk, D. C., & Kerns, R. D. (Eds.). (1985). *Health, illness, and families: A life-span perspective.* New York: John Wiley.

Venters, M. H., Jacobs, D. R., Luepker, R. V., Maiman, L. A., & Gillum, R. F. (1984). Spouse concordance of smoking patterns: The Minnesota heart survey. *American Journal of Epidemiology, 120,* 608-616.

Waxman, M., & Stunkard, A. J. (1980). Calorie intake and expenditure of obese boys. *Journal of Pediatrics, 96,* 187-193.

Weakland, J. (1977). "Family somatics": A neglected edge. *Family Process, 16,* 263-272.

Weisz, G., & Bucher, B. (1980). Involving husbands in treatment of obesity: Effects on weight loss, depression, and marital satisfaction. *Behavior Therapy, 11,* 643-650.

World Health Organization. (1976). *Statistical indices of family health* (No. 589). New York: Author.

Wynne, L. C., Cromwell, R., & Matthysse, S. (1978). *The nature of schizophrenia: New approaches to research and treatment.* New York: John Wiley.

Zitter, R. E., & Fremouw, W. J. (1978). Individual versus partner consequation for weight loss. *Behavior Therapy, 9,* 808-813.

Zuckerman, D. M., Kasl, S. V., & Osterfeld, A. M. (1984). Psychosocial predictors of mortality among the elderly poor: The role of religion, well-being, and social contact. *American Journal of Epidemiology, 119,* 410-423.

8

Violence, Abuse, and Neglect in Families

RICHARD J. GELLES

In U.S. society, people are more likely to be killed and physically assaulted, abused and neglected, and sexually assaulted and molested in their own homes and by other family members than anywhere else or by anyone else. Family life and the home are thought to be warm, intimate, and stress reducing, the place to which people flee for safety. In reality, the family is often a location of significant interpersonal and social stress that can lead to conflict and often to violence.

Historical Patterns of Family Violence

Women and children have been subjected to physical violence throughout the history of Western society. In ancient times, infants had no rights until the "right to live" was bestowed on them, typically as part of some formal cultural ritual carried out by their fathers (Radbill, 1980). When the right to live was withheld, infants were abandoned or left to die. Although we do not know how often children were killed or abandoned, we do know that infanticide was widely accepted among ancient and prehistoric cultures. Infanticide continued through the 18th and 19th centuries; illegitimate children continue to run the greatest risk of infanticide even today.

Killing children was not the only form of abuse inflicted by generations of parents. Since prehistoric times, children have been mutilated, beaten, and

183

maltreated. Such treatment was not only condoned but often mandated as the most appropriate child-rearing method (Greven, 1991).

The subordinate status of women in the United States and in most of the world's societies is well documented. Because physical force and violence are used as the last resort to keep subordinate groups in their place, the history of women in many societies has been one in which women have been victims of physical assault. A Roman husband could chastise, divorce, or kill his wife. Although legend has it that Blackstone's codification of English common law in 1768 asserted that a husband had the right to "physically chastise" an errant wife, provided that the stick was no thicker than his thumb—and thus the "rule of thumb" was born (Davidson, 1978; Pleck, 1987)—such a passage cannot be found in Blackstone (Sommers, 1994).

Siblings have also been the victims of family violence. The first case of family violence described in the Bible is Cain killing Abel. There has been less historical and current interest in sibling violence or violence toward men than there has been concern with violence toward children and women in families. In part, this is because social concern for victims of family violence is tied to the perceived powerlessness and helplessness of the victims. Thus, there is greater social concern for violence toward infants and young children than violence toward adolescents or adult men.

Estimates of the Current Incidence and Frequency

Until the early 1960s, violence between family members was considered rare and committed only by mentally ill or otherwise disturbed individuals. Only the most sensational and lurid cases received public attention, and there was a general belief that, even though family violence was a significant personal trouble, it was not widespread, nor was it a social problem.

There are various forms of family violence, including the abuse and neglect of children, sexual abuse of children, violence between spouses and intimate partners, abuse and neglect of the elderly, violence between siblings, and courtship violence and abuse. Various techniques have been used in attempts to achieve an accurate estimate of abuse and neglect in families in the United States and other countries. Researchers have examined official reports of child maltreatment and other official records, including police reports, clinical case records, and self-report social survey data. Because of the various definitions of *abuse* and *neglect,* and the differing methodologies used to examine incidence and frequency, there are no definitive data on the extent of abuse and neglect in families. The following section briefly reviews some of the data for each of the major forms of family violence.

Child Maltreatment

The National Center on Child Abuse and Neglect (NCCAN) has conducted three surveys designed to measure the national incidence of reported and recognized child maltreatment (Burgdorf, 1980; NCCAN, 1988, 1996). A total of 2.9 million maltreated children were known by the agencies surveyed in 1993.

A second source of data on the extent of child maltreatment comes from the National Child Abuse and Neglect Data System (NCANDS). NCANDS is a national data collection and analysis project carried out by the U.S. Department of Health and Human Services, Office of Child Abuse and Neglect. In 1996, states received 2,025,956 reports of child maltreatment, representing just over 3 million individual child victims. Of the 970,000 child victims for whom maltreatment was indicated or substantiated and for whom there were data on the type of maltreatment, 229,332 experienced physical abuse, 500,032 experienced neglect, and 119,397 experienced sexual abuse (NCCAN, 1998).

The National Family Violence Surveys interviewed two nationally representative samples of families: 2,146 family members in 1976 and 6,002 family members in 1985 (Gelles & Straus, 1987, 1988; Straus & Gelles, 1986; Straus, Gelles, & Steinmetz, 1980). Violence and abuse were measured by asking respondents to report on their own behavior toward their children in the previous 12 months. Milder forms of violence, violence that most people think of as physical punishment, were, of course, the most common. However, even with the severe forms of violence, the rates were surprisingly high. Abusive violence was defined as acts that had a high probability of injuring the child. These included kicking, biting, punching, hitting or trying to hit a child with an object, beating up a child, burning or scalding, and threatening or using a gun or a knife. Slightly more than 2 parents in 100 (2.3%) admitted to engaging in one act of abusive violence during the year prior to the 1985 survey. In the previous year, 7 children in 1,000 were hurt as a result of an act of violence directed at them by a parent. Projecting the rate of abusive violence to all children under 18 years of age who live with one or both parents means that 1.5 million children experience acts of abusive physical violence each year, and 450,000 children are injured each year as a result of parental violence (Gelles & Straus, 1987).

Sexual Abuse of Children

Among the most dramatic changes taking place over the past few decades has been the increased attention to child sexual abuse. In a comprehensive review of studies on the incidence and prevalence of child sexual abuse, Peters, Wyatt, and Finkelhor (1986) report that estimates of the prevalence range from 6% to 62% for females and from 3% to 31% for males. They point out that this variation may be accounted for by a number of methodological factors, including differences in the definitions of *abuse,* sample characteristics, the interview format (e.g., in-person versus phone interview), and the number of questions used to elicit information about abuse experiences. Whatever the number, it is clear that sexual abuse is a problem that affects large numbers of children.

Child Homicide

The U.S. Advisory Board on Child Abuse and Neglect (1995) estimates that 2,000 children under the age of 18 are killed by parents or caretakers each year; it also suggests that this estimate is low. McLain and his colleagues (McLain, Sacks, & Frohlke, 1993) report that abuse and neglect kill 5.4 out of every 100,000 children under 4 years of age, but this estimate is also probably low as a result of misclassification of child deaths. A second estimate is that the rate of child death is 11.6 per 100,000 children under 4 years of age (U.S. Advisory Board on Child Abuse and Neglect, 1995). The National Committee to Prevent Child Abuse and Neglect estimates that 1,215 children were killed by parents or caretakers in 1995, a rate of 1.81 children per 100,000 (Daro, 1996).

Dating and Courtship Violence

The virtues of romantic love, a phenomenon considered synonymous with American dating patterns, have been extolled in poems, songs, romance novels, television soap operas, and folklore. Sadly, along with the moonlight cruises, the first kiss, the flirtations, and affections is also the fact that violence is very much a part of modern dating patterns. Studies that examine the possibility of violence in dating and courtship find that between 10% and 67% of dating relationships involve violence (Sugarman & Hotaling, 1989). Researchers have found that the rate of severe violence among dating couples ranges from about 1% to 27% each year (Arias, Samios, & O'Leary, 1987; Lane & Gwartney-Gibbs, 1985; Makepeace, 1983).

Partner Abuse

Although there is no official reporting system for partner violence, there are a number of sources of data on the extent of violence between spouses or intimate partners. The National Institute of Justice, an agency of the U.S. Department of Justice, collects data on victims of violent crime using the National Crime Victims Survey (NCVS).

According to data from the NCVS, in 1992-1993, 9 women in 1,000, or 1 million women each year, experience violence at the hands of an intimate (Bachman & Saltzman, 1995). The rate of violent victimization at the hands of a stranger was 7.4 per 1,000. The number of intimate victimizations and the rate dropped between 1993 and 1996; 1996 survey data projected that 837,899 women were victims of intimate victimizations, a rate of 7.5 per 1,000.

Straus and Gelles and their colleagues have carried out three national surveys of domestic violence: in-person interviews with a nationally representative sample of 2,143 respondents in 1976 (Straus et al., 1980); telephone interviews with a nationally representative sample of 6,002 respondents in 1985 (Gelles & Straus, 1988; Straus & Gelles, 1986); and telephone interviews with a nationally representative sample of 1,970 respondents in 1992 (Straus & Kaufman-Kantor, 1994). The rate of "minor violence" or violence that had a low probability of causing a physical injury declined from 100 per 1,000 women in 1975 to about 80 per 1,000 in 1985 and then rose to nearly 90 per 1,000 in 1992. More serious or severe acts of violence toward women (acts labeled "severe assaults" or "wife beating" by the investigators) declined from 38 per 1,000 in 1975 to 19 per 1,000 in 1992.

The National Violence Against Women (NVAW) survey involved telephone interviews with a nationally representative sample of 8,000 women and 8,000 men (Tjaden & Thoennes, 1998). The survey was conducted between November 1995 and May 1996. The NVAW survey assessed lifetime prevalence and annual prevalence (violence experienced in the previous 12 months). The NVAW survey used a "modified" version of the Conflict Tactics Scales to measure violence victimization. Nearly 52% of women surveyed (519 per 1,000, or 52,261,743 women) reported experiencing a physical assault as a child or adult. Nearly 56% of women surveyed (559 per 1,000, or 56,289,623 women) reported experiencing any form of violence, including stalking, rape, or physical assault. The rate of lifetime assault at the hands of an intimate partner was 221 per 1,000 for physical violence and 254 per 1,000 for any form of violence victimization. The rates of forms of violence less likely to cause an injury, such as pushing, grabbing, shoving, or slapping, were the highest (between 160 and 181 per 1,000), whereas the rates of the most severe forms of violence (e.g., used a gun, used a knife, beat up) were the lowest (85 per 1,000 for "beat up"; 7 per 1,000 for used a gun).

The annual prevalence or incidence of violence was 19 per 1,000 for physical assault (1,913,243 women) and 30 per 1,000 for any form of violence victimization (3,020,910 women). The annual prevalence of women victimized by intimate partners was 13 per 1,000 for physical assault (1,309,061) and 18 per 1,000 (1,812,546 women) for all forms of victimization.

Homicide of Intimates

Researchers generally report that intrafamilial homicides account for between 20% and 40% of all murders (Curtis, 1974). About 680 husbands and boyfriends are killed by their wives and girlfriends each year, and more than 1,400 wives and girlfriends are slain by their husbands or boyfriends (U.S. Department of Justice, 1994).

Elder Abuse

Pillemer and Finkelhor (1988) interviewed 2,020 community-dwelling (noninstitutionalized) elderly persons in the Boston metropolitan area. Overall, 32 elderly persons per 1,000 reported experiencing physical violence, verbal aggression, and/or neglect in the past year. The rate of physical violence was 20 per 1,000. Although the conventional view of elder abuse is that of middle-aged children abusing and neglecting their elderly parents, Pillemer and Finkelhor found that spouses were the most frequent abusers of the elderly and that roughly equal numbers of men and women were victims. Women, however, were the victims of the most serious forms of abuse such as punching, kicking, beating, and choking. More recently, the National Elder Abuse Incidence Survey found that approximately 450,000 elderly persons living in domestic settings were abused and/or neglected in 1996 (National Center on Elder Abuse, 1998).

Hidden Violence: Sibling and Parents

Although parent-to-child violence and partner violence have received the most public attention, physical fights between brothers and sisters are by far the most common form of family violence. It is rare, however, that parents, physicians, or social workers consider sibling fighting as a problematic form of family violence. However, violence between siblings often goes far beyond so-called normal violence; for example, at least 109,000 children use guns or knives in fights with siblings each year (Straus et al., 1980).

Parents are also hidden victims of family violence. Each year, according to Straus and Gelles's national surveys, between 750,000 and 1 million parents have violent acts committed against them by their teenage children (Cornell & Gelles, 1982).

The Costs of Family Violence

Deborah Daro (1988) estimates that the immediate cost of hospitalizing abused and neglected children is $20 million annually; rehabilitation and special education cost $7 million; and foster care costs are $460 million. In addition, there are short-term education, juvenile court, and private therapy costs. Longer term costs include $14.8 million for juvenile court and detention costs, $646 million for long-term foster care, and future lost earnings of abused and neglected children of between $658 million and $1.3 billion. Jack Westman (1994) extrapolated Daro's costs and includes estimates for hospitalization, rehabilitation and special education, foster care, social services case management, and court expenses. His cost estimate was between $8.4 and $32.3 billion each year, based on a range of $12,174 to $46,870 per maltreated child per year.

The costs of domestic violence are estimated to be between $1.7 billion (Straus, 1986) and $140 billion (Miller, Cohen, & Wiersema, 1994). These costs include medical costs; property loss; productivity losses at home, school, and work; and loss of quality of life.

The consequences of child abuse and neglect differ by the age of the child. During childhood, some of the major consequences of maltreatment include problematic school performance and lowered attention to social cues. Researchers have found that children whose parents are "psychologically unavailable" function poorly across a wide range of psychological, cognitive, and developmental areas (Egeland & Sroufe, 1981). Physical aggression, antisocial behavior, and juvenile delinquency are among the most consistently documented consequences of abuse in adolescence and adulthood (Aber, Allen, Carlson, & Cicchetti, 1990; Dodge, Bates, & Pettit, 1990; Widom, 1989a, 1989b, 1991). Evidence is more suggestive that maltreatment increases the risk of alcohol and drug problems (National Research Council, 1993).

Research on the consequences of sexual abuse finds that inappropriate sexual behavior, such as frequent and overt sexual stimulation and inappropriate sexual overtures to other children, is commonly found among victims of sexual abuse (Kendall-Tackett, Williams, & Finkelhor, 1993). Widom (1995) has found that people who were sexually abused during childhood are at higher risk of arrest for committing crimes as adults, including sex crimes, compared with people who did not suffer sexual abuse. However, this risk is no greater than the risk of arrest for victims of other childhood maltreatment, with one exception. Victims of sexual abuse are more likely to be arrested for prostitution than are other victims of maltreatment.

As severe and significant as the consequences of child abuse and neglect are, it is also important to point out that the majority of children who are abused and neglected do not show signs of extreme disturbance. Despite having been physically, psychologically, or sexually abused, many children have effective coping abilities and thus are able to deal with their problems better than other maltreated children. There are a number of protective factors that insulate children from the effects of maltreatment. These include high intelligence and good scholastic attainment; temperament; cognitive appraisal of events; how the child views the maltreatment; having a relationship with a significant person; and the types of interventions, including placement outside of the home (National Research Council, 1993).

For women victims of domestic assault, the consequences also extend beyond physical injury. Research consistently reports a high incidence of depression and anxiety among samples of battered women as well as an increased risk of suicide attempts (Christopoulos et al., 1987; Gelles & Harrop, 1989; Hilberman, 1980; National Research Council, 1996; Schechter, 1983; Walker, 1984).

The consequences of family violence for society include the days lost from work by victims of spousal abuse, the medical care that victims require, and the investment of time by social and criminal justice agencies.

Factors Associated With Family Violence

The early thinking and writing on family violence was dominated by a mental illness model (Gelles, 1973). Abuse and neglect were thought to be caused by certain personality factors, such as immaturity or impulsiveness, or by psychopathology. The assumption was that no psychologically normal person would physically abuse a wife or child. There are a number of problems with the psychopathological or mental illness model of family violence and abuse. First, most of the conclusions about the causes of family violence are based on studies of a limited number of cases, typically without comparison groups, and on studies that draw conclusions after the data are collected, rather than testing hypotheses developed prior to data collection. Second, such an explanation confuses the cause with the consequence: People who abuse their children or partners are mentally ill, we are told; we know they are mentally ill because they have committed an outrageous act of violence or abuse. A third problem is that the psychopathological model ignores the fact that certain societal factors are related to family violence. The remainder of this section examines those societal factors.

Gender

Outside the American family, violent men clearly outnumber violent women. In the home, however, women are frequently as violent as, or even more violent than, men. Not surprising, research on child abuse often finds that mothers are slightly more likely than fathers to abuse or kill their children (Gil, 1970; Parke & Collmer, 1975; Straus et al., 1980; Wolfner & Gelles, 1993). Of course, one obvious explanation for this is that mothers spend more time with their children than fathers do, so they have more opportunity to be violent and abusive. Moreover, regardless of the amount of time parents spend with children, mothers tend to be the ones who have the greatest responsibility for child rearing. Margolin (1992) found that when one controls for the amount of responsibility mothers and fathers have for child care, males are more likely to be abusive.

There is considerable debate about the comparative rates of husband and wife violence. Whereas some investigators report that the rate of wife-to-husband violence is about the same as the rate of husband-to-wife violence (Straus, 1998; Straus & Gelles, 1986), others explain that women are the disproportionate victims of family violence (Dobash & Dobash, 1979; Dobash, Dobash, Wilson, & Daly, 1992; Tjaden & Thoennes, 1998). If one goes by how much harm is done, who initiates the violence, and how easy it is for a victim to escape violence, women clearly are the disproportionate victims of domestic violence. Boys are the more violent siblings and offspring, and mothers and sisters are the more frequent targets of the young or adolescent boys' family violence.

Social Characteristics

There are two persistent myths concerning the relationship between social class and family violence. The first is that violence is *confined* to lower-class families. Because the poor are more likely to go to emergency rooms or clinics, they are more likely to come to the attention of the authorities if their child is bruised or battered. Similarly, clinics or emergency rooms are the most likely source of medical aid for lower-class battered women.

The second myth, virtually the opposite of the first, is that family violence cuts evenly across society. There is, of course, a grain of truth to this; family violence does occur in virtually every social category. *But* the distribution is far from even. Gelles (1992) found that the rate of severe or abusive violence toward children was 30 per 1,000 children in families with incomes above the official poverty line, whereas for children in families with incomes below the poverty line, the rate was 105 per 1,000 children. Similarly, the rate of abusive husband-to-wife violence was twice as high among those couples with below-poverty incomes compared with couples with incomes above the poverty line (Gelles, 1993).

Rates of family violence also vary by race. Both official report and self-report survey data report that the rates of intimate violence are higher in minority families (National Research Council, 1998). The rates of violence toward children and between husbands and wives are highest among Hispanics, compared with blacks and whites, and higher among blacks compared with whites (Hampton & Gelles, 1991; Hampton, Gelles, & Harrop, 1989; Straus & Smith, 1990). The higher rates of partner abuse in Hispanic families reflect the economic deprivation, youthfulness, and urban residence of Hispanics, because when these factors are controlled, there is no statistically significant difference between Hispanics and non-Hispanic whites. However, with regard to violence toward children, the differences between Hispanics, blacks, and whites persist even when demographic and socioeconomic factors are controlled.

Rates of family violence are highest in urban families, people with no religious affiliation, people with some high school education, blue-collar workers, people under the age of 30, and in homes where the husband is unemployed (Gelles & Straus, 1988; Straus et al., 1980).

Stress

The finding that homes where husbands are unemployed are the most likely to be violent suggests that stress is related to domestic assault. Financial problems, being a single parent, being a teenage mother, and sexual difficulties all are factors that are related to violence (Gelles, 1989; Gelles & Straus, 1988; Parke & Collmer, 1975; Straus et al., 1980).

Social Isolation

People who are socially isolated from neighbors and relatives are more likely to be violent in the home. One major source of stress reduction and an insulator to family violence is being able to call on friends and family for help, aid, and assistance. The more a family is integrated into the community and the more groups and associations it belongs to, the less likely it is to be violent (Milner & Chilamkurti, 1991; Straus et al., 1980).

The Cycle of Violence

The notion that abused children grow up to be abusing parents and violent adults has been widely expressed in the child abuse and family violence literature (Gelles, 1980). Kaufman and Zigler (1993) reviewed the literature that tested the intergenerational transmission of violence hypothesis and concluded that the best estimate of the rate of intergenerational transmission appears to be 30% (plus or minus 5%). Although a rate of 30% intergenerational transmission is substantially less than the majority of abused children, the rate is considerably more than the between 2% and 4% rate of abuse found in the general population (Straus & Gelles, 1986).

Evidence from studies of parental and partner violence indicate that while experiencing violence in one's family of origin is often correlated with later violent behavior, such experience is not the sole determining factor. When the cycle of violence occurs, it is likely the result of a complex set of social and psychological processes.

Factors Associated With
Sexual Abuse of Children

There has been a great deal of research on the characteristics of sexual abusers, but current research has failed to isolate characteristics, especially demographic, social, or psychological characteristics, that discriminate between sexual abusers and nonabusers (Quinsey, 1984).

One of the key questions raised in discussions about sexual abuse is whether all children are at risk for sexual abuse or whether some children, because of some specific characteristic (e.g., age or poverty status), are at greater risk than others. In their review of studies on prevention, Finkelhor and Baron (1986) conclude that it is currently not clear what factors increase children's risk for sexual abuse. It appears that girls are at greater risk, but boys are also victimized. Girls are more likely to be victimized if they have at some time been separated from their mothers (e.g., if they ever lived away from their mother or their mother is ill or disabled) or if they report poor relationships with their mothers. As the researchers note, these factors may be consequences of sexual abuse as much as risk factors. The data point to the importance of mothers in protecting children from sexually aggressive men.

Theoretical Perspectives

A number of sociological and psychological theories may help explain the causes of family violence. They include the following.

Social Learning Theory

Social learning theory proposes that individuals who experienced violence are more likely to use violence in the home than are those who have experienced little or no violence. Children who experience violence themselves or who witness violence between their parents are more likely to use violence when they grow up. This finding has been interpreted to support the idea that family violence is learned. The family is the institution and social group where people learn the roles of husband and wife, parent and child. The home is the prime location where people learn how to deal with various stresses, crises, and frustrations. In many instances, the home is also the site where a person first experiences violence. Not only do people learn violent behavior, but they learn how to justify being violent. For example, hearing fathers say "This will hurt me more than it will hurt you" or mothers say "You have been bad, so you deserve to be spanked" contributes to how children learn to justify violent behavior.

Social Situational/Stress and Coping Theory

Social situational/stress and coping theory explains why violence is used in some situations and not in others. The theory proposes that abuse and violence occur because of two main factors. The first is structural stress and the lack of coping resources in a family. For instance, the association between low income and family violence indicates that an important factor in violence is inadequate financial resources. The second factor is the cultural norm concerning the use of force and violence. In contemporary American society, as well as many societies, violence in general, and violence toward children in particular, is normative (Straus et al., 1980). Thus, individuals learn to use violence both expressively and instrumentally as a means of coping with a pileup of stressor events.

Resource Theory

Another explanation of family violence is resource theory (Goode, 1971). This model assumes that all social systems (including the family) rest to some degree on force or the threat of force. The more resources—social, personal, and economic—a person can command, the more force he or she can muster. However, the fewer resources a person has, the more he or she will actually use force in an open manner. Thus, a husband who wants to be the dominant person in the family but has little education, has a job low in prestige and income, and lacks interpersonal skills may choose to use violence to maintain the dominant position. In addition, family members (including children) may use violence to redress a grievance when they have few alternative resources available. Thus, wives who have few social resources or social contacts may use violence toward their husbands in order to protect themselves.

Ecological Theory

Garbarino (1977) and Belsky (1980, 1993) proposed an ecological model to explain the complex nature of child maltreatment. The ecological model proposes that violence and abuse arise out of a mismatch of parent to child or family to neighborhood and community. For example, parents who are under a great deal of social stress and who have poor coping skills may have a difficult time meeting the needs of a child who is hyperactive. The risk of abuse and violence increases when the functioning of the children and parents is limited and constrained by developmental problems (e.g., children with learning disabilities and social or emotional handicaps) and when parents are under considerable stress or have personality problems (e.g., immaturity or impulsiveness). Finally, if there are few institutions and agencies in the community to support troubled families, then the risk of abuse is further increased.

Exchange Theory

Exchange theory proposes that partner abuse and child abuse be governed by the principle of costs and benefits. Abuse is used when the rewards are

greater than the costs (Gelles, 1983). The private nature of the family, the reluctance of social institutions and agencies to intervene—despite mandatory
child abuse reporting laws and mandatory arrest laws for partner violence—
and the low risk of other interventions reduce the costs of abuse and violence.
The cultural approval of violence as both expressive and instrumental behavior raises the potential rewards for violence. The most significant reward is
social control, or power.

Sociobiology Theory

A sociobiological or evolutionary perspective of family violence suggests
that violence toward human or nonhuman primate offspring is the result of
the reproductive success potential of children and parental investment. The
theory's central assumption is that natural selection is the process of differential reproduction and reproductive success (Daly & Wilson, 1980). Males can
be expected to invest in offspring when there is some degree of parental certainty (how confident the parent is that the child is his own genetic offspring);
females are also inclined to invest under conditions of parental certainty. Parents recognize their offspring and avoid squandering valuable reproductive
effort on someone else's offspring. Thus, Daly and Wilson (1985) conclude
that parental feelings are more readily and more profoundly established with
one's own offspring than in cases in which the parent-offspring relationship
is artificial. Children not genetically related to the parent (e.g., stepchildren
or adopted or foster children) or children with low reproductive potential
(e.g., handicapped or retarded children) are at the highest risk for infanticide
and abuse (Burgess & Garbarino, 1983; Daly & Wilson, 1980; Hrdy, 1979).
In addition, large families can dilute parental energy and lower attachment to
children, thus increasing the risk of child abuse and neglect (Burgess, 1979).

Smuts (1992) applied an evolutionary perspective to male aggression
against females. Smuts (1992), Daly and Wilson (1988), and Burgess and
Draper (1989) argue that male aggression against females often reflects male
reproductive striving. It has been postulated that both human and nonhuman
male primates use aggression against females to intimidate females so that
they will not resist future male efforts to mate with them and to reduce the
likelihood that females will mate with other males. Thus, males use aggression to control female sexuality to their reproductive advantage.

The frequency of male aggression varies across societies and situations
depending on the strength of female alliances, the support women can receive
from their families, the strength and importance of male alliances, the degree of equality in male-female relationships, and the degree to which males
control the economic resources within a society. Male aggression toward

females, both physical violence and rape, is high when female alliances are weak, when females lack kin support, when male alliances are strong, when male-female relationships are unbalanced, and when males control societal resources.

Feminist Theory

Feminist theorists (e.g., Dobash & Dobash, 1979; Pagelow, 1984; Yllö, 1983, 1988) see violence toward women as a unique phenomenon that has been obscured and overshadowed by what they refer to as a "narrow" focus on family violence. The central thesis of this theory is that economic and social processes operate directly and indirectly to support a patriarchal (male-dominated) social order and family structure. Patriarchy is seen as leading to the subordination of women and causes the historical pattern of systematic violence directed against women.

A Model of Sexual Abuse

Finkelhor (1984) reviewed research on the factors that have been proposed as contributing to the sexual abuse of children and has developed what he calls a "Four Precondition Model of Sexual Abuse." His review suggests that all the factors relating to sexual abuse can be grouped into one of four preconditions that need to be met before sexual abuse can occur. The preconditions are as follows:

1. A potential offender needs to have some motivation to abuse a child sexually.
2. The potential offender has to overcome internal inhibitions against acting on that motivation.
3. The potential offender has to overcome external impediments to committing sexual abuse.
4. The potential offender or some other factor has to undermine or overcome a child's possible resistance to sexual abuse.

Interventions

Protecting Children

All 50 states enacted mandatory reporting laws for child abuse and neglect by the late 1960s. These laws require certain professionals (or in some states, all adults) to report cases of suspected abuse or neglect. When a report comes in, state protective service workers investigate to determine whether the child is in need of protection and the family is in need of help or assistance. Although a wide array of options are available to child protection workers, they typically have two basic ways to protect a victim of child abuse: (a) removing the child and placing him or her in a foster home or institution or (b) providing the family with social support, such as counseling, food stamps, day care services, and so on.

Neither solution is ideal, and there are risks in both. For instance, a child may not understand why he or she is being removed from the home. Children who are removed from abusive homes may be protected from physical damage, but they still suffer emotional harm. The emotional harm arises from the fact that abused children still love and have strong feelings for their parents and do not understand why they have been removed from their parents and homes. Often, abused children feel that they are responsible for their own abuse. Abused children frequently require special medical and/or psychological care, and it is difficult to find a suitable placement for them. They could well become a burden for foster parents or institutions that have to care for them. Therefore, the risk of abuse might even be greater in a foster home or institution than in the home of the natural parents.

Leaving children in an abusive home and providing social services involves another type of risk. Most protective service workers are overworked, undertrained, and underpaid. Family services, such as crisis day care, financial assistance, suitable housing, and transportation services, are often limited. This can lead to cases in which children who were reported as abused, investigated by state agencies, and supervised by state agencies are killed during the period the family was supposedly being monitored. Half of all children who are killed by caretakers are killed *after* they have been reported to child welfare agencies (Gelles, 1996).

Only a handful of evaluations have been made of prevention and treatment programs for child maltreatment. In Elmira, New York, Olds, Henderson, Tatelbaum, and Chamberlin (1986) evaluated the effectiveness of a family support program during pregnancy and the first 2 years after birth for low-income, unmarried, first-time teenage mothers. Of the sample of poor unmarried teenage girls who received no services during their pregnancy period, 19% were reported for subsequent child maltreatment. Of those poor unmarried teenage mothers who were provided with the full complement of nurse home visits during their pregnancy and for the first 2 years after birth, 4% had confirmed cases of child abuse and neglect reported to the state child protection agency. Subsequent follow-ups of the home health visiting intervention demonstrated the long-term effectiveness of this intervention. However, the effectiveness varied depending on the populations receiving the service, the community context, and who made the visits (nurses or others) (Olds et al., 1999).

Daro and Cohn (1988) reviewed evaluations of 88 child maltreatment programs that were funded by the federal government between 1974 and 1982. They found that there was no noticeable correlation between a given set of services and the likelihood of further maltreatment of children. In fact, the more services a family received, the worse the family got and the more likely children were to be maltreated. Lay counseling, group counseling, and parent-education classes resulted in more positive treatment outcomes. The optimal treatment period appeared to be between 7 and 18 months. The projects that were successful in reducing abuse accomplished this by separating children from abusive parents, either by placing them in foster homes or by requiring the maltreating adult to move out of the house.

The National Academy of Sciences panel on "Assessing Family Violence Interventions" identified 78 evaluations of child maltreatment intervention programs that met the panel's criteria for methodologically sound evaluation research. The one commonality of the 78 evaluations of child abuse and neglect prevention and treatment programs was, in scientific terms, a failure to reject the null hypothesis. Although it may be too harsh a judgment to say that these programs have not and do not work as intended, the National Research Council (1998) report did come to the following conclusion regarding social service interventions:

> Social service interventions designed to improve parenting practices and provide family support have not yet demonstrated that they have the capacity to reduce or prevent abusive or neglectful behaviors significantly over time for the majority of families who have been reported for child maltreatment. (p. 118)

Protecting Women

There are a number of options available to women who want to either escape or be protected from partner violence. One option is to call the police. The best-known assessment of intervention into domestic violence is the Minneapolis Police Experiment (Sherman & Berk, 1984). This study was designed to examine whether arresting men for violent attacks on their partners would decrease the risk of further violence. This study called for the police to randomly assign incidents of misdemeanor family assaults to one of three treatments: arrest, separation, or advice/mediation. Those households receiving the arrest intervention had the lowest rate (10%) of recidivism (relapse into violent behavior), and those who were separated had the highest (24%).

Replications of the Minneapolis study, however, found that, contrary to the evidence from Minneapolis, arrest had no more effect in deterring future arrests or complaints of violence than did separation or counseling (Berk, Campbell, Klap, & Western, 1992; Dunford, Huizinga, & Elliott, 1990; Pate & Hamilton, 1992; Sherman & Smith, 1992). The replications did find that men who were employed when they were arrested were less likely to be violent after they were arrested than were men who were not arrested. However, men who were unemployed when they were arrested were actually more likely to be violent after they were arrested, compared with unemployed men who were not arrested.

A second possibility for women who want to be protected from partner violence is for the woman to go to a shelter or safe house. *If* a shelter is nearby, *if* the woman knows how to get to it, and *if* there is room, shelters provide physical protection, social support, counseling, legal aid, and even occupational counseling. Shelters are the most cost-efficient form of intervention into domestic violence. Researchers find that the effects of shelters seem to depend on the attributes of the victims. When a victim is actively engaged in taking control of her life, a shelter stay can dramatically reduce the likelihood of new violence. For some victims, a shelter stay may have no impact, and for others it may actually lead to an escalation of violence when they return home (Berk, Newton, & Berk, 1986).

Bowker (1983) talked to women who had been beaten and who managed to get their partners to stop being violent. Among the things these women did were to talk to friends and relatives, threaten their husbands, aggressively defend themselves from their husbands, go to shelters, call social service agencies, call the police, and various other actions. No one action worked best. Bowker concluded that, ultimately, the crucial factor was the woman's taking a stand and showing her determination that the violence had to stop.

Researchers have also evaluated group programs developed for violent men. Some of the earliest studies appeared to show that group counseling for batterers was effective in reducing subsequent violence (Dutton, 1986; Gondolf, 1987; Pirog-Good & Stets, 1986). However, a recent review of the research on the effectiveness of men's counseling programs found no overall effectiveness of such programs and found that no particular facet of programs, such as length or type of program, was effective in reducing men's violence (Levesque, 1998).

Prevention

At present, the vast majority of programs (e.g., shelters, crisis day care centers, police intervention programs, and parent support groups) aimed at dealing with family violence are treatment programs that are implemented *after* the abusive incident. What is needed, and what has not been attempted on any large scale, are services that would prevent violence and abuse before they begin. But such prevention programs require sweeping changes in both society and the family. After the conclusion of their national survey of family violence, Straus et al. (1980) proposed the following steps for the *prevention of violence:*

1. Eliminate the norms that legitimize and glorify violence in the society and the family.
2. Reduce violence-provoking stress created by society.
3. Integrate families into a network of kin and community.
4. Change the sexist character of society.
5. Break the cycle of violence in the family.

These proposals call for such fundamental changes in society and family life that many people resist them and argue that they could not work. But not making such changes continues the harmful and deadly tradition of family violence.

DISCUSSION QUESTIONS

1. Why has it been difficult to assess the incidence and frequency of family violence? How could a more thorough assessment of family violence be achieved?

2. Which factors do you think are the strongest predictors of family violence? Justify your response.

3. What are some of the myths associated with family violence?

4. Compare and contrast two theoretical explanations of family violence. What are the strengths and weaknesses of each theoretical perspective?

5. What policies and programs are needed to most effectively deal with partner abuse? What issues are involved in such interventions?

SUGGESTED READINGS

Belsky, J. (1993). Etiology of child maltreatment: A developmental-ecological approach. *Psychological Bulletin, 114,* 413-434.

Finkelhor, D. (1986). *A sourcebook on child sexual abuse.* Beverly Hills, CA: Sage.

Gelles, R. J. (1996). *The book of David: How preserving families can cost children's lives.* New York: Basic Books.

Smuts, B. (1992). Male aggression against women: An evolutionary perspective. *Human Nature, 3,* 1-44.

Tjaden, P., & Thoennes, N. (1998). *Prevalence, incidence, and consequence of violence against women: Findings from the National Violence Against Women Survey.* Denver, CO: Center for Policy Research.

REFERENCES

Aber, J. L., Allen, J. P., Carlson, V., & Cicchetti, D. (1990). The effects of maltreatment on development during early childhood: Recent studies and their theoretical, clinical, and policy implications. In D. Cicchetti & V. Carlson (Eds.), *Child maltreatment: Theory and research on causes and consequences* (pp. 579-619). New York: Cambridge University Press.

Arias, I., Samios, M., & O'Leary, K. D. (1987). Prevalence and correlates of physical aggression during courtship. *Journal of Interpersonal Violence, 2,* 82-90.

Bachman, R., & Saltzman, L. (1995). *Violence against women: Estimates from the redesigned survey.* Washington, DC: U.S. Department of Justice, Bureau of Justice Statistics.

Belsky, J. (1980). Child maltreatment: An ecological integration. *American Psychologist, 35,* 320-335.

Belsky, J. (1993). Etiology of child maltreatment: A developmental-ecological approach. *Psychological Bulletin, 114,* 413-434.

Berk, R. A., Campbell, A., Klap, R., & Western, B. (1992). The deterrent effect of arrest incidents of domestic violence: A Bayesian analysis of four field experiments. *American Sociological Review, 57,* 698-708.

Berk, R. A., Newton, P., & Berk, S. F. (1986). What a difference a day makes: An empirical study of the impact of shelters for battered women. *Journal of Marriage and the Family, 48,* 481-490.

Bowker, L. H. (1983). *Beating wife beating.* Lexington, MA: Lexington Books.

Burgdorf, K. (1980). *Recognition and reporting of child maltreatment.* Rockville, MD: Westat.

Burgess, R. L. (1979). *Family violence: Some implications from evolutionary biology.* Paper presented at meetings of the American Society of Criminology, Philadelphia.

Burgess, R. L., & Draper, P. (1989). The explanation of family violence: The role of biological, behavioral, and cultural selection. In L. Ohlin & M. Tonry (Eds.), *Family violence: Crime and justice: A review of research* (Vol. 11, pp. 59-116). Chicago: University of Chicago Press.

Burgess, R. L., & Garbarino, J. (1983). Doing what comes naturally? An evolutionary perspective on child abuse. In D. Finkelhor, R. Gelles, M. Straus, & G. Hotaling (Eds.), *The dark side of the families: Current family violence research* (pp. 88-101). Beverly Hills, CA: Sage.

Christopoulos, C., Cohn, D. A., Shaw, D. S., Joyce, S., Sullivan-Hanson, J., Kraft, S. P., & Emery, R. (1987). Children of abused women: Adjustment at time of shelter residence. *Journal of Marriage and the Family, 49*, 611-619.

Cornell, C. P., & Gelles, R. J. (1982). Adolescent to parent violence. *Urban Social Change Review, 15*, 8-14.

Curtis, L. (1974). *Criminal violence: National patterns and behavior.* Lexington, MA: Lexington Books.

Daly, M., & Wilson, M. (1980). Discriminative parental solicitude: A biosocial perspective. *Journal of Marriage and the Family, 42*, 277-288.

Daly, M., & Wilson, M. (1985). Child abuse and other risks of not living with both parents. *Ethology and Sociobiology, 6*, 197-210.

Daly, M., & Wilson, M. (1988). *Homicide.* New York: Aldine DeGruyter.

Daro, D. (1988). *Confronting child abuse: Research for effective programming.* New York: Free Press.

Daro, D. (1996). Current trends in child abuse reporting and fatalities: NCPCA's 1995 annual fifty state survey. *APSAC Advisor, 9*, 21-24.

Daro, D., & Cohn, A. H. (1988). Child maltreatment evaluation efforts: What have we learned? In G. T. Hotaling, D. Finkelhor, J. T. Kirkpatrick, & M. A. Straus (Eds.), *Coping with family violence: Research and policy perspectives* (pp. 275-287). Newbury Park, CA: Sage.

Davidson, T. (1978). *Conjugal crime: Understanding and changing the wife beating pattern.* New York: Hawthorn.

Dobash, R. E., & Dobash, R. (1979). *Violence against wives.* New York: Free Press.

Dobash, R. P., Dobash, R. E., Wilson, M., & Daly, M. (1992). The myth of sexual symmetry in marital violence. *Social Problems, 39*, 71-91.

Dodge, K. A., Bates, J. E., & Pettit, G. S. (1990). Mechanisms in the cycle of violence. *Science, 250*, 1678-1683.

Dunford, F. W., Huizinga, D., & Elliott, D. S. (1990). The role of arrest in domestic assault: The Omaha Police Experiment. *Criminology, 28*, 183-206.

Dutton, D. G. (1986). The outcome of court-mandated treatment for wife assault: A quasi-experimental evaluation. *Violence and Victims, 1*, 163-176.

Egeland, B., & Sroufe, L. A. (1981). Attachment and early child maltreatment. *Child Development, 52*, 44-52.

Finkelhor, D. (1984). *Child sexual abuse: New theory and research.* New York: Free Press.

Finkelhor, D., & Baron, L. (1986). High risk children. In D. Finkelhor (Ed.), *A sourcebook on child sexual abuse* (pp. 60-88). Beverly Hills, CA: Sage.

Garbarino, J. (1977). The human ecology of child maltreatment. *Journal of Marriage and the Family, 39*, 721-735.

Gelles, R. J. (1973). Child abuse as psychopathology: A sociological critique and reformulation. *American Journal of Orthopsychiatry, 43,* 611-621.

Gelles, R. J. (1980). Violence in the family: A review of research in the seventies. *Journal of Marriage and the Family, 42,* 873-885.

Gelles, R. J. (1983). An exchange/social control theory. In D. Finkelhor, R. Gelles, M. Straus, & G. Hotaling (Eds.), *The dark side of families: Current family violence research* (pp. 151-165). Beverly Hills, CA: Sage.

Gelles, R. J. (1989). Child abuse and violence in single parent families: Parent-absence and economic deprivation. *American Journal of Orthopsychiatry, 59,* 492-501.

Gelles, R. J. (1992). Poverty and violence toward children. *American Behavioral Scientist, 35,* 258-274.

Gelles, R. J. (1993). *Husband to wife violence by income.* Mimeographed.

Gelles, R. J. (1996). *The book of David: How preserving families can cost children's lives.* New York: Basic Books.

Gelles, R. J., & Harrop, J. W. (1989). Violence, battering, and psychological distress among women. *Journal of Interpersonal Violence, 4,* 400-420.

Gelles, R. J., & Straus, M. A. (1987). Is violence towards children increasing? A comparison of 1975 and 1985 national survey rates. *Journal of Interpersonal Violence, 2,* 212-222.

Gelles, R. J., & Straus, M. A. (1988). *Intimate violence.* New York: Simon & Schuster.

Gil, D. G. (1970). *Violence against children: Physical child abuse in the United States.* Cambridge, MA: Harvard University Press.

Gondolf, E. W. (1987). Evaluating progress for men who batter: Problems and prospects. *Journal of Family Violence, 2,* 95-108.

Goode, W. (1971). Force and violence in the family. *Journal of Marriage and the Family, 33,* 624-636.

Greven, P. (1991). *Spare the child: The religious roots of punishment and the psychological impact of physical abuse.* New York: Knopf.

Hampton, R. L., & Gelles, R. J. (1991). A profile of violence toward black children. In R. L. Hampton (Ed.), *Black family violence* (pp. 21-34). Lexington, MA: Lexington Books.

Hampton, R. L., Gelles, R. J., & Harrop, J. W. (1989). Is violence in black families increasing? A comparison of 1975 and 1985 national survey rates. *Journal of Marriage and the Family, 51,* 969-980.

Hilberman, E. (1980). Overview: "The wife-beater's wife" reconsidered. *American Journal of Psychiatry, 137,* 1336-1346.

Hrdy, S. B. (1979). Infanticide among animals: A review, classification, and examination of the implications for reproductive strategies of females. *Ethology and Sociobiology, 1,* 13-40.

Kaufman, J., & Zigler, E. (1993). The intergenerational transmission of abuse is overstated. In R. J. Gelles & D. R. Loseke (Eds.), *Current controversies on family violence.* Newbury Park, CA: Sage.

Kendall-Tackett, K. A., Williams, L., & Finkelhor, D. (1993). The impact of sexual abuse on children: A review and synthesis of recent empirical literature. *Psychological Bulletin, 113,* 164-180.

Lane, K. E., & Gwartney-Gibbs, P. A. (1985). Violence in the context of dating and sex. *Journal of Family Issues, 6,* 45-59.

Levesque, D. (1998). *Violence desistance among battering men: Existing intervention and the application of the Transtheoretical Model of Change.* Unpublished doctoral dissertation, University of Rhode Island, Kingston.

Makepeace, J. M. (1983). Life events stress and courtship violence. *Family Relations, 32,* 101-109.

Margolin, L. (1992). Beyond maternal blame: Physical child abuse as a phenomenon of gender. *Journal of Family Issues, 13,* 410-423.

McLain, P., Sacks, J., & Frohlke, R. (1993). Estimates of fatal child abuse and neglect, United States, 1979-1988. *Pediatrics, 91,* 338-343.

Miller, T. R., Cohen, M. A., & Wiersema, B. (1994). *Crime in the United States: Victims costs and consequences.* Unpublished manuscript, National Public Service Research Institute, Washington, DC.

Milner, J. S., & Chilamkurti, C. (1991). Physical child abuse perpetrator characteristics: A review of the literature. *Journal of Interpersonal Violence, 6,* 345-366.

National Center on Child Abuse and Neglect. (1988). *Study findings: Study of national incidence and prevalence of child abuse and neglect: 1988.* Washington, DC: U.S. Department of Health and Human Services.

National Center on Child Abuse and Neglect. (1996). *Study findings: Study of national incidence and prevalence of child abuse and neglect: 1993.* Washington, DC: U.S. Department of Health and Human Services.

National Center on Child Abuse and Neglect. (1998). *Child maltreatment 1996: Reports from the states to the National Center on Child Abuse and Neglect.* Washington, DC: U.S. Government Printing Office.

National Center on Elder Abuse. (1998). *The national elder abuse incidence study.* Washington, DC: American Public Human Services Association.

National Research Council. (1993). *Understanding child abuse and neglect.* Washington, DC: National Academy Press.

National Research Council. (1996). *Understanding violence against women.* Washington, DC: National Academy Press.

National Research Council. (1998). *Violence in families: Assessing prevention and treatment programs.* Washington, DC: National Academy Press.

Olds, D. L., Henderson, C. R., Kitzman, H. J., Eckenrode, J. J., Cole, R. E., & Tatelbaum, R. C. (1999). Prenatal and infancy home visitation by nurses: Recent findings. *Future of Children, 9,* 44-65.

Olds, D. L., Henderson, C. R., Jr., Tatelbaum, R., & Chamberlin, R. (1986). Preventing child abuse and neglect: A randomized trial of nurse home visitation. *Pediatrics, 77,* 65-78.

Pagelow, M. (1984). *Family violence.* New York: Praeger.

Parke, R. D., & Collmer, C. W. (1975). Child abuse: An interdisciplinary analysis. In M. Hetherington (Ed.), *Review of child development research* (Vol. 5, pp. 1-102). Chicago: University of Chicago Press.

Pate, A. M., & Hamilton, E. E. (1992). Formal and informal social deterrents to domestic violence: The Dade County Spouse Assault Experiment. *American Sociological Review, 57,* 691-697.

Peters, S. D., Wyatt, G. E., & Finkelhor, D. (1986). Prevalence. In D. Finkelhor (Ed.), *A sourcebook on child sexual abuse* (pp. 15-59). Beverly Hills, CA: Sage.

Pillemer, K., & Finkelhor, D. (1988). The prevalence of elder abuse: A random sample survey. *Gerontologist, 28,* 51-57.

Pirog-Good, M. A., & Stets, J. (1986). Programs for abusers: Who drops out and what can be done. *Response, 9,* 17-19.

Pleck, E. (1987). *Domestic tyranny: The making of American social policy against family violence from colonial times to the present.* New York: Oxford University Press.

Quinsey, V. L. (1984). Sexual aggression: Studies of offenders against women. In D. N. Weisstub (Ed.), *Law and mental health: International perspectives* (Vol. 1, pp. 84-121). New York: Pergamon.

Radbill, S. A. (1980). A history of child abuse and infanticide. In R. Helfer & C. Kempe (Eds.), *The battered child* (3rd ed., pp. 3-20). Chicago: University of Chicago Press.

Schechter, S. (1983). *Women and male violence.* Boston: South End.

Sherman, L. W., & Berk, R. A. (1984). The specific deterrent effects of arrest for domestic assault. *American Sociological Review, 49,* 261-272.

Sherman, L. W., & Smith, D. A. (1992). Crime, punishment, and stake in conformity: Legal and informal control of domestic violence. *American Sociological Review, 57,* 680-690.

Smuts, B. (1992). Male aggression against women: An evolutionary perspective. *Human Nature, 3,* 1-44.

Sommers, C. H. (1994). *Who stole feminism? How women have betrayed women.* New York: Simon & Schuster.

Straus, M. A. (1986). The cost of intrafamily violence. *Academic Medicine, 62,* 556-561.

Straus, M. A. (1998). The controversy over domestic violence by women: A methodological, theoretical, and sociology of science analysis. In X. B. Arriaga & S. Oskamp (Eds.), *Violence in intimate relationships.* Thousand Oaks, CA: Sage.

Straus, M. A., & Gelles, R. J. (1986). Societal change and change in family violence from 1975 to 1985 as revealed in two national surveys. *Journal of Marriage and the Family, 48,* 465-479.

Straus, M. A., Gelles, R. J., & Steinmetz, S. K. (1980). *Behind closed doors: Violence in the American family.* New York: Doubleday/Anchor.

Straus, M. A., & Kaufman-Kantor, G. (1994). *Change in spouse assault rates from 1975 to 1992: A comparison of three national surveys in the United States.* Paper presented at the 13th World Congress of Sociology, Bielefeld, Germany.

Straus, M. A., & Smith, C. (1990). Violence in Hispanic families in the United States: Incidence rates and structural interpretations. In M. A. Straus & R. J. Gelles (Eds.), *Physical violence in American families: Risk factors and adaptations in 8,145 families* (pp. 341-367). New Brunswick, NJ: Transaction Books.

Sugarman, D. B., & Hotaling, G. T. (1989). Dating violence: Prevalence, context, and risk factors. In M. A. Pirog-Good & J. E. Stets (Eds.), *Violence in dating relationships* (pp. 3-32). New York: Praeger.

Tjaden, P., & Thoennes, N. (1998). *Prevalence, incidence, and consequences of violence against women: Findings from the National Violence Against Women Survey.* Denver, CO: Center for Policy Research.

U.S. Advisory Board on Child Abuse and Neglect. (1995). *A nation's shame: Fatal child abuse and neglect in the United States.* Washington, DC: U.S. Department of Health and Human Services.

U.S. Department of Justice. (1994). *Uniform crime reports for the United States, 1991.* Washington, DC: U.S. Department of Justice, Federal Bureau of Investigation.

Walker, L. (1984). *The battered woman syndrome.* New York: Springer.

Westman, J. C. (1994). *Licensing parents: Can we prevent child abuse and neglect?* New York: Insight Books.

Widom, C. S. (1989a). Child abuse, neglect, and violent criminal behavior. *Criminology, 27,* 251-271.

Widom, C. S. (1989b). The cycle of violence. *Science, 244,* 160-166.

Widom, C. S. (1991). Childhood victimization and adolescent problem behaviors. In M. E. Lamb & R. Ketterlinus (Eds.), *Adolescent problem behaviors* (pp. 127-164). New York: Lawrence Erlbaum.

Widom, C. S. (1995). Victims of childhood sexual abuse: Later criminal consequences. *National Institute of Justice Research in Brief.* Washington, DC: U.S. Department of Justice, Office of Justice Programs.

Wolfner, G., & Gelles, R. J. (1993). A profile of violence toward children. *Child Abuse and Neglect: The International Journal, 17,* 197-212.

Yllö, K. (1983). Using a feminist approach in quantitative research. In D. Finkelhor, R. Gelles, M. Straus, & G. Hotaling (Eds.), *The dark side of families: Current family violence research* (pp. 277-288). Beverly Hills, CA: Sage.

Yllö, K. (1988). Political and methodological debates in wife abuse research. In K. Yllö & M. Bograd (Eds.), *Feminist perspectives on wife abuse* (pp. 28-50). Newbury Park, CA: Sage.

9

Family Stress and
Adolescent Substance Abuse

MICHAEL P. FARRELL
GRACE M. BARNES

Until recently, most researchers viewed parent-adolescent relations through a "social mold" perspective, seeing the adolescent's behavior as an outcome or consequence of the parent's child-rearing practices. However, over the past decade, there has been increasing interest in how parents are affected by the experience of raising adolescents (e.g., Ambert, 1992; Farrell & Rosenberg, 1981; Farrell, Rosenberg, & Rosenberg, 1993; Palkovitz, 1996). Ultimately, this change in perspective is leading to a bidirectional or "resonant" model of adolescent socialization, in which the behavior and psychological functioning of parents and adolescents are seen as reciprocally interdependent. One area in which this bidirectional model is applicable is in the relationship between family stress and adolescent substance abuse.

A number of researchers have found that stress in families contributes to substance abuse by adolescents (Chassin, Pillow, Curran, Molina, & Berrera, 1993; Clark, Lesnick, & Hegedus, 1997; Conger & Elder, 1994; Farrell, Barnes, & Banerjee, 1995; Wills, Vaccaro, & McNamara, 1992). For some adolescents, the effects are direct; for example, they use drugs or alcohol to escape from the stress and conflict at home (Hawkins, Catalano, & Miller, 1992). One study found that 34.9% of male and 38.5% of female alcohol us-

---

AUTHORS' NOTE: We would like to acknowledge David Blake for his assistance with bibliographical research for this chapter.

ers "drank to forget their troubles" (Windle, 1996). For others, the effects are indirect. For example, acutely stressful events, such as a parent's loss of a job, and chronic stress, such as that caused by extreme poverty, can have negative effects on parenting, which in turn can make an adolescent vulnerable to peer pressure to drink or use drugs.

On the other hand, family stress can also be a consequence of adolescent substance abuse. Once adolescents begin to drink heavily or use drugs regularly, their behavior can lead to a significant "pileup" of stressful events at home (Clark et al., 1997; Conger, 1997; Johnson & Pandina, 1993; Patterson, Reid, & Dishion, 1992). Heavy users are more likely to engage in risky behaviors (e.g., reckless driving or delinquency) that lead to undesirable consequences such as serious injuries, problems at school, unwanted pregnancy, or trouble with the law, all of which become new sources of stress for their parents (Windle, Shope, & Bukstein, 1996). Thus, adolescent alcohol and drug use can be both a cause and a consequence of stress in families.

Recent theory and research emphasize that alcohol and drug abuse unfold in a developmental sequence (e.g., Conger, 1997). Elliott, Huizinga, and Menard (1989) state it very simply: "Minor delinquency comes first, followed by alcohol use, serious delinquency, and serious drug use" (p. 189). It should be added that, after peaking in the mid- to late adolescent years, both delinquency and substance abuse decline for most people (Moffit, 1993). Most adolescents learn to drink in ways that are not viewed as problematic by them or their parents; however, for a significant minority, alcohol is a gateway to heavy drinking and drug abuse, which in turn are associated with numerous social, psychological, and health problems (Jessor, Donovan, & Costa, 1991; Kandel & Yamaguchi, 1993). Compared with other adolescents, heavy users of drugs and alcohol are more likely to be depressed, have low grades in school, drop out of high school, engage in crime and risky sexual encounters, have run-ins with the police, have automobile accidents, and experience injuries from risk-taking episodes (Hansen & O'Malley, 1996; Windle et al., 1996).

As the transition from childhood to adulthood progresses, adolescents come to rely less on their parents and more on their close friends for support and guidance, especially when it comes to lifestyle choices such as how to dress, where to seek entertainment, and whether or not to use drugs or alcohol (Berrera & Li, 1996). For some, the use of alcohol or drugs is a way to assert their autonomy, but the most common reason for drinking, given by 73% of respondents in a national sample, is "to have a good time with my friends" (O'Malley, Johnston, & Bachman, 1998). Thus, while family factors may play a significant role in the early stages of the developmental sequence, friends play an important role during the later stages. During this advanced stage of adolescence, even though the dynamics of friendship may encourage substance abuse, parental support and supervision can still play a part in buffering the impact of associating with heavy-drinking or drug-using friends (Bogenschneider, Wu, Raffaelli, & Tsay, 1998; Conger, 1997; Hawkins et al., 1992).

In this chapter, we first examine recent historical trends in adolescent alcohol and drug use. Because American society is becoming increasingly diverse, wherever possible we specify race and ethnic differences. Next we examine recent advances in theory and research on the role that families play in adolescent alcohol and drug use. Then we examine how adolescent alcohol and drug abuse contribute to stress within the family. Finally, we discuss the part that families can play in interventions to prevent substance abuse.

Recent Trends in Adolescent Alcohol and Drug Abuse

Even though all 50 states have made it illegal for persons under 21 to purchase alcohol, and they all outlaw the use of marijuana and other such mind-altering drugs, substance abuse is widespread among adolescents in American society. Despite the media and policy focus on hard drugs, alcohol is still the most commonly used substance, and between ages 12 and 20, the prevalence of alcohol use among adolescents accelerates at a rate that mirrors their increasing autonomy. Among high school seniors who participated in a representative national survey in late 1997, more than 80% reported that they drank "more than a few sips" of alcohol at some point during their lives, more than 50% reported that they drank in the last month, and about 30% reported they had five or more drinks in one sitting during the 2 weeks prior to completing the survey (Johnston, Bachman, & O'Malley, 1998).

Reviewing their annual surveys of representative national samples of about 50,000 high school seniors, researchers at the University of Michigan found that adolescent drug and alcohol use peaked in the late 1970s and early 1980s, declined over the 1980s, then for the most part leveled off (Johnston et al., 1998). However, there is evidence that some types of substance use increased in the 1990s. In 1980, 93% of high school seniors reported that they had "ever used" alcohol. This number declined to 80.4% in 1994, then leveled off near this figure for the next several years; in 1997, it was 81.7% (Johnston et al., 1998). Examining trends in the rates of heavy drinking, which they define as five or more drinks in one sitting in the previous 2 weeks, the Michigan researchers found that among the 1980 seniors, 41.2% reported they had at least one episode of heavy drinking. In 1993, this percentage dropped to 27.5%, then in 1997 it rose slightly to 30.2%.

In their periodic surveys of New York State high school students, researchers at the New York State Research Institute on Addictions have found similar trends (Barnes, Welte, Hoffman, & Dintcheff, 1997). In 1978, 92% of New York State 12th graders reported using alcohol at some point in their lives. By 1990, that figure had fallen to 75%, and in 1994 it was 77%. Using analyses of subgroups, these researchers found that between 1983 and 1990, alcohol consumption declined for all age, gender, and ethnic groups. However, between 1990 and 1994, it significantly increased among younger but not among older adolescents. For example, examining the mean number of days that high school students reported having alcohol-related problems in the past year, they found that it declined from 1.5 in 1983 to 1.2 in 1990; however, among the younger teens, it rose again dramatically in 1994, reaching a mean of approximately 2.0 days per year for the 17-year-olds. The alcohol-related problems included trouble with teachers and police because of drinking and driving a car after drinking a good bit—both of which are likely sources of stress in the families of the adolescents.

The most commonly used illicit drug is marijuana, and the proportion of adolescents using this drug has shown an even more dramatic pattern of decline and recovery over the 1980s and 1990s. In the 1980 national study of high school seniors, 60.3% reported they had ever used marijuana; in 1992, the proportion dropped to 32.6%, then it climbed again, reaching 49.6% in 1997 (Johnston et al., 1998). Although they are much less commonly used, hallucinogens, such as LSD, reveal a similar trend over this same time period. Once again, the regional data from New York State reflect these trends. In the 1978 New York survey, 54% of the high school seniors reported they had ever used marijuana; by 1990, that proportion had fallen to 24%, but in 1994 the proportion increased to 35%. Thus, there are signs that both heavy drinking and marijuana use increased in the 1990s, especially in the younger age groups.

Most researchers find that blacks are more likely than whites to abstain from alcohol and illicit drug use (Barnes et al., 1997; Gil, Vega, & Biafora, 1998; Hansen & O'Malley, 1996; Johnston et al., 1998; Vega, Zimmerman, Warheir, Apospori, & Gil, 1993). In most studies, the proportion of blacks who heavily use alcohol is less than half the proportion of whites. For example, in the 1991 national study, 32.9% of the white seniors compared with 11.8% of black seniors reported episodes of heavy drinking in the 2 weeks prior to the survey. In 1997, those proportions were 36.1% and 12.0%, respectively. In the New York studies, the researchers found that across all the surveys, 35% of whites compared with 20% of blacks reported episodes of heavy drinking at least once a month in the past year. Rates of alcohol use for Hispanic and Native American adolescents generally fall close to those of non-Hispanic whites (e.g., Barnes et al., 1997; Gil et al., 1998; O'Malley et al., 1998; Vega et al., 1993). Asian adolescents drink less than all other ethnic or racial groups (e.g., Bachman et al., 1991; Barnes et al., 1997; Windle et al., 1996). In the New York studies, when the researchers examined rates of marijuana use, they found signs that some of these differences by race and ethnicity may be diminishing. In 1978 and 1990, the researchers found that adolescent whites surpassed other ethnic groups in self-reported rates of marijuana use, but in the 1994 survey, blacks and Hispanics caught up to the whites (New York State Office of Alcoholism and Substance Abuse Services, 1996). In short, after a decade of decline, drug and alcohol abuse appear to be increasing again, especially among younger adolescents, and the increase appears to cut across all race and ethnic groups.

Over the past 20 years, gender roles have converged in numerous ways, and we might expect that male and female behaviors concerning rates of drug and alcohol use have also converged. Although there is some evidence that the percentage of females who use alcohol at some point in adolescence is converging with that of males, males still significantly outnumber females when it comes to drug abuse and heavy alcohol use (i.e., drinking five or more drinks at one sitting at least once a month), and these differences have remained stable across the past two decades. For example, in the national studies of high school seniors, the researchers found that in 1997, about 56.2% of the male and 48.9% of the female seniors reported using alcohol in the past 30 days (Johnston et al., 1998). When it comes to heavy drinking in the past 2 weeks, the proportions were 37.9% for males and 24.4% for females. The New York researchers found that the mean daily alcohol consumption for males was about twice that of females' consumption (1.26 vs. .62 drinks per day, respectively), and, not surprising, the mean number of days with alcohol-related problems for males was twice that of females (1.8 vs. .9) (Barnes et al., 1997). Thus, male adolescents drink more than females do, and they are more likely to bring stress into their families as a result of alcohol-related problems.

Family Socialization and Adolescent Substance Abuse

Numerous researchers have found that, regardless of family structure, several aspects of parental child-rearing practices influence adolescent drinking and drug use (for reviews, see Barnes, 1990; Hawkins et al., 1992). First, parents convey attitudes toward alcohol and drug use; these attitudes affect adolescent attitudes and their expectations about the effects of alcohol and drugs on mood, behavior, and health. Second, parents model patterns of alcohol and drug use that convey to children when, where, and how much alcohol is appropriate to consume. For example, some parents abstain from alcohol, some drink only on special occasions, others drink daily either at home or in a public place such as a tavern or bar, and some are alcoholics. Finally, parental supportiveness and the ways they supervise and reinforce their child's behavior during childhood and adolescence directly influence (a) whether adolescents become heavy alcohol or drug users and (b) their vulnerability to peer pressures to drink or use drugs. For example, Conger, Rueter, and Conger (1994) find that as economic pressures on a family increase, parents' behavior toward their children is likely to become more harsh and inconsistent. This kind of unsupportive parenting then makes substance abuse in an adolescent more likely (see also, Patterson et al., 1992).

Parents as Models

Social learning theorists propose that people are likely to imitate the behavior of those who have authority over them (e.g., Bandura & Walters, 1963). Deriving hypotheses from this theory, a number of researchers have proposed that parental attitudes toward alcohol and drugs, as well as their own patterns of consumption, have direct effects on the behavior of adolescents (e.g., Andrews, Hops, & Duncan, 1997; Chassin et al., 1993; Glynn, 1984; Koopmans & Boomsa, 1996). However, empirical research examining the direct effects of parental modeling on adolescent alcohol use has generated mixed results (see Barnes, 1990). Some have found effects (e.g., Pandina & Johnson, 1989); others have not (e.g., Barnes, Farrell, & Banerjee, 1994; Simons & Robertson, 1989). Recent research suggests that mothers' drinking behavior affects adolescents' drinking more than fathers' behavior (Chassin et al., 1993; Conger et al., 1994) and that adolescents are more likely to imitate parental drinking and drug use when the relationship between the parent and child is positive (e.g., Andrews et al., 1997). In our own research, we have found that heavy drinking by parents did not directly affect adolescent drinking, but it did have indirect effects through its impact on supportive parenting (Barnes, Reifman, Farrell, & Dintcheff, in press). Parents who drink heavily provide less support to their children, and the less support they provide, the more likely adolescents are to be heavy drinkers. Other researchers find evidence consistent with this model (e.g., Chassin et al., 1993; Conger et al.,

1994). Although researchers still are working to specify the conditions under which adolescents are most likely to follow their parents' example, the preponderance of evidence indicates that parental attitudes and modeling are factors that directly or indirectly influence adolescent drug and alcohol use.

Children of Alcoholics

An alcoholic parent not only models drinking behavior; he or she may create a stressful family environment that is adverse to meeting the developmental needs of children and adolescents (e.g., Chassin et al., 1993). This is particularly likely if the alcoholic parent also suffers from a psychiatric disorder, which occurs in approximately 37% of alcoholics (Zucker, Ellis, Bingham, & Fitzgerald, 1996). An alcoholic parent often abdicates the parental role and introduces stressful events into a family. Although family interaction may be subdued and instrumentally focused during "dry" periods, during the "wet" periods when the parent is drinking, emotions are high, parental conflict and episodes of violence are more likely, and family routines may be upended (Steinglass & Robertson, 1983).

Clinicians argue that these unpredictable cycles lead some children to take on parental responsibilities, such as household maintenance chores, bill paying, interfacing with service agencies, and caring for younger children. Other children in these circumstances take on tension management roles, such as scapegoat or clown, that help reduce the tension and conflict in the family system (e.g., Black, 1981; Fischer & Wampler, 1994). As a result of playing these roles, children in families of alcoholics learn a wide range of more or less adaptive "survival" strategies, including ignoring their own personal needs, denying their feelings, becoming overly responsible at home and in school, or getting into trouble to get attention. These theorists propose that, because of these survival strategies, children of alcoholics are likely to be depressed, to be anxious, to have low self-esteem, and to exhibit antisocial behavior.

Children of alcoholics also are more likely to drink and to become alcoholics themselves (Pollock, Schneider, Gabrielli, & Goodwin, 1987; Sher, Walitzer, Wood, & Brent, 1991). Studies of twins suggest that this effect is transmitted in part through modeling and in part through genetic inheritance (e.g., Koopmans & Boomsa, 1996). The personality characteristics that most often distinguish children of alcoholics are depression, anxiety, and impulsivity (e.g., Tweed & Ryff, 1991).

Recent research has attempted to identify the factors that make some children of alcoholics more resilient than others. Why do some children, even children in the same family, show different outcomes when growing up with an alcoholic parent? Research examining this question has focused on demographic characteristics of children and their families, biological and psychological characteristics of children, and the quality of the interpersonal relationship between the child and the nonalcoholic parent. In general, male children from low-income homes with few siblings are most at risk for problems (Roosa, Beals, Sandler, & Pillow, 1990). Children of heavy-drinking fathers in highly cohesive families show less emotional distress than children in families with low cohesion (Farrell et al., 1995). This latter finding is consistent with Wolin and his colleagues' theory that families who maintain rituals that reaffirm cohesion, such as celebrations of birthdays and holidays, can buffer the negative effects of an alcoholic parent on children (Wolin, Bennett, Noonan, & Teitelbaum, 1980).

Some research suggests that genetic factors play a part in the transfer of parental drinking patterns to children (e.g., Cloninger, Bohman, & Sigvardsson, 1981; Koopmans & Boomsa, 1996). Children of alcoholics or heavy drinkers may inherit a tolerance for the effects of alcohol that makes them more likely to become alcoholics or heavy drinkers themselves. In addition, they may inherit traits of temperament and cognitive functioning that make them more likely to have difficulties in adjusting to school and more prone to engage in delinquency and substance abuse. However, studies of twins raised apart suggest that genetic factors account for only a portion of the effects of parents on children, and family culture and patterns of socialization are of equal, if not more, importance (Barnes, 1990; Koopmans & Boomsa, 1996). Currently, researchers in the human genome project are attempting to map the function of more than 140,000 human genes. If these researchers discover more precise information about the genetic factors associated with heavy alcohol and drug abuse, theories of the genetic determinants of alcohol and drug use will receive more rigorous tests in the next decade.

Parental Support and Supervision

Beyond the effects of parental modeling and genetic inheritance, the socialization and developmental experiences of children in families from infancy onward affect their personalities and their relationships with their parents, which in turn affect their vulnerability to becoming heavy drinkers or drug abusers in adolescence (Barnes, 1990; Conger, 1997). As a number of theorists have proposed, and as researchers have consistently confirmed, supportive parenting is a critical factor influencing alcohol and drug use in adolescents (e.g., Barnes, 1990; Barnes & Farrell, 1992; Baumrind, 1990;

Steinberg, 1990; Wills, Mariani, & Filer, 1996). Loving, attentive, responsive parents develop strong emotional bonds with their children, and these bonds make children more responsive to parental expectations and less likely to be delinquent or rebellious in adolescence.

Family systems theorists suggest that parents who are too supportive in highly cohesive, "enmeshed" families may constrain adolescent development, leading to rebelliousness and problem behavior (e.g., Olson et al., 1983). There may be some support for this theory in small samples of clinically diagnosed adolescents; however, in studies of the general population, the more cohesion and support adolescents perceive in their families, the less likely they are to drink heavily, use drugs, or engage in other delinquent behavior (e.g., Farrell & Barnes, 1993). Open communication between parents and child, which is highly correlated with supportive parenting, is also found to reduce alcohol and drug use (Barnes & Farrell, 1992). On the other end of the parental support spectrum, adolescents who perceive that their parents are unresponsive to their feelings, ignore their achievements, do not help them with decision making, and do not spend time with them are more likely to rebel against conventional expectations, drink heavily, and use drugs.

Theorists have also proposed that parental controls and sanctions influence adolescent problem behavior and substance abuse (e.g., Baumrind, 1990; Rollins & Thomas, 1979; Steinberg, 1990). By "control," we mean overt attempts by parents to set limits on and punish adolescent misbehavior. In their review of research, Rollins and Thomas (1979) proposed that the effects of parental control are curvilinear; problem behaviors are more likely when control is either too low or too high. However, in part because the control construct has been inconsistently operationalized, empirical tests of the effects of control have yielded inconsistent results (Seydlitz, 1993). Attempts to control adolescent behavior have been operationalized as reasoning and explaining rules and punishments (inductive control), responding with anger and punishment when adolescents behave in unacceptable ways (coercive control), and knowing the whereabouts and the friends of adolescents (monitoring). In our own research, we found no evidence that inductive control affects adolescent substance abuse or delinquency (Barnes & Farrell, 1992). We found only a linear relationship between adolescent drinking and coercive control, and the effects are the opposite of what theory would predict. That is, we found that the more coercive control a parent practices, the more adolescents drink and use drugs. However, we also found that the more parents monitor a child's whereabouts and his or her friends, the less likely the adolescent is to use alcohol and drugs (Barnes & Farrell, 1992; Barnes et al., in press).

Peer Culture and Adolescent Substance Abuse

Whereas adolescents' access to alcohol comes mainly through their homes, access to drugs comes mainly through their informal peer network. Often, the dealer who sells the drugs or the person who supplies the alcohol is a classmate, friend, or neighbor. One of the strongest predictors of rates of adolescent drug and alcohol use is the adolescent's perception of drug and alcohol use by his or her closest friends. Although, in part, this correlation may be a result of selective perception or projection on the part of the adolescent, there is a great deal of evidence that peer models influence adolescent substance abuse (e.g., Bahr, Marcos, & Maughan, 1995; Barnes & Farrell, 1992; Barnes, Farrell, & Banerjee, 1994; Vega et al., 1993). Particularly as adolescents reach the ages of 16, 17, and 18, parental influence on alcohol and drug use matters less and the influence of friends matters more.

Although researchers agree that friends as well as parents play a part in adolescent drug and alcohol use, they are still sorting out how the effects of these two primary groups are interrelated. Some propose that peers and parents occupy separate domains in the lives of adolescents, and they each act as separate risk factors that have a cumulative impact on adolescents' alcohol and drug use (e.g., Hawkins et al., 1992). Others propose that families are the primary determinants of their child's behavior and that the friends that an adolescent chooses reflect attitudes and behaviors that he or she learns at home (e.g., Barnes, 1990; Elliott, Huizinga, & Ageton, 1985). Finally, some argue that drinking, drug use, and other delinquent behaviors are learned primarily from peers but parents can buffer or reduce these peer effects by careful supervision of their child and by maintaining a supportive relationship (e.g., Frauenglass, Routh, Pantin, & Mason, 1997; for a review, see Bogenschneider et al., 1998).

Recent longitudinal research suggests that the effects of supportive parenting, friends, and parental monitoring unfold sequentially (Barnes, Reifman, Farrell, Uhteg, & Dintcheff, 1994). In the early years of adolescence, roughly ages 12 to 15, supportive parenting has a direct effect on problem behaviors. The more supportive the parenting, the less adolescent alcohol and drug use. But as adolescents get older, supportive parenting has less of a direct effect and more of an indirect effect through its effect on parental monitoring. Supportive parenting affects the likelihood that adolescents will allow parental monitoring, which, in turn, leads to fewer problem behaviors, including drug and heavy alcohol use.

The vast majority of adolescents drink eventually, but they vary in how early they begin and in how rapidly they become regular or heavy users. In a recent analysis of the rates at which individual adolescents acquire problem drinking behaviors over a 6-year period (the slopes of their rates of acquisition), we found further confirmation of this sequential model linking parental support and monitoring. The level of parental support in year one influences the level of monitoring that adolescents allow, and this in turn influences the slope of the rate at which they acquire the pattern of heavy alcohol use over the subsequent 5 years (Barnes et al., in press).

Family Structure and
Adolescent Drug and Alcohol Use

Compared with the 1950s, today there is much greater diversity in the structure of families with adolescent children. The variations range from the 1950s ideal model, in which the father works while the mother stays home and cares for the children, to the dual-career parent model, the single-mother and single-father models, the cohabiting unmarried parents model, stepfamilies, and the gay and lesbian parents models. Each of these types of families has different kinds and degrees of stress when dealing with adolescent development. A recent comparison of adolescents in these different types of family structures reports that in comparison with adolescents in two-biological-parent families, those in single-father families and those in father-stepmother families are more than twice as likely to use drugs (Hoffman & Johnson, 1998). However, because most of the research on adolescent substance abuse to date has focused on comparisons of the two most common models, the single-mother and the two-parent families (usually grouping together the dual-worker and the traditional models), we limit our discussion to these two types of families.

Demographers estimate that at the turn of the 21st century, approximately one out of every two adolescents will have spent a portion of their childhood or adolescence in a single-mother home (Bumpass & Sweet, 1989). Reviews of studies done in the 1970s and 1980s indicate that adolescents growing up in single-mother families had more undesirable outcomes in the areas of academic achievement, conduct, psychological adjustment, self-esteem, and substance abuse (e.g., McLanahan & Sandefur, 1994; Wells & Rankin, 1991). However, recent meta-analyses of the effect sizes in these studies (Amato & Keith, 1991) show that across a wide range of outcomes, the differences between children in single-mother and in two-parent families are not large, and, while problematic outcomes may be somewhat more likely for adolescents in single-mother homes, the vast majority of these adolescents do as well as those in two-parent families. For example, McLanahan and Sandefur (1994), using the National Longitudinal Study of Youth data to examine how family structure affects idleness in young men in their late teens or early 20s, found that young men from single-mother homes are "more likely" to be idle (12% vs. 17%). However, these findings also mean that more than 80% of both types of young men are not idle. The relatively weak effects and the inconsistencies in findings led researchers in the 1990s to raise questions about why some adolescents in single-mother homes do fine while others do poorly (e.g., Farrell, Barnes, & Reifman, 1997; Furstenberg & Harris, 1993; McLanahan & Sandefur, 1994; Thomas, Farrell, & Barnes, 1996).

The Hazards of Single-Mother Families

There are several factors that may play a part in accounting for the relationship between family structure and adolescent behavior. First, because they are more likely to have lower incomes, single-mother families are more likely to live in poor neighborhoods (McLanahan & Sandefur, 1994). As adolescents in these neighborhoods become independent, they are more likely to encounter a deviant street culture where they observe drinking, drug use, prostitution, and other forms of delinquency and crime. The culture of the street then shapes their attitudes and behavior. A single mother may be less effective in monitoring an adolescent and controlling his or her exposure to this street culture than two parents would be. Second, single-parent families are often formed by separation and divorce. Parental conflict during the process of disengagement and after a divorce is a factor that may contribute to traumatic stress in families, which in turn may lead to neglecting the needs of children, rebellious behavior, and negative outcomes in adolescents (Amato & Rezac, 1994; Simons, Whitbeck, Beaman, & Conger, 1994; Wallerstein & Kelly, 1980). Third, divorce and low income in single-mother families are likely to lead to household moves that disrupt support networks for both the adolescent and the parent (McLanahan & Sandefur, 1994). Without support from neighbors, teachers, or extended family members, single parents may have more difficulty meeting the needs of an adolescent and providing supervision of him or her (Farrell, Barnes, & Fuller, 1997). Finally, a single parent caught between the demands of work and family life without the support of a spouse may experience role overload. Because of the overload of demands, the single parent may be less available to socialize the adolescent into appropriate behavior, provide supportive parenting, or monitor adolescent involvement with peers. Current researchers are exploring the relative importance of each of these factors, but it is premature to report the findings.

In our own recent research, we examined whether there are race and gender differences in the effects of single-mother families on adolescent alcohol and drug use and whether supportive parenting by nonresident fathers reduces the incidence of substance abuse in adolescents (Farrell, Barnes, & Fuller, 1997; Farrell, Barnes, & Reifman, 1997; Thomas et al., 1996). Comparing black and white adolescents raised in two-biological-parent families with those raised in single-mother families, we found that family structure affected alcohol and drug use in white males but not in black males or either group of females. Other researchers have found a similar pattern of differences by race: Among black adolescent males, family structure has negligible effects on adolescent behavior, but among white males, the effects are significant (e.g., Gil et al., 1998).

Not all children in single-mother families lack contact with their fathers, and supportive parenting by a nonresident father seems to buffer the effects of single-mother families on white males. White adolescent males in single-mother families who report that they receive emotional support and guidance from a nonresident father are no more likely to abuse alcohol or drugs than are those who live with two biological parents. On the other hand, the heaviest drinking and drug use by white males occurs in families of single mothers without supportive parenting from a nonresident father (Farrell, Barnes, & Fuller, 1997; Thomas et al., 1996).

As has already been discussed, black males use drugs and alcohol less than white males do, and black males with two parents drink and use drugs the least (Farrell, Barnes, & Fuller, 1997; Mason, Cauce, Gonzales, & Hiraga, 1994). Comparing males in these two-biological-parent families with those in single-mother families with and without father involvement, surprisingly, we find higher rates of drug and alcohol use when the nonresident father is involved (Thomas et al., 1996). On the other hand, sons of black single mothers without father involvement use drugs and alcohol no more than those with two biological parents do. Preliminary analyses of our data suggest that extended family support may be important as a buffer for black single-mother families (Farrell, Barnes, & Fuller, 1997). In their study of black single-mother families, Mason and his colleagues (Mason et al., 1994) found that highly supportive single mothers also buffered the effects of peer pressure to use alcohol and drugs. In general, these findings suggest that there are different types of single-mother families, and their effects on adolescent substance use depend on the support that mothers and adolescents receive from significant others.

Effects of Adolescent Substance Use on Families

The social mold perspective on families and children leads researchers to treat parental behavior as the "cause" of adolescent behavior. As we have seen, when it comes to explaining substance abuse, there is consistent evidence for this perspective from both cross-sectional and longitudinal studies. However, other sources play a role in adolescent substance abuse, including the norms of the adolescent's friendship groups and the sanctioning of substance abuse by the popular culture. Parents are sometimes as much the victims as they are the "cause" of their children's heavy drinking or drug use.

A number of studies have asked adolescents to report how frequently they have had conflicts with family members, friends, teachers, or legal authorities because of their drinking, and how often they have "passed out," skipped school, or engaged in delinquent activities. Heavy drinkers scored significantly higher than those who drink moderately or less. For example, in a study of a sample of more than 900 mostly white, suburban high school students and their parents, Windle (1996) reported that 23.6% of the adolescents were classified as problem drinkers, meaning they drank heavily and reported having five or more adverse events in the past 6 months as a consequence of their heavy drinking. Males were about twice as likely as females to fall into this category (17.3% of the males vs. 8.4% of the females). Both male and female problem drinkers were more likely than their classmates to use marijuana and other illicit drugs. Problem drinking for both males and females was associated with more stressful events in their lives, and for girls it was associated with more parental distress for their mothers. Thus, available evidence suggests that problem drinking by adolescents is a significant source of stress in families.

Implications

Stress, conflict, and negative affect in families can lead to adolescent substance use; once this substance use becomes heavy, it has consequences that can "pile up" stress in families. After these cycles reach the point where an adolescent becomes a problem drinker, they are very difficult to bring under control. However, our review has led to some conclusions about what parents can do to reduce the chances of heavy drinking and drug use by their adolescent children.

By the time adolescents are seniors in high school, alcohol use is widespread among their peers. Although light to moderate use does not directly lead to problematic outcomes for the adolescent or the family, it nevertheless can lead to heavy drinking and drug use, which can be very problematic. The earlier that an adolescent begins drinking, the greater the risks that he or she will become a heavy drinker and use drugs. Thus, if parents wish to reduce the chances of problem drinking and drug use in their children, it is important that they intervene early.

In their intervention, parents should take into account several factors. First, adolescents are influenced by their parents' attitudes toward alcohol and drugs as well as by their behavior. Beliefs, norms, and parental patterns of substance use that adolescents observe in their home affect their behavior. Second, how parents treat their children matters. The more responsive and supportive parents are to their children, and the more open the communication between them, the less likely adolescents are to become heavy drinkers and drug users. For families having difficulties in these areas, counseling or parent training programs can be helpful (e.g., Patterson et al., 1992; Roosa et al., 1990). Supportive parenting is particularly important in the pre-adolescent years; parental support in these years lays the foundation for the adolescent parent-child relationship. However, inductive reasoning as a control technique does not seem to affect adolescent behavior, and coercive punishment may actually backfire. The more coercive the punishment, the more likely the child is to use alcohol or drugs.

As adolescents mature, they are more influenced by peers, and the lifestyles of their friends have significant effects on the adolescent's drinking and drug use. Nevertheless, the more parents monitor the activities of the adolescent, the less likely they are to drink heavily or use drugs, even if their friends are using. In late adolescence, monitoring requires cooperation from the adolescent, and the extent to which an adolescent will allow monitoring depends on the degree of supportive parenting experienced in earlier periods of development.

Heavy drinking and drug use are more common among white males than among black males, and white males in single-mother families are particularly likely to use substances. However, supportive parenting by a nonresident father reduces the likelihood of heavy drinking or drug use in these white sons of single mothers. Black males in single-mother families are not affected in the same way as white males. In general, black males use drugs and alcohol less than white males do, and family structure has less of an impact on their rates of use. This relative resilience of black males in the face of risk factors is consistent with other research comparing race and ethnic groups (e.g., Vega et al., 1993). The fact that race and ethnic groups may be different in their susceptibility to drug and alcohol use suggests that we should be careful about overgeneralizing. What works in preventing substance abuse for one group may not work for another.

DISCUSSION QUESTIONS

1. What factors do you think are the strongest predictors of adolescent substance abuse? Justify your response.

2. Why are adolescents considered at higher risk for substance abuse than other age groups?

3. In what ways is the relationship between adolescent substance abuse and family process bidirectional?

4. What are the "pros" and "cons" of removing adolescents from their families for treatment of substance abuse?

5. Based on the research reviewed in this chapter, what are the implications for designing a prevention program for adolescents at risk for substance abuse?

SUGGESTED READINGS

Black, C. (1981). *It will never happen to me: Children of alcoholics as youngsters, adolescents, adults.* New York: Ballantine.

Collins, R. L., Leonard, K. E., & Searles, J. S. (1990). *Alcohol and the family: Research and clinical perspectives.* New York: Guilford.

Glynn, T. J. (1984). Adolescent drug use and family environment: A review. *Journal of Drug Issues, 2,* 271-295.

Kandel, D. B., & Yamaguchi, K. (1993). From beer to crack: Developmental patterns of drug involvement. *American Journal of Public Health, 83,* 851-855.

O'Malley, P. M., Johnston, L. D., & Bachman, J. G. (1998). Alcohol use among adolescents. *Alcohol Health & Research World, 22,* 85-94.

REFERENCES

Amato, P. R., & Keith, B. (1991). Parental divorce and the well-being of children: A meta-analysis. *Psychological Bulletin, 110,* 26-46.

Amato, P. R., & Rezac, S. J. (1994). Contact with nonresident parents, interparental conflict, and children's behavior. *Journal of Family Issues, 15,* 191-207.

Ambert, A. (1992). *The effects of children on parents.* New York: Haworth.

Andrews, J. A., Hops, H., & Duncan, S. C. (1997). Adolescent modeling of parent substance use: The moderating effect of the relationship with the parent. *Journal of Family Psychology, 11,* 259-270.

Bachman, J. G., Wallace, J. M., O'Malley, P. M., Johnston, L. D., Kurth, C. L., & Neighbors, H. W. (1991). Racial/ethnic differences in smoking, drinking, and illicit drug use among American high school seniors, 1976-89. *American Journal of Public Health, 81*(3), 372-377.

Bahr, S. J., Marcos, A. C., & Maughan, S. L. (1995). Family, educational, and peer influences on the alcohol use of female and male adolescents. *Journal of Studies on Alcohol, 56*(4), 457-468.

Bandura, A., & Walters, R. H. (1963). *Social learning and personality development.* New York: Holt, Rinehart & Winston.

Barnes, G. M. (1990). Impact of the family on adolescent drinking patterns. In R. L. Collins, K. E. Leonard, & J. S. Searles (Eds.), *Alcohol and the family: Research and clinical perspectives* (pp. 137-161). New York: Guilford.

Barnes, G. M., & Farrell, M. P. (1992). Parental support and control as predictors of adolescent drinking, delinquency, and related problem behaviors. *Journal of Marriage and the Family, 54,* 763-776.

Barnes, G. M., Farrell, M. P., & Banerjee, S. (1994). Family influences on alcohol and other problem behaviors among black and white adolescents in a general population sample. *Journal of Research on Adolescence, 4,* 183- 201.

Barnes, G. M., Reifman, A. S., Farrell, M. P., & Dintcheff, B. A. (in press). The effects of parenting on the development of adolescent alcohol misuse: A six-wave latent growth model. *Journal of Marriage and the Family.*

Barnes, G. M., Reifman, A. S., Farrell, M. P., Uhteg, L., & Dintcheff, B. A. (1994). Longitudinal effects of parenting on alcohol misuse among adolescents. *Alcoholism: Clinical and Experimental Research, 18,* 507.

Barnes, G. M., Welte, J. W., Hoffman, J. H., & Dintcheff, B. A. (1997). Changes in alcohol use and alcohol-related problems among 7th to 12th grade students in New York State, 1983-1994. *Alcoholism: Clinical and Experimental Research, 21,* 916-922.

Baumrind, D. (1990). Effective parenting during the early adolescent transition. In P. A. Cowan & M. Hetherington (Eds.), *Family transition* (pp. 111-164). Hillsdale, NJ: Lawrence Erlbaum.

Berrera, M., Jr., & Li, S. A. (1996). The relation of family support to adolescents' psychological distress and behavior problems. In G. Pierce, B. Sarason, & I. G. Sarason (Eds.), *Handbook of social support and the family* (pp. 313-343). New York: Plenum.

Black, C. (1981). *It will never happen to me: Children of alcoholics as youngsters, adolescents, adults.* New York: Ballantine.

Bogenschneider, K., Wu, M., Raffaelli, M., & Tsay, J. C. (1998). "Other teens drink, but not my kid": Does parental awareness of adolescent alcohol use protect adolescents from risky consequences? *Journal of Marriage and the Family, 60,* 356-373.

Bumpass, L. L., & Sweet, J. A. (1989). Children's experience in single-parent families: Implications of cohabitation and marital transitions. *Family Planning Perspectives, 21,* 256-260.

Chassin, L., Pillow, D. R., Curran, P., Molina, B. S., & Berrera, M., Jr. (1993). Relation of parental alcoholism to early adolescent substance use: A test of three mediating mechanisms. *Journal of Abnormal Psychology, 102,* 3-19.

Clark, D. B., Lesnick, L., & Hegedus, A. M. (1997). Traumas and other adverse life events in adolescents with alcohol abuse and dependence. *Journal of the American Academy of Child and Adolescent Psychiatry, 36,* 1744-1752.

Cloninger, C. R., Bohman, M., & Sigvardsson, S. (1981). Inheritance of alcohol abuse: Cross-fostering of adopted men. *Archives of General Psychiatry, 38,* 861-868.

Conger, R. D. (1997). The social context of substance abuse: A developmental perspective. In E. B. Robertson, S. Sloboda, G. M. Boyd, L. Beatty, & N. J. Kozel (Eds.), *Rural substance abuse: State of knowledge and issues* (NIDA Research Monograph No. 168, pp. 6-36). Rockville, MD: National Institutes of Health.

Conger, R. D., & Elder, G. H., Jr. (1994). *Families in troubled times: Adapting to change in rural America.* Hawthorne, NY: Aldine.

Conger, R., Rueter, M., & Conger, K. J. (1994). The family context of adolescent vulnerability and resilience to alcohol use and abuse. *Sociological Studies of Children, 6,* 55-86.

Elliott, D. S., Huizinga, D., & Ageton, S. S. (1985). *Explaining delinquency and drug use.* Beverly Hills, CA: Sage.

Elliott, D. S., Huizinga, D., & Menard, S. (1989). *Multiple problem youth: Delinquency, substance use, and mental health problems.* New York: Springer-Verlag.

Farrell, M. P., & Barnes, G. M. (1993). Social systems and social support: Effects of family cohesion and adaptability on parent and child functioning. *Journal of Marriage and the Family, 55,* 119-132.

Farrell, M. P., Barnes, G. M., & Banerjee, S. (1995). Family cohesion as a buffer against the effects of problem-drinking fathers on psychological distress, deviant behavior, and heavy drinking in adolescents. *Journal of Health and Social Behavior, 36,* 377-385.

Farrell, M. P., Barnes, G. M., & Fuller, P. (1997, November). *Factors contributing to well-functioning single mother families: Effects of race, father involvement, and extended family support on delinquency, illicit drug use, and heavy drinking in adolescents.* Paper presented at the 59th annual conference of the National Council on Family Relations, Arlington, VA.

Farrell, M. P., Barnes, G. M., & Reifman, A. (1997, August). *When single mother families work well: Effects of race, gender, and involvement of non-resident fathers on growth curves of adolescent delinquency, illicit drug use, and heavy drinking.* Poster presented at the annual meeting of the American Sociological Association, Toronto, Canada.

Farrell, M. P., & Rosenberg, S. D. (1981). *Men at midlife.* Boston: Auburn House.

Farrell, M. P., Rosenberg, S. D., & Rosenberg, H. J. (1993). Changing texts of male identity from early to late middle age. In J. Demick, K. Bursik, & R. Dibiase (Eds.), *Parental development* (pp. 203-224). Hillsdale, NJ: Lawrence Erlbaum.

Fischer, J. L., & Wampler, R. S. (1994). Abusive drinking in young adults: Personality type and family roles as moderators of family-of-origin influences. *Journal of Marriage and the Family, 56,* 469-479.

Frauenglass, S., Routh, D. K., Pantin, H. M., & Mason, C. A. (1997). Family support decreases influence of deviant peers on Hispanic adolescents' substance use. *Journal of Clinical Child Psychology, 26*(1), 15-23.

Furstenberg, F. F., Jr., & Harris, K. M. (1993). When and why fathers matter: Impacts of father involvement on the children of adolescent mothers. In R. I. Lerman & T. J. Ooms (Eds.), *Young unwed fathers' changing roles and emerging policies* (pp. 117-138). Philadelphia: Temple University Press.

Gil, A. G., Vega, W. A., & Biafora, F. (1998). Temporal influences of family structure and family risk factors on drug use initiation in a multiethnic sample of adolescent boys. *Journal of Youth and Adolescence, 27,* 373-394.

Glynn, T. J. (1984). Adolescent drug use and family environment: A review. *Journal of Drug Issues, 2,* 271-295.

Hansen, W. B., & O'Malley, P. M. (1996). Drug use. In R. J. DiClemente, W. B. Hansen, & L. E. Ponton (Eds.), *Handbook of adolescent health risk behavior* (pp. 161-192). New York: Plenum.

Hawkins, J. D., Catalano, R. E., & Miller, J. Y. (1992). Risk and protective factors for alcohol and other drug problems in adolescence and early adulthood: Implications for substance abuse prevention. *Psychological Bulletin, 112,* 64-105.

Hoffman, J. P., & Johnson, R. A. (1998). A national portrait of family structure and adolescent drug use. *Journal of Marriage and the Family, 60,* 633-645.

Jessor, R., Donovan, J. E., & Costa, F. M. (1991). *Beyond adolescence: Problem behavior and young adult development.* New York: Cambridge University Press.

Johnson, V., & Pandina, R. J. (1993). A longitudinal examination of the relationship among stress, coping strategies, and problems associated with alcohol abuse. *Alcohol: Clinical & Experimental Research, 17,* 696-702.

Johnston, L. D., Bachman, J. G., & O'Malley, P. M. (1998). *National survey results on drug use from the Monitoring the Future Study, 1975-1997: Vol. 1. Secondary school students* (DHHS Publication No. NIH 98-4345). Rockville, MD: National Institute on Drug Abuse.

Kandel, D. B., & Yamaguchi, K. (1993). From beer to crack: Developmental patterns of drug involvement. *American Journal of Public Health, 83,* 851-855.

Koopmans, J., & Boomsa, D. I. (1996). Familial resemblance in alcohol use: Genetic or cultural transmission? *Journal of Studies on Alcohol, 57,* 19-28.

Mason, C. A., Cauce, A. M., Gonzales, N., & Hiraga, Y. (1994). Adolescent problem behavior: The effect of peers and the moderating role of father absence and mother-child relationship. *American Journal of Community Psychology, 22,* 723-744.

McLanahan, S., & Sandefur, G. D. (1994). *Growing up with a single parent: What hurts, what helps?* Cambridge, MA: Harvard University Press.

Moffit, T. E. (1993). Adolescence-limited and life course persistent antisocial behavior: A developmental taxonomy. *Psychological Review, 100,* 674-701.

New York State Office of Alcoholism and Substance Abuse Services. (1996). *The New York State school survey: Alcohol and other drug use findings, 5th grade through 12th grade, 1994—Statewide youth survey report.* New York: Author.

Olson, D. H., McCubbin, H. I., Barnes, H., Larsen, A., Muxen, M., & Wilson, M. (1983). *Families: What makes them work.* Beverly Hills, CA: Sage.

O'Malley, P. M., Johnston, L. D., & Bachman, J. G. (1998). Alcohol use among adolescents. *Alcohol Health & Research World, 22,* 85-94.

Palkovitz, R. J. (1996). Parenting as a generator of adult development: Conceptual issues and implications. *Journal of Social and Personal Relationships, 13,* 571-592.

Pandina, R. J., & Johnson, V. (1989). Familial drinking history as a predictor of alcohol and drug consumption among adolescent children. *Journal of Studies of Alcohol, 30,* 245-253.

Patterson, G. R., Reid, J. B., & Dishion, T. J. (1992). *Antisocial boys.* Eugene, OR: Castalia.

Pollock, V. E., Schneider, L. S., Gabrielli, W. F., & Goodwin, D. W. (1987). Sex of parent and offspring in the transmission of alcoholism: A meta-analysis. *Journal of Nervous and Mental Disease, 175,* 668-673.

Rollins, B. C., & Thomas, D. L. (1979). Parental support, power, and control techniques in the socialization of children. In W. R. Burr, R. Hill, F. I. Nye, & I. L. Reiss (Eds.), *Contemporary theories about the family* (Vol. 1, pp. 317-364). New York: Free Press.

Roosa, M. W., Beals, J., Sandler, I. N., & Pillow, D. R. (1990). The role of risk and protective factors in predicting symptomatology in adolescent self- identified children of alcoholic parents. *American Journal of Community Psychology, 18,* 725-741.

Seydlitz, R. (1993). Complexity in the relationship among direct and indirect parental controls and delinquency. *Youth and Society, 24,* 243-275.

Sher, K. J., Walitzer, K., Wood, P. K., & Brent, E. E. (1991). Characteristics of children of alcoholics: Putative risk factors, substance use and abuse, and psychopathology. *Journal of Abnormal Psychology, 100,* 427-448.

Simons, R. L., & Robertson, J. F. (1989). The impact of parenting factors, deviant peers, and coping style upon adolescent drug use. *Family Relations, 38,* 273-281.

Simons, R. L., Whitbeck, L. B., Beaman, J., & Conger, R. D. (1994). The impact of mother's parenting, involvement by nonresidential fathers, and parental conflict on the adjustment of adolescent children. *Journal of Marriage and the Family, 56,* 356-374.

Steinberg, L. (1990). Autonomy, conflict, and harmony in the family relationship. In S. S. Feldman & G. R. Elliot (Eds.), *At the threshold: The developing adolescent* (pp. 259-276). Cambridge, MA: Harvard University Press.

Steinglass, P., & Robertson, A. (1983). The alcoholic family. In B. Kissin & H. Begleiter (Eds.), *The pathogenesis of alcoholism: Psychosocial factors* (pp. 243-307). New York: Plenum.

Thomas, G., Farrell, M. P., & Barnes, G. M. (1996). The effects of single-mother families and nonresident fathers on delinquency and substance abuse in black and white adolescents. *Journal of Marriage and the Family, 58,* 884-894.

Tweed, S., & Ryff, C. (1991). Adult children of alcoholics: Profiles of wellness amidst distress. *Journal of Studies on Alcohol, 52,* 133-141.

Vega, W. A., Zimmerman, R. S., Warheir, G. J., Apospori, E., & Gil, A. G. (1993). Risk factors for early adolescent drug use in four ethnic and racial groups. *American Journal of Public Health, 83,* 185-189.

Wallerstein, J. D., & Kelly, J. B. (1980). *Surviving the breakup: How children and parents cope with divorce.* New York: Basic Books.

Wells, L. E., & Rankin, J. H. (1991). Families and delinquency: A meta-analysis of the impact of broken homes. *Social Problems, 38,* 71-93.

Wills, T. A., Mariani, J., & Filer, M. (1996). The role of family and peer relationships in adolescent substance use. In G. Pierce, B. Sarason, & I. G. Sarason (Eds.), *Handbook of social support and the family* (pp. 521-549). New York: Plenum.

Wills, T. A., Vaccaro, D., & McNamara, G. (1992). The role of life events, family support, and competence in adolescent substance use: A test of vulnerability and protective factors. *American Journal of Community Psychology, 20,* 349-375.

Windle, M. (1996). An alcohol involvement typology for adolescents: Convergent validity and longitudinal stability. *Journal of Studies of Alcohol, 57,* 627-637.

Windle, M., Shope, J. T., & Bukstein, O. (1996). Alcohol use. In R. J. DiClemente, W. B. Hansen, & L. E. Ponton (Eds.), *Handbook of adolescent health risk behavior* (pp. 115-159). New York: Plenum.

Wolin, S. J., Bennett, L. A., Noonan, D. L., & Teitelbaum, M. A. (1980). Disrupted family rituals: A factor in the intergenerational transmission of alcoholism. *Journal of Studies on Alcohol, 41,* 199-214.

Zucker, R. A., Ellis, D. A., Bingham, C. R., & Fitzgerald, H. E. (1996). The development of alcoholic subtypes: Risk variation among alcoholic families during the early childhood years. *Alcohol Health & Research World, 20,* 46-54.

10

Mental Illness and Families

STEPHEN M. GAVAZZI
ANGIE M. SCHOCK

This chapter focuses on ways that families are affected by the stressors associated with the development of major mental disorders in one or more family members. Hence, a major goal of this chapter is to incorporate a family-oriented perspective regarding mental disorders. This is in contrast to an enormous and well-established body of research on individuals coping with mental disorders.

A family-oriented perspective on major mental disorders focuses on the entire family as the unit of analysis, including assessment, treatment, and research. By adopting a family system perspective, information is gained about all family members—that is, how they interact as a system in coping with one or more of their members suffering from a mental disorder. From a systems perspective, questions regarding assessment, treatment, and research are reformulated within a family system framework (i.e., "What do interaction patterns look like in families that contain a member or members suffering from a mental disorder?" "How do we help such families?" and "What is the effect of the mental disorder and/or its treatment on this family?").

Following a demographic and historical overview of mental disorders, we attempt to document the progress that has been made in such areas as (a) understanding the impact of individual and family life-cycle issues, (b) shifting the focus toward family strengths, (c) combining genetic and family environmental factors, and (d) the role of consumer-driven and grassroots organizations and advocacy initiatives.

229

Epidemiology of Mental Illness

Percentage of the U.S. Population

The National Institute of Mental Health (NIMH) Epidemiological Catchment Area (ECA) study (Reiger, Burke, & Burke, 1990) and more recently the National Comorbidity Survey (NCS) (Kessler et al., 1994) have supplied gross estimates of the prevalence of mental disorders in the U.S. population. According to the NCS, which interviewed more than 8,000 people between the ages of 15 and 54, nearly half of all respondents (44.2%) experienced a psychiatric disorder at least once in their life (Kessler et al., 1994), and 29% indicated having had experienced a mental disorder within the past year. For youth, mean prevalence rates for preschoolers, preadolescents, and adolescents were approximated to be 12%, 15%, and 18%, respectively (NIMH, 1991; Roberts, Attkisson, & Rosenblatt, 1998).

Sex Differences

There appear to be several gender differences in the vulnerability to mental illnesses. For example, the NCS found that women showed higher prevalence rates for affective disorders and anxiety disorders, whereas men showed high rates for substance abuse (Kessler et al., 1994) and antisocial personality disorders (Reiger et al., 1988). However, because men are more likely to self-medicate with alcohol and illicit drugs as a form of coping with psychological stress, it has been suggested that the rates of depression may actually be similar for males and females (Kessler et al., 1994).

In addition, women are more likely to use the health care system to treat distress and dysfunction (Glied & Kofman, 1995), and they are also more likely to use primary care providers and outpatient services. In contrast, men seek treatment through specialists and inpatient care. Also, there seems to be an interaction between sex and marital status; married women and unmarried men (single, widowed, or divorced) are more likely to experience mental disorders than single women (single, widowed, or divorced) and married men (Balcom & Healey, 1990; Gove, 1972).

It should be noted that the terminology and theoretical frameworks used by professionals to describe individual and family functioning often pathologize the relational styles and coping strategies of women (Bograd, 1990). Furthermore, it is important to note that the stigma of mental illness may be greater for men than for women, and thus men and women report, seek, and react to mental illness in different ways.

Age

Results of the NCS suggest that persons between 25 and 34 years of age have the highest rate of mental illness, with prevalence declining at later ages (Kessler et al., 1994). However, between 15% and 25% of the elderly suffer from a mental disorder (Cross-National Collaborative Group, 1992; Robins & Reiger, 1991; Roybal, 1984), and there is some evidence to suggest that the total number of physical and psychological complaints increases with advanced age (Brody & Kleban, 1983; Watson & Wright, 1984). For example, mental illness rates among individuals in nursing homes may approximate 90% (Smyer, Shea, & Streit, 1994).

One possible conclusion is that nursing homes are being used as a "dumping ground" for elderly family members who display psychiatric symptomology, thereby greatly inflating the rate of mental disorders among nursing home residents. But it is also possible that a significant portion of mental disturbances in older people goes undetected in the general population (emphasizing the need for epidemiological efforts that would help clarify these conflicting data).

Because psychiatric impairment of youth has only recently been acknowledged (Mash & Barkley, 1996), mental illness among children and adolescents is a relatively new area of study. Reports indicate that rates of serious emotional disturbances among children and adolescents are between 9% and 13% (Friedman, 1996), suggesting that nearly 75 million children in the United States have a mental disorder. In addition, rates are thought to differ among different age cohorts (preschoolers, preadolescents, and adolescents) (Roberts et al., 1998).

Ethnicity and Socioeconomic Status

Studies have consistently shown that almost all mental disorders decline with increased education and income (Bruce, Takeuchi, & Leaf, 1991; Canino et al., 1987; Robins & Reiger, 1991). However, socioeconomic status (SES) is more strongly related to anxiety disorders than affective disorders. Specifically, the prevalence of anxiety disorders significantly increases with decreasing income levels, yet this negative relationship was not found between rates for affective disorders and income. Hence, the lack of resources among less financially advantaged individuals may contribute to increased experiences of apprehension and agitation that are associated with anxiety disorders. In contrast, Bruce et al. (1991) found that individuals with incomes below the federal poverty level showed increased risk for a number of mental disorders.

Etiology

It is difficult to discuss the etiology (i.e., the study of the causes or origins) of mental disorders without adopting a family-oriented perspective, because all family members are a part of the system that may contribute to an individual's mental illness. Moreover, at minimum, it is necessary to involve at least one parent (mother, father, or both) in understanding individual psychopathology because even molecular, genetic-based research studies have at their core the implication of family heritage. Thus, most studies of the etiology of mental disorders focus on the relationship between the development of mental disorders and selected behaviors occurring inside the family system.

Interestingly, family experiences related to coping with a mental illness have changed dramatically over the past several decades, and this historical evolution is largely related to how family members are viewed as contributing to the onset of a disorder. According to Marsh (1998), this evolution can be grouped into three distinct phases. First, during the "institutional era" prior to World War II, the majority of mentally ill patients resided in institutions and were isolated from family; thus, little attention was given to the family's etiological role. The second phase, which lasted into the mid-1980s, was characterized by the deinstitutionalization of the mentally ill and often resulted in their returning to live with their families. Concurrent with this residential shift, professionals and the larger society began to shift the responsibility for the development of mental illness (often characterized as outright blame) onto families. More recently, however, a third phase has emerged in which families are actively involved with professionals in helping to ameliorate the impact of mental illness within the family. In this approach, there is a decided emphasis placed on not holding the family accountable for the onset of the family member's illness; instead, the disorder is portrayed as more likely a result of a combination of genetic factors and environmental influences (Rende & Plomin, 1993).

Much of our understanding of family stress and coping responses to mental disorders evolved from research conducted by family therapists on families that contained a member who had a major mental disorder—usually schizophrenia (Broderick & Schrader, 1981; Hoffman, 1981; Nichols & Schwartz, 1991). Much of this early research focused on the mother's role, usually in terms of how her illness may have contributed to her offspring's dysfunction.

Caplan and Hall-McCorquodale (1985), in a review of the literature, found that more than 70 forms of child psychopathology were attributed to mothers; none were attributed to fathers.

Research, however, has gradually expanded to investigate the impact of fathers (Phares & Compas, 1992), and the association between marital functioning and the development of psychopathology within the family (Davila & Bradbury, 1998; Phares & Compas, 1992). This trend reflects the growing emphasis placed on exploring the important link between family interactional patterns—including family-based stressors, family support, and relationship quality in the family—and the etiology of mental disorders.

Researchers who have focused on family stressors and mental illness have found interrelationships between interparental and parent-child conflict, maternal physical and mental health, divorce, parental death, and typical, everyday stressors (Compas, 1987; Forehand, Biggar, & Kotchick, 1998; Weller, Weller, Fristad, & Bowes, 1991). For example, Forehand and colleagues (1998) reported that in their sample of 285 families of adolescents (ages 11-15), more than half of the mothers reported experiencing two or more family stressors, and adolescents from those families with multiple stressors showed more depressive symptoms 6 years later compared with adolescents from less stressful family environments.

Several studies involving family support suggest that family supportive behaviors are related to the mental health of children and adolescents (Cole & McPherson, 1993; Garrison, Jackson, Marsteller, McKeown, & Addy, 1990). For instance, Sheeber, Hops, Alpert, Davis, and Andrews (1997) found that less supportive family environments and greater family conflict were associated with adolescent depressive symptomology. Similar results have been found when general family relationship quality is examined (Hops, Lewinsohn, Andrews, & Roberts, 1990; Puig-Antich et al., 1993). For example, depressed adolescents report poorer quality relationships with parents and siblings (Puig-Antich et al., 1993).

More recently, research and therapy efforts have been advanced through a focus on communication patterns such as "communication deviance" and "expressed emotion." Communication deviance (CD) refers to dysfunctional patterns of communication displayed by parents with schizophrenic sons or daughters. Such dysfunctional interaction patterns are thought to be of two basic types: "fragmented" (when family communications are described in ways such as erratic, disruptive, and awkward) and "amorphous" (when family communications are labeled in ways such as vague, confused, and intrusive) communications (Singer & Wynne, 1963, 1965a, 1965b). In a recent review, Miklowitz and Stackman (1992) reported that more than a dozen studies have found that higher levels of CD are more prevalent among parents of schizophrenics compared with parents of nonschizophrenic children. Specifically, children of parents who do not communicate in clear fashion during family discussions are at a greater risk for developing schizophrenia later in life.

The work on expressed emotion (EE), originating from the efforts of a British research team (cf. Brown, Birley, & Wing, 1972; Brown, Monck, Carstairs, & Wing, 1962), has been very influential in providing a family-oriented perspective on mental disorders. EE is a concept that has been used to describe (a) the level of emotional (over)involvement between family members and (b) the degree to which families display critical comments about the family member who has a mental disorder (Vaughn & Leff, 1976a, 1976b).

Although by definition the EE construct involves family members' reactions to a mentally ill family member, more recent work suggests that EE should be considered as reflecting a bidirectional process (Kavanagh, 1992; Miklowitz, 1995; Scazufca & Kuipers, 1998). In other words, critical and overprotective attitudes may, in fact, represent the way in which a family member is coping with the stress and burden of the mental illness rather than causing the disorder. In addition, this form of family response must be considered in light of the patient's behaviors (King, 1998). For instance, in one study of interactions between family members, it was found that negative communication exchanges were just as likely to be initiated by the patient as by the parents (Hahlweg et al., 1989).

Some researchers have attempted to gain a more complete understanding of exactly why EE is associated with psychiatric relapse (Barrowclough, Johnston, & Tarrier, 1994; Brewin, MacCarthy, Duda, & Vaughn, 1991; Hooley, 1998; Hooley & Licht, 1997). In other words, what is the *process* by which high levels of EE lead to a greater likelihood of relapse? It is thought that high-EE parents and spouses tend to make internal, stable, controllable attributions about the abnormal behavior of a mentally ill family member, whereas low-EE parents and spouses perceive the individual's behavior to be out of his or her control and a product of the illness (Hooley, Orley, & Teasdale, 1986). In other words, high-EE relatives tend to believe that the ill family member is responsible for and able to control problem behaviors caused by the illness.

One implication, therefore, would call for the education of family members regarding the severity and origin of the actual symptoms of a particular disorder in order to decrease family EE levels and thus improve the chances of recovery for mentally ill individuals. The recognition that abnormal behaviors are distinct from the individual's personality and largely out of that person's control would increase the possibility that family members would act in a less critical fashion toward the patient (Fristad, Gavazzi, & Soldano, 1999). As a result, educating family members about mental illness is thought to be a highly effective intervention strategy for changing family relationships.

Assessment

Understanding the impact of mental disorders requires that professionals begin any intervention with a thorough assessment of both the strengths and limitations of families. Specifically, mental health professionals must have a reliable and valid understanding of what family members have (and do not have) at their disposal in terms of coping with and adapting to a member that is mentally ill.

One way to assess these strengths and limitations is by focusing on the stressors facing the family at any given point in time. These stressors are often described as "burdens" associated with having a family member suffering from a mental disorder. The burdens faced by family members have been characterized as being *subjective* and *objective* (Hoenig & Hamilton, 1966). Subjective burdens generally have to do with perceptions about the illness, whereas objective burdens usually center on observable and countable stressors related to mental disorders (Bailey & Garralda, 1987; Maurin & Boyd, 1990). Objective burdens usually are measured in terms of the economic hardships faced by families—often calculated by a family's outright payment or copayment for medical expenses, as well as by lost wages suffered as a result of having to provide functional assistance to the mentally ill family member. Many other family efforts regarding the care and treatment of members (e.g., providing transportation, food, clothing, payment of insurance) should also be calculated into objective burdens.

The argument has been made that all family activities related to helping a family member with a mental disorder should be seen not as burdens but, rather, as "resource contributions" (i.e., viewing families as one of many service providers in the mental health delivery system) (Franks, 1990). However, this reframing of families as resource providers may be counterproductive if it leads to policy-making decisions that increase the objective and subjective burdens experienced by families (Hatfield, 1987; Lefley, 1989).

Because families provide many resources to mentally ill relatives, there has been a movement to increase the availability of services to both the patient and the family. "Family-friendly" services, however, have been criticized by both researchers and practitioners. These criticisms include (a) the lack of family involvement in treatment planning, (b) the unavailability of professionals and specific programs for families, and (c) the inadequate handling of emergency situations (Marsh, 1998).

One of the most severe subjective burdens on the family members is the stigma attached to mental disorders. The negative public perceptions of mental disorders are heightened by the media's continued propagation of inaccurate and stereotypical descriptions of individuals with mental disorders (Flynn, 1987). For example, in a recent book, *Media Madness: Public Images of Mental Illness,* Wahl (1995) notes that mental illness is the most commonly cited disability portrayed in the contemporary media.

Psychological burdens related to the stigma of mental disorders include lower self-esteem levels, reduced social contacts, job loss, and family relationship difficulties (Fuchs, 1986; Leete, 1987; Mittleman, 1985; Wahl & Harman, 1989). In addition, individuals with mental disorders and their families must interact with a mental health system that is organized in ways that are often not conducive to proper and efficient care delivery (Hatfield, 1987; Meyerson & Herman, 1987). This is more true in the case of a family member with a chronic mental disorder. Family members must also interact with mental health professionals who may hold negative attitudes about both individuals with mental disorders and their families (Minkoff, 1987; Mirabi, Weinman, Magnetti, & Keppler, 1985; Morrison, 1979).

It has been argued that research on family burden has provided only half of the picture; that is, family *strengths* have been neglected (Doornbos, 1996; Hawley & DeHaan, 1996; Walsh, 1996). The term *resiliency* is used in the family literature on psychopathology to characterize the strengths that a family develops during the course of coping with a mental illness. For example, in a recent nationwide study, Marsh and colleagues (1996) asked 131 family members of patients with a serious mental illness to respond to a set of open-ended questions concerning the development of personal, family, and patient resilience. Results showed that 99.2%, 87.8%, and 75.6% of the respondents, respectively, reported the presence of some form of personal, family, and patient resilience. Examples of resiliency dimensions included family support, family bonding, insight and caregiving competencies, and gratification through advocacy initiatives for constructive changes in the mental health system. Thus, through the acquisition of both coping strategies and support networks, family members often grow and change in very positive ways as a result of a family member's mental illness (Goldberg-Arnold, Fristad, & Gavazzi, 1999).

Theoretical Perspectives and Summary of Research Findings

According to Hahlweg and Goldstein (1987), much of the current family-oriented research on mental disorders follows the "vulnerability-stress model" (also referred to as the "diathesis-stress model"), originally developed by Rosenthal (1970) and subsequently advanced by Zubin and Spring (1977).

> According to this model, a predisposition to a disorder, such as schizophrenia, is inherited and forms the basis for various indices of vulnerability to the disorder. This vulnerability is modified by all life events that increase or decrease the likelihood that a major psychiatric disorder, such as schizophrenia, will emerge in early adulthood. The stress-vulnerability model is also applicable to the post-onset stage of psychiatric disorder because vulnerability continues to be modified in association with variations in remission from the acute phase of the disorder, and this vulnerability interacts with various intercurrent life events, within and outside of the family, to modify the risk for subsequent episodes of the disorder. (Hahlweg & Goldstein, 1987, p. 2)

Studies using a family-oriented perspective on mental disorders are organized into three categories. The first category includes studies that have examined how the presence of a mental disorder in a parent puts his or her offspring at risk of also developing a mental disorder (genetic linkage research). The second category reviews studies that assess the relationship between various family environmental factors and the subsequent mental health status of family members. Finally, the third category examines those studies that attempt to combine aspects of both genetic linkage and family context in the development of mental disorders.

Genetic Linkage Research

Genetic linkage research usually explores the relationship between the presence of a mental disorder in one family member and the concurrent or eventual manifestation of mental illness in other family members. Generally, two types of study designs have been used: The "top-down" design involves studying the children of mentally ill adults, and the "bottom-up" design looks at the adult relatives of children with mental disorders (Birmaher et al., 1996; Eley, in press). Although these approaches are useful in examining the tendency of mental illnesses to aggregate in families, the unique contributions of genetic and family environmental influences remain unclear. Therefore, studies of twins and children who have been adopted have been implemented to increase our understanding of how shared genes can cause mental illness among family members. For example, researchers often compare disorder rates among monozygotic (twins sharing 100% of their genes) and dizygotic (twins sharing only 50% of their genes) twins to evaluate the influence of heritability: If disorder rates are significantly higher among monozygotic twins, then heritability is deemed an important factor. Similarly, adoption studies generally compare the adjustment and mental health similarity among twins who have been reared in separate environments. Results of twin and adoption studies do suggest a genetic link in many different mental illnesses such as personality disorders, mood disorders, autism, and substance abuse (Mash & Dozois, 1996). However, it is likely that the extent of the genetic contribution may vary across specific disorders.

Predominant in this line of research, then, are those studies assessing the connection between parental mental health status and the "high genetic risk" status of their offspring (Mednick & Schulsinger, 1968). Goodman's (1984) review contains multiple examples of studies that have generated solid empirical support of this perspective. Specifically, the outcome of high-risk status is usually viewed from the perspective of the offspring of a mentally ill parent developing (a) the same or similar mental disorder and/or (b) other adjustment difficulties.

Research on Family Environment

A number of family environmental factors are related to the development of mental disorders, including family support (Cole & McPherson, 1993; Sheeber et al., 1997) and stressful events within the family (Forehand et al., 1998; Weller et al., 1991). There has also been a substantial body of research on family communication patterns, including affective style (Miklowitz, Goldstein, & Nuechterlein, 1995), communication deviance (Doane, 1978), and expressed emotion (Butzlaff & Hooley, 1998). As a result, there is some evidence linking family environment variables to the development and course of a family member's mental illness.

Cummings and Davies (1999) have proposed an interpersonal model to explain the family transmission of depression that accounts for and integrates many different family variables. Interpersonal approaches focus on the dynamic, reciprocal interaction between depressive social contexts and individuals over time (Cummings & Davies, 1999), and family members often serve as primary influencing agents.

More recently, Cummings and Davies have added to this interpersonal approach by including research on attachment theory and, as a result, have proposed an "emotional security hypothesis" model. This model emphasizes emotional security as a mediating variable between parental psychopathology, family process, and child adjustment. In other words, parent-child interactions can increase the child's susceptibility to psychopathology by threatening his or her emotional security. Furthermore, the child contributes to his or her own emotional security, and thus is an active respondent to both family events and interactions.

Although Cummings and Davies (1999) have presented this interpersonal approach in relation to families coping with depressive disorders, this theoretical model can be used to describe the relationship between family environment and other mental disorders as well. Most important, the model reflects efforts toward an integrated framework encompassing numerous family factors that describe the association between family context and psychopathology.

Combining Genetic Linkage and Family Environment Efforts

Rende and Plomin (1995) conclude that the most promising direction for future investigation will be the examination of how heredity and environmental influences contribute—both separately and in interaction with one another—to the development of psychopathology. Specifically, these authors outline important avenues for future research such as (a) the identification of genes and nonshared family environmental influences and (b) how an individual's genetic predisposition can actively lead to the development of at-risk family environments.

Interventions

Therapy

The family therapy profession has greatly influenced the family-oriented perspective regarding major mental disorders. Some of the family therapy field's earliest writings had directly and indirectly been used to blame families for "causing" the mental disorder of one or more of their members; residual effects of these earlier works still exist. Blaming attitudes can be seen, for instance, in a particular school of family therapy known as the Milan model (Selvini Palazzoli, Boscolo, Cecchin, & Prata, 1978). One current version of the Milan model holds that much of the blame for mental disorders in individuals resides in the "dirty games" that family members play with each other in the course of their interactions (Selvini Palazzoli & Prata, 1989). From this perspective, therapeutic interventions are designed to disrupt unhealthy family interactions in order to eliminate symptoms of the mental disorder.

Such family-pathology-based theories and therapies have been criticized for causing additional problems. Such outcomes are thought to stem from (a) the therapist's directly communicating to family members that they are "crazymaking" and are to blame for the mental disorder (Goldstein, 1981) or (b) communication messages that are contradictory and, consequently, unable to be responded to by family members (Lefley, 1989).

Most family therapists have moved away from such positions of blame. Examples of this trend can be found in those family therapists who use a "psychoeducational approach" to work with mental disorders in a family context (McFarlane, 1991). A psychoeducational approach typically includes three elements—education, training in coping skills, and social support—but the relative emphasis placed on each component may vary (Marsh, 1998). Within this approach, family members are encouraged to learn all they can about the mental disorder, becoming fully educated about the facts surrounding assessment and treatment. Nonblaming attributions about mental disorders and knowledge about the disorder's symptoms, course, and treatment are thought to be indicators of the effectiveness of psychoeducational programming (cf. Gavazzi, Fristad, & Law, 1997). As opposed to therapeutic approaches designed to eliminate a particular disorder, the psychoeducational approach largely seeks to prevent the *return* of the disorder, as well as to alleviate the pain and suffering of family members.

Research has documented the effectiveness of these psychoeducational approaches in the treatment of adults who suffer from schizophrenia (Hogarty et al., 1991), depression (Holder & Anderson, 1990), bipolar disorder (Honig, Hofman, Rozendaal, & Dingemans, 1997), or any mood disorder (Clarkin, Haas, & Glick, 1988). Research concerning the use of psychoeducational programming with families of impaired children and adolescents is indicating success in the treatment of mood disorders (Brent, Poling, McKain, & Baugher, 1993; Fristad, Gavazzi, Centolella, & Soldano, 1996; Fristad, Gavazzi, & Soldano, 1998).

Social Policy

The most significant and powerful impact on social attitudes and policy-making decisions regarding mental disorders has resulted from the work of grassroots organizations such as the National Alliance for the Mentally Ill (NAMI) and its related affiliates. NAMI has the dual focus of (a) advocating for patient (and family) rights and (b) providing general public education about mental disorders (Howe & Howe, 1987). The efforts of NAMI have resulted in a number of important issues being brought to the forefront. These issues include (a) broadening the quality of care, (b) augmenting our understanding of treatment difficulties associated with dual diagnosis and involuntary hospitalization, and (c) maximizing outreach to other self-help organizations and advocacy groups.

More recently, NAMI has been involved in the development of educational programming about mental illness and increased advocacy efforts regarding more effective service delivery for mental health needs. NAMI now disseminates a "Family-to-Family Educational Program" that allows trained volunteers to provide a 12-week course focusing on the treatment of mental illness and coping skills that are necessary for family members to effectively join in treatment efforts. In addition, NAMI has launched its Program of Assertive Community Treatment (PACT) Across America, a new advocacy initiative based on research findings and designed to endorse community-based treatment options.

Professional groups have also played a role in social policy efforts. In particular, the Group for the Advancement of Psychiatry has been heavily involved with educating both professional and lay audiences about critical issues associated with mental disorders and families. Perhaps most notable is a book published in cooperation with "Dear Abby" columnist Abigail van Buren that covers many of the problems and concerns of families in the initial and advanced stages of dealing with a family member diagnosed with a mental disorder (Group for the Advancement of Psychiatry, 1986).

Future Directions

In the first edition of this book, future directions regarding both research and intervention strategies concerning the family-oriented perspective on mental disorders were discussed in terms of (a) the need to focus on issues, including the training of mental health professionals, to better recognize the particular stresses, coping styles, and subsequent adaptation levels of family members dealing with the presence of mental disorders (Holden & Lewine, 1982; Lefley, 1987, 1988); (b) the successful use of support groups and other community-based self-help efforts (Barbee, Kasten, & Rosenson, 1991; Wintersteen & Young, 1988); and (c) the use of collaborative models of care that empower families (Backer & Richardson, 1989; Bernheim, 1989; Chamberlin, Rogers, & Sneed, 1989; Spaniol, Zipple, & Fitzgerald, 1984). We acknowledge that great strides have been made with regard to these issues. At the same time, other issues noted in the first edition of this book, including the health insurance industry's use of managed care strategies to contain the costs of health and mental health services by severely restricting or eliminating mental health benefits, continue to negatively affect the needs of mentally ill persons and their families.

Our analysis of the present situation now includes a new list of future directions for research and intervention efforts. The first consideration concerns how individual and family life-cycle stages may assist researchers and clinicians who are studying mental illness and families. Second, we need to increase our understanding of the roles of the father and the mother in coping with their child's illness. Third, newer and more integrative theoretical models could help to clarify the unique influence and relative effect that particular variables have in the development of psychopathology. Finally, a consideration of family strengths (in addition to burdens) may facilitate the development of coping strategies that can be translated into effective interventions, such as the future use of family-based interventions that adopt a psycho-educational approach.

DISCUSSION QUESTIONS

1. Discuss some of the reasons for gender differences in mental illness.

2. What changes, if any, should be made in how society views the mentally ill?

3. What family factors do you feel are most influential in explaining mental illness?

4. Give some examples of subjective and objective burdens that family members must cope with when caring for a mentally ill family member. What types of community services could be provided to these families?

5. Describe how psychoeducational approaches could be useful with families of the mentally ill.

SUGGESTED READINGS

Gorman, J. (1996). *The new psychiatry: The essential guide to state-of-the-art therapy, medication, and emotional health.* New York: St. Martin's.

Group for the Advancement of Psychiatry. (1986). *A family affair: Helping families cope with mental illness.* New York: Brunner/Mazel.

Hatfield, A. B. (1990). *Family education in mental illness.* New York: Guilford.

Kaslow, F. W. (1996) *Handbook of relational diagnoses and dysfunctional patterns.* New York: John Wiley.

Koplewicz, H. S. (1996). *It's nobody's fault: New hope and help for difficult children and their parents.* New York: Random House.

REFERENCES

Backer, T. E., & Richardson, D. (1989). Building bridges: Psychologists and families of the mentally ill. *American Psychologist, 44,* 546-550.

Bailey, D., & Garralda, M. E. (1987). The use of the social stress and support interview in families with deviant children: Methodological issues. *Social Psychiatry, 22,* 209-215.

Balcom, D. A., & Healey, D. (1990). The context for couples treatment of wife abuse. In M. P. Mirkin (Ed.), *The social and political contexts of family therapy* (pp. 121-137). Boston: Allyn & Bacon.

Barbee, J. G., Kasten, A. M., & Rosenson, M. K. (1991). Toward a new alliance: Psychiatric residents and family support groups. *Academic Psychiatry, 15,* 40-49.

Barrowclough, C., Johnston, M., & Tarrier, N. (1994). Attributions, expressed emotion, and patient relapse: An attributional model of relatives' response to schizophrenic illness. *Behavior Therapy, 25,* 67-88.

Bernheim, K. F. (1989). Psychologists and families of the severely mentally ill: The role of family consultation. *American Psychologist, 44,* 561-564.

Birmaher, B., Ryan, N. D., Williamson, D. E., Brent, D. A., Kaufman, J., Dahl, R. E., Perel, J., & Nelson, B. (1996). Child and adolescent depression: A review of the past 10 years: Part I. *Journal of the American Academy of Child and Adolescent Psychiatry, 121,* 241-258.

Bograd, M. (1990). Scapegoating mothers: Conceptual errors in systems formulations. In M. P. Mirkin (Ed.), *The social and political contexts of family therapy* (pp. 69-87). Boston: Allyn & Bacon.

Brent, D. A., Poling, K., McKain, B., & Baugher, M. (1993). A psychoeducational program for families of affectively ill children and adolescents. *Journal of the American Academy of Child and Adolescent Psychiatry, 121,* 770-774.

Brewin, C. R., MacCarthy, B., Duda, K., & Vaughn, C. E. (1991). Attribution and expressed emotion in the relatives of patients with schizophrenia. *Journal of Abnormal Psychology, 100,* 546-554.

Broderick, C. B., & Schrader, S. S. (1981). The history of professional marriage and family therapy. In A. S. Gurman & D. P. Kniskern (Eds.), *Handbook of family therapy* (pp. 5-35). New York: Brunner/Mazel.

Brody, E. M., & Kleban, M. H. (1983). Day-to-day mental and physical health symptoms of older people: A report on health logs. *Gerontologist, 23,* 75-85.

Brown, G. W., Birley, J. L. T., & Wing, J. K. (1972). Influence of family life on the course of schizophrenic disorders: A replication. *British Journal of Psychiatry, 121,* 241-258.

Brown, G. W., Monck, E. M., Carstairs, G. M., & Wing, J. K. (1962). Influence of family life on the course of schizophrenic disorders. *British Journal of Preventive and Social Medicine, 16,* 55-68.

Bruce, M. L., Takeuchi, D. T., & Leaf, P. J. (1991). Poverty and psychiatric status: Longitudinal evidence from the New Haven Epidemiologic Catchment Area Study. *Archives of General Psychiatry, 48,* 470-474.

Butzlaff, R. L., & Hooley, J. M. (1998). Expressed emotion and psychiatric relapse: A meta-analysis. *Archives of General Psychiatry, 55,* 547-552.

Canino, G. J., Bird, H. R., Shrout, P. E., Rubio-Stipec, M., Bravo, M., Martinez, R., Sesman, M., & Guevara, L. (1987). The prevalence of specific psychiatric disorders in Puerto Rico. *Archives of General Psychiatry, 44,* 727-735.

Caplan, P. J., & Hall-McCorquodale, I. (1985). Mother-blaming in major clinical journals. *American Journal of Orthopsychiatry, 55,* 345-353.

Chamberlin, J., Rogers, J. A., & Sneed, C. S. (1989). Consumers, families, and community support systems. *Psychosocial Rehabilitation Journal, 12,* 93-106.

Clarkin, J. F., Haas, G. L., & Glick, I. D. (1988). *Affective disorders and the family.* New York: Guilford.

Cole, D. A., & McPherson, A. E. (1993). Relation of family subsystems to adolescent depression: Implementing a new family assessment strategy. *Journal of Family Psychology, 7,* 119-133.

Compas, B. (1987). Stress and life events during childhood and adolescence. *Clinical Psychology Review, 7,* 275-302.

Cross-National Collaborative Group. (1992). The changing rate of major depression. *Journal of the American Medical Association, 268,* 3098-3105.

Cummings, E. M., & Davies, P. T. (1999). Depressed parents and family functioning: Interpersonal effects and children's functioning and development. In T. Joiner & J. Coyne (Eds.), *The interactional nature of depression* (pp. 299-327). Washington, DC: American Psychological Association.

Davila, J., & Bradbury, T. N. (1998). Psychopathology and the marital dyad. In L. L'Abate (Ed.), *Family psychopathology: The relational roots of dysfunctional behavior.* New York: Guilford.

Doane, J. A. (1978). Family interaction and communication deviance in disturbed and normal families: A review of research. *Family Process, 17,* 357-376.

Doornbos, M. M. (1996). The strengths of families coping with serious mental illness. *Archives of Psychiatric Nursing, 10,* 214-220.

Eley, T. C. (in press). Contributions of behavioral genetics research: Quantifying genetic, shared, environmental, and non-shared environmental influences. In M. W. Vasey & M. R. Dadds (Eds.), *The developmental psychopathology of anxiety.* New York: Oxford University Press.

Flynn, L. M. (1987). The stigma of mental illness. In A. B. Hatfield (Ed.), *Families of the mentally ill: Meeting the challenges* (pp. 53-60). San Francisco: Jossey-Bass.

Forehand, R., Biggar, H., & Kotchick, B. A. (1998). Cumulative risk across family stressors: Short- and long-term effects for adolescents. *Journal of Abnormal Child Psychology, 26,* 119-128.

Franks, D. D. (1990). Economic contribution of families caring for persons with severe and persistent mental illness. *Administration and Policy in Mental Health, 18,* 9-18.

Friedman, R. M. (1996). *Prevalence of serious emotional disturbance in children and adolescents.* Unpublished paper, Center for Mental Health Services, Washington, DC.

Fristad, M., Gavazzi, S. M., Centolella, D., & Soldano, K. (1996). Psychoeducation: An intervention strategy for families of children with mood disorders. *Contemporary Family Therapy, 18,* 371-383.

Fristad, M. A., Gavazzi, S. M., & Soldano, K. W. (1998). Multi-family psychoeducation groups for childhood mood disorders: Program description and preliminary efficacy data. *Contemporary Family Therapy, 20*(3), 385-402.

Fristad, M. A., Gavazzi, S. M., & Soldano, K. W. (1999). Naming the enemy: Learning to differentiate mood disorder "symptoms" from the "self" that experiences them. *Journal of Family Psychotherapy, 10,* 81-88.

Fuchs, L. (1986). First person account: Three generations of schizophrenia. *Schizophrenia Bulletin, 12,* 744-747.

Garrison, C. Z., Jackson, K. L., Marsteller, F., McKeown, R., & Addy, C. (1990). A longitudinal study of depressive symptomology in young adolescents. *Journal of the American Academy of Child and Adolescent Psychiatry, 29,* 581-585.

Gavazzi, S. M., Fristad, M., & Law, J. C. (1997). The Understanding Mood Disorders Questionnaire. *Psychological Reports, 81,* 172-174.

Glied, S., & Kofman, S. (1995). *Women and mental health: Issues for health reform.* New York: Commonwealth Fund, Commission on Women's Health.

Goldberg-Arnold, J. S., Fristad, M. A., & Gavazzi, S. M. (1999). Family psychoeducation: Giving caregivers what they want and need. *Family Relations, 48,* 411-417.

Goldstein, M. J. (1981). *New developments in interventions with families of schizophrenics.* San Francisco: Jossey-Bass.

Goodman, S. H. (1984). Children of disturbed parents: The interface between research and intervention. *American Journal of Community Psychiatry, 12,* 663-687.

Gove, W. (1972). The relationship between sex roles, marital status, and mental illness. *Social Forces, 51,* 38-44.

Group for the Advancement of Psychiatry. (1986). *A family affair: Helping families cope with mental illness.* New York: Brunner/Mazel.

Hahlweg, K., & Goldstein, M. J. (1987). *Understanding major mental disorders: The contribution of family interaction research.* New York: Family Process Press.

Hahlweg, K., Goldstein, M. J., Nuechterlein, K. H., Magana, A. B., Mintz, J., Doane, J. A., Miklowitz, D. J., & Snyder, K. S. (1989). Expressed emotion and patient-relative interaction in families of recent-onset schizophrenics. *Journal of Consulting and Clinical Psychology, 57,* 11-18.

Hatfield, A. B. (1987). The expressed emotion theory: Why families object. *Hospital and Community Psychiatry, 38,* 341.

Hawley, D. R., & DeHaan, L. (1996). Toward a definition of family resilience: Integrating life-span and family perspectives. *Family Process, 35,* 283-298.

Hoenig, J., & Hamilton, M. W. (1966). The schizophrenic patient in the community and his effect on the household. *International Journal of Social Psychiatry, 12,* 165-176.

Hoffman, L. (1981). *Foundations of family therapy.* New York: Basic Books.

Hogarty, G. E., Anderson, C. M., Reiss, D. J., Kornblith, S. J., Greenwald, D. P., Ulrich, R. F., & Carter, M. (1991). Family psychoeducation, social skills training, and maintenance chemotherapy in the aftercare of schizophrenia. *Archives of General Psychiatry, 48,* 340-347.

Holden, D. F., & Lewine, R. R. (1982). How families evaluate mental health professionals, resources, and effects of illness. *Schizophrenia Bulletin, 8,* 626-633.

Holder, D., & Anderson, C. M. (1990). Psychoeducational family intervention for depressed patients and their families. In G. I. Keitner (Ed.), *Depression and families: Impact and treatment* (pp. 157-184). Washington, DC: American Psychiatric Press.

Honig, A., Hofman, A., Rozendaal, N., & Dingemans, P. (1997). Psychoeducation in bipolar disorder: Effect on expressed emotion. *Psychiatry Research, 72,* 17-22.

Hooley, J. M. (1998). Expressed emotion and locus of control. *Journal of Nervous and Mental Disease, 186,* 374-378.

Hooley, J. M., & Licht, D. M. (1997). Expressed emotion and causal attributions in the spouses of depressed patients. *Journal of Abnormal Psychology, 106,* 298-306.

Hooley, J. M., Orley, J., & Teasdale, J. D. (1986). Levels of expressed emotion and relapse in depressed patients. *British Journal of Psychiatry, 148,* 642-647.

Hops, H., Lewinsohn, P. M., Andrews, J. A., & Roberts, R. (1990). Psychosocial correlates of depressive symptomology among high school students. *Journal of Clinical Child Psychology, 19,* 211-220.

Howe, C. W., & Howe, J. W. (1987). The National Alliance for the Mentally Ill: History and ideology. In A. B. Hatfield (Ed.), *Families of the mentally ill: Meeting the challenges* (pp. 23-42). San Francisco: Jossey-Bass.

Kavanagh, D. J. (1992). Recent development in expressed emotion and schizophrenia. *British Journal of Psychiatry, 160,* 601-620.

Kessler, R. C., McGonagle, K. A., Zhao, S., Nelson, C. B., Hughes, M., Eshleman, S., Wittchen, H., & Kendler, K. S. (1994). Lifetime and 12-month prevalence of DSM-III-R psychiatric disorders in the United States. *Archives of General Psychology, 51,* 8-19.

King, S. (1998). Is expressed emotion cause or effect? A longitudinal study. *International Clinical Psychopharmacology, 13* [Suppl. 1], S107-S108.

Leete, E. (1987). A patient's perspective on schizophrenia. In A. B. Hatfield (Ed.), *Families of the mentally ill: Meeting the challenges* (pp. 81-90). San Francisco: Jossey-Bass.

Lefley, H. P. (1987). The family's response to mental illness in a relative. In A. B. Hatfield (Ed.), *Families of the mentally ill: Meeting the challenges* (pp. 3-21). San Francisco: Jossey-Bass.

Lefley, H. P. (1988). Training professionals to work with families of chronic patients. *Community Mental Health Journal, 24,* 338-357.

Lefley, H. P. (1989). Family burden and family stigma in major mental illness. *American Psychologist, 44,* 556-560.

Marsh, D. T. (1998). *Serious mental illness and the family: The practitioner's guide.* New York: John Wiley.

Marsh, D. T., Lefley, H. P., Evans-Rhodes, D., Ansell, V. I., Doerzbacher, B. M., LaBarbera, L., & Paluzzi, J. E. (1996). The family experience of mental illness: Evidence for resilience. *Psychiatric Rehabilitation Journal, 20,* 3-12.

Mash, E. J., & Barkley, R. A. (1996). *Child psychopathology.* New York: Guilford.

Mash, E. J., & Dozois, D. J. (1996). Child psychopathology: A developmental systems perspective. In E. J. Mash & R. A. Barkley (Eds.), *Child psychopathology* (pp. 3-63). New York: Guilford.

Maurin, J. T., & Boyd, C. B. (1990). Burden of mental illness on the family: A critical review. *Archives of Psychiatric Nursing, 4,* 99-107.

McFarlane, W. R. (1991). Family psychoeducational treatment. In A. S. Gurman & D. P. Kniskern (Eds.), *Handbook of family therapy* (Vol. 2, pp. 363-395). New York: Brunner/Mazel.

Mednick, S. A., & Schulsinger, F. (1968). Some premorbid characteristics related to breakdown in children with schizophrenic mothers. In D. Rosenthal & S. Kety (Eds.), *The transmission of schizophrenia* (pp. 469-475). New York: Pergamon.

Meyerson, A. T., & Herman, G. H. (1987). Systems resistance to the chronic patient. In A. T. Meyerson (Ed.), *Barriers to treating the mentally ill* (pp. 21-33). San Francisco: Jossey-Bass.

Miklowitz, D. J. (1995). The evolution of family-based psychopathology. In R. H. Mikesell, D. D. Lusterman, & S. H. McDaniel (Eds.), *Integrating family therapy: Handbook of family psychology and systems theory.* Washington, DC: American Psychological Association.

Miklowitz, D. J., Goldstein, M. J., & Nuechterlein, K. H. (1995). Verbal interactions in families of schizophrenic and bipolar affective patients. *Journal of Abnormal Psychology, 104,* 268-276.

Miklowitz, D. J., & Stackman, D. (1992). Communication deviance in families of schizophrenic and other psychiatric patients: Current state of the construct. In E. F. Walker, R. H. Dworkin, & B. Cornblatt (Eds.), *Progress in experimental personality and psychopathology research* (pp. 1-46). New York: Springer.

Minkoff, K. (1987). Resistance of mental health professionals to working with the chronic mentally ill. In A. T. Meyerson (Ed.), *Barriers to treating the mentally ill* (pp. 3-19). San Francisco: Jossey-Bass.

Mirabi, M., Weinman, M., Magnetti, S., & Keppler, K. (1985). Professional attitudes toward the mentally ill. *Hospital and Community Psychiatry, 36,* 404-405.

Mittleman, G. (1985). First person account: The pain of parenthood of the mentally ill. *Schizophrenia Bulletin, 11,* 300-303.

Morrison, J. (1979). Attitudes of community gatekeepers and psychiatric social workers toward mental illness. *Journal of Community Psychology, 7,* 147-150.

National Institute of Mental Health. (1991). *Implementation of the national plan for research on child and adolescent mental disorders* (PA-91-46). Washington, DC: U.S. Department of Health and Human Services.

Nichols, M. P., & Schwartz, R. C. (1991). *Family therapy: Concepts and methods* (2nd ed.). Boston: Allyn & Bacon.

Phares, V., & Compas, B. E. (1992). The role of fathers in child and adolescent psychopathology: Make room for daddy. *Psychological Bulletin, 111,* 387-412.

Puig-Antich, J., Kaufman, J., Ryan, N. D., Williamson, D. E., Dahl, R. E., Lukens, E., Phil, M., Todak, G., Ambrosini, P., Rabinovich, H., & Nelson, B. (1993). The psychosocial functioning and family environment of depressed adolescents. *Journal of the American Academy of Child and Adolescent Psychiatry, 32,* 244-253.

Reiger, D. A., Boyd, J. H., Burke, J. D., Rae, D. S., Myers, J. K., Kramer, M., Robins, L. N., George, L. K., Karno, M., & Locke, B. Z. (1988). One month prevalence of mental disorders in the United States. *Archives of General Psychiatry, 45,* 977-986.

Reiger, D. A., Burke, J. D., Jr., & Burke, K. C. (1990). Comorbidity of affective and anxiety disorders in the NIMH Epidemiologic Catchment Area Program. In J. D. Maser & C. R. Cloninger (Eds.), *Comorbidity of mood and anxiety disorders* (pp. 113-122). Washington, DC: American Psychiatric Press.

Rende, R., & Plomin, R. (1993). Families at risk for psychopathology: Who becomes affected and why? *Development and Psychopathology, 5,* 529-540.

Rende, R., & Plomin, R. (1995). Nature, nurture, and the development of psychopathology. In D. Cicchetti & D. J. Cohen (Eds.), *Developmental psychopathology: Vol. 1. Theory and methods* (pp. 291-314). New York: John Wiley.

Roberts, R. E., Attkisson, C. C., & Rosenblatt, A. (1998). Prevalence of psychopathology among children and adolescents. *American Journal of Psychiatry, 155,* 715-725.

Robins, L. N., & Reiger, D. A. (Eds.). (1991). *Psychiatric disorders in America: The Epidemiologic Catchment Area Study.* New York: Free Press.

Rosenthal, D. (1970). *Genetic theory and abnormal behavior.* New York: McGraw-Hill.

Roybal, E. R. (1984). Federal involvement in mental health care for the aged. *American Psychologist, 39,* 163-166.

Scazufca, M., & Kuipers, E. (1998). Stability of expressed emotion in relatives of those with schizophrenia and its relationship with burden of care and perception of patients' social functioning. *Psychological Medicine, 28,* 453-461.

Selvini Palazzoli, M., Boscolo, L., Cecchin, G., & Prata, G. (1978). *Paradox and counterparadox.* New York: Jason Aronson.

Selvini Palazzoli, M., & Prata, G. (1989). *Family games: General models of psychotic processes in the family.* New York: Norton.

Sheeber, L., Hops, H., Alpert, A., Davis, B., & Andrews, J. (1997). Family support and conflict: Prospective relations to adolescent depression. *Journal of Abnormal Child Psychology, 25,* 333-344.

Singer, M., & Wynne, L. (1963). Differentiating characteristics of parents of childhood schizophrenics, childhood neurotics, and young adult schizophrenics. *American Journal of Psychiatry, 120,* 234-243.

Singer, M., & Wynne, L. (1965a). Thought disorder and family relations of schizophrenics: III. Methodology using projective techniques. *Archives of General Psychiatry, 12,* 187-200.

Singer, M., & Wynne, L. (1965b). Thought disorder and family relations of schizophrenics: IV. Results and implications. *Archives of General Psychiatry, 12,* 201-212.

Smyer, M. A., Shea, D. G., & Streit, A. (1994). The provision and use of mental health services in nursing homes: Results from the national medical expenditures survey. *American Journal of Public Health, 84,* 284-287.

Spaniol, L., Zipple, A., & Fitzgerald, S. (1984). How professionals can share power with families: Practical approaches to working with families of the mentally ill. *Psychosocial Rehabilitation Journal, 8,* 77-84.

Vaughn, C. E., & Leff, J. P. (1976a). The influence of family and social factors on the course of psychiatric illness: A comparison of schizophrenic and depressed neurotic patients. *British Journal of Psychiatry, 129,* 125-137.

Vaughn, C. E., & Leff, J. P. (1976b). The measurement of expressed emotion in the families of psychiatric patients. *British Journal of Social and Clinical Psychology, 15,* 157-165.

Wahl, O. F. (1995). *Media madness: Public images of mental illness.* New Brunswick, NJ: Rutgers University Press.

Wahl, O. F., & Harman, C. R. (1989). Family views of stigma. *Schizophrenia Bulletin, 15,* 131-139.

Walsh, F. (1996). The concept of family resilience: Crisis and challenge. *Family Process, 35,* 261-281.

Watson, W. L., & Wright, L. M. (1984). The elderly and their families: An interactional view. In E. I. Coppersmith (Ed.), *Families with handicapped members* (pp. 75-87). Rockville, MD: Aspen.

Weller, R. A., Weller, E. B., Fristad, M. A., & Bowes, J. M. (1991). Depression in recently bereaved prepubertal children. *American Journal of Psychiatry, 148,* 1536-1540.

Wintersteen, R. T., & Young, L. (1988). Effective professional collaboration with family support groups. *Psychosocial Rehabilitation Journal, 12,* 19-31.

Zubin, J., & Spring, B. J. (1977). Vulnerability: A new view of schizophrenia. *Journal of Abnormal Psychology, 86,* 103-126.

11

Economic Stress and Families

JONATHAN J. FOX
SUZANNE BARTHOLOMAE

The quality of marital and family life is largely a function of the economic resources available to individuals and families. Resources are used to meet our most basic needs—clothing, shelter, and food—and if resources are plentiful, they can be easily allocated to satisfy the comforts and luxuries we desire. Unfortunately, most families possess limited resources and must manage them in an effort to meet their needs and desires. The level and management of resources can be sources of stress or comfort. Resources can result in stress when there is (a) disagreement about their use and (b) concern about their availability. Comfort can be derived from resources not only when they are in abundance but also when they can be relied on to help solve problems and provide a sense of security.

Economic Stress Defined

Resources, frequently measured by family income, often define economic status. Threats to family income such as job loss, divorce, retirement, or disability can contribute to economic stress, which may be more specifically defined as the hardship, pressure, tension, or strain experienced as a result of changes in an individual's or family's financial affairs. Economic stress, also referred to by family researchers as economic distress, economic hardship, economic strain, economic pressure, or financial strain, can be the product of (a) the inability to meet financial obligations, (b) the uncertainty of income sources, (c) the instability of employment, and/or (d) the inadequacy of earnings to meet needs and desires. Economic stress can also be the product of conditions in the general economy at the national, regional, or local level (e.g., recession, unemployment, or poverty rates) (Adler et al., 1994; Klebanov, Brooks-Gunn, & Duncan, 1994; MacFadyen, MacFadyen, & Prince, 1996). Economic stress can be normative, resulting from expected milestones in the family life cycle such as marriage or the birth of a child, or situational, stemming from unexpected events such as divorce, forced retirement, or catastrophic illness. Economic stress associated with life events may be temporary (e.g., a short-term drop in income resulting from job loss) or chronic (e.g., a long-term income loss as a result of a permanent work-limiting disability).

Resources determine not only family economic well-being but also how families cope with economic stress. In the event of normative stressors, most individuals are able to marshal available resources that enable them to adapt and cope with change (Blaney, 1985; Hamilton, Croman, Hoffman, & Renner, 1990; McCubbin et al., 1980).

Economic stress in the family manifests itself directly by influencing individual well-being and indirectly by influencing family interaction (Conger et al., 1990; Elder & Caspi, 1988). Therefore, this chapter approaches economic stress in two parts. The first part examines the impact of economic stress on individuals, marriage, and family systems. The second part provides an overview of financial planning prescriptions to help alleviate financial stress encountered across the family life cycle.

Economic Stress and the Individual

Psychological and Social Impact

As previously mentioned, research indicates that economic factors (e.g., unemployment, low income) have a negative effect on the mental health and well-being of individuals (Adler et al., 1994; Klebanov et al., 1994; MacFadyen et al., 1996; Takeuchi, Williams, & Adair, 1991). Reactions to economic stress appear to have common psychological and social costs. Studies consistently show a relationship between economic strain and distress, including increased levels of anger, hostility, depression, anxiety, somatic complaints, and poorer physical health (Hamilton et al., 1990; Keith, 1993; Kessler, House, & Turner, 1987; Krause, 1987; Pearlin, Lieberman, Menaghan, & Mullan, 1981; Peirce, Frone, Russel, & Cooper, 1994;

Vinokur, Price, & Caplan, 1996). Furthermore, social costs include diminished relationship quality (marital, parent-child, friendships) through strain and disruption and changes in social activities, support, and networks (Voydanoff, 1990).

Several factors can ease the psychological and social damage brought about by economic stress. The way an individual defines the situation is important, as are the resources and supports available (McCubbin et al., 1980). Important resources drawn on include individual (e.g., education), psychological (e.g., coping skills), social (e.g., social support), relational (e.g., marital relationship), and material (e.g., income) resources (Elder & Caspi, 1988; Hamilton et al., 1990). In addition, there are several behavioral strategies that individuals and families can employ to cope with economic stress, including social support, cognitive restructuring, and self-help strategies (Gomel, Tinsley, Parke, & Clark, 1998; Guelzow, Bird, & Koball, 1991). In the context of stress, demographic characteristics such as gender, race, income, education, and marital status have been conceptualized as both economic and social resources. For example, marital status has both economic (e.g., combined incomes if both spouses work) and social (e.g., support and comfort from spouse) aspects and can improve or maintain the psychological well-being of married individuals under economic distress (Hamilton et al., 1990).

Ethnic Minority Groups

Ethnic minority groups often lack the social, legal, and economic supports afforded the majority culture. Whether structural discrimination or a lack of meaningful and equal employment opportunities, such circumstances greatly influence the economic behaviors and outcomes of ethnic group members (Burden & Klerman, 1984). Compared with whites, ethnic minority groups have lower income earnings and greater rates of poverty, placing them at a distinct economic disadvantage (DaVanzo & Rahman, 1993; Taylor, Chatters, Tucker, & Lewis, 1990). However, ethnic minority groups have resources, including family structures, family dynamics, value systems, and child-rearing practices, that traditionally have served as buffers of economic stress (Gomel et al., 1998; Taylor et al., 1990; Vega, 1991). For example, black families historically have dealt with economic adversity with the help of extended kin networks, reciprocal intergenerational relations, and strong bonds with the community, church, and friends (Taylor et al., 1990). These various social networks provide direct and in-kind assistance to moderate the impact of economic stressors (Taylor et al., 1990; Wilson & Tolson, 1990; Winkler, 1993).

Evidence regarding ethnic minority groups suggests that there are variations in the access, sources, and utilization of resources (Gomel et al., 1998; Wilson & Tolson, 1990; Winkler, 1993). The recency of immigration and the level of acculturation will determine the accessibility and use of formal and informal resources (Gomel et al., 1998) (see Chapter 15). Among Hispanic households, the incidence of nonnuclear family members contributing to family income is much greater than in white households, indicating a cultural variation of where resources originate (Angel & Tienda, 1982). Another example of unique resource utilization among ethnic minority groups is found among black single mothers who often "double up" with a relative as a living arrangement (Hao, 1995; Winkler, 1993). Unfortunately, research that examines ethnic differences in reaction to economic stress is sparse (Gomel et al., 1998). However, strikingly similar reactions occur among black, Latino, and white families, indicating common patterns of dealing with economic stress (Gomel et al., 1998).

Theoretical Perspectives

Several explanations have been offered to explain why there appears to be a common reaction to economic stress. First, the stress hypothesis refers to the notion that psychological distress is positively associated with economic stress (e.g., an increase in an individual's level of depression as a result of overindebtedness). Two possible relationships exist: (a) Individuals with poorer health or psychological functioning are more likely to have higher economic risk (e.g., lower socioeconomic status), or (b) higher economic risk somehow brings about the poor health or psychological dysfunction of individuals (Johnson, 1991; MacFadyen et al., 1996; Palmore, 1981). Research showing support for the stress hypothesis is inconsistent because it attempts to identify causality, which is difficult to test, requiring longitudinal data and more sophisticated statistical techniques.

It is critical to note the importance of the accumulation or "pileup" of economic stressors (MacFadyen et al., 1996). Consider a recently divorced woman adjusting to a lower standard of living. If she was unemployed prior to the divorce, she experiences the stress of finding a job. Adding to the economic stress, she also finds she has lost the social support she previously enjoyed via the couples' mutual friends and her former in-laws. Thus, her psychological stress may not result from the decline in income per se; rather, it is the culmination of low income, unemployment, lack of social support, and being recently divorced.

A second explanation for the relationship between economic stressors and psychological well-being is the accentuation hypothesis (Elder & Caspi, 1988). This hypothesis suggests that an individual's unstable characteristics are accentuated under economic stress. For example, studies of individuals and families during the depression found that men who were not moody and irritable prior to the 1930s stayed balanced when faced with economic decline, whereas explosive characteristics were accentuated during economic stress (Elder & Caspi, 1988).

Marital Status

Marital status is also instrumental in explaining the vulnerability and exposure to financial stress, with single (never married), divorced, separated, and widowed individuals being more likely to suffer from financial stress than married persons (Hamilton et al., 1990; Keith, 1993; Keith & Lorenz, 1989; Pearlin & Johnson, 1977; Pearlin et al., 1981). Because of the greater financial risk among the unmarried, the risk of diminished mental health is also greater. In general, economic stress is associated with greater levels of depression and lower life satisfaction and morale among the unmarried (Pearlin & Johnson, 1977).

Several factors contribute to the variation of economic stress by marital groups. First, marriage can serve a protective function during economic hardship by providing social support, which includes such characteristics as commitment, companionship, security, and emotional support. Couples who exchange supportive behavior when under economic stress experience less emotional distress than nonsupportive couples (Conger, Rueter, & Elder, 1999). Another positive effect of marriage results from the economic support provided. The sources, types, and levels of income vary by marital status groups, with married persons generally having higher household incomes (Ross, Mirowsky, & Goldsteen, 1990). In contrast, female-headed households with children have the lowest incomes. Furthermore, female-headed households are most prevalent among blacks, followed by Hispanics, whites, and Asians (DaVanzo & Rahman, 1993). While a higher standard of living may result from a marital union, this is not to say that dual-income families do not experience economic stress.

Marital status is also instrumental in explaining gender differences in financial stress (Keith, 1993). There are economic as well as socioemotional benefits to marriage for both men and women; however, women may benefit more economically from marriage while men benefit more socioemotionally (Ross et al., 1990). An economic aspect of marriage important to men is the role of breadwinner, whose personal identity is strongly rooted in the provider role and may explain men's greater distress during periods of financial strain (Kelvin & Jarrett, 1985). The greater psychological stress experienced by men during economic hardship also is thought to be a product of women's lesser commitment to work, with various family roles and responsibilities providing satisfaction for them (Voydanoff, 1990).

Although marriage can be a costly decision for women, the overall economic gain usually outweighs other marital status options. Women occupy economically vulnerable positions as widows, divorcées, or single mothers. In addition, because women often withdraw from or reduce participation in the labor market when they get married, they limit potential employment options and earnings that would be needed if they divorce (Holden & Smock, 1991). The effects can be long term; for example, the chance of collecting a pension among divorced and widowed women who do not work outside the home is decreased (DeViney, 1995).

With the increased number of female-headed households and higher rates of poverty among these groups, economic stress is an especially salient issue. As a family structure, female-headed households are more likely to have low incomes and suffer from psychological distress (Pearlin & Johnson, 1977). These women must often also deal with job discrimination, limited labor force participation (interrupted by childbearing), inconsistent child support, and the high cost of child care (Pett & Vaughan-Cole, 1986). In addition, economic stress as a result of income loss after divorce is well documented (e.g., Holden & Smock, 1991). Duncan and Hoffman (1985) estimate a 30% to 50% drop in family income and a 20% to 30% drop in per capita income among women following divorce, compared with only 7% for men.

Compared with married women, divorced women are more likely to depend on (a) income from personal earnings; (b) public transfers such as welfare and food stamps; and (c) private transfers such as child support, alimony, and assistance from parents and relatives. Divorced women who rely on public transfers and who are insecure about future income experience greater stress and have more difficulty in the overall adjustment to divorce (Kitson, 1992; Weiss, 1984). Longitudinal research suggests that the economic hardship experienced by divorced women (and children) is prolonged, with remarriage being the most effective means of recovery (Holden & Smock, 1991).

The incidence of poverty is high among widows as well, and with the increasing longevity of women, there is a greater likelihood of women being widowed and exposed to negative financial consequences later in life. For example, among women age 65 or older living alone, the percentage considered poor was 23.8%, 57.5%, and 50.7% among whites, blacks, and Hispanics, respectively, compared with 14.5%, 44.4%, and 39.9% among white, black, and Hispanic males, respectively (U.S. Bureau of the Census, 1996). Several studies indicate that widowhood negatively affects the economic status of women, thus leaving them vulnerable to the stress associated with deprivation (Bound, Duncan, Laren, & Oleninick, 1991; Brubaker, 1991; Umberson, Wortman, & Kessler, 1992). Age and work experiences are important factors in the financial situation of widows. Younger widows with a work history do not suffer as great a decline in economic status (Brubaker, 1991). The lack of financial preparation prior to widowhood is another factor associated with diminished well-being (O'Bryant & Morgan, 1989). In terms of the impact of economic stress on well-being, economic strain is the primary cause of depression in widowhood (Umberson et al., 1992).

Ethnic minorities are a population of special concern in regard to economic stress. The proportion of married persons in the black population has dramatically declined over the past few decades. African Americans are more likely to be single, divorced, or separated and less likely to remarry after divorce, compared with whites (Taylor et al., 1990). Among Hispanics, there is a higher percentage of female-headed households compared with whites, and marital dissolution has been on the rise among this group (DaVanzo & Rahman, 1993; Vega, 1991). Although these marital patterns increase the economic risk of these groups, there appear to be cultural mechanisms supporting these families. For example, among black single mothers, the availability of social support from kin and the community is often more prevalent because single parenting is more normative (Taylor et al., 1990).

Economic Stress and Marriage

When two people marry, they bring with them their individual attitudes, values, and behaviors toward money. As a result, a common and frequent area of conflict among couples is money (Goodman, 1986; Williams & Berry, 1984), and marital problems are more likely to be experienced by those who disagree about finances. Furthermore, conflict among married couples is lowest when they share control over financial decisions, without one partner dominating (Blumstein & Schwartz, 1983). Dynamic elements of the decision-making process include spousal contribution to the budget, the level of involvement, interest and expertise in the purchase, and who was most influential in previous purchasing decisions (Kircherler, 1988). Happily married couples have been found to agree more often and to be less hostile and more cooperative.

When couples employ systematic money management strategies, conflict during tough financial times can be reduced or eliminated. For example, the frequency of financial arguments is reduced when couples use financial management strategies such as record keeping, goal-setting practices, and savings (Godwin, 1994; Lawrence, Thomasson, Wozniak, & Prawitz, 1993). Furthermore, disagreement over family finances has been positively associated with the frequency of communication for both men and women, with greater levels of communication associated with decreased intensity of disagreements over finances (Williams & Berry, 1984). Disagreement over family finances for men has been associated with their own management practices; men who engage in proactive financial management activities experience less intense disagreements (Williams & Berry, 1984). Money in U.S. society is a highly personal topic that makes communication about finances a difficult challenge. For example, remarried couples have been found to be reluctant to discuss their finances prior to marriage; this is true even among individuals who identified money as a major source of disagreement contributing to their previous divorce (Lown, 1984).

Stress from family finances affects marital quality—a concept generally indicating happiness and satisfaction with marriage. When a couple faces economic hardship, the quality of the marital relationship often declines (Conger et al., 1990; Conger et al., 1999; Lorenz, Conger, Simon, Whitbeck, & Elder, 1991). Economic loss results in increased financial disputes and thus greater marital tension and discord (Liker & Elder, 1983). Economic loss is related to an increase in the negative exchanges and a reduction in the positive exchanges that occur between spouses (Conger et al., 1990). For example, financial strain among unemployed couples affects the marital relationship through spousal withdrawal of social support and social undermining (Vinokur et al., 1996). Economic strain increases husbands' hostility and decreases their supportiveness and warmth (Conger et al., 1990). Other reactions to economic stress in interpersonal relationships include lowered self-esteem and competitiveness between spouses.

Some couples are more resilient to economic stress than others. As previously mentioned, the exchange of supportive behaviors between couples eases the tensions related to economic stress. Effective problem-solving skills among couples under economic pressure also help reduce marital conflict and thus marital distress (Conger et al., 1999). Couples involved in a satisfying marital relationship have been found to more successfully cope with financial difficulties (Conger et al., 1999). For example, couples who had strong marital bonds prior to the depression were better able to successfully adapt to economic pressure (Liker & Elder, 1983). It also has been found that money management strategies can improve marital quality; for example, newlywed couples who use financial goal-setting practices and strict record keeping are more satisfied in their marriage (Godwin, 1994; Lawrence et al., 1993).

The mechanisms through which marital relations are affected by economic stress are thought to work in several ways (Elder & Caspi, 1988). First, economic stress is directly related to heightened marital discord (Olson et al., 1983). Second, economic stress may affect marital relations directly by disrupting social interactions (Elder & Caspi, 1988). For example, economic stress may increase the level of tension and the number of conflicts between spouses. In addition, economic stress has been found to influence communication and cooperation between spouses, decreasing levels of warmth and increasing hostility and competitiveness among couples (Conger et al., 1990). Third, personality changes take place in individuals as a result of economic stress; such individual changes affect the marital relationship. For example, a study of couples during the Great Depression found weakened marital ties as a result of negative changes in the husband's behavior (Elder & Caspi, 1988).

Marital stability, characterized by the duration of a marriage, also has been correlated with economic factors. Across several studies, various factors have been negatively related to marital disruption (Holden & Smock, 1991; Weiss, 1984). For example, individuals with greater levels of education may be better equipped (e.g., have better problem-solving skills) to handle the stress associated with financial strain. Money management among couples has also been associated with marital stability. Greater commitment is found among couples who pool their finances rather than keep their accounts separate. The majority of married couples prefer to pool their financial accounts; 10% or less prefer separate accounts (Blumstein & Schwartz, 1983).

Economic Stress and Family Relationships

The detrimental effect of economic stress on family functioning and family relationships has been well documented. Economic stress has been found to decrease family satisfaction and cohesion (Voydanoff, 1990). However, how well families cope is influenced by how they define their economic situation; the greater the perceived economic hardship by family members, the poorer the family relationships (Gomel et al., 1998).

Parents experiencing economic stress may find that the quality of their parenting suffers. Parental well-being is affected by economic stress, which influences parenting behaviors, child-rearing practices, and the quality of parent-child interactions (Takeuchi et al., 1991). For example, economic stress affects parenting practices by reducing affective support (Ho, Lempers, & Clark-Lempers, 1995), increasing inconsistent and arbitrary discipline (Elder & Caspi, 1988; Elder, Conger, Foster, & Ardelt, 1992), and lowering levels of supportiveness (Lempers & Clark-Lempers, 1990). Levels of maternal warmth and social support and the provision of child learning experiences in the home are negatively affected by economic stress (Klebanov et al., 1994).

Economic stress has been associated with specific child outcomes (Conger et al., 1992; Elder et al., 1992; Hagquist, 1998), both short and long term, as a result of limited resources, limited opportunities, and diminished human capital development. Children who experience economic stress have greater levels of depression, more impulsive and antisocial behaviors (Takeuchi et al., 1991), and decreased levels of self-esteem (Ho et al., 1995). Fathers' negativity resulting from economic pressure increases children's risk of depression and aggression (Elder et al., 1992), whereas maternal financial stress decreases the quality of the mother-child relationship, resulting in greater levels of depression and loneliness (Lempers & Clark-Lempers, 1997). Adolescents who regularly worry about their family's financial condition more frequently report suffering from various somatic complaints, including stomachaches, loss of appetite, depression, sleeplessness, and lack of concentration (Hagquist, 1998). In addition, compared with other types of stress (e.g., school, social, health, and so on), economic stress is the most strongly related to the adolescent's self-perceived health. Adolescents' perception of their relationship with their parents also is negatively affected by economic stress (Ho et al., 1995), because parents and children frequently disagree about control over money (Bachman, 1983). In contrast, adolescents' agreement over family finances increases their satisfaction with family life and their own money management skills (Williams & Prohofsky, 1986).

Economic stress within the family system amplifies the fragility and interdependence of each member. The dynamics of a family under stress has several qualities (Elder & Caspi, 1988); individual members of the family system (mother/wife, husband/father, and child) are affected directly by economic stress and will adapt according to their personal and social environment and resources. For example, unstable work may increase the depression or unhappiness of a single mother if she lacks adequate social support or if the unstable work increases her preexisting feelings of self-doubt (Gomel et al.,

1998). In addition, the way an individual functions in relationships may be altered as a result of economic distress. For example, a husband who is laid off may displace his individual hostility and anger into arguments with his wife. Under economic stress, alterations in the roles and responsibilities of family members may also occur. If a family experiences an income loss, other family members may be required to contribute household resources by engaging in the role of earner (Elder & Caspi, 1988). With a loss in income, families may have to reduce consumption; for example, leisure activities may be suspended.

Coping With Normative Economic Stressors

Financial planning, when used by individuals and families, can decrease family vulnerability and exposure to economic stress. Keeping pace with inflation (Guadagno, 1983) and balancing work and family (Nickols, 1994; Poduska, 1992) have been identified as the primary normative economic stressors facing American family financial managers. Today, as the baby boom cohort approaches and moves into their 50s, financial decisions of families are likely to be dominated by concerns over adequate savings for retirement and children's education (Kennickell, Starr-McCluer, & Sunden, 1997).

In the life-cycle model developed by Ando and Modigliani (1963), families are assumed to maximize lifetime satisfaction by spreading their consumption and income over family stages. Such a life-cycle model of balancing high- and low-income periods with saving and investing is designed to increase a family's satisfaction and decrease economic stress. The consumption path that results over time is expected to be smooth and stable, for the family maintains a standard of living with the use of savings during low-income periods.

The family economic life cycle can be described in three key stages identified by the relationship between expenditure and earning levels. First, in the family formation stage, families are expected to accumulate debt through the use of installment and consumer credit to meet expenditures that exceed earnings. In the second stage, as household heads approach peak earning years, families plan to accumulate wealth in anticipation of a substantial decrease in earned income. Reduced or stabilized expenditures and income that exceeds expenditures mark this second stage. In the third stage, consumption expenditures are again expected to outpace earnings as families tap savings and investments for expenditures in retirement.

Actual consumption patterns, however, are often affected by changing family needs and wants, situational stressors, and significant historical events (Fox, 1995). Thus, the pure life-cycle savings approach to family spending and saving patterns in many cases has not proven to be a valid depiction of actual household behavior. In fact, most empirical tests of the model refute the life-cycle savings hypothesis. Part of the gap between the theory of household resource allocation over time and actual resource allocation is explained by the nonnormative factors that are so prevalent among American families, including unanticipated unemployment, divorce, casualty losses, and unanticipated health care expenses (Fan, Chang, & Hanna, 1992). Regardless of the lack of empirical support, the life-cycle planning perspective continues to serve as a useful tool in building a financial foundation for coping with both normative and situational economic stressors.

A basic life-cycle savings model predicts that spending will outpace income in the household formation stage as a result of the purchase of a home and the expenses of child rearing. During this period, families accumulate significant amounts of debt. Planning for the payment of and worrying about the possible default on this debt could easily become a source of stress within many families. As income increases with workplace experience and household formation nears completion, immediate financial demands are expected to subside and families have an opportunity to accumulate savings and pay off debt accumulated in the formation stage. During these peak earning years, however, many families are challenged by the repayment of accumulated debt, college education expenses, and deferring the proper amount of consumption toward a period of anticipated reduced earnings in retirement. Families use tax planning, investment, and asset protection strategies to move assets from one point in the life cycle to another. Unfortunately, the complexity of these financial strategies can often become the source of additional economic stress in families (Aldana & Liljenquist, 1998). At the end of the family financial life cycle, families face the problem of living on reduced incomes and distributing excess assets among family members and/or favorite charities. These wealth transfers, and planning for them, can easily become an additional source of family stress and conflict through competition for assets.

Based on this family economic life-cycle model, normative economic changes facing American families can be anticipated and addressed. Sound financial planning strategies allow families to avoid and/or relieve much of the stress involved in financial transitions. Overall, the level of stress and financial dissatisfaction experienced by a family encountering a normative life event is largely determined by the level and management of resources available to a family, implying that the ability to obtain and manage resources can lessen the impact of stressor events. A strong relationship exists between measures of financial well-being and improved financial management skills, including cash management and the use of futuristic planning styles (Porter & Garman, 1993). The following guidelines for dealing with economic stress over the three financial life-cycle stages are based on a general financial planning model emphasizing goal setting and evaluation of progress toward these goals.

Phase 1: Debt Accumulation

Families in the household formation stage typically make up 30% of the U.S. population, yet they hold nearly 60% of the debt (Kapoor, Dlabay, & Hughes, 1999, p. 156). Nearly 9 out of 10 American household heads under the age of 45 hold some form of debt, whereas only 3 out of 10 over the age of 75 hold any debt (Kennickell et al., 1997). In testing their financial strain survey, Aldana and Liljenquist (1998) found that meeting debt obligations and credit card use were two of five factors reflecting financial strain. A key measure of financial distress used in the financial services industry is the frequency of late payments made by credit users. For families with heads younger than 45, about 8% report making debt payments at least 60 days late. For families with heads older than 54, the frequency of late payments is closer to 4% (Kennickell et al., 1997).

Of the various types of debt identified by the purpose and source of the funds borrowed, the most threatening to the long-term financial well-being of the family is high-interest consumer credit used to purchase nondurable goods and services. These nondurable goods include items that typically do not last longer than the payment period and yield no economic return while being held. Going out to dinner on the high-interest credit card is the classic example. Americans are expected to carry more than $660 billion in consumer credit or credit-card debt in the year 2000 (Kapoor et al., 1999, p. 162). Of all credit-card holders, 48% carry an outstanding balance on their cards, with an average balance of $1,500 (Kennickell et al., 1997). The average American household head has 9 credit cards, including bank, gas, retail, and phone cards. With these cards, Americans are expected to charge more than $830 billion in the year 2000, nearly twice what was charged in 1990 (Kapoor et al., 1999, p. 160). Because of these debt levels, it is not surprising that the rate of personal bankruptcies is at an all-time high. A total of 1,378,071 nonbusiness bankruptcies were reported for the year ending March 31, 1999 (Administrative Offices of the U.S. Courts, 1999), implying that nearly 1.5% of U.S. households filed for personal bankruptcy in the preceding year.

Prior to the passage of the Equal Credit Opportunity Act (ECOA) in 1975, discrimination by creditors based on gender, race, and ethnicity was an accepted practice. Since the passage of the ECOA, the availability of credit to previously underserved families has steadily increased. Credit usage levels now appear to be similar across groups defined by race, gender, or ethnicity (Bowen, Lago, & Furry, 1997). Although blacks and Hispanics appear more likely to borrow to finance a car, whites report a slightly higher overall frequency of credit use (Bowen et al., 1997).

Financial satisfaction and credit practices and attitudes appear to be directly related (Lown & Ju, 1992). Families with higher debt-to-income ratios were less satisfied with their overall financial situation, whereas those using credit cards for convenience instead of installment purchases, and those comfortable maintaining large total amounts of debt, were more satisfied with their finances (Lown & Ju, 1992). Furthermore, worries about debt repayment and meeting financial emergencies are associated with lower perceived levels of financial well-being (Porter & Garman, 1993).

Much of the stress that can come with debt can be avoided if families follow a plan of debt management. Surprisingly, Godwin and Koonce (1992) found that lower-income newlyweds held more positive attitudes toward formal financial planning practices than their higher-income counterparts. Lower-income couples were shown to be more likely to budget and were more optimistic about their future prospects through the use of financial planning practices. As part of these practices, planning credit use requires (a) establishing credit goals or debt limits; (b) exploring, understanding, and making good choices between the various sources of credit; and (c) being able to make fair comparisons between the costs of different types of credit (Garman & Forgue, 1997).

Financial ratios are commonly used as guides for manageable debt levels when setting credit goals. Debt ratios are also used as indicators of families at risk of default and bankruptcy (DeVaney, 1994; Lytton, Garman, & Porter, 1991). The most commonly used debt ratios are the debt-to-income ratio and the debt-to-equity ratio. The debt-to-income guideline is usually set near 20%, implying that families can manage debt payments equal to one fifth of their take-home income. The debt-to-equity ratio is the ratio of total debt to net worth, not including any equity or debt related to the home. Both of these ratios will vary significantly through the family life cycle, and the usefulness of these measures is more in monitoring changes over time than as a point-in-time measure. For example, a very high debt-to-income ratio may reflect rational and planned use of credit for a college student; however, families running a continued long-term deficit may be headed for financial difficulties.

Once goals and tolerable debt levels are set, credit options and sources can be studied. Sources range from the most informal (relatives and friends) to the formal (bank or banklike institutions). In the formal lending sector, banks and credit unions typically lend to average or better-than-average credit-risk individuals, forcing poor credit-risk individuals to use consumer finance companies that demand higher interest rates and fees. Historically, young, less educated, single-parent, and ethnic minority households have constituted the clientele for high-interest, high-fee-lending institutions—often known as part of the "alternative financial sector" (Caskey, 1997). Sales finance companies are typically tied to the financing of a specific product (e.g., an automobile through GMAC) and cater to average or above-average credit-risk borrowers. Within the family, typically between parent and child, debt financing may provide a mutually beneficial opportunity. Related parties considering a loan between one another will use different information than that used by a bank or lending institution. In this case, both the borrower and lender face potential gains relative to the formal financial sector. Lenders (parents) may earn higher rates than financial instruments of similar risk, while borrowers (children) may pay lower rates than those offered in the formal sector. Certainly, these intrafamily financial arrangements are fertile ground for conflict and stress; however, if debt is managed using contractual arrangements similar to those in the formal sector, families stand to gain financially by lending money to each other.

Most salient in the credit decision is determining the actual cost of credit. In the simplest form, the cost of credit is represented by the interest rate, known as the cost of money. The effective interest rate, or cost of money, is compared through the calculation of the annual percentage rate (APR)—the ratio of the average finance charge to the average outstanding balance in any single period. Stated more simply, the APR is the ratio of the cost of the money to the amount borrowed. If no interest or finance charges are paid by the borrower, then the APR is zero. If the sum of the interest and finance charge is equal to half of the amount borrowed, then the APR is 50%. Unfortunately, the calculation of the APR is typically not so simple. Finance charges can be easily hidden in document preparation fees or loan origination charges, and outstanding balances can be calculated in many ways. Many balance calculation methods overstate the actual amount borrowed and increase the total cost of the loan to the consumer. Many of the problems of comparing the cost of credit were greatly alleviated with the passage of the Truth-in-

Lending Act (TILA) in 1969. The act requires lenders in the formal sector to report the cost of money as an annual percentage rate, including all fees and finance charges. Although this act protects borrowers in the formal sector, those in the informal or "alternative financial" credit sector have no such protection.

Phase 2: Repaying Debt and Saving for Retirement

During the wealth accumulation stage of the family financial life cycle, when income is expected to exceed consumption, family financial managers plan to retire debt accumulated in the previous stage and invest any surplus in financial assets. Ideally, these investments will be chosen to match the risk tolerance and financial savvy of the family financial manager. During this stage in the family financial life cycle, families encounter economic stress as a result of not having adequate resources for (a) debt repayment or (b) meeting expenses such as children's college tuition and impending retirement.

Families burdened and stressed by debt repayment have limited options. For example, if the specific source of stress is a negative credit report, then there is little a family can do other than wait for the negative items to clear the report. Credit bureaus report negative information for 7 years and bankruptcy information for 10 years. Within these periods, companies offering "credit repair" services cannot erase negative items. Consumers do have the option of adding a written statement of up to 100 words to explain any negative information in their reports.

For families who are burdened with debt, the most important action is to accurately determine what is owed. Once a clear picture of the extent of the debt problem is drawn, families can allocate savings toward debt repayment, retiring the highest APR loans first, thus "investing" in the highest return assets earlier. This method of thinking of debt repayment in terms similar to saving for future financial goals helps financial managers justify an emphasis on debt repayment early in the financial life cycle, potentially relieving some of the stress involved in delaying savings for retirement and longer-range financial goals.

Nonprofit organizations such as Consumer Credit Counseling Services (CCCS) can assist families with the debt management process. Typically, CCCS will help families reestablish payment terms for debt with payments that are more manageable. Often the counseling service will collect a lump-sum payment and redistribute the payments to the family's creditors, thus relieving the stress involved in having direct contact with creditors. However, there are significant drawbacks to using such a debt management system. The process itself will likely be reported as a negative event in credit bureau files, and participants must agree to discontinue any use of credit while in the debt management process.

As families struggle to retire debt from the formation stage, they encounter significant additional educational expenses as children approach college age. The education spending pressures have risen steadily over the past two decades as tuition increases have consistently outpaced increases in wages. The collective hopelessness is expressed in families' unwillingness to even plan for and begin saving for a child's education. Lee, Hanna, and Siregar (1997) found that only 28% of households with children under the age of 18 had saved anything for education goals. However, households headed by college-educated Hispanic or Asian individuals were more likely to be saving for expected education expenses. Churaman (1992) reported that only 14% of two-parent families and 11% of single-parent families had saved money for children's college education. Churaman (1992) reported even lower education-saving rates for black families, with only 8% of black and 14% of otherwise similar white households saving specifically for college. The standard planning advice, as with any other long-term financial goal, is to estimate anticipated expenditures and start saving as early as possible to take advantage of compound interest and the time value of money. However, the complexities of the college financial aid system and a history of dramatic increases in the cost of college education have pushed educational planning out of the financial plans of most families (Churaman, 1992).

Todd and DeVaney (1997) describe the competing pressures families face in planning for their retirement and the college education of their children, finding that about 25% of all families use retirement assets to pay for college expenses. College-educated parents with at least two children in college were more likely to use retirement savings to pay for college costs; higher-income families were least likely to tap retirement funds for education. Of the households in the Todd and DeVaney study, 58% reported that they wished they had started saving sooner for retirement.

Recent empirical studies of the adequacy of retirement savings consistently find that American families are underfinancing their retirement. These families will need to either increase savings or reduce living standards below expected levels upon retirement. Yuh, Montalto, and Hanna (1998), using 1995 nationally representative data of households with heads over the age of 35, estimated that only 52% of households are on track for retirement at preretirement consumption levels. In this study, the adequacy of retirement savings varied significantly across many demographic groups. For example, only 39% of black, non-Hispanic households and 40% of households headed by unmarried women were found to be adequately prepared for retirement. Another study found that those most adequately prepared for retirement were families headed by white males with longer planning horizons who owned financial assets and planned to retire at or after age 65 (Li, Montalto, & Geistfeld, 1996). Moore and Mitchell (1998) show in their analysis that American families need to save an additional 16% of preretirement earnings to maintain standards of living at preretirement levels. Hira and Mugenda (1998) found that nearly 57% of nonretired households were dissatisfied with their current level of savings, yet surprisingly only 28% of nonretired households were dissatisfied with their perceived ability to meet long-term financial goals.

The formal process of retirement planning is outlined by Garman and Forgue (1997) and can be used to determine adequate levels of savings to meet retirement spending needs. As with all financial planning prescriptions, the process begins with goal setting. Goals are set based on income needs in retirement. Income replacement ratios are often used as crude, yet easy, substitutes for accurate estimates of spending needs in retirement. However, there are many plausible explanations for both increased and decreased income needs in retirement, and an individual income need projection level should be set by each family. Once an income level is set, current retirement resources available to the family can be evaluated. These sources typically come from anticipated Social Security benefits, employer-provided defined benefit pensions, and personal savings and/or resources in defined contribution retirement plans.

Defined retirement benefits typically are based on a set formula of years of service and salary earned. Social Security benefits are based on such a formula. The retirement benefits earned in defined contribution programs are very different and are determined by the amount the individual worker decides to save and where the savings are placed (certificates of deposit, stocks, bonds, mutual funds, or any other investment asset). Current employer practice is moving away from defined benefit plans and toward defined contribution plans (Employee Benefit Research Institute, 1997), thus shifting the planning and retirement-saving burden more toward families. Currently, there are proposals to move the Social Security system to a defined contribution plan, which would further place the planning burden on families to carefully manage their own finances.

Households headed by women, blacks, and Hispanics have been found to be investing less in higher-risk, higher-return assets such as stocks and small businesses (Bajtelsmit, Bernasek, & Jiankoplos, 1999; Embrey & Fox, 1997; Gutter, Fox, & Montalto, in press). While not having such volatile investments in a retirement portfolio may be comforting, it has been shown to be costly, because portfolios without stocks and business assets historically have underperformed (Siegel, 1994). The implications could be grim for fe-male-, black-, and Hispanic-headed households, for business earnings will not be equally distributed through the retirement investment portfolios of all families, placing the financial security of these households in jeopardy.

Once anticipated retirement resources are evaluated, they are subtracted from retirement needs and a savings gap is estimated. Additional annual con-tributions needed to fill this gap are then calculated, and investment decisions are made to match individual investor risk-tolerance levels and specific fi-nancial goals in retirement. In this final part of the retirement planning and saving process, a wide range of tax, investment, and insurance planning tools are available to families. It is at this point that many of the complexities of the financial planning process are presented to the family financial manager. In fact, the sheer breadth of the field of financial planning appears to be a source of economic stress in families. Aldana and Liljenquist (1998) confirm that the lack of financial education and understanding about financial matters is a significant determinant of financial strain. It has further been shown that those receiving professional advice about finances and retirement are more satisfied with their current financial situation (Porter & Garman, 1993; Todd & DeVaney, 1997). Furthermore, the delivery of this counseling, financial education, and/or advice has been shown to have the greatest impact when given in one-on-one sessions between family financial managers and trusted and known professionals (Gorham, DeVaney, & Bechman, 1998; Koonce, 1990).

Phase 3: Living in Retirement and Planning for Intergenerational Transfers

A recent survey reports that 41% of individuals found adjusting to retire-ment to be a financially difficult process, whereas only 12% of newlyweds and 23% of new parents reported difficulties with financial adjustments (Pollan & Levine, 1995). Similarly, Hira and Mugenda (1998) report that 35% of retirees were dissatisfied with their current level of savings. Whether or not retirement is perceived as a negative life event has been found to de-pend on the characteristics of the retiree. Retiree characteristics found to be predictive of a stressful retirement include lower socioeconomic status, less education, inadequate income, and poor physical and mental health (Blau, Oser, & Stephens, 1982; Bosse, Aldwin, Levenson, & Workman-Daniels,

1991). Bosse et al. (1991) found poor health and family finances to be predictors of stress during retirement. Logue (1991) reports a higher prevalence of financial stress in black, involuntarily retired women, with educated homeowners showing less financial strain. Logue also concluded that one in six retired women was financially stressed. Retirement was perceived as most stressful for those who experienced a significant financial decline after work stoppage, classifying retirement as a burdensome event (Bosse et al., 1991).

However, for the majority of currently retired Americans, financial stress and dissatisfaction levels appear to be minimal when compared with those in other stages of the family financial life cycle. Compared with younger and employed Americans, retirees have been shown to pay closer attention to their long-range financial plans. Davis and Carr (1992) found retirees, in comparison with other age groups, to be least likely to use formal or informal written budgets; however, these same retirees were found to be most likely to have a budget that covered a period longer than 1 month. In analyzing family readiness for financial emergencies, Hira, Fanslow, and Vogelsang (1992) found that the most satisfied household money managers tended to be retired, holding a higher net worth, and covered by a broad range of insurance products.

A more significant family stressor in retirement may be the lack of preparation for widowhood. One study found that more than half of widowed women (60%) had not discussed the management of their finances with their husband prior to his death, leaving them relatively unaware of their financial position and experiencing higher levels of stress and dissatisfaction with finances (Morgan, 1986).

In the simplest form of the family life-cycle savings model, families are assumed to hold no bequest motives, with every dollar spent during the lifetimes of the immediate family members. Clearly, an important extension of this life-cycle framework is the consideration of the impact and process of passing wealth between generations (Modigliani, 1988).

From infancy to early adulthood or longer, family members depend on the transfer of resources among each other. Certainly, intergenerational transfers from parent to child are greatest when the child is still dependent and not involved in market activity. However, this relationship has been shown to extend even further. Investigations into the pattern of parental support to children across the life span maintain that parents contribute financial support well into later life, yet support does decline with age (Cooney & Uhlenberg, 1992; Troll, Miller, & Atchley, 1979). Using data from the National Survey of Households and Families, Cooney and Uhlenberg (1992) examined the trajectory of support from parents to children and found an increased likelihood of children receiving financial support during their early to late 20s; however, support continuously declined throughout adulthood. In addition, children were found to turn to parents during times of economic stress, with well over half of respondents through age 45 naming a parent as someone they would call in case of a financial emergency. The nature and extent of young adults' dependence on financial support from parents is dependent on several factors. Child dependence on parents has likely increased because of delayed marriage and prolonged college attendance; however, higher levels of maternal employment and divorce have cut short the resources available to adult children, resulting in decreased dependence (Cooney & Uhlenberg, 1992).

Stress resulting from the estate planning or the intergenerational transfer portion of a family financial plan likely comes directly from (a) the perceived legal complexities associated with asset transfers before and after death and (b) the changing roles of family members in the financial management process (Edwards, 1991). The goal of estate planning is to maximize the compliance with the decedents' wants while minimizing the erosion of wealth through taxes and transaction costs.

Ramaglia and MacDonald (1999) outline the steps in the estate planning process. The first step is to compile financial records and determine the total value of the estate. Even in consideration of the complex tax legislation related to estates and the wide range and technical nature of trusts used in estate planning, valuation of assets is often the most difficult part of the estate planning process. Although assets such as stocks and bonds are easy to value, families typically own other assets that are difficult to value such as businesses, partnerships, and works of art. After valuation, the second step in the estate planning process is to write a will, naming beneficiaries, an executor, and a guardian or trustee to protect the interests of minor children. Once beneficiaries are designated, the impact of estimated federal and state estate and inheritance taxes can be calculated. Finally, on the basis of these estimates, families consider various strategies of interfamily gifting, life insurance, and charitable contributions to reduce anticipated estate taxes and preserve wealth while passing it to intended heirs.

The assistance of competent and honest financial and legal professionals is more critical in the estate planning process than in any other stage of the family financial life cycle. A solid estate plan will result from the integration of legal documents drafted in conjunction with the decedent's asset allocation and desired asset distribution upon death. These legal documents also will need to be periodically recast to address changes in tax policies, family structure, and family assets. Dealing with the economic property of a deceased or aging family member can easily become a stressor among surviving family members. However, as with the challenges faced in other financial life-cycle stages, financial planning can be used as an effective means of relieving family economic stress.

Summary

Economic stress exacts many social and psychological costs on the quality of individual and family life. Family financial planning is a general preventive strategy that can help reduce these social and psychological costs, thereby enhancing the well-being of family life. With the impending move of the baby boom cohort through the Social Security system as many retire, the need for sound and secure family financial planing is critical. Furthermore, with an increasing proportion of the population anticipating bequests, inheritance will provide new opportunities and challenges for family dynamics. With preventive planning and preparation, these family financial issues can be disposed of. Among those who do not plan and prepare, programs and policies can intervene in an effort to maintain the quality of family life.

DISCUSSION QUESTIONS

1. What are the key demographic differences in vulnerability and exposure to economic stress?

2. What are the primary economic stressors in families today? Is there adequate empirical evidence to reflect family economic trends to support your conclusions? You may want to consult *The Statistical Abstract of the United States,* accessed through the World Wide Web at *http://www.census.gov,* as an excellent source of such empirical evidence.

3. Is it a good idea for family members to lend money to one another? What is the potential impact of intrafamily loans on family stress levels? What are the issues that should be discussed before embarking on this financial arrangement?

4. What are the economic stressors families face in retirement? What are the critical components of a plan to help families avoid these stressors?

5. Who are the critical participants in an estate plan? What communication
   strategies should families use when anticipating intergenerational transfers of wealth?

SUGGESTED READINGS

Bowen, C. F., Lago, D. J., & Furry, M. M. (1997). Money management in families: A review of the literature with a racial, ethnic, and limited income perspective. *Advancing
the Consumer Interest, 9,* 32-42.

Bryant, W. K. (1990). *The economic organization of the household.* New York: Cambridge University Press.

Conger, R. D., Conger, K. J., Elder, G. H., Lorenz, F. O., Simons, R. L., & Whitbeck, L. B.
(1992). A family process model of economic hardship and adjustment of early adolescent boys. *Child Development, 63,* 526-541.

Garman, E. T., & Forgue, R. E. (1997). *Personal finance* (5th ed.). Boston: Houghton
Mifflin.

Kapoor, J. R., Dlabay, L. R., & Hughes, R. J. (1999). *Personal finance* (5th ed.). Boston:
Irwin/McGraw-Hill.

Ramaglia, J. A., & MacDonald, D. B. (1999). *Personal finance: Tools for decision making.* Cincinnati, OH: South-Western College.

Voydanoff, P., & Majka, L. C. (1988). *Families and economic distress: Coping strategies
and social policy.* Newbury Park, CA: Sage.

REFERENCES

Adler, N. E., Boyce, T., Chesney, M. A., Cohen, S., Folkman, S., Kahn, R. L., & Syme,
S. L. (1994). Socioeconomic status and health: The challenge of gradient. *American
Psychologist, 49,* 15-25.

Administrative Offices of the United States Courts. (1999). *News release: Second quarter 1999 shows slight drop in bankruptcy filings* [On-line; retrieved May 21]. Available: http://www.uscourts.gov/Press_Releases/pr052199.pdf

Aldana, S. G., & Liljenquist, W. (1998). Validity and reliability of a financial strain survey. *Financial Counseling and Planning, 9,* 11-18.

Ando, A., & Modigliani, F. (1963). The life cycle hypothesis of saving. *American Economic Review: Aggregate Implications and Tests, 53,* 55-84.

Angel, R., & Tienda, M. (1982). Determinants of extended household structure: Cultural
pattern or economic need? *American Journal of Sociology, 6,* 1360-1383.

Bachman, J. G. (1983, Summer). Premature affluence: Do high school students earn too
much? *Economic Outlook USA,* pp. 64-67.

Bajtelsmit, V., Bernasek, A., & Jiankoplos, N. (1999). Gender differences in defined contribution pension decisions. *Financial Services Review, 8,* 1-10.

Blaney, P. (1985). Stress and depression in adults: A critical review. In T. Field, P. McCabe, & N. Schniederman (Eds.), *Stress and coping* (pp. 263-283). Hillsdale, NJ: Lawrence Erlbaum.

Blau, A. S., Oser, S. T., & Stephens, R. C. (1982). Patterns of adaptation in retirement: A comparative analysis. In A. Kolker & P. E. Ahmed (Eds.), *Coping with medical issues: Aging* (pp. 119-138). New York: Elsevier Biomedical.

Blumstein, P., & Schwartz, P. (1983). *American couples: Money, work, sex.* New York: William Morrow.

Bosse, A., Aldwin, C. M., Levenson, M. R., & Workman-Daniels, K. (1991). How stressful is retirement? Findings from a normative age study. *Journal of Gerontology, 46,* 9-14.

Bound, J., Duncan, G. J., Laren, D. S., & Oleninick, L. (1991). Poverty dynamics in widowhood. *Journal of Gerontology, 46,* S115-S124.

Bowen, C. F., Lago, D. J., & Furry, M. M. (1997). Money management in families: A review of the literature with a racial, ethnic, and limited income perspective. *Advancing the Consumer Interest, 9,* 32-42.

Brubaker, T. H. (1991). Families in later life: A burgeoning research area. In A. Booth (Ed.), *Contemporary families: Looking forward, looking back.* Minneapolis, MN: National Council on Family Relations.

Burden, D. S., & Klerman, L. V. (1984). Teenage parenthood: Factors that lessen economic dependence. *Social Work, 29,* 11-16.

Caskey, J. P. (1997). *Lower income Americans, higher cost financial services.* Madison, WI: Filene Research Institute.

Churaman, C. V. (1992). Financing of college education by minority and white families. *Journal of Consumer Affairs, 26,* 324-350.

Conger, R. D., Conger, K. J., Elder, G. H., Lorenz, F. O., Simons, R. L., & Whitbeck, L. B. (1992). A family process model of economic hardship and adjustment of early adolescent boys. *Child Development, 63,* 526-541.

Conger, R. D., Elder, G. H., Lorenz, F. O., Conger, K. J., Simons, R. L., Whitbeck, L. B., Huck, S., & Melby, J. N. (1990). Linking economic hardship to marital quality and instability. *Journal of Marriage and the Family, 52,* 643-656.

Conger, R. D., Rueter, M. A., & Elder, G. H. (1999). Couple resilience to economic pressure. *Journal of Personality and Social Psychology, 76,* 54-71.

Cooney, T. M., & Uhlenberg, P. (1992). Support from parents over the life course: The adult child's perspective. *Social Forces, 71,* 63-84.

DaVanzo, J., & Rahman, M. O. (1993). American families: Trends and correlates. *Population Index, 59,* 350-386.

Davis, E. P., & Carr, R. A. (1992). Budgeting practices over the life cycle. *Financial Counseling and Planning, 3,* 3-16.

DeVaney, S. A. (1994). The usefulness of financial ratios as predictors of household insolvency: Two perspectives. *Financial Counseling and Planning, 5,* 5-24.

DeViney, S. (1995). Life course, private pension, and financial well-being. *American Behavioral Scientist, 39,* 172-185.

Duncan, G. J., & Hoffman, S. D. (1985). A reconsideration of the economic consequences of marital dissolution. *Demography, 22*(4), 485-497.

Edwards, K. P. (1991). Planning for family asset transfers. *Financial Counseling and Planning, 2,* 55-78.

Elder, G. H., & Caspi, A. (1988). Economic stress in lives: Developmental perspectives. *Journal of Social Issues, 44,* 25-45.

Elder, G. H., Conger, R. D., Foster, E. M., & Ardelt, M. (1992). Families under economic pressure. *Journal of Family Issues, 13,* 5-37.

Embrey, L., & Fox, J. J. (1997). Gender differences in the investment decision making process. *Financial Counseling and Planning, 8,* 33-39.

Employee Benefit Research Institute. (1997). *Defined contribution plan dominance grows across sectors and employer sizes while mega defined benefit plans remain strong: Where we are and where we are going* (Issue Brief No. 190). Washington, DC: Author.

Fan, X. J., Chang, Y. R., & Hanna, S. (1992). Optimal credit use with uncertain income. *Financial Counseling and Planning, 3,* 125-132.

Fox, J. J. (1995). Household demand system analysis: Implications of unit root econometrics for modeling, testing, and policy analysis. *Consumer Interests Annual, 41,* 195-201.

Garman, E. T., & Forgue, R. E. (1997). *Personal finance* (5th ed.). Boston: Houghton Mifflin.

Godwin, D. D. (1994). Antecedents and consequences of newlyweds' cash flow management. *Financial Counseling and Planning, 5,* 161-190.

Godwin, D. D., & Koonce, J. C. (1992). Cash flow management of low-income newlyweds. *Financial Counseling and Planning, 3,* 17-42.

Gomel, J. N., Tinsley, B. J., Parke, R. D., & Clark, K. M. (1998). The effects of economic hardship on family relationships among African American, Latino, and Euro-American families. *Journal of Family Issues, 19,* 436-467.

Goodman, M. (1986). Americans and their money. *Money, 15,* 159-166.

Gorham, E. E., DeVaney, S. A., & Bechman, J. C. (1998). Adoption of financial management practices: A program assessment. *Journal of Extension, 36* [On-line]. Available: http://www.joe.org/joe/1998august/a5.html

Guadagno, M. A. (1983). Economic stress: Family financial management. In H. McCubbin & C. Figley (Eds.), *Stress and the family* (pp. 201-217). New York: Brunner/Mazel.

Guelzow, M. G., Bird, G. W., & Koball, E. H. (1991). An exploratory path analysis of the stress process for dual-career men and women. *Journal of Marriage and the Family, 53,* 151-164.

Gutter, M. S., Fox, J. J., & Montalto, C. P. (1999). Racial differences in investor decision making. *Financial Services Review, 8*(3), 149-162.

Hagquist, C. E. I. (1998). Economic stress and perceived health among adolescents in Sweden. *Journal of Adolescent Health, 22,* 250-257.

Hamilton, V. L., Croman, C. L., Hoffman, W. S., & Renner, D. S. (1990). Hard times and vulnerable people: Initial effects of plant closing on autoworkers' mental health. *Journal of Health and Social Behavior, 31,* 123-140.

Hao, L. (1995). How does a single mother choose kin and welfare support? *Social Science Research, 24,* 1-27.

Hira, T. K., Fanslow, A. M., & Vogelsang, R. (1992). Determinants of satisfaction with preparations for financial emergencies. *Financial Counseling and Planning, 3,* 43-62.

Hira, T. K., & Mugenda, O. (1998). Predictors of financial satisfaction: Differences between retirees and non-retirees. *Financial Counseling and Planning, 9,* 75-83.

Ho, C. S., Lempers, J. D., & Clark-Lempers, D. S. (1995). Effects of economic hardship on adolescent self-esteem: A family mediation model. *Adolescence, 30,* 117-131.

Holden, K. C., & Smock, P. J. (1991). The economic costs of marital dissolution: Why do women bear a disproportionate cost? *Annual Review of Sociology, 17,* 51-78.

Johnson, T. P. (1991). Mental health, social relations, and social selection: A longitudinal analysis. *Journal of Health and Social Behavior, 32,* 408-423.

Kapoor, J. R., Dlabay, L. R., & Hughes, R. J. (1999). *Personal finance* (5th ed.). Boston: Irwin/McGraw-Hill.

Keith, P. M., & Lorenz, F. O. (1989). Financial strain and health of unmarried older people. *Gerontologist, 29,* 684-691.

Keith, V. M. (1993). Gender, financial strain, and psychological distress among adults. *Research on Aging, 15,* 123-147.

Kelvin, P., & Jarrett, J. E. (1985). *Unemployment: Its social psychological effects.* London: Cambridge University Press.

Kennickell, A. B., Starr-McCluer, M., & Sunden, A. E. (1997). Family finances in the U.S.: Recent evidence from the Survey of Consumer Finances. *Federal Reserve Bulletin, 83,* 1-24.

Kessler, R. C., House, J. S., & Turner, J. B. (1987). Unemployment and health in a community sample. *Journal of Health and Social Behavior, 28,* 51-59.

Kircherler, E. (1988). Diary reports on daily economic decisions of happy versus unhappy couples. *Journal of Economic Psychology, 9,* 327-357.

Kitson, G. C., with Holmes, W. M. (1992). *Portrait of divorce: Adjustment to marital breakdown.* New York: Guilford.

Klebanov, P. K., Brooks-Gunn, J., & Duncan, G. J. (1994). Does neighborhood and family poverty affect mothers' parenting, mental health, and social support? *Journal of Marriage and the Family, 56,* 441-455.

Koonce, J. C. (1990). Helping low-income elderly with money management. *Journal of Extension, 28* [On-line]. Available: http://www.joe.org/joe/1990fall/a3.html

Krause, N. (1987). Chronic strain, locus of control, and distress in older adults. *Psychology and Aging, 2,* 375-382.

Lawrence, F. C., Thomasson, R. H., Wozniak, P. J., & Prawitz, A. D. (1993). Factors relating to spousal financial arguments. *Financial Counseling and Planning, 4,* 85-94.

Lee, S., Hanna, S., & Siregar, M. (1997). Children's college as a saving goal. *Financial Counseling and Planning, 8,* 33-36.

Lempers, J. D., & Clark-Lempers, D. (1990). Economic hardship, parenting, and distress in adolescence. *Child Development, 60*, 25-39.

Lempers, J. D., & Clark-Lempers, D. (1997). Economic hardship, family relationships, and adolescent distress: An evaluation of a stress-distress mediation model in mother-daughter and mother-son dyads. *Adolescence, 32*, 339-356.

Li, J., Montalto, C. P., & Geistfeld, L. V. (1996). Determinants of financial adequacy for retirement. *Financial Counseling and Planning, 7*, 39-48.

Liker, J. K., & Elder, G. H. (1983). Economic hardship and marital relations in the 1930s. *American Sociological Review, 48*, 343-359.

Logue, B. J. (1991). Women at risk: Predictors of financial stress for retired women workers. *Gerontologist, 31*, 657-665.

Lorenz, F. O., Conger, R. D., Simon, R. L., Whitbeck, L. B., & Elder, G. H. (1991). Economic pressure and marital quality: An illustration of the method variance problem in the causal modeling of family processes. *Journal of Marriage and the Family, 53*, 375-388.

Lown, J. M. (1984). Financial management practices of remarried families. In C. A. Dickson (Ed.), *Proceedings of the Western Regional Home Management-Family Economics Educators* (pp. 52-56). Honolulu, HI: Western Regional Home Management-Family Economics Educators.

Lown, J. M., & Ju, I. (1992). A model of credit use and financial satisfaction. *Financial Counseling and Planning, 3*, 105-124.

Lytton, R. H., Garman, E. T., & Porter, N. M. (1991). How to use financial ratios when advising clients. *Financial Counseling and Planning, 2*, 3-24.

MacFadyen, A. J., MacFadyen, H. W., & Prince, N. J. (1996). Economic stress and psychological well-being: An economic psychology framework. *Journal of Economic Psychology, 17*, 291-311.

McCubbin, H. I., Joy, C. B., Cauble, A. E., Comeau, J. K., Patterson, J. M., & Needle, R. H. (1980). Family stress and coping: A decade review. *Journal of Marriage and the Family, 42*, 855-872.

Modigliani, F. (1988). The role of intergenerational transfers and life cycle saving in the accumulation of wealth. *Journal of Economic Perspectives, 2*, 15-40.

Moore, J. F., & Mitchell, O. S. (1998). *Projected retirement wealth and savings adequacy in the Health and Retirement Study* (Pension Research Council Working Paper No. 98-1). Philadelphia: Warton School of the University of Pennsylvania.

Morgan, L. A. (1986). The financial experience of widowed women: Evidence from the LRHS. *Gerontologist, 25*, 351-357.

Nickols, S. Y. (1994). Work/family stresses. In P. McKenry & S. Price (Eds.), *Families and change: Coping with stressful events* (pp. 66-87). Thousand Oaks, CA: Sage.

O'Bryant, S. L., & Morgan, L. A. (1989). Financial experience and well-being among mature widowed women. *Gerontologist, 29*, 245-251.

Olson, D. H., McCubbin, H. I., Barnes, H., Larsen, A., Muxen, M., & Wilson, M. (1983). *Families: What makes them work.* Beverly Hills, CA: Sage.

Palmore, E. (1981). *Social patterns in normal aging: Findings from the Duke longitudinal study.* Durham, NC: Duke University Press.

Pearlin, L., & Johnson, J. (1977). Marital status, life-strains, and depression. *American Sociological Review, 42,* 704-715.

Pearlin, L. I., Lieberman, M. A., Menaghan, E. G., & Mullan, J. T. (1981). The stress process. *Journal of Health and Social Behavior, 22,* 337-356.

Peirce, R. S., Frone, M. R., Russel, M., & Cooper, M. L. (1994). Relationship of financial strain and psychosocial resources to alcohol use and abuse: The mediating role of negative affect and drinking motives. *Journal of Health and Social Behavior, 35,* 291-308.

Pett, M. A., & Vaughan-Cole, B. (1986). The impact of income issues and social status on post-divorce adjustment of custodial parents. *Family Relations, 35,* 103-111.

Poduska, B. (1992). Money, marriage, Maslow's hierarchy of needs. *American Behavioral Scientist, 35,* 756-770.

Pollan, S. M., & Levine, M. (1995). The rise and fall of retirement. *Worth, 4*(1), 72.

Porter, N. M., & Garman, E. T. (1993). Testing a conceptual model of financial well-being. *Financial Counseling and Planning, 4,* 135-164.

Ramaglia, J. A., & MacDonald, D. B. (1999). *Personal finance: Tools for decision making.* Cincinnati, OH: South-Western College.

Ross, C. E., Mirowsky, J., & Goldsteen, K. (1990). The impact of the family on health: The decade in review. *Journal of Marriage and the Family, 52,* 1052-1078.

Siegel, J. J. (1994). *Stocks for the long run: A guide to selecting for long-term growth.* Burr Ridge, IL: Irwin Professional.

Takeuchi, D. T., Williams, D. R., & Adair, R. K. (1991). Economic stress in the family and children's emotional and behavioral problems. *Journal of Marriage and the Family, 53,* 1031-1041.

Taylor, R. J., Chatters, L. M., Tucker, M., & Lewis, E. (1990). Developments in research on black families: A decade review. *Journal of Marriage and the Family, 52,* 993-1014.

Todd, K. J., & DeVaney, S. A. (1997). Financial planning for retirement by parents of college students. *Financial Counseling and Planning, 8,* 25-32.

Troll, L. E., Miller, S. J., & Atchley, R. C. (1979). *Families in later life.* Belmont, CA: Wadsworth.

Umberson, D., Wortman, C. B., & Kessler, R. C. (1992). Widowhood and depression: Explaining long-term gender differences in vulnerability. *Journal of Health and Social Behavior, 33,* 10-24.

U.S. Bureau of the Census. (1996). *Current population reports: Special studies: 65+ in the United States* (P-23-190). Washington, DC: U.S. Government Printing Office.

Vega, W. A. (1991). Families in later life: A burgeoning research area. In A. Booth (Ed.), *Contemporary families: Looking forward, looking back* (pp. 297-306). Minneapolis, MN: National Council on Family Relations.

Vinokur, A. D., Price, R. H., & Caplan, R. D. (1996). Hard times and hurtful partners: How financial strain affects depression and relationship satisfaction of unemployed persons and their spouses. *Journal of Health and Social Behavior, 71,* 166-179.

Voydanoff, P. (1990). Economic distress and family relations: A review of the eighties. *Journal of Marriage and the Family, 52,* 1099-1115.

Weiss, R. S. (1984). The impact of marital dissolution on income and consumption in single-parent households. *Journal of Marriage and the Family, 46,* 115-127.

Williams, F. L., & Berry, R. E. (1984). Intensity of family disagreement over finances and associated factors. *Journal of Consumer Studies and Home Economics, 8,* 33-53.

Williams, F. L., & Prohofsky, S. S. (1986). Teenagers' perception of agreement over family expenditures, employment, and family life. *Journal of Youth and Adolescence, 15,* 243-257.

Wilson, M. N., & Tolson, T. J. (1990). Familial support in the black community. *Journal of Clinical Child Psychology, 19,* 347-355.

Winkler, A. E. (1993). The living arrangements of single mothers with dependent children: An added perspective. *American Journal of Economics and Sociology, 52,* 1-18.

Yuh, Y., Montalto, C. P., & Hanna, S. (1998). Are Americans prepared for retirement? *Financial Counseling and Planning, 9,* 1-12.

12

Divorce as a Family Stressor

DAVID H. DEMO
MARK A. FINE
LAWRENCE H. GANONG

Divorce is widely viewed as a serious problem. The word *divorce* conjures up images of divided families, vulnerable children, failed marriages, forgotten commitments, long and expensive legal battles, resentment, hostility, bitterness, and economic hardship. It is understandable that people do not think positively about divorce. Children do not grow up dreaming that they will divorce one day. Nor do most children hope that their parents will divorce and live apart. Yet increasing numbers of children in the United States are living this scenario, growing up in what researchers call binuclear families. From 1970 to 1994, the percentage of white children living with two parents (including stepparents) fell from 90% to 80%; for African American children, the percentage declined from 60% to 33%; and for Hispanic children, the percentage decreased from 80% to 65% (Teachman, 2000).

Our first objective in this chapter is to consider different perspectives for thinking about divorce and to challenge some assumptions, attitudes, and beliefs about how families are affected by divorce. For example, a common belief is that children and adults experience severe, long-term postdivorce adjustment problems. Although some studies of small clinical samples support this belief (e.g., Wallerstein & Blakeslee, 1990), studies of larger and more representative samples suggest moderate and short-term effects for adults (Booth & Amato, 1991) and children (Acock & Demo, 1994; Amato, 2000). As researchers continue to explore the mechanisms by which divorce influences family members, attention is being focused on a number of previously unasked questions. For example, could postdivorce adjustment problems be at least partly attributable to the social stigma associated with divorce and to society making divorce an experience that is socially divisive, legally tormenting, financially expensive, and emotionally exhausting? How are children's development and well-being influenced by the experience of parental divorce and its accompanying life transitions, and how are they affected by *pre*divorce family experiences such as marital conflict, parent-child conflict, family tension and stress, alcoholism, abuse, and parental neglect and abandonment? How is adult well-being influenced by pre- and postdivorce family processes and resources? How do economic circumstances change? What are the consequences of economic changes for family members? Why are some marriages more prone to divorce? These questions suggest that it would be better to conceptualize divorce as a process rather than as an event.

Our second objective in this chapter is to illustrate the variable nature of adjustment to divorce (Fine, 2000). As feminist researchers emphasize, family life is perceived, defined, and experienced differently by each family member (e.g., Ferree, 1990). Rather than a unitary or "core" family reality, there are multiple and sometimes conflicting realities. Understanding divorce requires us to understand the perspectives of all family members regarding their pre- and postdivorce family histories, relationships, and experiences.

Our third objective is to describe interventions that may facilitate divorce adjustment. Because divorce is a process that occurs within larger social, legal, and cultural systems, it is important to consider possible changes in those systems that may ease the stress of divorce and provide greater support for individuals and families. In particular, we consider family life education and mediation. Our discussion is guided by feminist, social exchange, and life-course theories.

History and Context

Although it is commonly believed that the divorce rate was low through the 1950s and then soared in recent decades, historical analyses indicate that the divorce rate increased steadily from the mid–19th century through the 1970s (Cherlin, 1992). The divorce rate then stabilized at a high level in the early 1980s and declined modestly through the 1990s (Teachman, 2000). About 50% of first marriages formed in the 1990s will end in divorce.

There are several reasons why the divorce rate rose dramatically after World War II. One important consideration is that the nuclear family of the late 1940s and 1950s—the family that is often used as a standard by which contemporary families are judged—was an aberration (Cherlin, 1992). Following the instability and hard times of the Great Depression and World War II, high value was placed on family life, contributing to a short-term drop in the divorce rate. The postwar economic boom stimulated growth in the middle class, the standard of living improved, marriage and birth rates rose, and divorce rates dropped.

Although the male-breadwinner, female-homemaker marriages of the late 1940s and 1950s were much *more* susceptible to divorce than marriages begun earlier, mid-20th-century marriages are viewed with nostalgia (Coontz, 1992), partly because they were significantly *less* likely than contemporary marriages to end in divorce. Often overlooked in such simple historical comparisons, however, is that "traditional" marriages are characterized by inequities and burdens for women, who often perform disproportionate shares of unpaid domestic work, child care, caregiving for aging parents, and other aspects of family labor in addition to wage labor (Demo & Acock, 1993). Thus, although "traditional" marriages during this period were less likely than contemporary marriages to end in divorce, this stability had costs.

During the 1960s and 1970s, the climate in the United States contributed to an increasing emphasis on individualism. From the late 1950s to the late 1980s, singlehood, cohabitation, childlessness, and nonmarital sexual relations became more acceptable, while opposition to abortion and divorce weakened (Thornton, 1989). For many, concerns with self-fulfillment and careerism diminished their commitment to family, rendering marriage and other intimate relationships vulnerable (Schnaiberg & Goldenberg, 1989).

Economic factors also contributed to rising divorce rates. Changing work patterns, diminished occupational opportunities, men's declining labor force involvement, stagnant wages for white men and declining wages for African American men over the past two decades, and massive underemployment for millions of lower-income wage earners have led to domestic upheaval for many families (Coontz, 1997; Teachman, 2000). Even though women earn less than men do for the same work, their reduced economic dependence on men has made divorce an acceptable alternative for women in unhappy marriages. Heckert, Nowak, and Snyder (1998) observed that compared with "traditional" marriages in which the husband earned the majority of family income and marriages (primarily in low-income families) in which wives earned substantially more than husbands (75%-100% of family income), the greatest likelihood of marital disruption occurred for marriages in which wives earned 50% to 75% of family income. For the latter group, women's economic independence may have enhanced the attractiveness of leaving an unhappy marriage. It is important to note, however, that in many families, particularly those with lower incomes, wives' earnings relieve economic pressure, stabilize marriage, and prevent marital dissolution (Heckert et al., 1998). Women's economic independence plays a central role in marital and family dynamics, and there is evidence for the idea that women's earnings have a nonlinear influence on the probability of marital disruption.

Although many observers have argued that individuals find it harder to maintain happy marriages now than they did before, the evidence is not conclusive. Perhaps a more plausible explanation of the increase in the divorce rate in the late 1960s and 1970s is that many individuals, especially women, recognized that marriage was not meeting their personal needs (Bernard, 1972). In this context, it is not surprising that two thirds of recent divorces have been initiated by women (Ahrons, 1994; Braver, 1998). But the relationship between marital quality and attitudes toward divorce is bidirectional. Research indicates that divorce is more likely to occur in marriages in which partners hold favorable attitudes toward divorce (Amato, 1996), but adopting favorable attitudes toward divorce may erode marital quality over time by decreasing marital interaction and increasing marital conflict (Amato & Rogers, 1999).

Another factor undermining marital stability is that individuals often have unrealistic, idealistic, and romanticized notions about marriage. The coexistence of these conditions—personal fulfillment being strongly valued, lofty expectations not being satisfied, and perceiving that desirable alternatives are available—increases the probability of divorce. The fact is the divorce rate in the United States is likely to remain higher than in the past.

Proneness to Divorce

The reasons why some couples stay together while others do not are complicated. There is consistent evidence that several demographic, life-course, and marital processes contribute to a higher probability of divorce, including parental divorce (Amato, 1996), cohabitation prior to marriage (Axinn & Thornton, 1992), premarital childbearing, early age at marriage, childlessness during marriage, lower income and socioeconomic status (White, 1990), negative affect in marital interaction (Gottman, 1994), and marital hostility (Matthews, Wickrama, & Conger, 1996). Among the important factors protecting marriages from divorce are shared leisure time (Hill, 1988); many more positive than negative marital interactions (Gottman, 1994); the presence of children, particularly sons (Katzev, Warner, & Acock, 1994); fathers' engagement in child rearing (Morgan, Lye, & Condran, 1988); marital happiness (Booth, Johnson, & Edwards, 1983); and the accumulation of assets (Booth, Johnson, White, & Edwards, 1986).

Unfortunately, we know much less about how family processes and relationships relate to the likelihood of divorce than we do about the influence of demographic and life-course factors (White, 1990). Drawing largely on exchange theory, Hill (1988) formulated the "attachment hypothesis" that frequent and pleasurable shared leisure time provides short-term benefits by drawing couples together and provides long-term benefits by preventing marital breakup. Couples with more shared leisure time were significantly less likely to divorce.

Hill's (1988) study also clarified the counteracting mechanisms by which children influence marital stability. Children facilitate marital stability because parents may want to stay together "for the sake of the children," and parents may fear that divorce would reduce their involvement with their children. Conversely, the presence of children restricts couples' leisure time, undermining marital happiness and destabilizing the marriage. Compared with couples with no children, parents spent a mean of 7 to 10 fewer hours per week in shared leisure. Thus, children both contribute to and detract from marital stability. These findings underscore the importance of examining multiple marriage and family processes to explain marital dissolution.

From a social exchange perspective, shared leisure time is one of many rewards of marriage. Others include social status, emotional gratification, sexual pleasure, and the accumulation of property and economic assets. Costs of marriage include the time and energy invested in household labor, wage labor, emotional labor, and child care. According to social exchange theory, low marital quality occurs when the costs of marriage exceed the rewards. When the marriage is not profitable, and when outcomes fall below the level that the individual perceives could be obtained in some other relationship, one or both parties may choose to divorce (Sabatelli & Shehan, 1993).

Another underutilized approach for uncovering the causes of divorce is asking divorced people for their accounts of "what went wrong" in their marriages. The accounts of formerly married people reveal reasons for divorce that are often overlooked in historical or demographic studies. For example, wives report more dissatisfaction with marriage than husbands do (Spanier & Thompson, 1984). Common complaints by wives include their husband's authoritarianism, mental cruelty, verbal and physical abuse, excessive drinking, lack of love, neglect of children, emotional and personality problems, and extramarital sex (Bloom, Niles, & Tatcher, 1985). More men than women describe themselves as having problems with alcohol, drugs, or physical abuse that contributed to the divorce. It is common for women and men to share the views that communication problems, unhappiness, and incompatibility led to the divorce. Former spouses' descriptions of their marriages underscore that gender differentiation and power imbalances in marriage, work, and parenthood often have undesirable, even harsh, consequences for family members.

Divorce and Its Aftermath

Although public disapproval of divorce has softened, divorced individuals still confront stigma. Gerstel (1990) found that although most divorced individuals did not think their friends or family disapproved of their divorce, they still lost friends and felt as if friends and others assessed and attributed blame. In response, elaborate accounts are developed to explain the divorce to self and to others (Hopper, 1993).

Gerstel (1990) illustrated how the circumstances associated with social disapproval are different for women than they are for men. Compared with childless women, mothers experienced harsher disapproval, particularly if they had young children; men, however, did not perceive any differences in social reactions based on their parental status. Men who had been sexually involved outside the marriage prior to separation reported greater disapproval than did other men. Gerstel (1990) concluded that the processes associated with social rejection and stigma reflect "a gender-based ideology of divorce—and marriage" (p. 464).

The broader structure of pre- and postdivorce social networks provides further illustrations of gender-based beliefs, expectations, opportunities, and constraints. Women are expected to be "kin-keepers," while men are encouraged to be independent, with social networks that are dominated by ties with friends (Milardo, 1987). Compared with men, women typically interact more frequently with kin during marriage, and they are more likely to sustain these ties postdivorce. Although both women's and men's social networks become smaller and less dense following divorce (Rands, 1988), women typically have fewer friends postdivorce (Hetherington, Cox, & Cox, 1982). These patterns impair the ability of social networks to provide support for individuals coping with divorce. Men are disadvantaged because they are less likely than women to have intimate friends and less likely to receive support from kin and nonkin (Spanier & Thompson, 1984). Women are disadvantaged because their strong involvement with their families reduces their levels of social participation and recreation (Milardo, 1987).

Economic Consequences

Women are more likely to be economically disadvantaged after divorce than men are. Of course, some women and men fare better than others, and predivorce standard of living is critical in measuring economic decline postdivorce. However, there is a clear pattern that the economic well-being of divorced women and their children plunges in comparison with predivorce levels; divorced men, on the other hand, often enjoy a better financial situation postdivorce (Peterson, 1996).

For a significant proportion of women, the economic result of divorce is poverty. Morgan (1989) found that more than one fourth of divorced women fall into poverty during the 5 years following the end of their marriage. Postdivorce poverty is especially common among women who had lower family incomes while married (Holden & Smock, 1991), but the proportional change in income is most severe for women who were relatively well-off during marriage. Furthermore, most women's economic plight following divorce is not short-lived. Despite high levels of female employment prior to separation and even higher levels postseparation, economic hardship typically extends for at least 5 years following divorce (Weiss, 1984). Five years after divorce, women's family income is still only 71% of predivorce income (Duncan & Hoffman, 1985). Although economic recovery is faster for women with higher predivorce incomes, the way most women recover financially is to remarry (Duncan & Hoffman, 1985).

For most men, by contrast, divorce has only short-term economic costs and usually contributes to an *improved* standard of living within a short period. One year after divorce, men's income is 90% of their predivorce income (Duncan & Hoffman, 1985). Examining a national sample, Duncan and Hoffman found that men's income-to-needs ratio improved 13% over predivorce levels by the first year postdivorce and improved to 24% over predivorce levels by the second year following divorce.

The economic costs of divorce are greater for women because most marriages and divorces involve children, and mothers continue to devote substantially more time to caring for children than fathers do (Acock & Demo, 1994; Marsiglio, 1993). The time women invest in child care and other unpaid family labor restricts their educational and occupational opportunities as well as their income. Women are less likely to work if they have young children, and family demands prompt many employed women to reduce the time spent in paid work (Ferree, 1990). Furthermore, most children reside with their mothers postdivorce. Another major reason for women's economic disadvantage after divorce is that compliance of child support awards by fathers is rare.

Many mothers receive irregular or incomplete child support payments, and 25% receive nothing (U.S. Bureau of the Census, 1989). Even when fathers comply fully, child support awards are typically too low to meet the costs of rearing children, and they are not indexed for inflation (Pirog-Good & Brown, 1996).

Institutionalized sexism and gender discrimination in the wage workplace also contribute to women's sustained postdivorce economic decline. Most employment opportunities for women are in low-paying or temporary work, jobs that offer little advancement. Women's lower earnings relative to men's, combined with the inadequacies of child support payments and the lack of affordable day care, doom most women and their families to long periods of economic hardship following divorce.

Psychological Adjustment

In some cases, it is fairly straightforward to think of changes associated with divorce, such as postdivorce changes in the size or composition of friendship networks or in income, as consequences of divorce. But some changes may predate the divorce, and other changes are more difficult to assess. For example, how do we determine whether an adult's postdivorce adjustment is attributable to chronic strains associated with single parenting, long-term mental or physical health problems, family conflict or abuse that occurred prior to the divorce, or some combination of these (and perhaps other) factors?

Although several studies have examined the course of adult mental health following divorce, most involve cross-sectional designs, rely on clinical or convenience samples, or fail to include control groups. Still, there are some consistent findings. In a rare longitudinal study, Coysh, Johnston, Tschann, Wallerstein, and Kline (1989) examined a predominantly white, middle- and higher-income clinical sample of divorced adults. They found that an important predictor of both women's and men's postdivorce psychological adjustment was their predivorce adjustment. For both genders, better coping and emotional functioning prior to divorce were associated with more effective coping and less anger and emotional distress after divorce. Preseparation communication and shared decision making regarding child rearing also were associated with more cooperative involvement between parents after divorce.

Coysh and colleagues (1989) also found important differences in the ways that women and men responded to family experiences preceding and following divorce. Although both women and men who were involved in relationships with new partners were doing much better psychologically and emotionally than others without such relationships, women were bothered more by pre- and postdivorce family issues, tensions, and conflicts. For men, "new relationships were able to undo, with surprising rapidity, the narcissistic injury engendered by the divorce" (p. 68). In contrast, "women appear to be more affected by the residual hostility from the past marriage and problematic relations between partners and children in their new marriages or relationships" (p. 68).

Similarly, Farnsworth, Pett, and Lund (1989) found that recently divorced women were more likely than men to report feelings of helplessness, avoidance, anger, guilt, and confusion. Gove and Shin (1989) observed that it is common for divorced women to feel trapped, to wish they could change their lives and get away from it all. Examining changes over time, Doherty, Su, and Needle (1989) reported slight improvements in men's psychological well-being during the predivorce to postdivorce period (ranging from 1 to 4 years), whereas women's psychological well-being declined significantly over the same period, and their use of alcohol and other drugs increased.

White women appear to be more severely affected by divorce than African American women are (Gove & Shin, 1989). The evidence on race differences in adjustment to divorce is limited, but it appears that compared with their white counterparts, African American women receive more social support postdivorce (Cherlin, 1992). Kitson (1992) suggests that although African Americans view divorce as regrettable, the higher divorce rate among African Americans prompts greater acceptance and less stigma. For those who remarry, there are few and small differences in the psychological adjustment of whites and African Americans (Fine, McKenry, Donnelly, & Voydanoff, 1992).

There are a number of possible explanations for gender differences in postdivorce adjustment. Women, in general, are more deeply committed to marriage, parenthood, and family life than men are; women devote substantially more time and energy to these activities than men do; and "women's well-being seems to be tied more closely to the emotional make-up of marriage" (Thompson & Walker, 1989, p. 846). Having invested more in the relationship, it is reasonable that the dissolution of the relationship inflicts greater emotional pain for women than for men. Other factors certainly contribute to women's postdivorce distress, including their worsened economic position and the chronic stresses associated with coordinating employment and single parenting (Demo & Acock, 1996b).

As bleak a picture as this paints for many divorced women, there is considerable evidence to suggest that divorce is a short-term crisis, with stress increasing as the divorce approaches, then subsiding postdivorce as life is re-organized and individuals adjust to new routines and lifestyles (Booth & Amato, 1991). Consistent with other studies (Coysh et al., 1989), Booth and Amato (1991) found that predivorce well-being is an important factor in the adjustment process. Many divorced women may feel that even with the de-mands placed on them, they prefer their current situation to the lives they had when they were married.

Children's Adjustment

Perhaps no issue surrounding divorce generates more concern or stirs more controversy than children's adjustment to divorce, and the research literature on the subject is voluminous (e.g., see Amato, 1993, 2000; Fine, 2000; Simons, 1996). Our main purpose here is to briefly summarize what we know about how children are influenced by divorce and the processes associated with divorce, and to offer some explanations for these patterns.

As is the case for most adults, the evidence suggests that most children and adolescents experience emotional adjustments for 1 to 2 years during the pe-riod leading up to and immediately following parental separation and divorce (Hetherington et al., 1982). This is usually the period when marital and fam-ily conflict intensify, when legal battles are fought, and when relationships with residential and nonresidential parents are restructured and renegotiated. On average, however, the adjustment of children and adolescents in post-divorce families is only marginally lower than that of their counterparts in continuously intact two-parent families (Acock & Demo, 1994; Amato, 2000; Demo & Acock, 1996a). Differences in children's psychological well-being within family types tend to be far greater than differences between fam-ily types. For example, on measures of self-esteem, some children in first-marriage families score near the top of the scale, some in the middle, and some near the bottom. But, on average, their scores are very similar to the scores of children living in single-parent families. Also, adolescents appear to adjust more readily to parental divorce than younger children do (Demo & Acock, 1988).

There are additional similarities in the adjustment processes of children and adults. As with adults, the type of legal custody arrangement does not ap-pear to affect children's well-being (Furstenberg & Cherlin, 1991). More im-portant to children's postdivorce adjustment are the provision of economic resources; having positive, nurturing relationships with both parents; and having low levels of parental and family conflict (Demo, 1992; McLanahan

& Sandefur, 1994). Children's predivorce adjustment is also related to the course of their well-being through the divorce process (Cherlin et al., 1991).

It is widely speculated that reduced involvement with nonresidential parents is damaging to children's well-being. Heightening this concern are studies showing that, in most cases, paternal involvement following divorce is infrequent and that fathers' contact typically diminishes over time (King, 1994; Maccoby & Mnookin, 1992). But the broader picture is both more complex and more encouraging. Children live in a wide variety of family situations following parents' divorce, including arrangements in which nonresidential fathers (especially African American fathers) maintain regular contact with their children (King & Heard, 1999; Mott, 1990). Many children change residences (some several times) to live with a different parent (Amato, 2000); children living with their fathers typically have relatively frequent contact with nonresidential mothers (Maccoby & Mnookin, 1992); and most children and adolescents adapt well to diverse forms of postdivorce family life (Buchanan, Maccoby, & Dornbusch, 1996; King & Heard, 1999). These patterns demonstrate that traditional definitions of family structure (e.g., father-present or father-absent) and broad generalizations of postdivorce parenting (e.g., deadbeat dads) obscure substantial temporal and cultural variation in residential and visitation processes (King & Heard, 1999).

There is also some evidence that the frequency of contact with the nonresidential parent has little effect on children's well-being (Furstenberg & Cherlin, 1991; King, 1994). One plausible explanation for this is that the frequency of parental contact may be unrelated to the history and/or quality of the relationship. For example, although low levels of paternal involvement appear to be the norm for children in mother-only families, for some children this means seeing less of a nurturing and supportive father, whereas for others it means seeing less of a detached or abusive father. On the other hand, the *quality* of children's relationships with both parents affects their adjustment to divorce. One study found that children are more likely to feel close to nonresidential mothers than to nonresidential fathers (Peterson & Zill, 1986), but research linking the quality of these relationships to children's well-being is sparse and inconclusive. There is consistent evidence, however, that children's adjustment is enhanced if they have a good relationship with at least one of their parents (Hetherington, Bridges, & Insabella, 1998).

A serious problem confronting many children following divorce is prolonged economic hardship. Although children's postdivorce residential arrangements are variable and change over time, roughly two thirds of children live with their mother, 10% live with their father, and the remainder have dual residences or live in other arrangements (Maccoby & Mnookin, 1992). As we have seen, most women and children experience a sharp, long-term decline in their standard of living. Economic hardship is associated with lowered parental well-being, less effective and less supportive parenting, inconsistent and harsh discipline, and distress and impaired socioemotional functioning in children (Elder, Nguyen, & Caspi, 1985). It should be clear, however, that these adverse effects are products of chronic financial stress and are experienced by children in divorced and nondivorced families alike.

Multiple Family Transitions and Children's Adjustment

Although research indicates that most children and adolescents who experience their parents' divorce score in the normal range on measures of adjustment, a small but growing minority may be at prolonged risk because of multiple transitions in family living arrangements. Typically, researchers have conceptualized and measured family structure in terms of (a) the marital histories of the parents and (b) who is presently living in the household (e.g., intact, single-parent, or stepparent families). An alternative to this operationalization of family structure has been proposed by Capaldi and Patterson (1991), who argue that family structure can be conceptualized in terms of the number of times that a child experiences a parenting transition. Children who have lived continuously with both of their biological parents have experienced no parenting transitions (0PT); those who have experienced the divorce of their parents have experienced one parenting transition (1PT); those who have experienced the divorce and subsequent remarriage of their residential parent have experienced two parenting transitions (2PT); and those who have experienced two or more divorces and/or remarriages involving their residential parent have experienced multiple parenting transitions (MPT). Capaldi and Patterson found that there was a positive linear relationship between adjustment problems and the number of parenting transitions among fourth-grade boys.

A series of studies by Kurdek, Fine, and Sinclair (1994, 1995) support the parenting transition approach. Across samples, sexes, and measures of adjustment, children in the 0PT group had higher levels of adjustment than did other children, and children in the MPT group fared worse than the other groups. Contrary to the model, however, children in the 2PT group were generally as well adjusted as those in the 1PT group. Najman et al. (1997) found, in a prospective, longitudinal study, that children of mothers who experienced no partner changes (i.e., married mothers who remained married or single mothers who remained single) had the fewest behavior problems. These findings support the parenting transition hypothesis in that fewer parenting changes were associated with better outcomes. These findings indicate the importance of considering not just the present family structure but also changes over time, as well as the importance of distinguishing between divorced single mothers and never-married single mothers.

Despite its limited empirical support base, the parenting transition approach provides an example of how the family structure and family process approaches can be integrated. Parenting transitions can be thought of as family processes in the sense that they cause stress and uncertainty in children's (and parents') lives and because they lead to changes in parenting behaviors and other family interactions. At the same time, as conceptualized by Capaldi and Patterson (1991), parenting transitions—because they are operationalized by marriage and divorce—also can be considered to be elements of family structure. The parenting transition approach moves away from considering structure to be based solely on who is and is not living in the household and toward considering the stresses that accrue as family members experience changes. Given the prevalence of divorce and serial transitions for children and adults, an important intervention question is how family life education and family mediation may help in restructuring the divorce process to minimize its harmful effects.

Interventions

The past two decades have seen the rise of what has been called the "divorce industry," consisting of professionals from a variety of fields who make their living from divorce (Bohannon, 1984). The divorce industry has led to the development of new professions such as family mediation and to expanded opportunities for attorneys, therapists, school counselors, family life educators, and social workers, among others. In this section, we consider two types of interventions that attempt to improve the lives of those who have experienced divorce: family life education for divorcing parents and family mediation. These two were selected because they are becoming increasingly popular and can potentially affect large numbers of divorced families.

Family Life Education for Divorcing Parents

In no arena is the "divorce industry" more apparent than in the area of family life education for divorcing parents. Partly because of an increased awareness of the stresses that divorce places on children, attention has been focused on helping children adjust. In recent years, the most frequent way this has been addressed is by educational programs developed to help parents help their children cope with divorce. Blaisure and Geasler (1996) reported that 299 new programs were developed between 1992 and 1994. Most of these programs are court mandated (Fine et al., 1999), and it is these programs that we consider.

The modal educational program for divorcing parents consists of a single 2-hour session, charging participants a fee ranging from $21 to $30, and is offered one or more times per month (Blaisure & Geasler, 1996). Although curricula vary, issues that are typically covered include (a) postdivorce reactions of children and parents, (b) children's needs and reactions to divorce at different ages, (c) the benefits of cooperative postdivorce parenting, and (d) the costs of placing children "in the middle" of parents' disputes (Braver, Salem, Pearson, & DeLuse, 1996).

The quality of the evaluations of these programs has lagged far behind programmatic development (Braver, Smith, & DeLuse, 1997). Evaluations of these programs, when conducted, have primarily consisted of "consumer satisfaction" questionnaires that ask participants how satisfied they were with various aspects of the program (Blaisure & Geasler, 1996). Results from these questionnaires typically show that consumers are very satisfied with the programs (Blaisure & Geasler, 1996; Fine et al., 1999; Kramer & Washo, 1993; McKenry, Clark, & Stone, 1999), which is not surprising given that clients usually report having positive experiences with a wide range of interventions.

Client satisfaction does not necessarily mean that the programs are successful in fostering behavioral change. Unfortunately, we know relatively little about the short- and long-term effectiveness of these parenting education programs. The few studies that have been done have suggested some limited positive impacts. Kramer and Washo (1993), over a 3-year period, found that parents with initially high levels of parental conflict reported a significant decline in their ex-spouse's triangulating child-rearing behaviors (e.g., blaming the other parent for the divorce in front of the child) at follow-up. However, there were no program effects on parents' reports of adaptive child-rearing behaviors or parent-child relationship quality. Furthermore, although children were reported as being better adjusted at the follow-up than they were at the time of the program, this improvement occurred in both the educational and comparison groups. Arbuthnot and Gordon (1996) found that over a 6-month follow-up period, parents learned useful parenting and communication skills, and children were exposed to less parental conflict. However, there were few differences between the parent education and comparison groups in child adjustment.

Because these educational programs have political and intuitive appeal, it is likely that the absence of evaluation will not deter their widespread implementation. However, as noted by Braver et al. (1996), without sound evaluation findings, courts and legislatures will find it increasingly difficult to justify mandating such programs. Thus, evaluations of these programs that extend beyond consumer satisfaction are much needed.

Given that the primary targets of parent education for divorcing parents are *children,* one might wonder why children themselves are not the direct recipients of intervention. Clearly, there are a number of reasons why parents are the direct recipients of these educational sessions, including that they are more amenable to such interventions, they hopefully have both the insight and motivation to benefit from the material presented, and it is logistically easier to require adults to attend such a session than children. Nevertheless, there are a number of programs developed for children whose parents are divorced or divorcing (Grych & Fincham, 1992). Many of these are school-based programs that focus on helping children adapt socially and emotionally; become aware of their feelings about themselves, their parents, and the divorce; express their feelings in appropriate ways; learn to cope with frustration; learn to get along with others; and enhance their self-esteem. There is some evidence that these group interventions are effective (Grych & Fincham, 1992), but few programs have been adequately evaluated in controlled studies, and findings from the evaluation studies that have been conducted are not clear-cut.

Divorce Mediation

Mediation is one of a class of alternative dispute-resolution approaches (they are alternative because they are less adversarial than traditional legal procedures). Divorce mediation consists of an impartial third party helping a divorcing or divorced couple identify, discuss, and, hopefully, resolve disagreements related to the divorce (Emery, 1995; Margulies, 1992). Mediation has grown rapidly and is now mandated in several states (Emery, 1995). Mediation usually addresses five areas of potential conflict: (a) property division, (b) spousal support, (c) child support, (d) custody, and (e) visitation (Emery, 1995; Margulies, 1992). Successful mediation allows the divorcing couple to maintain control of decisions in these domains.

Mediation is built around the principle of cooperative negotiation, whereas the U.S. legal system is adversarial, viewing the parties as disputants who compete with each other for limited resources. In contrast to therapy, mediation targets more specific, pragmatic, and concrete issues. Emery (1995) has described the core of mediation as "renegotiating family relationships" (p. 379). The negotiation of relationships is not achieved by exploring psychological issues but by helping the (ex-)partners agree on issues regarding child rearing.

Research on the effectiveness of mediation is still in its early stages, but there is preliminary evidence that mediation leads to more positive outcomes than litigation does. Studies have suggested that (a) fewer mediated agreements return to court after the divorce than do other types of agreements (Emery, Matthews, & Wyer, 1991); (b) compliance with mediated agreements is greater than compliance with adjudicated agreements (Emery, 1995); (c) participants are typically satisfied with mediation, with fathers being more satisfied with mediated than litigated settlements but mothers being similarly satisfied with both types of agreements (Emery, Matthews, & Kitzmann, 1994); (d) the psychological adjustment of parents and children is not related to whether parents participate in mediation or litigation, although the follow-up periods have typically been quite short; (e) mediation may be less costly than litigation (Kelly, 1990), partly because settlements can be made in less time (Emery et al., 1991); and (f) in mediated, as opposed to litigated, agreements, nonresidential parents are more likely to remain in contact with children, child support is more likely to be paid, and parents are more satisfied with postdivorce arrangements (Grych & Fincham, 1992).

Despite these findings, the practice of mediation is not without its critics. First, some have expressed concern that men's greater power places women at a disadvantage in negotiating and that mediators do not take power differentials into account (Menzel, 1991). On the other hand, noting that women are more satisfied than men are with both litigated and mediated settlements, Emery (1995) has suggested that it is not that women are disadvantaged in mediation but, rather, that men are disadvantaged in litigation. Thus, men have more to gain in mediation than they often do in litigation, which leads them to be more satisfied with mediated agreements. By contrast, women typically fare as well in both types of settlements.

Second, mediation is an appropriate strategy for only certain couples. Spouses who cannot communicate and problem solve with each other, whether because one or both spouses have personality characteristics that prohibit cooperative problem solving or the couple has dysfunctional interactional patterns, are inappropriate candidates for mediation.

Third, there has been controversy regarding who can be effective mediators. Mediators generally fall into one of two groups: lawyers and mental health professionals. Some have argued that lawyers are best suited to be mediators because of their knowledge of the law; others have suggested that mental health professionals are better suited because they have knowledge of the psychological and emotional aspects of how children, parents, and families cope with divorce. Emery (1995) speculates that mediation will not become a separate profession but will develop further within both the mental health and legal professions.

Finally, there is some controversy as to whether mediation should be mandated, used only in select cases, or be voluntary. As Emery (1995) notes, there are some cases when mediation may be inappropriate, such as when child or spouse abuse has occurred. Nevertheless, given that mandating mediation requires that a couple attend a session but does not mean that the parties must reach a settlement, there are strong reasons to require mediation, except in selected cases.

Conclusions

Divorce and binuclear families are becoming normative experiences as we enter the 21st century, and recent research provides compelling evidence that the divorce process needs to be rethought. Although there is considerable variation in children's and adults' emotional adjustment to divorce, most children and adults adapt well to a variety of postdivorce family forms and function in the normal ranges of adjustment. Among the small percentage who experience lingering difficulties, the problems can often be traced to poor adjustment preceding the divorce; predivorce family tension, stress, conflict, and hostility; postdivorce economic decline; and multiple transitions in family structure.

Divorce is more widely accepted and less stigmatized today than it has been in the past, but it still tends to be viewed negatively and is often blamed for many individual and societal problems. Opposition to divorce also has legal and political implications as efforts surface to toughen divorce laws and make it more difficult for couples to obtain divorces. The evidence reviewed here suggests that divorce is a prevalent (and sometimes even necessary) aspect of family life and that little will be gained (and many people will be hurt) by restricting divorce and pathologizing postdivorce family types. A much more fruitful approach would be for family researchers, practitioners, and policy makers to focus attention and resources on processes that help to explain marital dissolution and its consequences. For example, what can be done to facilitate more meaningful, enjoyable, and rewarding paternal involvement in child rearing, marriage, and family life? Paternal involvement has a variety of benefits for fathers as well as for their wives and children. Two immediate benefits are more equitable marriages and a reduced risk of marital dissolution. But should divorce occur, a history of sustained and supportive predivorce paternal involvement increases the likelihood that fathers will continue to provide emotional and financial resources for their children in the years following divorce. Without the disruption of resources, the severity of the stresses is reduced and any potential crisis may be averted.

Another important question is how wage work and unpaid domestic work can be reorganized and better balanced so that women and men divide labor equitably. Eliminating discrimination that women face in wage work, enhancing employment opportunities for women and men, emancipating men from the pressures and strains of work absorption, and coordinating family work so that it is divided equitably are viable avenues and formidable challenges for strengthening marriages and families. These questions broaden the focus on divorce as a social problem to a comprehensive concern with how society and families can be changed to attach greater importance to, and provide more support for, mutually fulfilling marriages.

Public and scholarly attention also needs to be devoted to interventions designed to educate and better prepare divorcing adults—parents and nonparents alike—for the stresses, transitions, economic responsibilities and difficulties, and coparenting challenges they will face in a variety of postdivorce family forms. Client satisfaction with educational programs for divorcing parents is impressive, but resources for offering and expanding such programs are scarce, and little research has evaluated the short- and long-term impact of these programs on parenting effectiveness, parent-child relationships, or child well-being. Programs designed specifically for children are also needed. Finally, there is preliminary evidence that divorce mediation has numerous advantages over conventional adversarial divorces. The challenge as we begin the new millennium will be to explore these and other interventions as ways of normalizing divorce, facilitating healthy adjustment, and embracing family diversity.

DISCUSSION QUESTIONS

1. Marriage and divorce are gendered social processes. Explain how these processes are experienced differently by women and men, and why this is important for understanding postdivorce adjustment and coparenting.

2. A popular belief is that postdivorce family forms are not well suited to meet the needs of family members. To what extent does the research evidence support this belief?

3. There have been some recent efforts to make it harder for couples to obtain a divorce. Do you support these legislative efforts? Why or why not?

4. Should parents who are divorcing be required to attend a parenting education program or should they be allowed to choose whether they wish to attend? Explain your answer.

5. What are some advantages and disadvantages of divorce mediation compared with the more typical legal process? Give an example of a couple for whom divorce mediation is likely to be very effective and another example of a couple for whom divorce mediation is unlikely to be effective (and might even be harmful).

SUGGESTED READINGS

Arbuthnot, J., & Gordon, D. A. (1997). Divorce education for parents and children. In L. VandeCreek, S. Knapp, & T. J. Jackson (Eds.), *Innovations in clinical practice: A sourcebook* (Vol. 15, pp. 341-364). Sarasota, FL: Professional Resource Press.

Arditti, J. A. (1999). Rethinking relationships between divorced mothers and their children: Capitalizing on family strengths. *Family Relations, 48,* 109-119.

Arendell, T. (1995). *Fathers and divorce.* Thousand Oaks, CA: Sage.

Buehler, C., & Gerard, J. M. (1995). Divorce law in the United States: A focus on child custody. *Family Relations, 44,* 439-458.

Seltzer, J. A., & Brandreth, Y. (1994). What fathers say about involvement with children after separation. *Journal of Family Issues, 15,* 49-77.

REFERENCES

Acock, A. C., & Demo, D. H. (1994). *Family diversity and well-being.* Thousand Oaks, CA: Sage.

Ahrons, C. (1994). *The good divorce: Keeping your family together when your marriage comes apart.* New York: HarperCollins.

Amato, P. R. (1993). Children's adjustment to divorce: Theories, hypotheses, and empirical support. *Journal of Marriage and the Family, 55,* 23-38.

Amato, P. R. (1996). Explaining the intergenerational transmission of divorce. *Journal of Marriage and the Family, 58,* 628-640.

Amato, P. R. (2000). Diversity within single-parent families. In D. H. Demo, K. R. Allen, & M. A. Fine (Eds.), *The handbook of family diversity* (pp. 149-172). New York: Oxford University Press.

Amato, P. R., & Rogers, S. J. (1999). Do attitudes toward divorce affect marital quality? *Journal of Family Issues, 20,* 69-86.

Arbuthnot, J., & Gordon, D. A. (1996). Does mandatory divorce education for parents work? *Family and Conciliation Courts Review, 34,* 60-81.

Axinn, W. G., & Thornton, A. (1992). The relationship between cohabitation and divorce: Selectivity or causal influence? *Demography, 29,* 357-374.

Bernard, J. (1972). *The future of marriage.* New York: World.

Blaisure, K. R., & Geasler, M. J. (1996). Results of a survey of court-connected parent education programs in U.S. counties. *Family and Conciliation Courts Review, 34,* 23-40.

Bloom, B. L., Niles, R. L., & Tatcher, A. M. (1985). Sources of marital dissatisfaction among newly separated persons. *Journal of Family Issues, 6,* 359-373.

Bohannon, P. (1984). *All the happy families: Exploring the varieties of family life.* New York: McGraw-Hill.

Booth, A., & Amato, P. (1991). Divorce and psychological stress. *Journal of Health and Social Behavior, 32,* 396-407.

Booth, A., Johnson, D., & Edwards, J. N. (1983). Measuring marital instability. *Journal of Marriage and the Family, 45,* 387-394.

Booth, A., Johnson, D., White, L., & Edwards, J. N. (1986). Divorce and marital instability over the life course. *Journal of Family Issues, 7,* 421-442.

Braver, S. L. (1998). *Divorced dads: Shattering the myths.* New York: Tarcher Putnam.

Braver, S. L., Salem, P., Pearson, J., & DeLuse, S. R. (1996). The content of divorce education programs: Results of a survey. *Family and Conciliation Courts Review, 34,* 41-59.

Braver, S. L., Smith, M. C., & DeLuse, S. R. (1997). Methodological considerations in evaluating family court programs: A primer using divorced parent education programs as a case example. *Family and Conciliation Courts Review, 35,* 9-36.

Buchanan, C. M., Maccoby, E., & Dornbusch, S. M. (1996). *Adolescents after divorce.* Cambridge, MA: Harvard University Press.

Capaldi, D. M., & Patterson, G. R. (1991). Relations of parental transitions to boys' adjustment problems: I. A linear hypothesis; II. Mothers at risk for transitions and unskilled parenting. *Developmental Psychology, 27,* 489-504.

Cherlin, A. J. (1992). *Marriage, divorce, and remarriage* (Rev. and enlarged ed.). Cambridge, MA: Harvard University Press.

Cherlin, A. J., Furstenberg, F. F., Jr., Chase-Lansdale, L. P., Kiernan, K. E., Robins, P. K., Morrison, D. R., & Teitler, J. O. (1991). Longitudinal effects of divorce in Great Britain and the United States. *Science, 252,* 1386-1389.

Coontz, S. (1992). *The way we never were: American families and the nostalgia trap.* New York: Basic Books.

Coontz, S. (1997). *The way we really are: Coming to terms with America's changing families.* New York: Basic Books.

Coysh, W. S., Johnston, J. R., Tschann, J. M., Wallerstein, J. S., & Kline, M. (1989). Parental postdivorce adjustment in joint and sole physical custody families. *Journal of Family Issues, 10,* 52-71.

Demo, D. H. (1992). Parent-child relations: Assessing recent changes. *Journal of Marriage and the Family, 54,* 104-117.

Demo, D. H., & Acock, A. C. (1988). The impact of divorce on children. *Journal of Marriage and the Family, 50,* 619-648.

Demo, D. H., & Acock, A. C. (1993). How much have things really changed? Family diversity and the division of domestic labor. *Family Relations, 42,* 323-331.

Demo, D. H., & Acock, A. C. (1996a). Family structure, family process, and adolescent well-being. *Journal of Research on Adolescence, 6,* 457-488.

Demo, D. H., & Acock, A. C. (1996b). Singlehood, marriage, and remarriage: The effects of family structure and family relationships on mothers' well-being. *Journal of Family Issues, 17,* 388-407.

Doherty, W. J., Su, S., & Needle, R. (1989). Marital disruption and psychological well-being: A panel study. *Journal of Family Issues, 10,* 72-85.

Duncan, G. J., & Hoffman, S. D. (1985). Economic consequences of marital instability. In M. David & T. Smeeding (Eds.), *Horizontal equity, uncertainty, and economic well-being* (pp. 427-467). Chicago: University of Chicago Press.

Elder, G., Nguyen, T., & Caspi, A. (1985). Linking family hardship to children's lives. *Child Development, 56,* 361-375.

Emery, R. E. (1995). Divorce mediation: Negotiating agreements and renegotiating relationships. *Family Relations, 44,* 377-383.

Emery, R. E., Matthews, S., & Kitzmann, K. (1994). Child custody mediation and litigation: Parents' satisfaction and functioning a year after settlement. *Journal of Consulting and Clinical Psychology, 62,* 124-129.

Emery, R., Matthews, S. G., & Wyer, M. M. (1991). Child custody mediation and litigation: Further evidence on the differing views of mothers and fathers. *Journal of Consulting and Clinical Psychology, 59,* 410-418.

Farnsworth, J., Pett, M. A., & Lund, D. A. (1989). Predictors of loss management and well-being in later life widowhood and divorce. *Journal of Family Issues, 10,* 102-121.

Ferree, M. M. (1990). Beyond separate spheres: Feminism and family research. *Journal of Marriage and the Family, 52,* 866-884.

Fine, M. A. (2000). Divorce and single parenting. In C. Hendricks & S. S. Hendricks (Eds.), *Sourcebook of close relationships* (pp. 139-152). Thousand Oaks, CA: Sage.

Fine, M. A., Coleman, M., Gable, S., Ganong, L. H., Ispa, J., Morrison, J., & Thornburg, K. R. (1999). Research-based parenting education for divorcing parents: A university-community collaboration. In T. R. Chibocos & R. M. Lerner (Eds.), *Serving children and families through community-university partnerships: Success stories* (pp. 251-258). Norwell, MA: Kluwer.

Fine, M. A., McKenry, P. C., Donnelly, B. W., & Voydanoff, P. (1992). Perceived adjustment of parents and children: Variations by family structure, race, and gender. *Journal of Marriage and the Family, 54,* 118-127.

Furstenberg, F. F., Jr., & Cherlin, A. J. (1991). *Divided families: What happens to children when parents part.* Cambridge, MA: Harvard University Press.

Gerstel, N. (1990). Divorce and stigma. In C. Carlson (Ed.), *Perspectives on the family: History, class, and feminism* (pp. 460-478). Belmont, CA: Wadsworth.

Gottman, J. M. (1994). *What predicts divorce?* Hillsdale, NJ: Lawrence Erlbaum.

Gove, W. R., & Shin, H. (1989). The psychological well-being of divorced and widowed men and women: An empirical analysis. *Journal of Family Issues, 10,* 122-144.

Grych, J. H., & Fincham, F. (1992). Interventions for children of divorce: Toward greater integration of research and action. *Psychological Bulletin, 111,* 434-454.

Heckert, D. A., Nowak, T. C., & Snyder, K. A. (1998). The impact of husbands' and wives' relative earnings on marital disruption. *Journal of Marriage and the Family, 60,* 690-703.

Hetherington, E. M., Bridges, M., & Insabella, G. M. (1998). What matters? What does not? Five perspectives on the association between marital transitions and children's adjustment. *American Psychologist, 53,* 167-184.

Hetherington, E. M., Cox, M., & Cox, R. (1982). Effects of divorce on parents and children. In M. E. Lamb (Ed.), *Nontraditional families* (pp. 233-288). Hillsdale, NJ: Lawrence Erlbaum.

Hill, M. S. (1988). Marital stability and spouses' shared time: A multidisciplinary hypothesis. *Journal of Family Issues, 9,* 427-451.

Holden, K. C., & Smock, P. J. (1991). The economic costs of marital dissolution: Why do women bear a disproportionate cost? *Annual Review of Sociology, 17,* 51-78.

Hopper, J. (1993). The rhetoric of motives in divorce. *Journal of Marriage and the Family, 55,* 801-813.

Katzev, A. R., Warner, R. L., & Acock, A. C. (1994). Girls or boys: Relationship of child gender to marital instability. *Journal of Marriage and the Family, 56,* 89-110.

Kelly, J. B. (1990). Is mediation less expensive? Comparison of mediated and adversarial divorce costs. *Mediation Quarterly, 8,* 15-26.

King, V. (1994). Nonresident father involvement and child well-being: Can dads make a difference? *Journal of Family Issues, 15,* 78-96.

King, V., & Heard, H. E. (1999). Nonresident father visitation, parental conflict, and mothers' satisfaction: What's best for child well-being? *Journal of Marriage and the Family, 61,* 385-396.

Kitson, G. C. (1992). *Portrait of divorce: Adjustment to marital breakdown.* New York: Guilford.

Kramer, L., & Washo, C. A. (1993). Evaluation of a court-mandated prevention program for divorcing parents. *Family Relations, 42,* 179-186.

Kurdek, L. A., Fine, M. A., & Sinclair, R. J. (1994). The relation between parenting transitions and adjustment in young adolescents: A multi-sample investigation. *Journal of Early Adolescence, 14,* 412-432.

Kurdek, L. A., Fine, M. A., & Sinclair, R. J. (1995). School adjustment in sixth graders: Parenting transitions, family climate, and peer norm effects. *Child Development, 66,* 430-445.

Maccoby, E. E., & Mnookin, R. H. (1992). *Dividing the child: Social and legal dilemmas of custody.* Cambridge, MA: Harvard University Press.

Margulies, S. (1992). *Getting divorced without ruining your life.* New York: Fireside.

Marsiglio, W. (1993). Contemporary scholarship on fatherhood: Culture, identity, and conduct. *Journal of Family Issues, 14,* 484-509.

Matthews, L. S., Wickrama, K. A. S., & Conger, R. D. (1996). Predicting marital instability from spouse and observer reports of marital interaction. *Journal of Marriage and the Family, 58,* 641-655.

McKenry, P. C., Clark, K. A., & Stone, G. (1999). Evaluation of a parent education program for divorcing parents. *Family Relations, 48,* 129-137.

McLanahan, S., & Sandefur, G. (1994). *Growing up with a single parent: What hurts, what helps.* Cambridge, MA: Harvard University Press.

Menzel, K. E. (1991). Judging the fairness of mediation: A critical framework. *Mediation Quarterly, 9,* 3-20.

Milardo, R. M. (1987). Changes in social networks of women and men following divorce: A review. *Journal of Family Issues, 8,* 78-96.

Morgan, L. A. (1989). Economic well-being following marital termination: A comparison of widowed and divorced women. *Journal of Family Issues, 10,* 86-101.

Morgan, S. P., Lye, D., & Condran, G. (1988). Sons, daughters, and the risk of marital disruption. *American Journal of Sociology, 94,* 110-129.

Mott, F. L. (1990). When is a father really gone? Paternal-child contact in father-absent homes. *Demography, 27,* 499-517.

Najman, J. M., Behrens, B. C., Andersen, M., Bor, W., O'Callaghan, M., & Williams, G. M. (1997). Impact of family type and family quality on child behavior problems: A longitudinal study. *Journal of the American Academy of Child and Adolescent Psychiatry, 36,* 1357-1365.

Peterson, J. L., & Zill, N. (1986). Marital disruption, parent-child relationships, and behavior problems in children. *Journal of Marriage and the Family, 48,* 295-307.

Peterson, R. R. (1996). A re-evaluation of the economic consequences of divorce. *American Sociological Review, 61,* 528-536.

Pirog-Good, M. A., & Brown, P. R. (1996). Accuracy and ambiguity in the application of state child support guidelines. *Family Relations, 45,* 3-10.

Rands, M. (1988). Changes in social networks following marital separation and divorce. In R. M. Milardo (Ed.), *Families and social networks* (pp. 127-146). Newbury Park, CA: Sage.

Sabatelli, R. M., & Shehan, C. L. (1993). Exchange and resource theories. In P. G. Boss, W. J. Doherty, R. LaRossa, W. R. Schumm, & S. K. Steinmetz (Eds.), *Sourcebook of family theories and methods: A contextual approach* (pp. 385-411). New York: Plenum.

Schnaiberg, A., & Goldenberg, S. (1989). From empty nest to crowded nest: The dynamics of incompletely launched young adults. *Social Problems, 36,* 251-266.

Simons, R. L. (Ed.). (1996). *Understanding differences between divorced and intact families: Stress, interaction, and child outcome.* Thousand Oaks, CA: Sage.

Spanier, G. B., & Thompson, L. (1984). *Parting: The aftermath of separation and divorce.* Beverly Hills, CA: Sage.

Teachman, J. D. (2000). Diversity of family structure: Economic and social influences. In D. H. Demo, K. R. Allen, & M. A. Fine (Eds.), *The handbook of family diversity* (pp. 32-58). New York: Oxford University Press.

Thompson, L., & Walker, A. J. (1989). Gender in families: Women and men in marriage, work, and parenthood. *Journal of Marriage and the Family, 51,* 845-871.

Thornton, A. (1989). Changing attitudes toward family issues. *Journal of Marriage and the Family, 51,* 873-893.

U.S. Bureau of the Census. (1989). *Child support and alimony: 1985* (Supplemental Report; Current Population Reports, P-23, No. 154). Washington, DC: Government Printing Office.

Wallerstein, J. S., & Blakeslee, S. (1990). *Second chances: Men, women, and children a decade after divorce.* New York: Ticknor & Fields.

Weiss, R. (1984). The impact of marital dissolution on income and consumption in single-parent households. *Journal of Marriage and the Family, 46,* 115-127.

White, L. K. (1990). Determinants of divorce: A review of research in the eighties. *Journal of Marriage and the Family, 52,* 904-912.

13

Remarriage and Recoupling

A Stress Perspective

MARGARET CROSBIE-BURNETT
KATRINA M. McCLINTIC

Remarriage and the creation of stepfamilies have been common practices for centuries. However, until the dramatic rise in the divorce rate in the 1970s, nearly all remarriages occurred after the death of a spouse. Today, nearly all remarriages occur after divorce; two thirds of divorced women and three quarters of divorced men remarry (Bumpass, Sweet, & Casto-Martin, 1990). Women are not only less likely to remarry, they also remarry less quickly in all age groups; the mean length of time between divorce and remarriage is 3.6 years for men and 3.9 years for women. Rates of remarriage decline with age for both men and women; rates of remarriage for divorced women peaked in 1965 and then declined steadily until 1985 (Glick, 1989a). Of the 1.5 million divorced men and women who do remarry each year, 61% marry divorced, 35% marry single, and 4% marry widowed partners. Nearly 5% of remarriages (twice the percentage of first marriages) are interracial, including all racial combinations. When we examine remarriages as a subset of all marriages, we find that 49% of European American and 40% of African American marriages are a remarriage for one or both partners (Wilson & Clarke, 1992).

Contrary to popular myth, the divorce rate for remarriages (49%) is only slightly higher than the divorce rate for first marriages (47%; Martin & Bumpass, 1989); this rate tends to be highest in families with children from previous relationships (Tzeng & Mare, 1995). It is not surprising that

303

remarrieds and first-marrieds report comparable levels of marital satisfaction (Vemer, Coleman, Ganong, & Cooper, 1989). However, wives in both groups report less marital satisfaction than husbands do (Ihinger-Tallman & Pasley, 1987), though sex roles are more egalitarian in second marriages than in first (Ishii-Kuntz & Coltrane, 1992).

It should be noted that remarriage is *not* synonymous with the creation of stepfamily households. Only one half of the 11 million households of re-marrieds include minor children and are therefore defined as stepfamilies by the U.S. Bureau of the Census. However, most of the other half of remarried households include step-relationships. These households include homes with stepchildren who have reached majority age and may or may not be liv-ing at home and noncustodial homes that minor children visit. In addition to the stepfamilies formed by the remarriage of one or two parents, an increas-ing number of stepfamilies are created when unmarried mothers marry for the first time, and a small number of stepfamilies are formed when gay and les-bian parents recouple. It is estimated that in the United States, 3 million gay men and lesbians are parents (Harvard Law Review Association, 1990); an unknown percentage of these parents cohabit with a same-sex partner, form-ing either custodial or noncustodial stepfamily households.

If we examine the stepfamily demographic statistics from the child's per-spective, we find that in any one year, 7% of minor children (nearly 6 million) live with a legally married parent and stepparent, and another 2.5% live with a parent who is cohabiting with a partner (Sweet, 1991). These percentages do not include young adult stepchildren who are living in the parental home or children who visit a stepfamily household formed by the noncustodial par-ent's recoupling. In addition, another 5% of minor children live in step-families but were born to the remarried couple (Glick, 1989b). Projections suggest that about one third of today's children will live in a stepfamily be-fore they reach the age of 18 (Seltzer, 1994), and about 45% of these children will be either a stepchild or a stepparent during their lives (Ganong & Coleman, 1988).

Definitions

The rest of this chapter addresses the stepfamilies formed by the recoupling of parents. It will not include the recoupling of childless adults. It is the pres-ence of step-relationships that makes stepfamilies different from other two-parent families. Although nearly all of the research on stepfamilies has been conducted with samples of legally remarried European American spouses, the term *recoupling* is used because it is more inclusive than *remarriage*. Recoupling includes heterosexual and homosexual cohabitors and first marriages of parents.

Stepfamily is defined as a family in which at least one of the recoupling adults has one or more children from a prior relationship and the children spend time in the adult's household. *Extended stepfamily network* is defined as the households that are linked together by traditional extended family *and* by biological ties between children and their nonresidential parent.

Costs and Benefits

There are costs and benefits to recoupling at both the societal and individual levels. Economically, recoupling with a wage earner usually means a higher standard of living (Hill, 1992), particularly for women and their children. The consequent decreased economic distress has been associated with decreased psychological distress for divorced women (Shapiro, 1996). However, the recoupling of a child's noncustodial father is likely to result in less financial and emotional support from him (Ahrons & Wallisch, 1987).

Unfortunately, stepfamilies have a higher incidence of spouse abuse (Kalmuss & Seltzer, 1986) and child abuse and neglect than biological families do (Daly & Wilson, 1991; Giles-Sims, 1997). Adolescents seem to face particular challenges in adjusting to a parent's remarriage (Hetherington, 1993); they are considered to be at risk for externalizing behaviors (Anderson, Greene, Hetherington, & Clingempeel, 1999) as well as suicidal behavior (Rubenstein, Halton, Kasten, Rubin, & Stechler, 1998). Although research results are not totally consistent, having a stepfather in the home appears to have a positive effect for boys, but girls do not fair as well as boys in stepfather or in stepmother families (Emery, 1988). Family theorists are struggling to ascertain the reasons for these findings. Hypotheses include the interruption of close parent-daughter relationships and sexual tension between stepfathers and stepdaughters.

A Family Stress Theory of Recoupling

In this chapter, a model of family stress and coping that has both sociological and psychological components will be used to integrate the theory and research on stepfamilies and to suggest interventions that can promote adjustment to recoupling and stepfamily living (see Figure 13.1). The model is

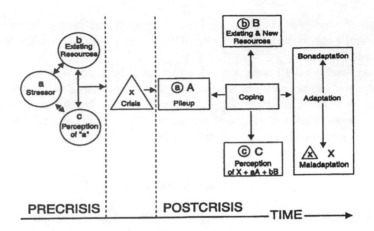

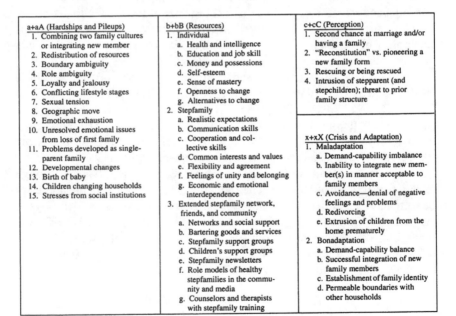

a+aA (Hardships and Pileups)	b+bB (Resources)	c+cC (Perception)

1. Combining two family cultures or integrating new member
2. Redistribution of resources
3. Boundary ambiguity
4. Role ambiguity
5. Loyalty and jealousy
6. Conflicting lifestyle stages
7. Sexual tension
8. Geographic move
9. Emotional exhaustion
10. Unresolved emotional issues from loss of first family
11. Problems developed as single-parent family
12. Developmental changes
13. Birth of baby
14. Children changing households
15. Stresses from social institutions
	1. Individual
	  a. Health and intelligence
	  b. Education and job skill
	  c. Money and possessions
	  d. Self-esteem
	  e. Sense of mastery
	  f. Openness to change
	  g. Alternatives to change
	2. Stepfamily
	  a. Realistic expectations
	  b. Communication skills
	  c. Cooperation and collective skills
	  d. Common interests and values
	  e. Flexibility and agreement
	  f. Feelings of unity and belonging
	  g. Economic and emotional interdependence
	3. Extended stepfamily network, friends, and community
	  a. Networks and social support
	  b. Bartering goods and services
	  c. Stepfamily support groups
	  d. Children's support groups
	  e. Stepfamily newsletters
	  f. Role models of healthy stepfamilies in the community and media
	  g. Counselors and therapists with stepfamily training
		1. Second chance at marriage and/or having a family
		2. "Reconstitution" vs. pioneering a new family form
		3. Rescuing or being rescued
		4. Intrusion of stepparent (and stepchildren); threat to prior family structure<hr>**x+xX (Crisis and Adaptation)**
		1. Maladaptation
		  a. Demand-capability imbalance
		  b. Inability to integrate new member(s) in manner acceptable to family members
		  c. Avoidance—denial of negative feelings and problems
		  d. Redivorcing
		  e. Extrusion of children from the home prematurely
		2. Bonadaptation
		  a. Demand-capability balance
		  b. Successful integration of new family members
		  c. Establishment of family identity
		  d. Permeable boundaries with other households

Figure 13.1. The Double ABC-X Model as a Guide for the Assessment of Stepfamilies, Intervention With Stepfamilies, and Policy Change in Support of Stepfamilies

SOURCE: Based on the Double ABC-X Model (McCubbin & Patterson, 1983a) and the Contextual Model of Family Stress (Boss, 1987).

based on the Double ABC-X Model (McCubbin & Patterson, 1983a) and the Contextual Model of Family Stress (Boss, 1987).

The Stressor Event and Associated Hardships

Recoupling (see "a" in Figure 13.1) can be defined as a normative developmental stressor event (McCubbin & Patterson, 1983b) because it changes the family boundary by adding one or more new family members to the family group (the prior single-parent household) and because recoupling is now being conceptualized by some (Carter & McGoldrick, 1988; Crosbie-Burnett, 1989) as a normal part of a family's life cycle. Recoupling also creates pressure to change the structure of the family, allowing for the stepparent to have an adult role and, possibly, integrating stepsiblings into the subsystem of children with concomitant changes in birth order and/or sex ratio.

New Family Member(s)

The addition of a partner for the biological parent forces a reorganization of roles and relationships. First, the biological parent shares the family leadership role (to varying degrees) with the new adult. This means a redistribution of family power (Crosbie-Burnett & Giles-Sims, 1987; Giles-Sims & Crosbie-Burnett, 1989), which often includes a displacement of an older child, who was a coleader in the single-parent household, by the new stepparent. The entry of a new partner for the biological parent is also reported to threaten the relationships between that parent and the children (Visher & Visher, 1979). Both parties can experience the stepparent as "coming between" the biological parent and children, disrupting a bond that predated the recoupling. When two families are joined by a recoupling, two family cultures are brought together with the potential for discrepant values, habits, and interests. Integrating two family cultures requires negotiation and the creation of new family rituals and traditions. Family rituals and traditions have been identified as a characteristic of healthy families (McCubbin & McCubbin, 1987), and, by definition, new families have few or none.

Redistribution of Resources

A variety of resources—money, space, time, and affection—must be redistributed among family members if the family is to meet the needs of new, as well as original, family members. Stepchildren report that the acquisition of stepsiblings, which 40 to 50% of stepchildren experience (Bumpass, 1984), is a source of stress (Lutz, 1983). The distribution of money within the stepfamily and between households in the extended stepfamily network is a commonly reported source of stress for stepfamilies (Albrecht, 1979; Fishman, 1983; Goetting, 1982; Jacobson, 1993). Money-related stress is exacerbated because many couples are reluctant to discuss this delicate issue before recoupling (Dolan & Lowen, 1985).

Boundary Ambiguity

The ambiguity of boundaries between households that have biological parent-child ties linking them together suggests a third source of stress for these families (Boss & Greenberg, 1984). For example, is a nonresidential father with joint legal custody a member of the stepfamily? He has decision-making power that influences the functioning of the stepfamily.

To complicate matters further, stepfamily members themselves may disagree about who is and is not part of their family (Pasley, 1987). It is clear that there is an inherent boundary ambiguity for stepfamilies and an inherent tension between (a) the new stepfamily's need for boundary definition to enhance group cohesion and unity and (b) the needs of biological parents and children separated by households to include each other in "family" and to have permeable boundaries through which to maintain emotional ties.

Stepparent Role Ambiguity

Stepparent role ambiguity is a major source of stress (Fine, Ganong, & Coleman, 1997, 1999; Giles-Sims, 1984; Schwebel, Fine, & Renner, 1991). There are few social norms for the stepparent role, especially when the nonresidential biological parent is active in the child's life. Consequently, family members have their own individual (usually unspoken) expectations for the stepparent role, adding to the probability of conflict between members of the stepfamily and the entire extended stepfamily network. This discrepancy in perceptions of the stepparent role has been found particularly between the stepchild, who believes the stepparent should behave more as a friend, and the stepparent and parent, who believe the stepparent should play a parental role (Fine, Coleman, & Ganong, 1998). There have been mixed findings regarding the role of stepparent involvement in children's adjustment. While some studies have found that stepparent warmth or support is important to promote child and adolescent well-being (Crosbie-Burnett & Giles-Sims,

1994; Fine, Voydanoff, & Donnelly, 1993), others have found that children who report low involvement by their stepfathers also report being happier at home (Funder, Kinsella, & Courtney, 1992).

Disagreement concerning the amount and nature of the nurturance and discipline of children that the stepparent "should" perform are notorious sources of stress for stepfamilies (Cherlin, 1978; Ihinger-Tallman & Pasley, 1987; Visher & Visher, 1983). Both role clarity (Fine et al., 1997; Fine, Kurdek, & Hennigan, 1991) and role flexibility (Boss, 1980) may be crucial factors in the stepfamily's adjustment. There are a variety of roles to be filled, a variety of adults to fill them, and no clear role prescriptions delineating the division of labor (Crosbie-Burnett & Lewis, 1993). U.S. society adds to the ambiguity of the stepparent role by, for example, denying stepparents legal parental rights yet including stepparent income in computing Aid to Families With Dependent Children (AFDC) and college financial aid.

Stepchild Role Ambiguity and Loyalty Conflicts

The stepchild role is also ambiguous. Children do not know how they are *supposed* to relate to a stepparent, especially if their nonresidential biological parent is part of their lives. Yet the relationship between the stepparent and stepchild appears to be a key factor in stepfamily happiness (Crosbie-Burnett, 1984), marital quality (Fine & Kurdek, 1995), and stepchild adjustment (Furstenberg, Nord, Peterson, & Zill, 1983).

Having a biological parent and a stepparent of the same sex has been identified as a source of stress in the recoupling of heterosexual families. For example, children report feeling guilty for liking a stepparent better than the same-sex biological parent (Lutz, 1983). Jealousy and competition between the same-sex parents can heighten loyalty conflicts for children (Wallerstein & Kelly, 1980) and biological parents, who may be trying to coparent with a former spouse while building a marriage with a new spouse. It is not unusual for the nonresidential parent (and the relatives on that side of the extended family network) to be threatened by the recoupling and harass the remarrying couple's household in a variety of ways, including relitigating and demanding demonstrations of loyalty from the children. Although joint-custody arrangements are associated with better stepchild-stepparent relationships and more family cohesion than sole-custody arrangements, hostility within the coparental relationship is detrimental; it is associated with more loyalty conflicts and adjustment difficulties for adolescents in remarried families (Crosbie-Burnett, 1991).

Conflicting Life-Cycle Stages

Recoupling can bring together individuals who are in different life-cycle stages; this can cause stress and conflict. For example, the newlyweds need time alone, whereas children demand attention. The couple may want to create family cohesion by doing family activities, while the adolescent is attempting to individuate and desires more time with peers. A middle-aged stepfather who has reared one set of children and is ready to be finished with major parenting responsibilities may find himself with a new baby. The new couple may wish to purchase a home, but college tuition bills for stepchildren may stand in the way.

Sexual Tension

Recoupling often brings together children, adolescents, and adults of the opposite sex without benefit of the incest taboo. This potential for sexual tension is hypothesized to be one reason why girls are reporting more family-related stress than boys (Lutz, 1983), why they are reported by their residential mothers to have poorer well-being than boys (Crosbie-Burnett, 1988a), and why some studies are finding stepdaughters to have worse relations with stepfathers than stepsons do (Clingempeel, Ievoli, & Brand, 1984; Clingempeel & Segal, 1986; Peterson & Zill, 1986; Santrock, Warshak, Lindbergh, & Meadows, 1982). This delicate subject can be threatening to couples and children.

Resources

Resources (see "b" in Figure 13.1) are a combination of individual family members' strengths and assets, the family's capabilities of resistance vis-à-vis the stressor, and extrafamilial resources (McCubbin, 1979). They include health, intelligence, education, job skills, money and possessions, a spirit of cooperation, relationship skills, and networks and social support (Boss, 1987). A family's use of resources is a measure of its ability to cope with the stressor.

Individual

In addition to the above assets that individuals can bring to the stepfamily, individual resources that are particularly important in times of transition include self-esteem and a sense of control or mastery (Pearlin & Schooler, 1978), openness to change, and self-efficacy in successful adaptation. In recoupling, the addition of a second wage earner is particularly important because it usually improves the standard of living for the family, particularly for mothers and their children (Folk, Graham, & Beller, 1992; Hill, 1992). For stepchildren, having a nonresidential parent's household for either temporary or permanent "escape" also can be a resource.

Family

Family stress research has identified factors that promote the family resources of cohesion and integration (Olson & McCubbin, 1982) and are considered to help the family buffer the hardships associated with a stressor. These include common interests and values, agreement on role structure, affection, feelings of unity, collective as opposed to personal goals, and economic interdependence. By definition, many of these are missing in new stepfamilies. Bringing together two family cultures, and individuals at different stages in the family life cycle, lessens the probability of common interests and values and collective goals. Role and boundary ambiguity are a threat to feelings of unity and agreement on role structure. Sharing affection in the step-relationship takes time and can be awkward for stepfamilies, particularly those with adolescents. The flow of moneys between households in the extended stepfamily network may diminish economic interdependence within the stepfamily household by providing alternative sources of support.

Family stress research has identified additional resources that have been associated with successful adaptation. These resources seem to be particularly crucial for stepfamilies: flexibility and open communication (Henry & Lovelace, 1995), shared power and flexibility in the authority and status structure, and successful experience coping with past stressors such as divorce or poverty.

Extended Family and Friends

Even in our mobile society, extended family is still an important source of emotional support and other helping behaviors (McCubbin, Joy, Cauble, Patterson, & Needle, 1980; Unger & Powell, 1980). This appears to be true for stepfamilies as well (Booth & Edwards, 1992; Kennedy & Kennedy, 1993; Pasley & Ihinger-Tallman, 1982). A well-functioning extended stepfamily network can expand this traditional resource by sharing a variety of resources (e.g., child care, children's clothing, emotional energy, and skills) across the households of coparents as well as the households of extended biological kin.

Friends are, of course, an important source of social support (McCubbin, 1979). However, this may be an underutilized source of support in new stepfamilies because, in addition to the potential loss of this support associated with geographic moves at recoupling, there is a desire on the part of many remarried couples to "gloss over" problems in an effort to ward off a much-feared second divorce and to appear successfully "reconstituted" to friends and family.

Community Resources

Community resources refer to the support that the community provides to help families under stress. The adequacy of these supports depends on the fit between the family and the community (Hansen & Hill, 1964; Mechanic, 1974). Unfortunately, the fit between the stepfamily and the community is often awkward at best and is more likely to be a hardship than a resource at the present time. For example, the interface between schools and stepfamilies is often problematic (Crosbie-Burnett, 1994). This problem of family-community fit is multiplied for gay and lesbian stepfamilies and sometimes for families of color, depending on their community.

Cherlin (1978) hypothesized the basis of stresses in stepfamilies as a function of the lack of institutionalization of remarriage and recoupling in society. This idea is supported by studies reporting not only a lack of norms for behavior for remarrieds (Goetting, 1980) but also a bias against stepfamily members (Bryan, Coleman, Ganong, & Bryan, 1986; Bryant, Coleman, & Ganong, 1988; Coleman & Ganong, 1987). This bias adds to the stepfamily's pressure to "pass" as an intact, nuclear family. Recently, it seems that perceptions of stepfamilies as "incomplete institutions" are waning, but the social stigma of being a stepparent, and a stepmother in particular, remains (Coleman, Ganong, & Cable, 1996).

On the more positive side, community resources are becoming more available as the numbers of stepfamilies increase and, therefore, the family form becomes normative. Stepfamily associations, newsletters, and support groups for remarrieds are becoming more prevalent. Mental health professionals are becoming more aware of the need for special training in the unique aspects of stepfamilies. Schools are beginning to recognize the need to respond to stepparents more positively; some schools now offer postdivorce support groups for children of divorce and recoupling (Crosbie-Burnett & Newcomer, 1990a, 1990b).

Perception of Recoupling

The subjective definition that the family makes of the stressor and its concomitant hardships (see "c" in Figure 13.1) is a reflection of the family members' values, histories, culture(s), religion(s), economics, and developmental stages. However, the definition or meaning given to a recoupling may be quite discrepant across family members. Discrepant perceptions must be added to the list of hardships because they add stress to the family (Coleman & Ganong, 1997).

Biological Parent

The biological parent may perceive the change as a "reconstitution"—a chance to become a legitimate family again. It is also a second (or subsequent) chance to have a good marriage or partnership. The recoupling also may mean help with child rearing and an increase in standard of living.

Stepparent

Some stepparents see themselves as rescuers of single parents and children and therefore anticipate appreciation. On the contrary, other stepparents see themselves as gaining a spouse but have no intention of parenting stepchildren; this may be in conflict with a biological parent's expectation that he or she is gaining a helpmate with parenting.

Previously single stepparents are entering their first coupling and are more likely to view the situation with all of the idealism of first-marrieds. There is preliminary evidence that previously single stepfathers try to perform a more traditional father role than stepfathers who had a prior family (Crosbie-Burnett, 1988a). Also, stepparents who are unable to have biological children of their own may be enthusiastic about becoming a "mom" or "dad."

For previously married stepparents, the recoupling can have a meaning similar to the biological parent's—a second chance. For stepparents who have "lost" their biological children through loss of custody, geographic mobility, and so on, the recoupling can mean being part of a family again.

Stepchildren

The largest discrepancies in the meaning of the recoupling may be found between adults and children. Understandably, children are anxious about the meaning of the recoupling for life in their own household(s) and for relationships with biological parents, grandparents, and other extended family. Some stepchildren, of course, anticipate the recoupling with the same optimism for a better life that the adults do. Others perceive the recoupling as a threat to family stability and see the stepparent as an intruder; this is especially true for the child who is being displaced as the single parent's confidant and helpmate in the household (Visher & Visher, 1979). Children who are not in poverty and who have a nonresidential parent who is active in their lives may perceive no need for a stepparent. For children who gain stepsiblings, the recoupling may mean a change in birth order, which children can find disconcerting (Ihinger-Tallman, 1987).

Crisis

A crisis response of disequilibrium (see "x" in Figure 13.1) so acute that the family system is immobilized, incapacitated, and unable to restore stability is likely to occur if the recoupling, interacting with the family's resources and the family members' meaning of the recoupling, is not accompanied by a major change in family structure and patterns of interaction. The stress of this change does not have to reach crisis proportions. A crisis response is likely if there is, for example, resistance by members of the prior single-parent family or if the integration of the stepparent inappropriately places him or her into an "instant parent that the children will love and obey" role. In a crisis state, the stepparent will have no appropriate role, and the family rules will not have changed or they will have changed too suddenly to accommodate the needs of all family members.

Typical signs of resistance to appropriate structural change in stepfamilies are (a) outright conflict; (b) avoidance (i.e., denial of negative feelings and denial of problems, especially by the adults) and literal avoidance of the stepparent by the children; and (c) elimination (redivorcing, which keeps the prior single-parent family structure intact). A variation of elimination in stepfamilies is the extrusion, or pushing out, of a particularly resistant child from the home (White & Booth, 1985) by sending him or her to live with the other biological parent or elsewhere.

If these initial attempts at adjustment do not eliminate the crisis, the family either breaks apart or begins to move into the adaptation phase by restructuring—changing roles, rules, goals, and patterns of interaction—and consolidation, in which family members must make the subsequent changes that are needed to accomplish a shared lifestyle, compromise, and meet individuals' needs. This is discussed below.

Pileup

Pileup (see "aA" in Figure 13.1) refers to additional demands on the family that are related to the initial stressor—prior strains, normative developmental changes, consequences of the family's attempt to cope with the initial stressor, and/or ambiguity about the family situation. Stepfamilies often experience a pileup of demands.

Initial Stressor

Additional demands directly related to the recoupling often include the biological parent's feeling "caught in the middle" as he or she attempts to facilitate the integration of the stepparent. Also, recoupling sometimes requires a geographic move, which results in the concomitant stresses associated with loss of peer group, change of school or work, and adaptation to a new community for the adult and children.

Prior Strains

Most individuals in stepfamilies have experienced the prior loss of the first family. There are often unresolved emotional issues related to that experience for both children and adults. For example, children who have been abandoned by a nonresidential parent may find it hard to trust a new stepparent.

There may also be pileup from a single-parent stage of the family. An overworked single parent may not have had the time or emotional energy to supervise children and adolescents, who may now be in trouble in school or with the law. Wallerstein and Kelly (1980) and Wallerstein and Blakeslee (1989) have documented how the family crisis of divorce can hamper children's normal development. Furthermore, the strain of poverty experienced by many single-mother families can leave financial and emotional problems that are not cured by a recoupling alone. If the recoupling was an effort to cope with an unhappy situation of a single parent, it too would be considered pileup.

Normative Developmental Changes

Difficulties of combining conflicting life-cycle stages at the time of re-coupling are frequent. As children continue to mature, they reach the stage of searching for their own identities. One common developmental issue for step-adolescents is a desire to know the nonresidential parent better. This has potential for placing new demands on the stepfamily, especially if relations with the other parent are strained or nonexistent.

The birth of a baby is a major transition for any family (LaRossa & LaRossa, 1981). In stepfamilies, a baby is symbolically important because he or she is the only family member who is biologically related to everyone in the household. However, there is no evidence that the birth of a new baby strengthens the bonds between stepfamily members (Ganong & Coleman, 1988).

Consequences of the Attempt to Cope With the Stressor

One common maladaptive coping mechanism in stepfamilies is the lack of acknowledgment of negative feelings, apparently because of the fear that showing these feelings will cause redivorce (Visher & Visher, 1983). Step-parents who have tried to "instantly" love their stepchildren in an effort to "reconstitute" a nuclear family and cannot do so report feeling guilty. An-other maladaptive coping mechanism used by stepparents is to become in-creasingly more authoritarian or more distant; this causes more problems and results in alienation of the stepchildren or of the stepparent, depending on the biological parent's alliance (Crosbie-Burnett & Giles-Sims, 1994; White & Booth, 1985).

Resistant children may choose or be sent to live with the other biological parent. This can cause a pileup of demands on the family if the child or either biological parent is unhappy with the change. The nonresidential parent who is unsupportive of the recoupling can also be a source of continual pileup of hardships by creating problems with respect to visitation, child support, and/ or relitigation.

Ambiguity About the Situation

Social ambiguity (McCubbin & Patterson, 1983a) is a chronic stress for stepfamilies; they look for models of realistic, healthy stepfamily function-ing in society and find virtually none. Our social institutions are based on nu-clear families. Society's ambivalence toward stepfamilies is evidenced in the inconsistencies in law and policy (Fine, 1997) and in the invisibility of healthy stepfamilies, who are camouflaged as "regular" two-parent families.

Family Adaptive Resources

Existing resources are those resources that the family still has available over time as it moves into the adaptation phase. Expanded family resources are those resources that are strengthened or developed in response to the stressor, crisis, and/or pileup (see "bB" in Figure 13.1). In stepfamilies, these might include venting emotions and "getting the cards on the table"; increased communication within and between households; the use of literature on recoupling; and assistance from counselors, support groups, or social agencies.

Family Definition and Meaning

The meaning (see "cC" in Figure 13.1) the family gives to the total situation—the crisis, pileup, and existing and new resources—is crucial in stepfamilies. For example, if children continue to see the recoupling as an invasion by the stepparent or stepsiblings, or if either adult perceives the recoupling as a move into an overwhelming situation and is feeling "worn down," *bonadaptation* (positive adaptation) is unlikely. Similarly, if family members continue to try to make the recoupling a "reconstitution" of a nuclear family and deny the need for functioning differently, bonadaptation is also unlikely. If the stepfamily can reevaluate their "failure" to make the family run smoothly, let go of self- and other-blaming, and perceive themselves as pioneers in a new family form, they may be open to the opportunity for growth.

Adaptation

The Double ABC-X Model has three units of analysis: the individual family member, the family unit, and the community. For stepfamilies, one might add the extended stepfamily network and a second community if children spend time in the homes of parents who live in different communities. Assessment of all units is crucial to understanding the family's process in response to the stressor and to predicting outcomes (see "xX" in Figure 13.1). According to the model, each unit has demands and capabilities. Bonadaptation occurs through these reciprocal relationships when the demand of one unit is met by the capabilities of another. When this happens, balance is achieved. *Maladaptation* occurs when a demand-capability imbalance exists. Assessment of each unit's demands and a search for a unit capable of meeting those demands would minimize imbalances and promote bonadaptation. There are imbalances to which stepfamilies are particularly vulnerable; these will be discussed below.

Balance Between Individual and Family

A stepparent may have capabilities that are being underused if he or she is not an integral part of the family. Alternatively, the addition of a stepparent with high demands may drain the already strained resources of the prior single-parent household. Individual developmental needs, especially of children, may go unmet because they are in conflict with the life cycle of a new marriage. The demands of a new stepmother to be "woman of the house" may be met with the family's inability to move a daughter out of that role. A study of changes in labor force participation of new stepmothers and remarrying biological mothers found that those women who decreased their participation had much lower levels of marital satisfaction than those women who did not (Crosbie-Burnett, 1988b). This suggests that trading in one's role in the workplace for an increased mother/wife role takes its toll on women's marital happiness.

Balance Between Stepfamily and Other Households in the Extended Stepfamily Network

A joint-custody, nonresidential parent may have demands on the stepfamily regarding decision-making power that the new stepfamily may be incapable of giving as a result of the demands of the new stepparent to be "in charge." Also, the adults in the stepfamily may want to move geographically to improve employment or living conditions, but this may mean decreasing a stepchild's visits with a nonresidential parent and/or grandparents.

Balance Between Family and Community

The community and its institutions (health care, school, workplace, government, etc.) make demands on families with the assumption that the families are intact, nuclear families (Crosbie-Burnett, 1994). The culture still defines stepfamilies as outside of the norm (Coleman & Ganong, 1987; Ganong & Coleman, 1997). These demands threaten family pride and cohesion. The stepfamily may turn to the community for support and understanding but too often find misunderstanding or, even worse, prejudice and discrimination.

Bonadaptation and Maladaptation

In stepfamilies, bonadaptation is characterized by the integration of the new family member(s) into the family by restructuring roles and rules and changing interaction patterns. The stepfamily may begin to experience a sense of unity by having a family identity of its own yet have permeable boundaries to allow for visitation. Children will have permission to enjoy all households of which they are a part. Family members will be able to resume developmental tasks and get their needs for a sense of control and affection met. These changes are facilitated by an important modification in the family's paradigm (Reiss & Oliveri, 1980), giving up the hope for "reconstitution of a nuclear family" and adopting a new, more realistic perspective on their family.

Maladaptation is characterized by divorce or separation, exclusion of children, or a disorganization of the family such that individuals cannot get their needs met and are therefore unable to proceed developmentally. It is possible for some family members (e.g., the couple) to have bonadaptation following recoupling while others (e.g., children) may be experiencing maladaptation (Brand & Clingempeel, 1987; White & Booth, 1985). Psychosomatic or behavioral symptoms of distress may appear. Given the many hardships and pileup demands, the lack of community resources, and the potential for problems with respect to perception of the recoupling, it is no wonder that stepfamilies experience a high rate of distress. The combined Double ABC-X Model and Contextual Model, with the empirical and clinical literature, suggest directions for maximizing the probability of bonadaptation and minimizing the probability of maladaptation for stepfamilies.

Cultural Variations

Nearly all of the findings reported above are based on dominant-culture stepfamilies. Though attention to the complexity of families described by the term *stepfamily* is increasing (Berger, 1998b), empirical research is minimal. The few studies with ethnic minorities have focused on comparisons between African Americans and European Americans in terms of remarriage rates (Smock, 1990; Wilson & Clarke, 1992), redivorce rates (Aguirre & Parr, 1982; Teachman, 1986), child support awards (Beller & Graham, 1986), mother-daughter relationships (Fox & Inazu, 1982), and adjustment of step-family members (Fine, McKenry, Donnelly, & Voydanoff, 1992). The Fine et al. (1992) study found similar levels of adjustment of parents and children in the two subsamples, suggesting that findings of studies of *adjustment* with dominant-culture stepfamilies may be generalizable to African American stepfamilies. However, this study does not suggest that family *processes* in these two groups are similar.

Noteworthy exceptions to these comparison studies are a study of inter-actions among family members in a variety of African American family structures (Barnes, 1985) and a clinician's report of racially intermarried stepfamilies in therapy (Baptiste, 1984). Perhaps this lack of research on family processes related to stress and coping in stepfamilies of color is a re-sult of the small numbers of family scholars of color and of the dominant cul-ture's conceptualization and definition of *stepfamily,* which is based on the legal definition of *stepparent.* Many types of ethnic minority families func-tion in ways that are different from the way family functioning is conceptual-ized in the legal system (Crosbie-Burnett & Lewis, 1993).

The sparse literature on gay and lesbian stepfamilies is limited to clinical observations of these families (Baptiste, 1987a, 1987b, 1995); an empirical study of relationship quality in lesbian couples with and without children (Koepke, Hare, & Moran, 1992); an empirical study of both social support and the correlates of couple and family happiness in gay male stepfamilies with adolescents (Crosbie-Burnett & Helmbrecht, 1993); and, most recently, a study using a group interview format to explore the experiences and issues faced by gay stepfamilies (Berger, 1998a) and a qualitative study on lesbian stepfamilies (Wright, 1998). In general, these writings suggest that homo-sexual stepfamilies must cope with the same stresses as heterosexual step-families as well as the additional stresses of homophobia and closeting.

Implications of the Model for Assessment, Intervention, and Policy

Assessment and Intervention

According to the Double ABC-X Model, assessment of stepfamily adjust-ment should cover the basic issues included under "Hardships and Pileups," "Resources," and "Perception" to understand the stepfamily's level of adap-tation to the recoupling (see Figure 13.1). The identification of hardships, used and untapped resources, and adaptive and maladaptive perceptions and attributions can then direct therapeutic or preventive interventions. For example, if the assessment of all family members reveals that the adolescent and the biological parent have very different role expectations for the stepparent than the stepparent has, then basic communication skills to share expectations and negotiate new roles and rules for interaction should decrease the hardship associated with the displacement of a child by the stepparent. Also, simply listing all of the resources that individuals bring to the stepfamily can be an empowering experience for the stepfamily. Finding stepfamily support groups for family members could increase the use of community resources, just as helping the stepfamily toward a "pioneering" perception of itself and away from the maladaptive "reconstitution" myth could generate a more realistic and optimistic meaning of the family's situation.

Policy

The Double ABC-X Model identifies possibilities for change in policy at many levels. At the national level, educational campaigns might reduce the negative connotation of "step-" in U.S. society and raise the public's awareness of stepfamily issues, including presenting healthy models of coping. Research on extended stepfamily networks could become a funding priority. Federal guidelines for student financial aid, AFDC, and children's health care need to be modified to reduce the financial burden of stepparents.

Though many improvements could be made at the federal level, state policy has been even less willing to recognize the role that residential stepparents play in stepfamilies (Mason & Simon, 1995). These laws could be modified to reflect stepparents' contributions to our children (Fine & Fine, 1992) by giving them some level of parental rights. Policies that reduce the legal ambiguity of the stepparent-stepchild relationship may help reduce ambiguity regarding the stepparent role in general (Fine, 1997).

At the local level, support groups and helping professionals trained in stepfamily issues could be identified and publicized. Free educational workshops for remarrying couples could prepare couples to cope with the hardships that are necessarily part of recoupling (e.g., role ambiguity) and help them to avoid others that are not (e.g., jealousy). Many of the policies and procedures of schools and colleges and the attitudes of school personnel are not supportive of stepchildren and their parents; these need to be modified (Crosbie-Burnett, 1994). Universities that train helping professionals should offer coursework in this family form. In a recent study on stepfamily therapy,

48.6% of those who found therapy unhelpful cited the problem as the therapist's lack of knowledge concerning stepfamily dynamics and issues (Visher,
Visher, & Pasley, 1997). Churches and temples should encourage their minis-
ters and rabbis to receive training in recoupling so that their premarital counseling would be more appropriate for this group.

Future Directions

Research

Nearly two decades of research with stepfamilies has taught us much about
European American custodial stepfamily households. The research should
now move from comparisons between recoupled families and other family
structures to identification of family processes that promote healthy
stepfamily coping. This search for an understanding of adaptive outcomes
calls for an increased use of qualitative research methods with well-functioning stepfamilies because qualitative methods may identify new, salient variables in the functioning of stepfamilies. This should lead to the creation of
theories based on stepfamilies rather than on intact families. These new theories can then serve as a basis for therapeutic interventions, the effectiveness
of which would be tested. In addition, examination of family functioning in
other cultures can shed light on how others have successfully answered the
needs of family members in nonnuclear structures (Crosbie-Burnett &
Lewis, 1993).

The topics of stepfamily research will expand in a variety of directions—
across social institutions, across types of stepfamily households, and across
age ranges. For example, the institutions of education and the law are being
influenced by the growing numbers of stepfamilies. A partnership between
policy makers and family scholars would be beneficial for the creation of appropriate policies for stepfamilies (Duran-Aydintug & Ihinger-Tallman,
1995). The stepfamily households of recoupled noncustodial parents, of gay
and lesbian stepfamilies, and of first-married mothers—about whom virtually nothing is known—should receive attention from researchers. Stepfamily relationships between adult children and elderly parents (Brody,
Litvin, Albert, & Hoffman, 1994; Coleman, Ganong, & Cable, 1997; Litvin,
Albert, Brody, & Hoffman, 1995) and between stepchildren and (step)grand-
parents (Gladstone, 1991; Henry, Ceglian, & Matthews, 1992; Henry,
Ceglian, & Ostrander, 1993; Kennedy & Kennedy, 1993) have recently become topics of increased interest.

Interventions

As more is learned about healthy stepfamily coping, educational and preventive programs and related literature should increase for both children and adults. Support groups for stepchildren in schools are increasing, and there is a small body of research describing and evaluating educational or preventive programs for stepfamilies (Hughes & Schroeder, 1997; Nicholson, Halford, & Sanders, 1998). There have been efforts to modify standard therapy models to address the particular stressors of stepfamilies (Atwood & Zebersky, 1995; Fausel, 1995; Lawton & Sanders, 1994; Papernow, 1994; Robinson, 1991; Tiesel, Miller, & Olson, 1995), as well as to develop specific techniques for use in therapy with stepfamilies (Clark, 1997; Wark & Jobalia, 1998). Most importantly, significant steps have been taken toward linking the growing empirical knowledge base about stepfamilies with appropriate assessment and treatment strategies (Bray & Harvey, 1995; Huntley, 1995; Martin, Martin, & Jeffers, 1992; Morrison & Stollman, 1995; Pasley, Dollahite, & Ihinger-Tallman, 1993). Efforts to articulate and integrate these various methods into theory- and research-based treatment models should now follow. This will eventually lead to studies on the efficacy of these approaches and attempts to disseminate them to clinicians in the community.

Summary

The numbers of stepfamilies are increasing because of remarriage after divorce, first marriage of parents, and cohabitation of heterosexual and homosexual parents. About 10% of minor children live in stepfamilies. Family stress theory was used in this chapter as a framework for integrating the empirical research and clinical reports on stepfamilies. Given our increasing knowledge of stepfamilies, directions for changes in the law, education, and therapy are becoming clear. The present model could be used as a basis for a comprehensive prevention and remediation program for the benefit of helping stepfamilies cope with stressors.

DISCUSSION QUESTIONS

1. Describe why remarriages, as compared with first marriages, may be described as stressful (i.e., What are some of the characteristics of remarriages that contribute to stress?).

2. How might the ABC-X Model be used for the development of programs and other interventions for remarried families? Explain your answer.

3. Describe the liabilities and resources that characterize remarried families and how they impair these families.

4. What are some of the cultural variations in remarried families? What could persons in different cultures learn from each other that would enhance the lives of remarried families?

5. Design a remarriage preparation class for individuals who have children and are planning on marrying.

SUGGESTED READINGS

Booth, A., & Dunn, J. (Eds.). (1994). *Step-families: Who benefits? Who does not?* Hillsdale, NJ: Lawrence Erlbaum.

Huntley, D. K. (Ed.). (1995). *Understanding stepfamilies: Implications for assessment and treatment.* Alexandria, VA: American Counseling Association Press.

Levine, I., & Sussman, M. B. (Eds.). (1997). *Stepfamilies: History, research, and policy.* NY: Haworth.

Papernow, P. L. (1992). *Becoming a stepfamily: Patterns of development in remarried families.* NY: Gardner.

Pasley, B. I., & Ihinger-Tallman, M. (1994). *Stepparenting: Issues in theory, research, and practice.* Westport, CT: Greenwood.

Sager, C. J., Brown, H. S., Crohn, H., Engel, T., Rodstein, E., & Walker, E. (1993). *Treating the remarried family.* NY: Brunner/Mazel.

Visher, E. B., & Visher, J. S. (1988). *Old loyalties, new ties: Therapeutic strategies with stepfamilies.* NY: Brunner/Mazel.

REFERENCES

Aguirre, B. E., & Parr, W. C. (1982). Husband's marriage order and the stability of first/second marriages of white and black women. *Journal of Marriage and the Family, 44,* 605-620.

Ahrons, C. R., & Wallisch, K. (1987). Parenting in the binuclear family: Relationships between biological and stepparents. In K. Pasley & M. Ihinger-Tallman (Eds.), *Remarriage and stepparenting: Current research and theory* (pp. 225-256). New York: Guilford.

Albrecht, S. (1979). Correlates of marital happiness among the remarried. *Journal of Marriage and the Family, 41,* 857-867.

Anderson, E. R., Greene, S. M., Hetherington, E. M., & Clingempeel, W. G. (1999). The dynamics of remarriage: Adolescent, parent, and sibling influences. In E. M. Hetherington (Ed.), *Coping with divorce, single parenting, and remarriage: A risk and resiliency perspective* (pp. 295-319). Mahwah, NJ: Lawrence Erlbaum.

Atwood, J. D., & Zebersky, R. (1995). Using social construction therapy with the REM family. *Journal of Divorce and Remarriage, 24,* 133-162.

Baptiste, D. A. (1984). Marital and family therapy with racially/culturally intermarried stepfamilies: Issues and guidelines. *Family Relations, 33,* 373-380.

Baptiste, D. A. (1987a). The gay and lesbian stepparent family. In F. Bozett (Ed.), *Gay and lesbian parenting* (pp. 112-137). New York: Praeger.

Baptiste, D. A. (1987b). Psychotherapy with gay/lesbian couples and their children in "stepfamilies": A challenge for marriage and family therapists. *Journal of Homosexuality, 14,* 223-238.

Baptiste, D. A. (1995). Therapy with a lesbian stepfamily with an electively mute child: A case report. *Journal of Family Psychotherapy, 6,* 1-14.

Barnes, A. S. (1985). *The black middle class family: A study of black subsociety, neighborhood, and home in interaction.* Bristol, IN: Wyndham Hall.

Beller, A. H., & Graham, J. W. (1986). Child support awards: Differentials and trends by race and marital status. *Demography, 23,* 231-245.

Berger, R. (1998a). The experience and issues of gay stepfamilies. *Journal of Divorce and Remarriage, 29,* 93-102.

Berger, R. (1998b). *Stepfamilies: A multi-dimensional perspective.* New York: Haworth.

Booth, A., & Edwards, J. (1992). Why remarriages are more unstable. *Journal of Family Issues, 13,* 179-194.

Boss, P. (1980). The relationship of psychological father presence, wife's personal qualities, and wife/family dysfunction in families of missing fathers. *Journal of Marriage and the Family, 42,* 541-549.

Boss, P. (1987). Family stress. In M. B. Sussman & S. Steinmetz (Eds.), *Handbook of marriage and the family* (pp. 695-723). New York: Plenum.

Boss, P., & Greenberg, J. (1984). Family boundary ambiguity: A new variable in family stress theory. *Family Process, 23,* 535-546.

Brand, E., & Clingempeel, W. (1987). Interdependencies of marital and stepparent-stepchild relationships and children's psychological adjustment: Research findings and clinical implications. *Family Relations, 36,* 140-145.

Bray, J. H., & Harvey, D. M. (1995). Adolescents in stepfamilies: Developmental family interventions. *Psychotherapy, 32,* 122-130.

Brody, E. M., Litvin, S. J., Albert, S. M., & Hoffman, C. J. (1994). Marital status of daughters and patterns of parent care. *Journal of Gerontology, 49,* S59-S103.

Bryan, L. R., Coleman, M. M., Ganong, L. H., & Bryan, S. H. (1986). Person perception: Family structure as a cue for stereotyping. *Journal of Marriage and the Family, 48,* 169-174.

Bryant, Z. L., Coleman, M., & Ganong, L. H. (1988). Race and family structure stereotyping: Perceptions of black and white nuclear and stepfamilies. *Journal of Black Psychology, 15,* 1-16.

Bumpass, L. (1984). Some characteristics of children's second families. *American Journal of Sociology, 90,* 608-623.

Bumpass, L. L., Sweet, J. A., & Casto-Martin, T. C. (1990). Changing pattern of remarriage. *Journal of Marriage and the Family, 52,* 747-756.

Carter, B., & McGoldrick, M. (Eds.). (1988). *The changing family life style* (2nd ed.). New York: Gardner.

Cherlin, A. (1978). Remarriage as an incomplete institution. *American Journal of Sociology, 84,* 634-650.

Clark, W. (1997). Joining with Jenga: An intervention for building trust with stepfamilies. *Journal of Family Psychotherapy, 8,* 73-75.

Clingempeel, W., Ievoli, R., & Brand, E. (1984). Structural complexity and the quality of stepfather-stepchild relationships. *Family Process, 23,* 547-560.

Clingempeel, W., & Segal, S. (1986). Stepparent-stepchild relations and the psychological adjustment of children in stepmother and stepfather families. *Child Development, 57,* 474-484.

Coleman, M., & Ganong, L. H. (1987). The cultural stereotyping of stepfamilies. In K. Pasley & M. Ihinger-Tallman (Eds.), *Remarriage and stepparenting: Current research and theory* (pp. 19-41). New York: Guilford.

Coleman, M., & Ganong, L. H. (1997). Stepfamilies from the stepfamily's perspective. *Marriage and Family Review, 26,* 107-121.

Coleman, M., Ganong, L. H., & Cable, S. M. (1996). Perceptions of stepparents: An examination of the incomplete institutionalization and social stigma hypotheses. *Journal of Divorce and Remarriage, 26,* 25-48.

Coleman, M., Ganong, L. H., & Cable, S. M. (1997). Beliefs about women's intergenerational family obligations to provide support before and after divorce and remarriage. *Journal of Marriage and the Family, 59,* 165-176.

Crosbie-Burnett, M. (1984). The centrality of the step relationship: A challenge to family theory and practice. *Family Relations, 33,* 459-463.

Crosbie-Burnett, M. (1988a). Impact of joint versus maternal legal custody, sex and age of adolescent, and family structure complexity on adolescents in remarried families. *Conciliation Courts Review, 26,* 47-52.

Crosbie-Burnett, M. (1988b). Relationship between marital satisfaction and labor force participation in remarrying couples. *Family Perspective, 22,* 347-359.

Crosbie-Burnett, M. (1989). Application of family stress theory to remarriage: A model for assessing and helping stepfamilies. *Family Relations, 38,* 323-331.

Crosbie-Burnett, M. (1991). Impact of joint versus sole custody and quality of co-parental relationship on adjustment of adolescents in remarried families. *Behavioral Sciences and the Law, 9,* 439-449.

Crosbie-Burnett, M. (1994). The interface between stepparent families and schools: Research, theory, policy, and practice. In K. Pasley & M. Ihinger-Tallman (Eds.), *Current issues in theory, research, and practice* (pp. 199-216). Westport, CT: Greenwood.

Crosbie-Burnett, M., & Giles-Sims, J. (1987). Marital power in stepfather families. *Journal of Family Psychology, 4,* 484-495.

Crosbie-Burnett, M., & Giles-Sims, J. (1994). Adolescent adjustment and stepparenting styles. *Family Relations, 43,* 394-399.

Crosbie-Burnett, M., & Helmbrecht, L. (1993). A descriptive empirical study of gay male stepfamilies. *Family Relations, 42,* 256-262.

Crosbie-Burnett, M., & Lewis, E. (1993). Use of African-American family structure and functioning to address the challenges of European-American post-divorce families. *Family Relations, 42,* 243-248.

Crosbie-Burnett, M., & Newcomer, L. (1990a). Group counseling children of divorce: The effects of a multimodal intervention. *Journal of Divorce, 13,* 69-78.

Crosbie-Burnett, M., & Newcomer, L. (1990b). A multimodal intervention for group counseling children of divorce. In E. R. Gerler, J. C. Ciechalski, & L. D. Parker (Eds.), *Elementary school counseling in a changing world* (pp. 41-52). Ann Arbor, MI: ERIC/ CAPS.

Daly, M., & Wilson, M. (1991). A reply to Gelles: Stepchildren are disproportionately abused, and diverse forms of violence can share causal factors. *Human Nature, 2,* 419-426.

Dolan, E., & Lowen, J. (1985). Remarried family: Challenges and opportunities. *Journal of Home Economics, 77,* 36-44.

Duran-Aydintug, C., & Ihinger-Tallman, M. (1995). Law and stepfamilies. In L. J. McIntyre & M. B. Sussman (Eds.), *Families and law* (pp. 169-192). New York: Haworth.

Emery, R. E. (1988). *Marriage, divorce, and children's adjustment.* Newbury Park, CA: Sage.

Fausel, D. F. (1995). Stress inoculation training for stepcouples. *Marriage and Family Review, 21,* 137-155.

Fine, M. A. (1997). Stepfamilies from a policy perspective: Guidance from the empirical literature. In I. Levin & M. B. Sussman (Eds.), *Stepfamilies: History, research, and policy* (pp. 249-264). New York: Haworth.

Fine, M. A., Coleman, M., & Ganong, L. H. (1998). Consistency in perceptions of the step-parent role among step-parents, parents, and stepchildren. *Journal of Social and Personal Relationships, 15,* 810-828.

Fine, M. A., & Fine, D. R. (1992). Recent changes in laws affecting stepfamilies: Suggestions for legal reform. *Family Relations, 41,* 334-340.

Fine, M. A., Ganong, L. H., & Coleman, M. (1997). The relation between role constructions and adjustment among stepfathers. *Journal of Family Issues, 18,* 503-525.

Fine, M. A., Ganong, L. H., & Coleman, M. (1999). A social constructionist multimethod approach to understanding the stepparent role. In E. M. Hetherington (Ed.), *Coping with divorce, single parenting, and remarriage: A risk and resiliency perspective* (pp. 273-294). Mahwah, NJ: Lawrence Erlbaum.

Fine, M. A., & Kurdek, L. A. (1995). Relation between marital quality and (step)parent-child relationship quality for parents and stepparents in stepfamilies. *Journal of Family Psychology, 9,* 216-223.

Fine, M. A., Kurdek, L. A., & Hennigan, L. (1991). Family structure, perceived clarity of (step)parent roles, and perceived self-competence in young adolescents. *Family Perspective, 25,* 261-282.

Fine, M. A., McKenry, P. C., Donnelly, B. W., & Voydanoff, P. (1992). Perceived adjustments of parents and children: Variations by family structure, race, and gender. *Journal of Marriage and the Family, 54,* 118-127.

Fine, M. A., Voydanoff, P., & Donnelly, B. (1993). Relations between parental control and warmth and child well-being in stepfamilies. *Journal of Family Psychology, 7,* 222-232.

Fishman, B. (1983). The economic behavior of stepfamilies. *Family Relations, 32,* 359-366.

Folk, K. F., Graham, J. W., & Beller, A. H. (1992). Child support and remarriage implications for the economic well-being of children. *Journal of Family Issues, 13,* 142-157.

Fox, G. L., & Inazu, J. K. (1982). The influence of mother's marital history on the mother-daughter relationship in black and white households. *Journal of Marriage and the Family, 44,* 143-153.

Funder, K., Kinsella, S., & Courtney, P. (1992). Stepfathers in children's lives. *Family Matters, 31,* 14-17.

Furstenberg, F., Nord, C., Peterson, J., & Zill, N. (1983). The life course of children of divorce: Marital disruption and parental contact. *American Sociological Review, 48,* 656-668.

Ganong, L. H., & Coleman, M. (1988). Do mutual children cement bonds in stepfamilies? *Journal of Marriage and the Family, 50,* 687-698.

Ganong, L. H., & Coleman, M. (1997). How society views stepfamilies. *Marriage and Family Review, 26,* 85-106.

Giles-Sims, J. (1984). The stepparent role: Expectations, behavior, and sanctions. *Journal of Family Issues, 5,* 116-130.

Giles-Sims, J. (1997). Current knowledge about child abuse in stepfamilies. *Marriage and Family Review, 26,* 215-230.

Giles-Sims, J., & Crosbie-Burnett, M. (1989). Adolescent power in stepfather families: A test of normative-resource theory. *Journal of Marriage and the Family, 51,* 1065-1078.

Gladstone, J. W. (1991). An analysis of changes in grandparent-grandchild visitation following an adult child's remarriage. *Canadian Journal on Aging, 10,* 113-126.

Glick, P. (1989a). The family life cycle and social change. *Family Relations, 38,* 123-129.

Glick, P. (1989b). Remarried families, stepfamilies, and stepchildren: A brief demographic profile. *Family Relations, 38,* 24-27.

Goetting, A. (1980). Former spouse–current spouse relationships: Behavioral expectations. *Journal of Family Issues, 1,* 58-80.

Goetting, A. (1982). The six stations of remarriage: Developmental tasks of remarriage after divorce. *Family Relations, 31,* 213-222.

Hansen, D. A., & Hill, R. (1964). Families under stress. In H. Christensen (Ed.), *Handbook of marriage and the family* (pp. 782-819). Chicago: Rand McNally.

Harvard Law Review Association. (1990). *Sexual orientation and the law.* Cambridge, MA: Harvard University Press.

Henry, C. S., Ceglian, C. P., & Matthews, D. W. (1992). The role behaviors, role meanings, and grandmothering styles of grandmothers and stepgrandmothers: Perceptions of the middle generation. *Journal of Divorce and Remarriage, 17,* 1-22.

Henry, C. S., Ceglian, C. P., & Ostrander, D. L. (1993). The transition to stepgrandparenthood. *Journal of Divorce and Remarriage, 19,* 25-44.

Henry, C. S., & Lovelace, S. G. (1995). Family resources and adolescent family life satisfaction in remarried family households. *Journal of Family Issues, 16,* 765-786.

Hetherington, E. M. (1993). An overview of the Virginia Longitudinal Study of Divorce
and Remarriage with a focus on early adolescence. *Journal of Family Psychology, 7,*
39-56.

Hill, M. S. (1992). The role of economic resources and remarriage in financial assistance
for children of divorce. *Journal of Family Issues, 13,* 158-178.

Hughes, R., Jr., & Schroeder, J. D. (1997). Family life education programs for
stepfamilies. *Marriage and Family Review, 26,* 281-300.

Huntley, D. K. (1995). *Understanding stepfamilies: Implications for assessment and
treatment.* Alexandria, VA: American Counseling Association.

Ihinger-Tallman, M. (1987). Sibling and stepsibling bonding in stepfamilies. In K. Pasley
& M. Ihinger-Tallman (Eds.), *Remarriage and stepparenting: Current research and
theory* (pp. 164-184). New York: Guilford.

Ihinger-Tallman, M., & Pasley, K. (1987). *Remarriage.* Newbury Park, CA: Sage.

Ishii-Kuntz, M., & Coltrane, S. (1992). Remarriage, stepparenting, and household labor.
Journal of Family Issues, 13, 215-233.

Jacobson, D. (1993). What's fair? Concepts of financial management in stepfamily
households. *Journal of Divorce and Remarriage, 19,* 221-238.

Kalmuss, D., & Seltzer, J. A. (1986). Continuity of marital behavior in remarriage: The
case of spouse abuse. *Journal of Marriage and the Family, 48,* 113-120.

Kennedy, G. E., & Kennedy, C. E. (1993). Grandparents: A special resource for children
in stepfamilies. *Journal of Divorce and Remarriage, 19,* 45-68.

Koepke, L., Hare, J., & Moran, P. B. (1992). Relationship quality in a sample of lesbian
couples with children and child-free lesbian couples. *Family Relations, 41,* 224-229.

LaRossa, R., & LaRossa, M. M. (1981). *Transition to parenthood: How infants change
families.* Beverly Hills, CA: Sage.

Lawton, J. M., & Sanders, M. R. (1994). Designing effective behavioral family interventions for stepfamilies. *Clinical Psychology Review, 14,* 463-496.

Litvin, S. J., Albert, S. M., Brody, E. M., & Hoffman, C. (1995). Marital status, competing demands, and role priorities of parent-caring daughters. *Journal of Applied Gerontology, 14,* 372-390.

Lutz, P. (1983). The stepfamily: An adolescent perspective. *Family Relations, 32,* 367-
375.

Martin, D., Martin, M., & Jeffers, P. (1992). *Stepfamilies: Understanding systems, assessment, and intervention.* San Francisco: Jossey-Bass.

Martin, T., & Bumpass, L. (1989). Recent trends in marital disruption. *Demography, 26,*
37-51.

Mason, M. A., & Simon, D. W. (1995). The ambiguous stepparent: Federal legislation in
search of a model. *Family Law Quarterly, 29,* 445-482.

McCubbin, H. I. (1979). Integrating coping behaviors into family stress theory. *Journal
of Marriage and the Family, 41,* 237-244.

McCubbin, H. I., Joy, C., Cauble, A., Patterson, J. M., & Needle, R. (1980). Family stress,
coping, and social support: A decade review. *Journal of Marriage and the Family, 42,*
855-871.

McCubbin, H. I., & McCubbin, M. A. (1987). Family stress theory and assessment: The T-Double ABCX Model of family adjustment and adaptation. In H. I. McCubbin & A. Thompson (Eds.), *Family assessment inventories for research and practice* (pp. 3-34). Madison: University of Wisconsin Press.

McCubbin, H. I., & Patterson, J. M. (1983a). The family stress process: The Double ABCX Model of adjustment and adaptation. In H. I. McCubbin, M. B. Sussman, & J. M. Patterson (Eds.), *Social stress and the family: Advances and developments in family stress theory and research* (pp. 7-38). New York: Haworth.

McCubbin, H. I., & Patterson, J. M. (1983b). Family transitions: Adaptation to stress. In H. I. McCubbin & C. R. Figley (Eds.), *Stress and the family* (Vol. 1, pp. 5-25). New York: Brunner/Mazel.

Mechanic, D. (1974). Social structure and personal adaptation: Some neglected dimensions. In G. Coehlo, D. Hamburg, & J. Adams (Eds.), *Coping and adaptation* (pp. 32-44). New York: Basic Books.

Morrison, K., & Stollman, W. (1995). Stepfamily assessment: An integrated model. *Journal of Divorce and Remarriage, 24,* 163-182.

Nicholson, J. M., Halford, K., & Sanders, M. (1998). Prevention of mental health problems in stepfamilies: Interventions for maintaining and enhancing the relationships and well being of stepfamily members. *Mental Health in Australia, 8,* 49-51.

Olson, D. H., & McCubbin, H. I. (1982). Circumplex Model of marital and family systems: V. Application to family stress and crisis intervention. In H. I. McCubbin, A. E. Cauble, & J. M. Patterson (Eds.), *Family stress, coping, and social support* (pp. 48-68). Springfield, IL: Charles C Thomas.

Papernow, P. L. (1994). Therapy with remarried couples. In G. Wheeler & S. Backman (Eds.), *On intimate ground: A Gestalt approach to working with couples* (pp. 128-165). San Francisco: Jossey-Bass.

Pasley, K. (1987). Family boundary ambiguity: Perceptions of adult stepfamily family members. In K. Pasley & M. Ihinger-Tallman (Eds.), *Remarriage and stepparenting: Current research and theory* (pp. 206-224). New York: Guilford.

Pasley, K., Dollahite, D. C., & Ihinger-Tallman, M. (1993). Bridging the gap: Clinical applications of research findings on the spouse and stepparent roles in remarriage. *Family Relations, 42,* 315-322.

Pasley, K., & Ihinger-Tallman, M. (1982). Remarried family life: Supports and constraints. In N. Stinnett, J. DeFrain, H. Lingren, G. Rowe, S. VanZandt, & R. Williams (Eds.), *Building family strengths: Vol. 4. Positive support systems* (pp. 367-383). Lincoln: University of Nebraska Press.

Pearlin, L., & Schooler, C. (1978). The structure of coping. *Journal of Health and Social Behavior, 19,* 2-21.

Peterson, J., & Zill, N. (1986). Marital disruption, parent-child relationships, and behavior problems in children. *Journal of Marriage and the Family, 48,* 295-307.

Reiss, D., & Oliveri, M. (1980). Family paradigm and family coping: A proposal for linking the family's intrinsic adaptive capacities to its responses to stress. *Family Relations, 29,* 431-444.

Robinson, M. (1991). *Family transformation through divorce and remarriage: A systemic approach.* London: Tavistock/Routledge.

Rubenstein, J. L., Halton, A., Kasten, L., Rubin, C., & Stechler, G. (1998). Suicidal behavior in adolescents: Stress and protection in different family contexts. *American Journal of Orthopsychiatry, 68,* 274-284.

Santrock, J., Warshak, R., Lindbergh, C., & Meadows, L. (1982). Children's and parents' observed social behavior in stepfather families. *Child Development, 53,* 472-480.

Schwebel, A., Fine, M., & Renner, M. (1991). A study of perceptions of the stepparent role. *Journal of Family Issues, 12,* 43-57.

Seltzer, J. A. (1994). Intergenerational ties in adulthood and childhood experience. In A. Booth & J. Dunn (Eds.), *Stepfamilies: Who benefits? who does not?* (pp. 89-96). Hillsdale, NJ: Lawrence Erlbaum.

Shapiro, A. D. (1996). Explaining psychological distress in a sample of remarried and divorced persons: The influence of economic distress. *Journal of Family Issues, 17,* 186-203.

Smock, P. J. (1990). Remarriage patterns of black and white women: Reassessing the role of educational attainment. *Demography, 27,* 467-473.

Sweet, J. A. (1991, November). *The demography of one-parent and step-families: Changing marriage, remarriage, and reproductive patterns.* Paper presented at the 5th Annual Wingspread Conference on Remarriage, Denver, CO.

Teachman, J. D. (1986). First and second marital dissolution: A decomposition exercise with whites and blacks. *Sociological Quarterly, 27,* 571-590.

Tiesel, J. W., Miller, B., & Olson, D. H. (1995). Systemic intervention with stepfamilies using the Circumplex Model. In D. K. Huntley (Ed.), *Understanding stepfamilies: Implications for assessment and treatment* (pp. 35-55). Alexandria, VA: American Counseling Association.

Tzeng, J. M., & Mare, R. D. (1995). Labor market and socioeconomic effects on marital stability. *Social Science Research, 24,* 329-351.

Unger, D., & Powell, D. (1980). Supporting families under stress: The role of social networks. *Family Relations, 29,* 566-574.

Vemer, E., Coleman, M., Ganong, L., & Cooper, H. (1989). Marital satisfaction in remarriage: A meta-analysis. *Journal of Marriage and the Family, 51,* 713-725.

Visher, E., & Visher, J. (1979). *Stepfamilies: A guide to working with stepparents and stepchildren.* New York: Brunner/Mazel.

Visher, E., & Visher, J. (1983). Stepparenting: Blending families. In H. I. McCubbin & C. R. Figley (Eds.), *Stress and the family* (Vol. 1, pp. 133-146). New York: Brunner/Mazel.

Visher, E. B., Visher, J. S., & Pasley, K. (1997). Stepfamily therapy from the client's perspective. *Marriage and Family Review, 26,* 191-213.

Wallerstein, J. S., & Blakeslee, S. (1989). *Second chances: Men, women, and children a decade after divorce.* New York: Ticknor & Fields.

Wallerstein, J., & Kelly, J. (1980). *Surviving the breakup.* New York: Basic Books.

Wark, L., & Jobalia, S. (1998). What would it take to build a bridge? An intervention for stepfamilies. *Journal of Family Psychotherapy, 9,* 69-77.

White, L., & Booth, A. (1985). The quality and stability of remarriages: The role of stepchildren. *American Sociological Review, 50,* 689-698.

Wilson, B. F., & Clarke, S. C. (1992). Remarriages: A demographic profile. *Journal of Family Issues, 13,* 123-141.

Wright, J. M. (1998). *Lesbian stepfamilies: An ethnography of love.* New York: Haworth.

14

Challenges and Life Experiences of Black American Families

VELMA McBRIDE MURRY

At all moments in time between 1880 and 1925—that is, from an adult generation born in slavery to an adult generation about to be devastated by the Great Depression of the 1930s and the modernization of southern agriculture afterward—the typical Afro-American family was lower-class in status and headed by two parents. This was so in the urban and rural South in 1880 and 1900 and in New York City in 1905 and 1925. It was just as common among farm laborers, sharecroppers, tenants, and northern and southern urban unskilled laborers and service workers. It accompanied the southern blacks in the great migration to the North that has so reshaped the twentieth century. (Gutman, 1976, p. 9)

The new millennium has prompted a time of reflection about changes that have occurred over the past 100 years. At the beginning of the 20th century, most white Americans had high hopes for the future based on the growth of the United States, evidenced by the emergence of industrialization, newly developed cities, increased employment, new conveniences, new ways of living, and new wealth. In sharp contrast, black Americans entered the 20th century with little hope for a better life. Rather, they were concerned about their quest for freedom, their lack of political and economic resources, and their continual defeat as they crusaded for equal rights and first-class citizenship (Logan & Cohen, 1967). Significant progress has occurred over the past 100 years; however, we end the 20th century with concerns about the "prevailing preference for white over black" that has intensified "overt demonstrations of structural and personal ethnocentrism and racism" (McAdoo, 1997, p. xix). In fact, many of the concerns expressed by black families at the beginning of the 20th century still exist, such as the widening economic and political power and equal rights between black and white Americans. Patterns of racial disparities have stimulated inquiry to determine issues such as the following: Why are black families in so much trouble? How have slavery, unfair treatment, affirmative action, and civil rights affected the life patterns of black families? What is the significance of race, ethnicity, culture, and skin color in understanding families' experiences? Why are there so many negative views about black families?

Responses to these questions differ depending on the theoretical approaches and paradigms used to study black families. Allen (1978), in his review of writings and research on black families, contended that the purpose of comparing American blacks and whites is to legitimate the idea that black families should look like white families. Unfortunately, in most instances, this notion continues to be the dominant focus even today, and, in general, the majority of empirical studies and theoretical explanations related to black families can be categorized as one of three conceptual perspectives. *Cultural equivalence* deemphasizes the distinctions between black and white families by using white middle-class family norms as the referent to which black families are compared; similarities between the groups are interpreted as support for shared values (Scanzoni, 1971). *Cultural deviance* emphasizes the norms and family patterns of white middle-class families as the referent to which black families are compared; deviation from the referent group is interpreted as pathological (Aldous, 1969). *Cultural variance* is applied if white middle-class norms are not the primary referents, and black cultural patterns are used primarily to explain black family life experiences (Jackson, 1971).

A hundred years ago, Du Bois (1899) asserted that the conditions of black families could not be fully understood until researchers assessed the influence of history and slavery, as well as the various social, economic, and political forces that affected their lives. This proposed approach provides a more accurate portrayal and illustrates the diversity in these families.

Early classic studies of the black community by black scholars, such as those of Du Bois (1908) and Drake St. Clair and Cayton (1945), highlighted the diversity in black American families and described them as adaptive, resilient, deviant, pathological, culturally distinctive, and "just like yours." What is apparent from these early studies is that just as black families are different from white families, black families are also different from each other. Therefore, the heterogeneity of black family life, with regard to value systems, lifestyles, and social class structure, makes it impossible to characterize with certainty what constitutes "*the* black family." Still, our understanding and ways of knowing about black American families are largely based on the premise that *all* black families are the same. Consequently, awareness about diversity within black families is very limited because most studies have been race comparative (i.e., white families' "normality" is used as a reference to substantiate black families' "abnormality"). In contrast, classic studies, such as those previously noted, are seldom used as the foundation for studying black families.

The traditional characterization of black families can be traced to Daniel Patrick Moynihan's (1967) monograph on "The Negro Family: The Case for National Action." Using results from the 1960 U.S. Census data, Moynihan reported that 25% of black households were headed by women and 25% of all black babies were born out of wedlock. On the basis of these data, Moynihan concluded that "the black family" structure was disintegrating and headed for extinction. Interestingly, the report did not focus on the majority of black families. For example, the same census data revealed that 75% of black families who were raising children lived in married, intact households. This report resulted in black families being described and studied as a group who are unstable, disorganized, void of values, and unable to replenish society with productive citizens. The image of black families highlighted in the Moynihan Report remains with us; black families are often described as single mothers and their children who are living in poverty, unemployed, welfare dependent, and residing in crime-infested neighborhoods (Downey, 1994; Glenn & Kramer, 1985; Jaynes & Williams, 1989; Wilson, 1987).

Studies of individual black family members also perpetuate images of homogeneity. For instance, black youth are often viewed as reared only in low-income urban neighborhoods, as lacking in motivation, and, consequently, as academic failures who engage in antisocial behaviors, including adolescent pregnancy, gang violence, and substance and drug use and abuse (Anderson, 1989; Furstenberg, Brooks-Gunn, & Morgan, 1987). These antisocial behaviors are often linked to family dysfunction and an unstable family structure, specifically father absence and lack of maternal control (Amato & Stolba, 1993; Aquilino, 1994). In fact, few studies of black families include adult males, even when they are present in the family. This lack of inclusion of black fathers, uncles, brothers, and grandfathers in studies continues to reinforce the traditional stereotype regarding the absence and invisibility of black men in families (McAdoo, 1988; Mirande, 1991).

Concern about the negative portrayal of black families has been expressed and challenged by scholars in numerous disciplines for several decades. A common theme is the need for studies of black families that include families that represent and characterize different levels of family functioning and processes (Allen, 1978; Billingsley, 1968; Brody & Flor, 1998; Hill, 1998).

Furthermore, to reduce the perpetuation of families' dysfunction, Massaquoi (1993) emphasized the need to consider patterns that occur most prevalently among black families, instead of the relentless pursuit of conveying unflattering and pessimistic views. In response to this challenge, this chapter highlights stressors that are ubiquitous to most families, including black Americans, living in the United States. These include financial strains, marriage, and parenting. However, the significant influence of racism in understanding how black families respond to these stressors is also emphasized. As pointed out by Peters and Massey's (1983) stress and coping models about black families, we *must* include the subtle influences of racism in order to understand family outcomes. Thus, everyday life experiences of black families are examined within the context of race-related stress with an emphasis on the extraordinary efforts that black families put forward to lead ordinary lives.

Demographic Picture of Black American Families

Blacks make up the largest ethnic minority group in the United States, including 30 million persons and accounting for 13% of the total population. Most black families reside in urban areas, and black Americans, on average, are younger than other ethnic groups. The median age of black Americans is 29 years, compared with 37.2 years for non-Hispanic whites. More than two thirds of black families, 67.1%, include children, compared with 55.6% of white families. In terms of age distributions of children, data show that 8.7% of America's black children, compared with 6.3% of white children, are under the age of 5, and 9.9% of black children and 6.7% of white children are ages 5 to 9 (Glick, 1999).

Conceptual Frameworks and Theoretical Perspectives

Family theories are general principles or concepts used to explain and organize information about families. Family theories are important because they affect research questions posed about families, drive the interpretation of data collected, influence prevention and intervention approaches, and direct social and family policy.

Traditional Models and Perspectives

As noted earlier, most approaches used to study black families are referred to as the *cultural equivalent, cultural deviant,* and *cultural variant* perspectives. These perspectives focus on addressing questions to determine "what is wrong with black families." Such information is thought to be useful in developing strategies for righting the wrong in black American families, as they are often characterized as having more problems and experiencing more stress and crises than families of other ethnic groups (Sudarkasa, 1993).

Black families' crises have been the feature of many research investigations, programs, and writings in the popular press and media. Typically highlighted is a cause-and-effect relationship between father absence and a multitude of social problems experienced by black mothers and children, including financial and social costs to society as a consequence of adolescent motherhood, juvenile delinquency, school dropout and failure, substance and drug abuse, gang violence, neighborhood crime, and the growing underclass and poverty occurring among black families (McLanahan & Booth, 1983; Wallerstein & Blakeslee, 1989; Wilson, 1987). Traditional models provide a plethora of information about "what is not working" in black families, in contrast to "what is working."

These approaches have been criticized because they offer a narrow view and restrict the consideration of other important issues that affect black families (Bowman, 1993; Dilworth-Anderson, Burton, & Johnson, 1993; McAdoo, 1997; Murry & Brody, 1999; Sudarkasa, 1993). Moreover, the cultural equivalent approach pulls our focus away from the crucial contributing role of the environment and the transactions between families and the environment. This approach constrains us to view all troublesome, nonmainstream behaviors and consequences as resulting from a deficit in the person or family, rather than as manifestations of parents' or individuals' desires and drives for mastery over challenging environments (Murry & Brody, 1999). In other words, the traditional models do not consider black families' strength and resiliency.

Resiliency Model

In recent years, the resiliency model has been used to study black American families (Dilworth-Anderson et al., 1993; Luster & McAdoo, 1996; McCubbin, Futrell, Thompson, & Thompson, 1998; Murry & Brody, 1999). *Resiliency* is defined as the power or ability to recover from adversity, illness, or depression. This model provides a framework that examines factors that explain families' abilities to endure and survive in the face of extraordinary challenges. It also considers how families' strengths shape the vulnerability and resiliency in children as well as other family members (McCubbin et al., 1998). Its central focus is in contrast to the traditional deficit and deviant models.

Risk, a major concept of the resiliency model, originated from investigations of epidemics and chronic diseases in the medical field. An assumption inherent in studies of resiliency is that problems can be prevented by identifying the processes that increase the risk of their occurrence (Hawkins, Catalano, & Miller, 1992). For example, high blood pressure, a high-fat diet, smoking, and too little exercise have been isolated as risk factors for cardiovascular problems (Vartianinen, Fallonen, McAlister, & Puska, 1990). A risk-focus approach, therefore, is useful in understanding human behavior, given that negative individual, familial, and environmental circumstances can have deleterious consequences for future developmental processes (Bogenschneider, 1996; Murry & Brody, 1999). Furthermore, social scientists have noted that as risk factors increase, in terms of accumulation of stressors and stress, the probability of dysfunctions escalates (Luster & Small, 1997; Sameroff, Seifer, Zax, Barocas, & Greenspan, 1992). Therefore, a reduction in the aforementioned risk factors would reduce cardiovascular problems.

Stress resilient models have recently been developed to explain how black families successfully meet the demands of children and families (Bowman & Howard, 1985; Murry & Brody, 1999; Peters, 1985; Peters & Massey, 1983; Spencer, 1984). Protective factors, a central concept of the stress resilient model, are described as the processes by which individuals develop adaptive ways of responding to crisis or stressful situations (Rutter, 1990). Social capital has also emerged as a significant concept in understanding how families manage stress and crisis. In this case, social capital refers to parents' ability to connect with social mechanisms that advance their children's and families' ability to succeed (i.e., educational systems, labor market) (Baldwin, Baldwin, & Cole, 1990; Coleman, 1988).

Family Stress Models

Family stress models are useful in studying ordinary life experiences of black Americans because they place these experiences in social and environmental contexts. In addition, several modifications of the family stress model have emerged to increase their application to black families. The social stress model, for example, examines change in families by integrating individual- and system-level variables to explain coping and competence in families. This model is applicable to black family patterns because it views stress as a social contextual variable and assumes that stress is "not the consequence of bad luck, unfortunate encounters, or unique circumstances" (Pearlin, 1982, p. 375). Stress is, instead, the consequence of engagement in social institutions whose very structure and functioning can engender and sustain patterns of conflict, confusion, and distress (Pearlin, 1982). Furthermore, the social stress model examines families from the micro- and macrolevel. An example of the application of this model is the linking of parent-child interaction or intrafamilial processes (micro) to social, economic, and political causes (macro).

The Mundane Extreme Environmental Stress (MEES) Model was designed by Peters and Massey (1983) to reflect the life experiences of black Americans living in the United States (see Figure 14.1). MEES is a modified version of the traditional ABC-X Model of family stress (Hill, 1963), which examines how families react to and manage stressors (stressful life events). Stressors may occur as a function of normative family transitions or result from misfortunes such as loss of income, the death of a family member, or chronic illness. Traditional family stress models, however, do not incorporate the life experiences of families who "live under continuous and varying stresses of oppression" (Peters & Massey, 1983, p. 195). What is more, the historical circumstances of blacks in the United States necessitate the revision of traditional stress models, so the constraints experienced by black families are given consideration as attempts are made to understand how they live, work, and survive in the United States. In fact, "stress [emerging from] racism is such a normal part of the everyday life of black people that some do not view discrimination, prejudice, or institutional racism as a special added stress[or], but as a normal part of everyday living" (Peters & Massey, 1983, p. 211).

Thus, in the MEES Model, racism is a major contextual variable and is perceived to be ubiquitous, constant, continuous, and mundane in the lives of black Americans. In comparison with the traditional ABC-X Model, the MEES Model includes an additional A factor that reflects the pervasive impact of racial discrimination. Therefore, each stressor experienced by black Americans, both external and internal, must be examined through the lenses of this component. The additional A factor represents chronic, unpredictable acts of racial discrimination. The D factor of the MEES Model reflects the

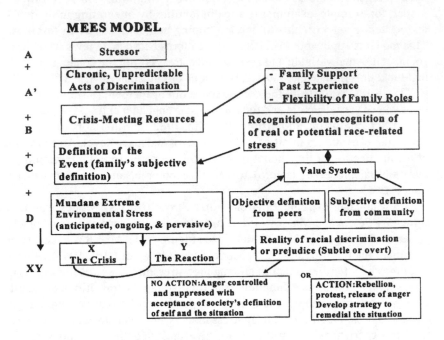

Figure 14.1. Formula for Conceptualization of Family Stress for Black American Families
SOURCE: Adapted from Peters and Massey (1983).

mundane, extreme environmental stress that is race related and occurs daily in the lives of black American families. The Y factor represents the processes by which black families experience and respond to the A and D factors.

Everyday Stressors and Unique Circumstances of Black Families

We know little about ordinary life experiences of black families. They are seldom included in the research literature, the treatment strategies proposed by practitioners, the coverage of families observed in the popular press, television, theater, or policies. Most black families are living ordinary lives, rearing children in a stable, cohesive, nurturing environment with firmly entrenched family values. In fact, national statistics on black Americans show that the majority of black families, *invisible families to the public view,* do not use drugs; have never been arrested, incarcerated, or jailed; are graduating from high school; and are employed. What follows, therefore, is a summary of empirical and theoretical writings about black families and the ordinary life experiences of black families.

Economic Stress and Strain

Economic stress and its negative impact on black families' life experiences has been of particular interest to researchers. There is evidence, for example, that unemployment, employment uncertainty, and not having enough money to "make ends meet" are associated with depression, anxiety, low self-esteem, lower marital quality, and more punitive parenting strategies (Conger et al., 1990; Elder, Conger, Foster, & Ardelt, 1992; McLoyd, 1989). The level of stress created in families as a result of economic hardships increases families' risk of maladaptive functioning.

Black families are at greater risk of experiencing economic hardship than families of other ethnic groups. For instance, the employment conditions of black Americans have been linked to a history of oppression and discrimination (Staples & Johnson, 1993). Data on economic trends that emerged during the recent recession provide support for this relationship. Specifically, in 1990-1991, black Americans were the only large ethnic group to suffer a net loss in jobs (Sharp, 1993). Comparison of data on income earnings in 1992 (U.S. Bureau of the Census, 1992) revealed that the lowest earning power occurred within married black couples in which there was a single breadwinner. When married black males are the single breadwinners in their family, the family's income is $166 below the median weekly income of married white males in the same employment situation. In contrast, married white males' weekly income is $17 above the median, and black women who are married and are major breadwinners earn less than married black males, white males, and white females.

The patterns described here provide strong evidence to question the extent to which the changing family structure of black families in recent years adequately explains the economic disparities between blacks and whites. This seems important because a reason often given for the widening income-earning gap between black and white families is the increased female-headed families in black communities. Darity, Myers, and Chung (1998) examined racial earning gaps by linking them to differential characteristics of blacks and whites and found that there are significant earning gaps among family heads. This gap, however, does not appear to be solely a function of welfare-induced labor force withdrawals or increased incidences of female-headed families. The earning gaps also cannot be attributed solely to black and white differences in characteristics (e.g., education) or to the deterioration of black families. These researchers concluded that the racial earning gap is a result of the continued disparities in the treatment of blacks.

> Racial discrimination is a more strongly influential factor in the determination of the widening racial gaps in earnings among family heads. The shift began toward the end of the Carter Presidential Administration and lasted into the Reagan and Bush Administrations. (Darity et al., 1998, p. 20)

Wilson (1987) also noted that the sources of poverty and the household composition of black families are linked to social structure rather than to families or individuals. For example, unemployment among black males, which has continued to increase since the 1960s, is associated not only with the economic well-being of male-headed households but also with the increase in female-headed families. The low employment rate of black males has also been linked to (a) the difficulty black women face in finding men to marry and (b) the toll that violence and drugs are taking on young black men. Homicide rates for young black Americans have increased to astronomical levels over the past decade (Weddle & McKenry, 1995).

Brody, Flor, and Gibson (in press) and McLoyd (1990) have suggested the need for researchers to consider the link between family financial pressure and developmental outcomes of black children. Being raised in poor neighborhoods in which few individuals are employed has an impact on how children are socialized, and families with few financial resources may feel helpless and unable to control stressful events that occur in their lives. Having few economic resources may also explain why some families are more present-oriented than future-oriented. When parents are confronting stressful life events such as inadequate financial resources, in addition to experiencing psychological distress, they may use "quick and decisive" methods of discipline (McLoyd, 1990), provide less affection, and exhibit more irritability toward their children (Brody & Flor, 1998). The day-to-day hassles associated with poverty may create psychological distress in parents, which in turn undermines parenting quality.

Poverty means living in poorer-quality neighborhoods, having limited exposure to high educational achievers, and having fewer role models who represent productive citizens. Families in these environments cope by building their children's self-esteem by engaging in positive parent-child interactions and by exhibiting high levels of parental nurturing (Brody & Flor, 1998; Luster & McAdoo, 1996; Murry & Brody, 1999).

Black Middle-Class Families

Although most research on black American families has been dominated by inquiries into the lives of those who are poor, the majority of black families are working class and middle class (Billingsley, 1992). However, with few exceptions (Landers-Potts, Murry, & Brody, 1999), their family life experiences remain unexplored. In 1993, 18% of black families in the United States had incomes in excess of $50,000, compared with 37% of white families (Smith & Horton, 1997). Although upwardly mobile black Americans have existed for as much as seven generations, the challenge of reaching and maintaining middle-class status continues to be an issue (McAdoo, 1997). Those blacks who had obtained middle-class status during slavery were often freedmen or women who were employed as skilled craftspeople; others were slaves who were able to work and buy their freedom. In addition, the offspring of the union of white males and black females, who were raised in the home of their white father and worked inside the house rather than in the fields, were also part of the black middle-class structure.

Because of the earning power discrepancy between black families and white families, the income earnings of black middle-class families resemble white lower-middle-class families. The majority of blacks who are middle class are employed in positions as administrative assistants, small business owners, police officers, teachers, and government bureaucrats (Collins, 1983; Landry, 1987; Wilson, 1995). One subgroup of black families that has reached economic parity with white families is young professionals ages 25 to 35; they are referred to as the "golden cohort" and have, in general, delayed childbearing to concentrate on their careers (Malveaux, 1981). Having middle-class status, however, does not eliminate everyday challenges and concerns for black families. Maintaining this social class status is tenuous because the income of most middle-class blacks does not allow for much excess in terms of ordinary expenses (Landry, 1987) or accumulated wealth (Jaynes & Williams, 1989; Oliver & Shapiro, 1995).

Another challenge for middle-class black Americans is neighborhood surroundings. Middle-class black Americans live in qualitatively different kinds of neighborhoods than middle-class whites do. Black middle-class families tend to live in neighborhoods that have more internal poverty rates and are located closer to high-poverty and high-crime areas than those of white middle-class families (Alba, Logan, & Bellair, 1994; Darden, 1987; Grossman & White, 1997). To manage this extraordinary challenge and foster neighborhood stability, many black middle-class residents "work to circumscribe the criminal activity that does exist by holding the neighborhood delinquents within the bonds of familial and neighborhood associations" (Pattillo, 1998, p. 747). Quiet neighborhoods exist by "integrating and establishing a truce between the networks of gang members and the business of drug dealing, on the one hand, and the activism of church leaders, block club members, and local political officials, on the other hand" (Pattillo, 1998, p. 747). Cooperation occurs because many of those engaging in criminal activity also want to live in a neighborhood that is relatively free from the threat of crime (Bursik & Grasmick, 1993). These adaptive patterns have also been associated with the coping strategies of black families living in stable low-income neighborhoods (Cloward & Ohlin, 1960).

Building and Maintaining
Couple and Family Relationships

Living Patterns

As with families of other racial groups in the United States, the living patterns and family forms of black families have changed tremendously over the past three decades (Farley & Allen, 1987). Some of the noted changes include increases in (a) the number of individuals living alone, (b) the rate of cohabiting couples, and (c) the number of families headed by women. Each of these trends has been more substantial for black families than for families of other ethnic groups (Glick, 1999).

Blacks, for example, are far less likely than whites or Hispanics to be in a marital relationship. At the beginning of the 20th century, however, most blacks lived in husband- or father-present households (Gutman, 1976), and in 1971, 64% of black households were married-couple families, compared with 42% in 1995 (U.S. Bureau of the Census, 1996). During the same period (1971-1995), the percentages of single-parent black families increased as a result of greater numbers of never-married, divorced, and widowed mother-headed families. Several social structural factors have been linked to the present living arrangements of black family members.

Challenges of the Marriage Marketplace

Today, Americans are marrying later and having sex earlier than in previous generations. Delayed marriage is often associated with increased societal demands for advanced educational training to obtain employment. Black Americans, particularly women, who want to marry someone of the same race are further challenged by the sex-ratio imbalance and shortage of employed black men. Among single black Americans ages 25 to 29, there are 98 men per 100 women; among those ages 30 to 34, there are 77 men per 100 women; and by ages 40 to 44, there are 65 men per 100 single women. There are an estimated 1.5 million more black women than black men (Staples & Johnson, 1993). This situation is seldom included in explanations for the increasing rates of single-mother-headed families (Murry, 1997); however, lack of eligible males is a stressor that carries with it the consequence of low marriage rates for black Americans. Actually, black women begin to outnumber black men beginning at age 18. This imbalance creates a "marriage squeeze" in which black women are squeezed out of the marriage market, giving black males greater bargaining power in mate selection. This gender power imbalance, as a consequence of sex-ratio imbalances, also affects black male/female relationships. Thus, low marriage rates among black Americans may not be a consequence of black women's and men's declining interest in marriage but a response to social structural circumstances that exist in wider society.

In addition to the sex-ratio imbalance, the mate selection criterion of middle-class black women also has been linked to low marriage rates. "Many black men are considered unacceptable unless they are good looking, have a college degree, are professionals, earn at least $90,000 annually, own a luxury automobile, and have other such resources" (Chapman, 1997, p. 275). Black males, however, are not to be "blamed" for their financial position in society (Wilson, 1989).

The limited pool of eligible black males and the fact that many are viewed as undesirable mates have been associated with consequences of institutional racism. For instance, limited access to health care has been linked to racial discrimination, which in turn is associated with high infant mortality, premature death, and poor health of black American males (Edelman, 1997). In addition, racism has been associated with the devastating rates of homicide, incarceration, high school dropouts, and drug abuse among black males

(Albrecht, Fossett, Cready, & Kiecolt, 1997). Mundane extreme environmental stress suggests the need to revisit the conclusion that the low marriage rate for blacks is a result of the lack of relationship commitment among black men and the lower value placed on marriage and family in the black community (South, 1993).

Low-income black American youth embrace many life goals held by their middle-class counterparts (i.e., to have a stable marriage, an economically secure spouse, and a family with children conceived and born in wedlock). According to Tucker and Mitchell-Kernan (1995), both black males and black females are cognizant of the challenges confronting them in achieving these goals because of the shortage of marriageable black men. Tucker and Mitchell-Kernan also reported that the marital aspirations of young adult black women have been lowered because of the inability to find someone that meets their standards; not having enough money to support a family was more readily cited by black males. Concern about being able to marry is warranted, given that the probability of *ever* marrying has declined more for blacks than for any other group. Between 1970 and 1990, the proportion of ever-married black women declined from 83% to 63% (U.S. Bureau of the Census, 1992). According to Norton and Moorman (1987), fewer than three out of four black women can expect to marry, compared with nine out of ten white women.

Marital Relationship Issues

Admittedly, a greater proportion of black families are headed by single parents; however, few attempts have been undertaken to study the experiences of the 43% of black couples who are married. For example, areas such as the factors that promote marital success in black couples, the impact of societal stressors (e.g., racism and discrimination) on black couples' marital relationships, and how black couples establish marital roles and negotiate the completion of marital tasks have historically been neglected. In addition, those factors that predict long-term marriages, and the processes associated with marital transitions and the adjustment of newlywed couples, have been studied less in black couples and other couples of color than in white couples.

Available studies show similarities and dissimilarities in the marital relationships of black marrieds and white marrieds. One of the few studies on newlyweds that included black couples revealed that income was positively related to feelings of marital competence for blacks but was negatively related to whites' perception of marital competence (Veroff, Sutherland,

Chadiha, & Ortega, 1993). That is, increased income was associated with *less* marital happiness for white newlyweds but *greater* marital happiness for black newlyweds. In addition, premarital cohabitation was negatively associated with marital happiness for blacks but not for whites (Veroff et al., 1993). Reasons for these racial differences were attributed to variations in the significance of professional career development for whites and the meaning of cohabitation for blacks. Specifically, the author noted that increased income has less effect on the marital happiness of whites because they exhibit greater career proneness than blacks because of greater employment and educational opportunities. Cohabitation has a greater effect on the marital happiness of blacks because they have different meanings of this form of living arrangement than whites do. Not surprising, the interpretations of these findings are similar to other racial comparative studies. When statistical differences emerge between blacks and whites, whites are used as the referent group to substantiate what is considered "normal."

In another study, Veroff, Hatchett, and Douvan (1992) examined the consequences and correlates of marital instability between black and white couples in early marriage. They found that for whites, marital process, life events, and role interference were the most predictive factors for marital instability; among blacks, situational factors were more significant predictors. For example, marriages of black couples were at greatest risk when wives were relatively young and when husbands' fathers had attained high levels of education and husbands' mothers' educational attainment was low.

Problems often encountered by black couples are reflections of living in a racist society (Pinkney, 1993). Findings from Hayes's (1988) study of black couples reveal a significant relationship between race and work-related stressors, successful marital relationships, and coping processes. High marital satisfaction occurs to the extent that black couples develop skills to manage racism, bigotry, and social pressures often encountered in workplace settings and other social settings. Staples and Johnson (1993), in their discussion of stable married black couples, highlighted the significance of couples adhering to the customs of their African heritage. Relationship characteristics that are central to building and maintaining quality black male and female relationships include understanding, honesty, warmth, open communication, sharing, respectability, independence, listening skills, support, and maturity (Aldridge, 1991). Strength and resiliency among black couples are also linked to emotional support from extended family and to connection with friends with whom they can interact and problem solve.

Conner (1998) conducted a study to identify correlates of marital satisfaction and longevity among black couples. Results of this descriptive study of stable black married couples revealed that the respondents looked forward to growing old together. Although both partners reported having satisfying marriages, wives perceived themselves and their spouse as slightly more satisfied than husbands viewed themselves and their spouse. Most of the couples reported problems associated with family, work, and spousal time together. Communication, shared responsibilities, and friendship were the most significant correlates of marital success. All couples in Conner's study agreed that black married couples endured more than white couples in building and maintaining marriages.

In another study, Ray (1988) identified the ways in which married black couples coped with family financial matters. Results from this study revealed the importance of couples developing effective financial-management strategies. These strategies included mutual respect and the ability to negotiate and resolve conflict. In general, skills that promote success in married black couples' relationships include discussing important issues in a loving manner, having satisfying sexual relations and intimacy, managing frustrations, and becoming friends. This sense of male/female togetherness may also enhance couples' marriages by increasing black husbands' sensitivity to gender-equity issues (Collins, 1990; Kane, 1992).

A plethora of studies in the past decade have focused on gender equity in the home. Most of these studies are based on data obtained from middle-class white couples, but available studies of black couples support the position of egalitarianism. That is, black husbands are more likely than white husbands to participate in household tasks and child care (Hossain & Roopnarine, 1993; Orbuch & Custer, 1995).

Orbuch and Eyster (1997) identified patterns that determine how black and white married couples negotiate household tasks and the degree to which these processes influence marital satisfaction. These researchers were particularly interested in the significance of race in understanding marital culture and the division of housework. Results from data obtained from 199 black and 174 white first-time married couples revealed that for both black and white couples, when wives' income was greater than that of their husbands' and when couples supported egalitarian norms regarding gender roles, husbands were more likely to participate in household tasks (Orbuch & Eyster, 1997). Findings also revealed that black couples perceived themselves as more egalitarian than white couples. In addition, black couples' perception about men and women sharing family and work roles was more favorable than white couples'. In fact, black wives reported more participation from their husbands in female-typed household tasks than white wives did. The authors interpreted the race effects as a function of black wives having greater resources relative to their husbands than white wives did. In addition, black women's resource base, more than white women's, is linked to increased opportunities to obtain structural resources and the need to garner resources as a result of employment instability experienced by their husbands.

Clark-Nicolas and Gray-Little (1991) have pointed out that personal resources such as education and financial stability are intricate to the marital success of black families. Education increases one's marketability and opportunities for employment and financial security; financial stability provides a sense of fulfillment and comfort and increases discretionary time and energy that can be redirected toward marital and family relationships.

Religion is another resource frequently linked to success in black families. Religion provides a system of meaning through which life events can be filtered and understood (Blaine & Crocker, 1995; Ellison, 1993; Peterson & Roy, 1985), and linking spiritual meaning to life events may foster coping capabilities and increase levels of social support (Sherkat & Reed, 1992). Attending church, praying, and reading the Bible have been linked to stronger subjective well-being in black families (Blaine & Crocker, 1995). Church attendance may provide social interactions that result in families under stress receiving positive reflective appraisals from individuals with similar values and experiences (Demo & Hughes, 1990; Ellison, 1993). The church also provides opportunities for individuals and families to attain positions of status and respect, which may be unavailable in mainstream white society (Demo & Hughes, 1990). Such roles may enhance coping abilities that can be applied not only in the church but also in the wider environment. Finally, the church provides role models for younger black family members and is a mechanism for racial socialization and political action (Taylor, Thornton, & Chatters, 1987).

Parenting Challenges of Black Americans

Parenting is traditionally defined as consistent interactions between parents and children that foster children's growth. This process is often characterized as nurturing, protecting, and guiding children. Unlike for parents in mainstream society, preparing children to be productive citizens for black parents requires that they teach their children to exist in a society where they are frequently devalued and at the same time to have self-pride in one's culture (McLoyd, 1990; Peters, 1985). Stevenson, Reed, Bodison, and Bishop (1997) characterize the parenting challenges of black Americans as rearing children in a "hope lost" society that expects and sees the worst in their children. Thus, racial socialization is a common component of black mothers' and fathers' parenting practices. Peters (1985) describes racial socialization as the "process of raising physically and emotionally healthy children who are black in a society in which being black has negative connotations" (p. 161). This suggests that the psychological well-being of black children is, in large part, dependent on racial socialization received from their family.

Ward (1996) characterized the parenting of black children as a "political act" (p. 86) because the parenting processes of blacks include messages about their children's world and their place in it. Black children are socialized based on cultural and political assumptions derived from their parents' experiences. Many black parents' daily child-rearing approaches, directly and indirectly, are powerful lessons of resistance—that is, scripted by black parents' own childhood socialization experiences of being marginalized.

Racial socialization also may occur, directly and indirectly, among parents of other ethnic groups, but its purpose and meaning differ from black parents'. For example, the impetus for white middle-class parents' discussions of race is their desire to promote views of equality among their children, whereas black parents' discussions are for the purpose of preparing their children for a racist, discriminatory, and prejudicial society. It has been found that when race-related topics were avoided, white parents noted that it was because race was not important; black parents avoided the topic because they believed their children were too young to understand racial issues (Thornton, Chatters, Taylor, & Allen, 1990).

Child-rearing practices of black parents that reflect race-related messages are both verbal and nonverbal. These messages transmit moral values and attitudes about racial issues in addition to conveying rules about conduct. Black parents also emphasize the importance of hard work, education, and self-pride in preparing their children for potential racial bias (Peters, 1985; Thornton et al., 1990). Racial socialization processes may also be shared indirectly by using culturally relevant words and phrases, telling stories, structuring children's environments by displaying culturally based art in the home, and influencing children's peer group affiliation. Many parenting practices promote resiliency in their children for the purpose of protecting them from the negative consequences associated with being assessed in terms of white standards. Internalization of negative self-images is less likely to occur when black parents skillfully weave messages about self-esteem and self-worth into moments of intimacy. This process cultivates resistance against beliefs, attitudes, and practices that can erode a black child's self-confidence and impair positive identity development (Kofkin, Katz, & Downey, 1995). Thus, resilient black children and families are those who can determine when, where, and how to resist oppression, as well as to know when, where, and how to accommodate to it (Ward, 1996).

Most studies on racial socialization have focused on racial identity and developmental outcomes of children and adolescents. The extent to which parents' racial identity affects their parenting practices, however, has not been examined. This issue is important because knowing more about parents' self-perception with regard to race may explain how and what black parents teach their children about race and may enhance our understanding of black children's growth and development (Bowman & Howard, 1985; Peters, 1985; Thornton et al., 1990). In fact, McLoyd (1998) has pointed out the need for research models on black children to incorporate the unique history of oppression experienced by black children's parents. To understand the development of black children and the challenges confronting black families, researchers should consider the linkages of parents' perception of race as well as experiences that can be linked to their skin color, including economic deprivation and the stigmatization of being of minority status (i.e., discrimination, prejudices, oppression, and racism).

Conclusion, Implications, and Recommendations

The information presented in this chapter highlights the need to critically review and revise the theoretical frameworks used to study black families. Conceptual frameworks determine the research focus, questions, and interpretation. Also emphasized is the need for future works to include a more representative presentation of black families. These approaches will enhance our understanding of why some black families are able to meet the continuing challenges and stress associated with everyday life experiences, including those specifically linked to discrimination and racism. The information presented in this chapter also suggests the need to broaden our definitions and expectations regarding healthy family functioning and to recognize that what has been traditionally viewed as chaotic, enmeshed, and dysfunctional in black families may actually reflect ways of adapting to social oppression (Murry, 1995). Given this, there is a need for the development of new models in the study of black families that will result in a restructuring of the image of black families that was established by earlier scholars. Such information has implications for policy, research, and intervention.

Social policy and intervention efforts should be derived from both empirical and theoretical formulation (Willie, 1993). The misrepresentation of black families in the Moynihan Report (Moynihan, 1967), for example, continues to influence the life of black American families. His characterization of the power structure of black families was offered void of a theoretical paradigm. Moynihan misunderstood the egalitarian patterns in black families and mislabeled it as matriarchy.

Those interested in the family life of black Americans, such as researchers, policy makers, educators, and practitioners, must be sensitive to the social, political, and economic realities of being black in America. These issues need to be at the forefront of one's awareness to more accurately understand how they are linked to stressful life events, life experiences, structural changes in families, and parenting techniques. In addition, ethnicity, culture, family structure, socioeconomic status, geographic residence, and family patterns must be considered in designing interventions.

DISCUSSION QUESTIONS

1. Compare and contrast the current theories and perspectives used to study black American families. Give an example of each and cite research studies to substantiate your example.

2. Discuss the paradigm shift that has occurred in the conceptualization of low marriage rates and increasing single-parent family structures among black American families. What are the basic tenets of the new paradigm?

3. How valid is the belief that black families are disintegrating?

4. Explore the meaning of parenting among black American families. Explain the concept of racial socialization and the extent to which it may be necessary for all children living in the United States.

5. Discuss the strengths in black American families and how they are linked to marital stability and family survival.

SUGGESTED READINGS

Angelou, M. (1983). *I know why the caged bird sings.* New York: Bantam.
Billingsley, A. (1992). *Climbing Jacob's ladder: The enduring legacy of African American families.* New York: Simon & Schuster.
Brisco, C. (1996). *Big girls don't cry.* New York: Ballantine.
Cose, E. (1993). *The rage of a privileged class: Why are middle class blacks angry? Why should Americans care?* New York: HarperCollins.

Taylor, R. J., Jackson, J. S., & Chatters, L. M. (1997). *Family life in black America.* Thousand Oaks, CA: Sage.

REFERENCES

Alba, R. D., Logan, J. R., & Bellair, P. E. (1994). Living with crime: The implications of racial/ethnic differences in suburban location. *Social Forces, 73,* 395-434.

Albrecht, C. M., Fossett, M. A., Cready, C. M., & Kiecolt, K. J. (1997). Mate availability, women's marriage prevalence, and husbands' education. *Journal of Family Issues, 18,* 429-452.

Aldous, J. (1969). Wives' employment status and lower class men as husbands-fathers: Support for the Moynihan thesis. *Journal of Marriage and the Family, 31,* 469-476.

Aldridge, D. P. (1991). *Focusing: Black male-female relationships.* Chicago: Third World Press.

Allen, W. (1978). The search for applicable theories of black family life. *Journal of Marriage and the Family, 40,* 111-129.

Amato, P., & Stolba, A. (1993). Extended single-parent households and children's behavior. *Sociological Quarterly, 34,* 543-549.

Anderson, E. (1989). Sex codes and family life among poor inner-city youths. *Annuals of the American Academy of Political and Social Science, 501,* 59-78.

Aquilino, W. S. (1994). The impact of childhood family disruption on young adults' relationship with parents. *Journal of Marriage and the Family, 56,* 295-313.

Baldwin, A. L., Baldwin, C., & Cole, R. E. (1990). Stress-resistant families and stress-resistant children. In J. Rolf, A. S. Master, D. Cicchetti, K. H. Nuechterlein, & S. Weintraub (Eds.), *Risk and protective factors in the development of psychopathology* (pp. 257-280). New York: Cambridge University Press.

Billingsley, A. (1968). *Black families in white America.* Englewood Cliffs, NJ: Prentice Hall.

Billingsley, A. (1992). *Climbing Jacob's ladder: The enduring legacy of African American families.* New York: Simon & Schuster.

Blaine, R., & Crocker, J. (1995). Religiousness, race, and psychological well-being: Exploring social psychological mediators. *Personality and Social Psychology Bulletin, 21,* 1031-1041.

Bogenschneider, K. (1996). An ecological risk/protective theory for building prevention programs, policies, and community capacity to support youth. *Family Relations, 45,* 127-138.

Bowman, P. (1993). The impact of economic marginality among African American husbands and fathers. In H. P. McAdoo (Ed.), *Family ethnicity: Strength in diversity* (pp. 120-137). Newbury Park, CA: Sage.

Bowman, P., & Howard, C. (1985). Race related socialization, motivation, and academic achievement: A study of black youths in three generation families. *Journal of American Academy of Child Psychiatry, 24,* 134-141.

Brody, G. H., & Flor, D. L. (1998). Maternal resources, parenting practices, and child competence in rural, single-parent African American families. *Developmental Psychology, 69,* 803-816.

Brody, G. H., Flor, D. L., & Gibson, N. M. (in press). Linking maternal efficacy beliefs, developmental goals, parenting practices, and child competence in single-parent African American families. *Child Development.*

Bursik, R., & Grasmick, H. (1993). *Neighborhood and crime.* Lexington, MA: Lexington Books.

Chapman, A. B. (1997). The black search for love and devotion: Facing the future against all odds. In H. P. McAdoo (Ed.), *Black families* (3rd ed., pp. 273-283). Thousand Oaks, CA: Sage.

Clark-Nicolas, P., & Gray-Little, B. (1991). Effects of economic resources on marital quality for black couples. *Journal of Marriage and the Family, 53,* 645-656.

Cloward, R. A., & Ohlin, L. E. (1960). *Delinquency and opportunity: A theory of delinquent gangs.* New York: Free Press.

Coleman, J. S. (1988). Social capital in the creation of human capital. *American Journal of Sociology, 94,* S95-S120.

Collins, P. H. (1990). *Black feminist thought.* Winchester, MA: Unwin Hyman.

Collins, S. M. (1983). The making of the black middle class. *Social Problems, 30,* 369-382.

Conger, R. D., Elder, G. H., Lorenz, F. O., Conger, K., Simons, R. L., Whitbeck, L. B., Huck, S., & Melby, J. N. (1990). Linking economic hardship to marital quality and instability. *Journal of Marriage and the Family, 52,* 643-656.

Conner, M. E. (1998). Level of satisfaction in African-American marriages: A preliminary investigation. In H. I. McCubbin, E. A. Thompson, A. I. Thompson, & J. A. Futrell (Eds.), *Resiliency in African-American families* (pp. 159-177). Thousand Oaks, CA: Sage.

Darden, J. T. (1987). Socioeconomic status and racial residential segregation: Blacks and Hispanics in Chicago. *International Journal of Comparative Sociology, 28,* 1-13.

Darity, W. A., Myers, S. L., Jr., & Chung, C. (1998). Racial earnings disparities and family structure. *Southern Economic Journal, 65,* 20-41.

Demo, D. H., & Hughes, M. (1990). Socialization and racial identity among black Americans. *Social Psychology Quarterly, 53,* 364-374.

Dilworth-Anderson, P., Burton, L., & Johnson, L. B. (1993). Reframing theories for understanding race, ethnicity, and families. In P. G. Boss, W. J. Doherty, R. LaRossa, W. R. Schumm, & S. K. Steinmetz (Eds.), *Sourcebook of family theories and methods: A conceptual approach.* New York: Plenum.

Downey, D. B. (1994). The school performance of children from single-mother and single-father families: Economic or interpersonal deprivation? *Journal of Family Issues, 15,* 129-147.

Drake St. Clair, W., & Cayton, H. (1945). *Black metropolis: A study of Negro life in a northern city.* New York: Harcourt Brace.

Du Bois, W. E. B. (1899). *The Philadelphia Negro: A social study.* Philadelphia: University of Pennsylvania.

Du Bois, W. E. B. (1908). *The Negro American family* (Atlanta Study No. 13). Atlanta, GA: Atlanta University.

Edelman, M. W. (1997). An advocacy agenda for black families and children. In H. P. McAdoo (Ed.), *Black families* (3rd ed., pp. 323-332). Thousand Oaks, CA: Sage.

Elder, G. H., Conger, R. D., Foster, E. M., & Ardelt, M. (1992). Families under economic pressure. *Journal of Family Issues, 13,* 5-37.

Ellison, C. G. (1993). Religious involvement and self-perception of black Americans. *Social Forces, 71,* 1027-1055.

Farley, R., & Allen, W. R. (1987). *The color line and the quality of life in America.* New York: Russell Sage.

Furstenberg, F. F., Jr., Brooks-Gunn, J., & Morgan, S. P. (1987). *Adolescent mothers in later life.* New York: Cambridge University Press.

Glenn, N. D., & Kramer, K. B. (1985). The marriages and divorces of the children of divorce. *Journal of Marriage and the Family, 49,* 811-825.

Glick, P. C. (1999). Demographic pictures of African American families. In H. P. McAdoo (Ed.), *Black families* (3rd ed.). Thousand Oaks, CA: Sage.

Grossman, R., & White, B. P. (1997, February 7). Poverty surrounds black middle class: Upscale neighborhood virtually an island. *Chicago Tribune,* Section C, p. 1.

Gutman, H. G. (1976). *The black family in slavery and freedom, 1750-1925.* New York: Pantheon.

Hawkins, J. D., Catalano, R. F., & Miller, J. Y. (1992). Risk and protective factors for alcohol and other drug problems in adolescence and early adulthood: Implications for substance abuse prevention. *Psychological Bulletin, 112,* 64-105.

Hayes, J. (1988, October). Staying married strategies. *Essence Magazine,* pp. 69-73.

Hill, R. (1963). Social stresses on the family. In M. B. Sussman (Ed.), *Sourcebook on marriage and the family.* Boston: Houghton Mifflin.

Hill, R. B. (1998). Understanding black family functioning: A holistic perspective. *Journal of Comparative Family Studies, 29,* 15-25.

Hossain, Z., & Roopnarine, J. L. (1993). Division of household labor and child care in dual-earner African-American families with infants. *Sex Roles, 29,* 571-583.

Jackson, J. (1971). But where are the men? *Black Scholars, 3,* 34-41.

Jaynes, G., & Williams, R. M. (Eds.). (1989). *A common destiny: Blacks and American society.* Washington, DC: National Academy Press.

Kane, E. W. (1992). Race, gender, and attitudes toward gender stratification. *Social Psychology Quarterly, 55,* 311-320.

Kofkin, J. A., Katz, P. A., & Downey, E. P. (1995, March). *Family discourse about race and the development of children's racial attitudes.* Paper presented at the biennial meeting of the Society for Research on Child Development, Indianapolis, IN.

Landers-Potts, M., Murry, V. M., & Brody, G. H. (1999, November). *Mothers' and teachers' perceptions of African American children's behavior.* Paper presented at the National Council on Family Relations, Irvine, CA.

Landry, B. (1987). *The new black middle class.* Berkeley: University of California Press.

Logan, R. W., & Cohen, I. S. (1967). *The American Negro: Old world background and new world experience.* New York: Houghton Mifflin.

Luster, T., & McAdoo, H. P. (1996). Family and child influences on educational attainment: A secondary analysis of the high/scope Perry Preschool data. *Developmental Psychology, 32,* 26-39.

Luster, T., & Small, S. (1997). A sexual abuse history and problems in adolescence: Exploring the effects of moderating variables. *Journal of Marriage and the Family, 59,* 131-142.

Malveaux, J. (1981, May). *Shifts in the occupational and employment of black women: Current trends and future implications.* Paper presented at the Conference on Black Working Women, University of California, Berkeley.

Massaquoi, H. (1993, August). The black family nobody knows. *Ebony, 48,* pp. 28-31.

McAdoo, H. P. (1997). *Black families.* Thousand Oaks, CA: Sage.

McAdoo, J. L. (1988). The roles of black fathers in the socialization of black children. In H. P. McAdoo (Ed.), *Black families* (2nd ed., pp. 257-267). Newbury Park, CA: Sage.

McCubbin, H. I., Futrell, J. A., Thompson, E. A., & Thompson, A. I. (1998). Resilient families in an ethnic and cultural context. In H. I. McCubbin, E. A. Thompson, A. I. Thompson, & J. A. Futrell (Eds.), *Resiliency in African-American families* (pp. 329-351). Thousand Oaks, CA: Sage.

McLanahan, S., & Booth, K. (1983). Mother-only families: Problems, prospects, and politics. *Journal of Marriage and the Family, 51,* 557-580.

McLoyd, V. C. (1989). Socialization and development in a changing economy: The effects of parental job and income loss on children. *American Psychologist, 44,* 293-302.

McLoyd, V. C. (1990). Minority children: Introduction to the special issue. *Child Development, 61,* 263-266.

McLoyd, V. C. (1998). Socioeconomic disadvantage and child development. *American Psychologist, 53,* 185-204.

Mirande, A. (1991). Ethnicity and fatherhood. In F. W. Bozett & S. M. H. Hanson (Eds.), *Fatherhood and families in cultural context* (pp. 53-82). New York: Springer.

Moynihan, D. P. (1967). The Negro family: The case for national action. In L. Rainwater & W. L. Rainwater (Eds.), *The Moynihan Report and the politics of controversy.* Cambridge: MIT Press.

Murry, V. M. (1995, November). *Strength and resiliency of black American families: Research update for practitioners.* Paper presented at the National Council on Family Relations, Portland, OR.

Murry, V. M. (1997). The impact of sexual activity and fertility timing on subsequent life experiences of African American high school graduates. *Families in Society: The Journal of Contemporary Human Services, 78,* 383-392.

Murry, V. M., & Brody, G. H. (1999). Self-regulation and self-worth of black children reared in economically stressed, rural, single mother-headed families: The contribution of risk and protective factors. *Journal of Family Issues, 20,* 458-484.

Norton, A. J., & Moorman, J. E. (1987). Current trends in marriage and divorce among American women. *Journal of Marriage and the Family, 49,* 3-14.

Oliver, M. L., & Shapiro, T. M. (1995). *Black wealth/white wealth: A new perspective on racial inequality.* New York: Routledge.

Orbuch, T. L., & Custer, L. (1995). The social context of married women's work and its impact on black husbands and white husbands. *Journal of Marriage and the Family, 57,* 333-345.

Orbuch, T. L., & Eyster, S. L. (1997). Division of household labor among black couples and white couples. *Social Forces, 76,* 301-333.

Pattillo, M. E. (1998). Sweet mothers and gangbangers: Managing crime in a black middle-class neighborhood. *Social Forces, 76,* 747-775.

Pearlin, L. I. (1982). The social contexts of stress. In L. Goldberger & S. Breznitz (Eds.), *Handbook of stress: Theoretical and clinical aspects* (pp. 367-379). New York: Free Press.

Peters, M. F. (1985). Racial socialization of young black children. In H. P. McAdoo & J. L. McAdoo (Eds.), *Black children.* Beverly Hills, CA: Sage.

Peters, M. F., & Massey, G. (1983). Chronic vs. mundane stress in family stress theories: The case of black families in white America. *Marriage and Family Review, 6,* 193-218.

Peterson, L. R., & Roy, A. (1985). Religiosity, anxiety, and meaning and purpose: Religion's consequences for psychological well-being. *Review of Religious Research, 27,* 49-62.

Pinkney, A. (1993). *Black Americans* (4th ed.). Englewood Cliffs, NJ: Prentice Hall.

Ray, E. C. (1988, October). Love is not enough. *Essence,* pp. 34-38.

Rutter, M. (1990). Psychosocial resilience and protective mechanisms. In J. Rolf, A. Masten, D. Cicchetti, K. Nuechterlein, & S. Weintraub (Eds.), *Risk and protective factors in the development of psychopathology* (pp. 181-214). Cambridge, UK: Cambridge University Press.

Sameroff, A. J., Seifer, R., Zax, M., Barocas, R., & Greenspan, S. (1992). *New approaches to mental health from birth to adolescence.* New Haven, CT: Yale University Press.

Scanzoni, J. (1971). *The black family in modern society.* Boston: Allyn & Bacon.

Sharp, R. (1993, September 14). In latest recession, only blacks suffered net employment loss. *Wall Street Journal,* p. 1.

Sherkat, D. E., & Reed, M. D. (1992). The effects of religion and social support on self-esteem and depression among the suddenly bereaved. *Social Indicators Research, 26,* 259-275.

Smith, J. C., & Horton, C. P. (1997). *Statistical record of black America* (4th ed.). Detroit, MI: Gale Research.

South, S. J. (1993). Racial and ethnic differences in the desire to marry. *Journal of Marriage and the Family, 55,* 357-370.

Spencer, M. B. (1984). Black children's race awareness, racial attitudes, and self-concept: A reinterpretation. *Journal of Black Psychology, 6,* 59-79.

Staples, R., & Johnson, L. B. (1993). *Black families at the crossroads: Challenges and prospects.* San Francisco: Jossey-Bass.

Stevenson, H. C., Reed, J., Bodison, P., & Bishop, A. (1997). Racism stress management: Racial socialization beliefs and the experience of depression and anger in African American youth. *Youth & Society, 29,* 197-222.

Sudarkasa, N. (1993). Female-headed African American households: Some neglected dimensions. In H. P. McAdoo (Ed.), *Family ethnicity: Strength in diversity* (pp. 81-89). Newbury Park, CA: Sage.

Taylor, R. J., Thornton, M. C., & Chatters, L. M. (1987). Black Americans' perceptions of the sociohistorical role of the church. *Journal of Black Studies, 18,* 123-138.

Thornton, M., Chatters, L., Taylor, R., & Allen, W. (1990). Sociodemographic and environmental correlates of racial socialization by black parents. *Child Development, 61,* 401-409.

Tucker, B. M., & Mitchell-Kernan, C. (1995). *The decline in marriage among African Americans.* New York: Russell Sage.

U.S. Bureau of the Census. (1992). *Marital status and living arrangements: March 1992* (Current Population Reports Series, P. 20, No. 468). Washington, DC: Government Printing Office.

U.S. Bureau of the Census. (1996). *The black population in the United States: March 1996* (Current Population Reports, P. 20, No. 398). Washington, DC: Government Printing Office.

Vartianinen, E., Fallonen, U., McAlister, A. L., & Puska, P. (1990). Eight-year follow-up results of an adolescent smoking prevention program: The North Korea Youth Project. *American Journal of Public Health, 80,* 78-79.

Veroff, J., Hatchett, S., & Douvan, E. (1992). Consequences of participating in a longitudinal study of marriage. *Public Opinion Quarterly, 56,* 315-327.

Veroff, J., Sutherland, L., Chadiha, L., & Ortega, R. (1993). Newlyweds tell their stories. *Journal of Social and Personal Relationships, 10,* 437-457.

Wallerstein, J. S., & Blakeslee, S. (1989). *Second chances: Men, women, and children a decade after divorce.* New York: Ticknor & Fields.

Ward, J. V. (1996). Raising resisters: The role of truth telling in the psychological development of African American girls. In B. J. Leadbeater & N. Way (Eds.), *Urban adolescent girls: Current research and future trends* (pp. 85-99). New York: New York University Press.

Weddle, K. D., & McKenry, P. C. (1995). Self-destructive behaviors of black youth: Suicide and homicide. In R. Taylor (Ed.), *Black youth: Perspectives on their status in the United States* (pp. 203-223). New York: Basic Books.

Willie, C. V. (1993). Social theory and social policy derived from the black family experience. *Journal of Black Studies, 23,* 451-459.

Wilson, F. H. (1995). Rising tide or ebb tide: Recent changes in the black middle class in the U.S., 1980-1990. *Research in Race and Ethnic Relations, 8,* 21-55.

Wilson, J. N. (1989). Child development in the context of the black extended family. *American Psychologist, 44,* 246-258.

Wilson, W. J. (1987). *The truly disadvantaged: The inner city, the underclass, and public policy.* Chicago: University of Chicago Press.

15

Immigrant Families and Sources of Stress

HECTOR BALCAZAR
ZHENCHAO QIAN

The Unique Experience of Immigrant Families

The experiences of immigrant families coming to the United States are as diverse as life itself. For centuries, immigrant families in pursuit of the American dream have taken many routes to arrive in the United States, across the Atlantic and the Pacific, across the Caribbean, and through the vast southern border with Mexico (Parrillo, 1991). Every immigrant family has a story to tell about their circumstances and the reasons and forms of departure from their homeland.

Many stories of immigrant families are filled with sadness, suffering, hope, and optimism. Memories about their decision to immigrate are closely linked to the human tragedies of war, devastation, persecution, repression, and poverty, as well as to the lack of social mobility and a strong desire for improvement. After their arrival, these same families' stories illustrate hope, freedom, opportunity, and, at the same time, difficulty in providing a better life for their families. Parrillo (1991) identified two characteristics or elements of the human spirit of immigrant families as they sought their destiny in the new land of America: (a) the individual's resolute quest for a better life and (b) the family's emotional and moral encouragement to carry on.

According to the 1990 census, new immigrants into the United States reached 7.3 million in the 1980s. The proportion of foreign-born individuals increased to 8% in 1990 from less than 5% in 1970 (Chiswick & Sullivan,

359

1995). Immigrants now make up almost one third of the population increase in the United States (Rumbaut, 1996). The recent influx of new immigrants is second only to the peak immigration in the first decade of the 20th century, when most immigrants were Europeans. Today, immigrants are diverse in their countries of origin, and they come from every country in the world. Most, however, are from Asia, Mexico, and other parts of Latin America and, thus, become racial minorities when they settle in the United States.

Understanding the Experience of
Immigrant Families: A Contemporary View

Because of the rapid increases in immigrant families, it is important to understand these families and the unique experiences that characterize the process of striving for a better life in a new society. These experiences are processes of transformation and as such involve multiple changes in which families are integrated into an existing social system, thereby creating new forms of social arrangements. At the microlevel, the individual family experiences a variety of changes as it copes with the challenges of the new environment. For example, the immigration process brings about physical, psychosocial, and cultural changes among family members as they adjust to the new social milieu (Roer-Strier, 1997). These transformations and their consequences for family well-being are major themes of this chapter. Specifically, this chapter focuses on stress and coping strategies related to immigrant adults, immigrant children, and children of immigrants, and because most recent immigrants are members of racial minorities, we only include literature related to immigrant families who are racial minorities.

With few exceptions, racial and ethnic minority immigrants do not speak English as a native language. English fluency is such an important aspect and determinant of adjustment in the United States; therefore, those who do not speak English often find themselves unprepared for fulfilling their dreams. Furthermore, immigrants have less (but more diverse) educational attainment than nonimmigrants, and the gap between the two groups has widened in recent years (Chiswick & Sullivan, 1995). A lack of schooling puts many immigrants in a disadvantaged position because the industrial restructuring that has occurred in recent decades requires workers to be educated, at least to some degree, in order to successfully compete in the labor market. These two factors—the inability to speak English and low educational attainment—handicap many immigrants. Consequently, these immigrants lack the job skills needed in the U.S. labor market and end up in low-paying and low-status jobs. As a result, 18% of immigrants in the United States live in households with incomes below the poverty level (Chiswick & Sullivan, 1995). This, of course, creates enormous stress for immigrant families—many of whom are classified as "working poor" but do not qualify for welfare programs.

Although the proportion of recent immigrants who live in poverty is greater than that of nonimmigrants, some immigrants, specifically those with higher levels of education and the ability to speak English, have done reasonably well. Compared with others, these immigrants have higher occupational attainments, higher earnings, lower unemployment rates, higher rates of geographic mobility within the United States, higher rates of naturalization, and lower fertility rates (Chiswick & Sullivan, 1995). However, educational credentials do not translate into equivalent income for immigrants and for white nonimmigrants.

Regardless of country of origin, language use, and socioeconomic status, many immigrants come to the United States to fulfill their dreams; some are successful and some are not. Despite varying degrees of socioeconomic success, many immigrant families are faced with enormous pressures as a result of living in the United States. For example, they need to deal with financial problems as a result of the insecure nature of employment; that is, they are less likely to secure jobs and also less likely to retain jobs once they have them (Farley, 1996). In addition, they experience acculturative stress; they need to deal with issues such as language problems, perceived discrimination, and conflict between their own cultural values and American values (Gill, Vega, & Dimas, 1994).

Acculturative stress may be stronger for immigrant families with school-age children, and it has become more evident as a result of increases in immigrant families with school-age children. For example, first- or second-generation children (immigrant children or children of immigrants) account for 15% of the school-age population (Landale & Oropesa, 1995). This percentage is even higher among Hispanics and Asian Americans: 59% of Hispanic children and 90% of Asian American children are members of the first or second generation (Landale & Oropesa, 1995). These families are often characterized by cultural and generational gaps between parents and children. As a result, these families tend to experience stress-related problems, including interpersonal conflict, role conflict, poor self-esteem, and intergenerational conflict.

In addition to economic and acculturation problems, recent immigrants face problems that extend beyond family members to the wider social system. The majority of immigrants are identified as members of a racial minority.

Thus, they also face the institutional discrimination that is encountered by nonimmigrant racial minorities (Benson, 1990).

Immigrants with low socioeconomic status are more likely to live in neighborhoods where minority nonimmigrants reside. Therefore, a ghetto culture exists that often prevents immigrants from moving up in socioeconomic status. Meanwhile, immigrants living outside their neighborhood experience the dual status of being a minority as well as an immigrant, often resulting in isolation and alienation from the larger society.

Despite the severe stress associated with immigration and acculturation, immigrants are often hesitant to seek mental health services even if they are failing to cope and/or adjust to their present environment. The primary reasons for these phenomena are (a) the lack of accessibility and availability of mental health services in areas where they live; (b) the cultural stigma attached to using services associated with mental health; and (c) the lack of culturally appropriate mental health services (Fong, 1998).

When individuals and families migrate to the United States, or to any other country, they experience disruptions in their supportive social networks, socioeconomic hardships, and a series of stress reactions as they attempt to become part of the social groups in a new country (Rogler, Cortes, & Malgady, 1991). Immigrant families undergoing the process of integration will have unique experiences, both positive and negative, related to these new social arrangements and modes of living in the new environment. In general, immigrant families experience many changes as a result of new living arrangements in a new country (Rogler et al., 1991).

Stress-coping models (Anderson, 1991; Cervantes & Castro, 1985; Lazarus, 1984; Lazarus & Folkman, 1984) provide a theoretical framework for understanding the dynamic and interactive factors that affect migration-induced adaptations experienced by immigrant families (Rogler et al., 1991). One important factor in this process is acculturation and its multiple dimensions; acculturative stress is a special type of stress associated with the process of acculturation.

The Concept of Acculturation and Acculturative Stress in the Immigration Process

Researchers interested in the interrelationship between cultural systems, cultural change, and the immigration process have explored the phenomenon of acculturation. Classical definitions of *acculturation* include those that identify acculturation as a series of phenomena that results when people of different cultures come into continuous firsthand contact and the resulting subsequent changes in the behaviors of either or both cultural groups (Berry, 1990; Redfield, Linton, & Herskovits, 1936). The acculturation process is not static, nor is it simply a process of reactions to changes within the cultural context of individuals. It involves an active series of social circumstances and adjustments that immigrants experience when being confronted with cultural changes or with changes in their cultural surroundings (Berry, Poortinga, Segall, & Dasen, 1992; Schmitz, 1997).

According to Berry (1990), depending on the nature of the contact, the immigrant group can experience four modes of acculturation: (a) *assimilation*, when the immigrant group loses the values of its original cultural identity and adopts the values of the dominant culture; (b) *separation*, when the immigrant group maintains strong values of its original cultural identity and avoids interaction with the dominant society or host culture; (c) *integration*, when the immigrant group maintains its cultural identity and, at the same time, becomes part of the larger society by acquiring the characteristics of the host culture; and (d) *marginalization* or *deculturation*, when the immigrant group loses its original cultural identity while also avoiding the dominant culture and showing no interest in the larger society.

Although these concepts were originally proposed at the group level, it is at the individual level where the modalities of acculturation have received the most attention. One way of understanding the process of acculturation at the individual level is by defining it on a continuum (Balcazar, Castro, & Krull, 1995; Castro, Cota, & Vega, 1999). On one side of this continuum is the "low-acculturated group," and on the opposite side is the "high-acculturated group." In between these groups is a third group identified as a "middle-acculturated group." Several factors can be used to categorize individuals into these groups. For example, among Hispanics, these elements are the language (Spanish vs. English) that subjects speak and write, the country where childhood was spent (childhood environment), the current circle of friends (Hispanic vs. non-Hispanic), and the pride of having a Latino/Hispanic background (Balcazar et al., 1995). Those individuals who would be assigned to the low-acculturated group would be characterized by speaking and reading only Spanish, having grown up in Mexico or Latin America, having only Hispanic friends, and being very proud of their Hispanic heritage. In contrast, the high-acculturated group would include those individuals with an Anglo-European cultural orientation. These individuals speak and write only English, were born and raised in the United States, have only Anglo-European friends, and feel very proud to be American. It is also possible to have individuals with a bicultural orientation and bilingual and ethnic identity that is a result of a combination of both cultural experiences (i.e., Hispanic and Anglo European) (Balcazar et al., 1995).

As cultural adjustments are made, some form of psychological conflict and social disintegration may occur. This type of conflict is called acculturative stress (i.e., the pain and suffering associated with the process of acculturation) (Berry, Kim, Minde, & Mok, 1987; Mena, Padilla, & Maldonado, 1987). Acculturative stress includes a wide range of behaviors and experiences, some of which can be pathological (Thomas, 1995). These include depression, anxiety, deviant behaviors, adjustment disorders, psychosomatic symptomatology, and substance abuse (Berry, 1986; Thomas, 1995).

The extent to which acculturative stress affects immigrants' mental health will depend on a variety of group and individual characteristics (Berry, 1990). For example, for some immigrants, acculturation enhances their lives and their mental health status, whereas for others, it creates a wide range of psychological and social problems. Positive or negative outcome largely depends on several factors that moderate the relationships between acculturation and stress, including psychological characteristics of the individual, demographic and social factors, modes of acculturation, and societal factors of the host country (Berry, 1990).

Recent studies conducted among Hispanic immigrant women revealed that different stressors may become prominent at various stages (low vs. high) of acculturation (Balcazar, Peterson, & Cobas, 1996; Balcazar, Peterson, & Krull, 1997; Peterson, Cobas, Balcazar, & Amling, 1998). That is, certain stressors may occur early in the acculturation process when individuals feel separated from their origins (e.g., from Mexico and family members who remained there) as well as later in the process when they increasingly become aware of and adjust to aspects of the U.S. culture that are in conflict with their own cultural background. In addition, stressful experiences may continue to exist for some immigrants who are confronted with oppression and prejudices of U.S. society (Peterson et al., 1998). The combination of greater stress, conflict, and diminished family connections, which often result from the acculturation process, may leave some immigrants more vulnerable to psychosocial and mental health problems (Balcazar et al., 1997; Berry, 1990; Thomas, 1995).

Other expressions of stress that are associated with immigrant experiences include culture shock and homesickness (Van Tilburg & Vingerhoets, 1997). When exposed to a new culture, a person experiences culture shock (Furnham, 1997), which results in unpleasant emotional reactions of surprise or shock. This surprise or shock can be the result of encountering an unexpected situation or of negative feelings toward the person's own culture, the foreign culture, or both. Elements of culture shock include the following: (a) strain as a result of efforts to make psychological adaptations; (b) a sense of loss and feelings of deprivation; (c) being rejected by and/or rejecting members of the new culture; (d) confusion regarding the individual's role expectations, values, feelings, and self-identity; (e) negative emotions in the form of surprise, anxiety, disgust, and indignation after realizing cultural differences; and (f) feelings of inability to cope with the new environment (Furnham, 1997; Oberg, 1960). Some elements of culture shock may be temporary and may not be experienced by all immigrants. Likewise, the transitory experience of culture shock does not always result in negative behavioral patterns and may, in the long run, prove to be beneficial to the immigrant's coping and adaptive skills.

Homesickness is a related concept that immigrants might experience. Furnham (1997) defines *homesickness* in several ways: a strong preoccupation with thoughts of home, a perceived need to go home, and a sense of grief for home. Homesickness brings about feelings of unhappiness and, in some circumstances, physical reactions in the form of disease or disorientation (Furnham, 1997).

Journeys of the Immigrant Family: Reflections on the Family's Structure and Function

A fundamental quest for many immigrants in the United States has been to preserve and enhance the well-being of their families. According to Parrillo (1991), immigrant families have their own unique social biographies. Each family brings cultural, socioeconomic, and religious backgrounds to the immigration experience; however, one fundamental similarity shared by almost all ethnic groups is the importance placed on preserving the family structure and its function as a core element of their existence in the new country.

Family structures of immigrants take many forms as they migrate to the United States. Some families arrive as part of a nuclear family, while others join extended families already living in the United States. In some circumstances (especially those immigrants from Mexico and other Central American countries), they enter the United States leaving behind members of their nuclear family, waiting for the opportunity to reunite in the new country.

Many immigrants come from cultures that highly value a more collective family structure. The family is the place for cherished traditions to be carried out, and it serves as an emotional shelter for family members (Parrillo, 1991) in both nuclear and close-knit extended families. Therefore, a wide network of kin obligations becomes integrated into the daily functioning of family life. Aunts, uncles, and other relatives who live in the same household or in close proximity assume many functions of the nuclear family, including taking care of children, doing household chores, and providing financial resources for shelter and food (Thomas, 1995).

Traditional family values of ethnic immigrant groups have played an important role in preserving the integrity of the family structure and have served as a source of emotional stability for families during difficult times. Research in the area of immigrant families has focused particular attention on family values that help immigrants cope with the stressors associated with the immigration process. Comparisons of ethnic minority families, particularly those who are low acculturated, and Anglo families have resulted in the identification of family values that differ between these two groups. For example, according to Anderson (1991), the traditional values (illustrated by Afrocentric values) of many ethnic groups differ from those of the majority Eurocentric culture in the following ways: (a) time (present here-and-now vs. *future*); (b) worldviews (systemic, holistic, spiritual, group/community, and harmony vs. *linear, materialistic, individualistic, and mastery*); (c) identity (self and community vs. *self*); (d) acquisition of knowledge (gained through introspection and faith vs. *known by measuring*); and (e) transmission of knowledge (oral vs. *written*).

For Hispanic families (particularly for low-acculturated families), these values are evident in (a) the preference for a group of familial orientation, compared with an individualistic orientation; (b) a cultural emphasis on harmony in interpersonal relationships and the avoidance of confrontation and conflict in relationships; (c) a strong loyalty, attachment, and solidarity with nuclear and extended family members; (d) a strong value for respect or deference and obedience to authority figures; (e) a preference for closeness in interpersonal space, as reflected in the desire for interpersonal warmth in social relations; (f) a present time orientation that values a focus on here-and-now activities; and (g) strong gender roles, including clear distinctions for appropriate behavior for men and women (Balcazar et al., 1995).

Discrepancies in cultural and familial values are often a source of conflict and stress. As families experience the process of acculturation and family life undergoes cultural transitions, family members' values begin to change. Parents and children may experience intergenerational conflicts in value systems; marital relations change; new roles for men and women are developed; and new patterns of work, discipline, and family life are established. How families cope with these stressful cultural transitions is an important area requiring further study (Roer-Strier, 1997).

Neighborhoods and Neighbors

Immigrants coming from a society different from the United States find it difficult to adjust. They may learn to function within their new society, but some will remain attached to the old country and attempt to pass on their native traditions to their children (Parrillo, 1991). Consequently, they face cultural clashes and often feel isolated in the new society. The theory of social isolation postulates that migration involves not only physical separation from the homeland but also separation from one's orienting set of mutual rights, obligations, and networks of social interaction, thereby causing the most tumultuous and destructive experiences associated with immigration (Kuo, 1976). Evidence strongly suggests that an immigrant who feels lonely and alienated tends to have symptoms of psychological distress (Fong, 1998).

To reduce social isolation and cultural shock, many immigrant families, especially those with low socioeconomic status, choose to live in neighborhoods where other fellow ethnic immigrants reside. The advantages of living together in one neighborhood are evident for immigrant families. Those who live with fellow ethnic families do not experience strong discrimination because there is little interaction with the larger society (Benson, 1990). Strong social support is readily available, and immigrant families have the opportunity of sharing similar experiences; thus, it is easier for them to confront cultural shock and isolation. In addition, it is also possible for them to build a network of relatives and friends who are accessible to each other and, consequently, can use social support from their ethnic community to promote adaptability to the larger society (Leslie, 1992).

Although these neighborhoods are often poor, beset by violence, drugs, and problems in nearby schools, immigrant children and children of immigrants who live in these neighborhoods are likely to be supervised by both their parents and the community, thus being subjected to strong social control (Zhou & Bankston, 1998). As a result, these children are more likely to develop their own ethnic identity than are those living in predominantly white suburban neighborhoods. Immigrant children who are from families associated with tightly knit social networks consistently report better psychological conditions, higher levels of academic achievement, and stronger educational aspirations than those in socially isolated families (Zhou, 1997). In contrast, immigrant children and children of immigrants living in socially isolated families are likely to experience family problems attributable to changed cultural standards. In addition, because of little support from neighbors and networks, their experiences of isolation accumulate to affect their everyday life and cause mental distress (Parrillo, 1991; Rogler et al., 1991).

Well-acculturated immigrant families often live in predominantly white neighborhoods. Immigrant children and children of immigrants from these families go to schools where there are few students in their racial or ethnic group. Although these immigrants adapt economically, their social adaptation may lag behind. It is likely that discrimination against them is commonplace in the neighborhoods, but because of their ethnic and native background, they may perceive greater discrimination than what actually exists (Mena et al., 1987). Thus, they are more likely to sense social isolation than those living in ethnically segregated neighborhoods and are more likely to concur with racial minority natives about the problems of racial discrimination. One coping strategy used by these families in dealing with this social isolation is to establish social networks and provide social support among themselves by sending their children to weekend ethnic language schools and to ethnic churches. These activities facilitate talking with others about their problems, thereby helping to reduce stress.

Stress Among Immigrant Children and Children of Immigrants

Children who came to the United States when they were very young and those who were born to recent immigrants experience the same kind of growing pains as children of native-born parents. Adolescence, in particular, is a developmental period during which children experience a dramatic change in their physical, intellectual, and social development. Immigrant children and children of immigrants, however, need to deal with much more than typical adolescents of native-born parents do.

These adolescents usually have parents who have difficulty communicating with them because of language barriers, depend on them to be intermediaries between their family and the larger society, and teach them cultural values of their country of origin that often contradict what they learn at school and in interactions with their peers. They often have low self-esteem and dislike their dual-status identity of being a racial minority and an immigrant. Moreover, they are often caught in the crossroads of cultural clashes generated by, on the one hand, their eagerness to conform to the norms of the mainstream society and, on the other, their obligation to fulfill their duties as an offspring of an immigrant.

Cultural and Generational Conflict

Immigrant children often find themselves living in two worlds. At school, they learn to be independent, spontaneous, outspoken, and aggressive. At

home, they learn to be interdependent, modest, and respectful. This difference in acculturation creates enormous stress for both parents and children.
Portes and Rumbaut (1996) used generational consonance and dissonance to
conceptualize the acculturation gaps between immigrant parents and their
children. Generational consonance indicates agreement in acculturation between immigrant parents and their children; generational dissonance occurs
when children disagree on the levels of parental acculturation and oppose parental guidance. Thus, generational dissonance can lead to intensified parent-
child conflict and stress.

English fluency is essential for immigrant families to succeed in the United
States. Immigrant parents who are not fluent in English are more likely to be
isolated from the mainstream society and face prejudice and discrimination
(Lieberson & Waters, 1988). Inside the immigrant families, parents' language skills also may create communication barriers between parents and
children. The children, being educated in the United States, often speak English and feel comfortable doing so because this is the language their friends
speak and the language of mainstream society. Gradually, some children feel
less willing and less able to speak the language they share with their parents,
and thus communication barriers are formed.

If a family does not address parent-child communication problems, the results might be serious conflicts and dysfunction in the family (Hong & Ham,
1992). Children who prefer to speak English at home often lose social support from their parents and community, and if their neighborhoods are not
similar to those of the children's peers, they are likely to rebel against their
parents' expectations and to assimilate into an oppositional culture (Portes &
Stepick, 1993; Waters, 1996). If this happens, children may have low motivation and low ability to perform well at school (Matute-Bianchi, 1991). In contrast, children who master both languages tend to excel in school and have
high self-esteem, because bilingual skills allow children to gain access to the
emotional and normative supports of ethnic groups (Fernandez & Nielsen,
1986; Matute-Bianchi, 1991; Sung, 1987; Tienda, 1984). However, the advantage of being bilingual diminishes with the increase in the duration of stay
in the United States (Fernandez & Nielsen, 1986).

Immigrant parents who do not speak English also tend to have lower levels
of education; thus, they have little opportunity to advance in the labor market.
Children of these immigrants are often uncomfortable with their parents' socioeconomic status, and this economic and social marginality puts strains on
parent-child relations. In a study of children of Vietnamese refugees, Zhou
and Bankston (1998) found that children often act as translators and intermediaries between their families and the larger society. Thus, children of

immigrant parents who do not speak English are confused about their family roles because they feel that they know more than their parents do and thus lose respect for their parents. As a result, parental supervision becomes less effective. Because these families often live in poor neighborhoods, these children are at high risk of being exposed to adversarial subcultures of marginalized native-born youths. Delinquency and gang activity occur when immigrant youths are poorly integrated into the family (Zhou & Bankston, 1998).

Another stressor that immigrant children and children of immigrants often face is the enormous pressure to excel in school. This is especially true for immigrant families from Asia. Many immigrants who were educated in their native countries quickly realize that educational attainment does not translate into the same earnings that their native counterparts with the same educational attainment acquire. Although these parents accept the fact that as immigrants they cannot compete as well, they place their hopes in their children, who they think can achieve a higher socioeconomic status with an American education.

Immigrant children and children of immigrants do not want to disappoint their parents. However, the native culture may put down high achievers at school (Zhou & Bankston, 1998). Good students are considered "geeks" and "nerds." The reality at schools, especially at public schools, and the expectations of parents often place the children in the middle. Furthermore, parents' high expectations often create distress within the family if children's wishes or talents do not match their parents' expectations or if their children simply want to be popular at school.

Many immigrant families come from countries where women are considered subordinate to men. Gender roles change dramatically when immigrant families move into the United States as a result of the greater employment opportunities for immigrant women. Despite these changes, however, women in immigrant families are still expected to obey traditional values regarding their family roles.

For many immigrant families, it is much more important for girls to obey their parents than it is for boys. Thus, social control is much tighter for girls than for boys. According to interviews among Vietnamese immigrant families (Zhou & Bankston, 1998), this ensures that girls will be obedient because women need to live up to higher behavioral standards than those expected of men, in addition to being highly educated so that they will be suitable wives to relatively high-status husbands. Clearly, female immigrant children and female children of immigrants often feel torn between a sense of independence encouraged by American society and a sense of obligation instilled by their parents (Fong, 1998).

Identity and Self-Esteem

Immigrants are challenged to cope in U.S. society, where socioeconomic and cultural environments differ significantly from those in their country of origin. In response to their new dual status as immigrants and members of racial/ethnic minorities, racial minority immigrants need to define their social identity based on their social similarity and dissimilarity with the reference groups that directly affect their experience (Rosenberg, 1979; Rumbaut, 1996). Their identification assimilation has important implications for their success in this society (Gordon, 1964).

Although they strive hard for survival and/or success, immigrant adults are realistic about their goals and are prepared for an unfavorable environment. They realize that their immigrant status does not help them in the job market and that the education received from their country of origin is not adequate for competition in their new society. Although they accept the fact that they are in an inferior position to excel socioeconomically in the United States, immigrant adults place their great hopes on their children, whom they expect to fulfill American dreams on their behalf.

Immigrant children and children of immigrants, especially those of Asian descent, often have been socialized to excel at school and to succeed in their professional careers, but they often find themselves unable to overcome the barriers that their parents' generation has experienced. Consequently, they are likely to develop goal-striving stress when "they believe that they possess opportunities for success equal to those of the dominant group members but in fact cannot overcome the consequences of segregation and other forms of *de facto* discrimination" (Kuo, 1976, p. 298). Dissonant social contexts as a result of discrimination and disparagement erode their self-esteem, which further impairs their capacity to respond to a stressful environment (Rosenberg, 1979; Rumbaut, 1996). In turn, low self-esteem makes them feel discriminated against without having any evidence of this in actuality (Kuo, 1976).

Children with low self-esteem tend to view their own racial or ethnic group as inferior and their immigrant status as shameful. For example, some Asian Americans prefer to be European American rather than Asian American (Phinney, 1989). In an experiment conducted in a classroom in San Francisco, Chinese American students were asked to list what they thought were their "American" qualities and what they thought were their "Chinese" qualities (Nee & Nee, 1974). Students listed everything that was interesting, creative, adventurous, sexy, and fun as American and everything that was dull, uncreative, old-fashioned, inhibiting, and repressive as Chinese. Similarly, those with low self-esteem do not feel American when their physical features are different and when their English is not good (U.S. Dept. of Health and Human Services, 1988). Gender is a main determinant of psychological well-being: Girls are much more likely than boys to report lower self-esteem, greater depression, and a greater level of parent-child conflict (Rumbaut, 1996).

On the other hand, children's psychological well-being is very much affected by the family context. Higher-status professional immigrant parents are more likely to positively affect their children's self-esteem. Children with high self-esteem are more likely to feel comfortable with their ethnicity and nativity and more likely to identify with their national origin than are children with low self-esteem (Rumbaut, 1996).

Research Implications and Programmatic Recommendations

Immigrant families are exposed to a variety of stressful experiences unique to the process of immigration. They come from distinct ethnic and social backgrounds and have very different migration histories and trajectories. The process of immigration is complex, and the forces affecting the lives of the immigrant family are multifaceted. Because of this complexity, new paradigms and theoretical models need to be developed to understand the dynamic and interactive factors affecting the migration-induced adaptations experienced by immigrant families. The acculturation phenomenon associated with the immigration experience and the stressors associated with this phenomenon (e.g., acculturative stress) need to be better understood. Stress-coping models specific to the immigration experience need to be developed to better understand the effects of different sources of stress affecting first- and second-generation immigrants.

Systematic information needs to be collected to document (a) how different subgroups of ethnic communities respond to the stressors resulting from the immigration process and (b) how they cope and favorably respond to preserve the integrity of family life. In-depth, longitudinal studies are needed to document the extent to which social and economic institutions are responsive to (a) the needs of first-generation immigrants and (b) the complex relationships that are established between these institutions and the immigrant families and ethnic communities. Integrated research needs to be added into the study of immigrant farmworkers and the different stressors affecting this vulnerable population of immigrants.

From a programmatic perspective, undergraduate and graduate curricula in universities and colleges must incorporate courses that present the immigration experience as a complex process that affects the lives of immigrant families in multiple ways. Social studies curricula must integrate the concepts of stress and coping into their courses that examine the process of immigration. The heterogeneity of the immigrant population and their different migration trajectories need to be recognized. Immigrants who are also members of an ethnic minority bring unique social, economic, and educational characteristics to the nation; therefore, efforts must be made to understand how these characteristics affect their experiences.

Programs at the community level must be more responsive to identifying those immigrants who are not coping and adjusting well to the immigration process. Culturally appropriate mental health services and culturally sensitive mental health professionals need to be enhanced to better serve the immigrant population.

Policy Recommendations

Today, immigration is a controversial topic. The immigration agenda has become a political tool to defend special social and economic interests. Immigration policies have become more stringent and have affected the lives of many immigrants, particularly those coming from Mexico, which represent proportionately the majority of immigrants to the United States. In this new climate of immigration reform, family-strengthening programs that are sensitive to the challenges and needs of immigrants are needed. Single-solution strategies that focus on one-shot approaches to ameliorate stressful events in the lives of immigrants are too simplistic. Policies that can strengthen the social, economic, and educational support network of immigrants should include all immigrants whose families are undergoing the different processes of acculturation.

Community health and social agencies need to recognize the importance of providing mental health support services for those immigrants suffering severe stress associated with the immigration process. The immigrant family as a system should be the focus of attention when providing services, including health services. A more holistic approach should be added to programs and interventions that address the needs of immigrants who suffer different types of immigration-induced stress.

DISCUSSION QUESTIONS

1. Immigrant families are exposed to different sources of stress than non-immigrant families are. What unique types of stress do immigrants to the United States experience?

2. How do English proficiency, socioeconomic status, family structure and composition, cultural factors, and level of education affect the immigration experience of individuals and families who come to the United States?

3. Why is it important for researchers and policy makers to understand the process of acculturation?

4. Jose is 12 years old, and he just arrived from Mexico with his parents. Yu is a 12-year-old girl from China. Her parents arrived in the United States when Yu was a 1-month-old baby. Can you identify the different challenges brought by Jose's and Yu's unique immigration experiences as they go through their adolescent experience in the United States?

5. In your opinion, what are the factors that can counterbalance the potentially negative effects of acculturative stress, cultural shock, and homesickness experienced by immigrants living temporarily or permanently in the United States?

SUGGESTED READINGS

Parrillo, V. N. (1991). The immigrant family: Securing the American dream. *Journal of Comparative Family Studies, 22,* 131-145.

Portes, A., & Rumbaut, R. G. (1996). *Immigrant America: A portrait.* Berkeley: University of California Press.

Thomas, T. (1995). Acculturative stress in the adjustment of immigrant families. *Journal of Social Distress and the Homeless, 4,* 131-142.

Van Tilburg, M., & Vingerhoets, A. (1997). *Psychological aspects of geographical moves: Homesickness and acculturative stress.* The Netherlands: Tilburg University Press.

Zhou, M. (1997). Growing up American: The challenge confronting immigrant children and children of immigrants. *Annual Review of Sociology, 23,* 63-95.

REFERENCES

Anderson, L. (1991). Acculturative stress: A theory of relevance to black Americans. *Clinical Psychology Review, 11,* 685-702.

Balcazar, H., Castro, F., & Krull, J. (1995). Cancer risk reduction in Mexican-American women: The role of acculturation, education, and health risk factors. *Health Education Quarterly, 22,* 61-84.

Balcazar, H., Peterson, G., & Cobas, J. (1996). Acculturation and health-related risk behaviors among Mexican-American pregnant youth. *American Journal of Health Behavior, 20,* 425-433.

Balcazar, H., Peterson, G., & Krull, J. (1997). Acculturation and family cohesiveness in Mexican-American pregnant women: Social and health implications. *Family and Community Health, 20,* 16-31.

Benson, J. E. (1990). Households, migration, and community context. *Urban Anthropology, 19,* 9-29.

Berry, J. (1986). The acculturation process and refugee behavior. In C. Williams & J. Westermeyer (Eds.), *Refugee mental health in resettlement countries* (pp. 25-37). Washington, DC: Hemisphere.

Berry, J. (1990). Psychology of acculturation. In J. J. Berman (Ed.), *Cross cultural perspectives* (Vol. 37, pp. 201-234). London: Lincoln.

Berry, J., Kim, U., Minde, T., & Mok, D. (1987). Comparative studies of acculturative stress. *International Migration Review, 21,* 491-511.

Berry, J., Poortinga, Y., Segall, M., & Dasen, P. (1992). *Cross-cultural psychology: Research and applications.* Cambridge, UK: Cambridge University Press.

Castro, F., Cota, M., & Vega, S. (1999). Health promotion in Latino populations: A sociocultural model for program planning, development, and evaluation. In R. M. Huff & M. V. Kline (Eds.), *Promoting health in multicultural populations* (pp. 137-168). Thousand Oaks, CA: Sage.

Cervantes, R., & Castro, F. (1985). Stress, coping, and Mexican-American mental health: A systematic review. *Hispanic Journal of Behavioral Sciences, 7,* 1-73.

Chiswick, B. R., & Sullivan, T. A. (1995). The new immigrants. In R. Farley (Ed.), *State of the union: America in the 1990s: Vol. 2. Social trends* (pp. 211-270). New York: Russell Sage.

Farley, R. (1996). *The new American reality: Who we are, how we got here, where we are going.* New York: Russell Sage.

Fernandez, R. M., & Nielsen, F. (1986). Bilingualism and Hispanic scholastic achievement: Some baseline results. *Social Science Research, 15,* 43-70.

Fong, T. P. (1998). *The contemporary Asian-American experience: Beyond the model minority.* Upper Saddle River, NJ: Prentice Hall.

Furnham, A. (1997). Culture shock, homesickness, and adaptation to a foreign culture. In M. Van Tilburg & A. Vingerhoets (Eds.), *Psychological aspects of geographical moves: Homesickness and acculturative stress* (pp. 17-37). The Netherlands: Tilburg University Press.

Gill, A. G., Vega, W. A., & Dimas, J. M. (1994). Acculturative stress and personal adjustment among Hispanic adolescent boys. *Journal of Community Psychology, 22,* 43-54.

Gordon, M. M. (1964). *Assimilation in American life.* New York: Oxford University Press.

Hong, G. K., & Ham, M. (1992). Impact of immigration on the family life cycle: Clinical implications for Chinese Americans. *Journal of Family Psychotherapy, 3,* 27-40.

Kuo, W. (1976). Theories of migration and mental health: An empirical testing on Chinese Americans. *Social Science and Medicine, 10,* 297-306.

Landale, N., & Oropesa, R. S. (1995). *Immigrant children and the children of immigrants: Inter- and intra-group differences in the United States* (Research Paper 95-02). East Lansing: Michigan State University.

Lazarus, R. S. (1984). Puzzles in the study of daily hassles. *Journal of Behavioral Medicine, 7,* 375-389.

Lazarus, R. S., & Folkman, S. (1984). *Stress, appraisal, and coping.* New York: Springer.

Leslie, L. A. (1992). The role of informal support networks in the adjustment of Central American immigrant families. *Journal of Community Psychology, 20,* 243-256.

Lieberson, S., & Waters, M. C. (1988). *From many strands: Ethnic and racial groups in contemporary America.* New York: Russell Sage.

Matute-Bianchi, M. E. (1991). Situational ethnicity and patterns of school performance among immigrant and non-immigrant Mexican-descent students. In M. Gibson & J. Ogbu (Eds.), *Minority status and schooling: A comparative study of immigrant and voluntary minorities* (pp. 236-251). New York: Garland.

Mena, F. J., Padilla, A. M., & Maldonado, M. (1987). Acculturative stress and specific coping strategies among immigrant and later generation college students. *Hispanic Journal of Behavioral Sciences, 9,* 207-225.

Nee, V. G., & Nee, B. D. B. (1974). *Longtime Californ': A documentary study of the American Chinatown.* Boston: Houghton Mifflin.

Oberg, J. (1960). Culture shock: Adjustment to new cultural environments. *Practical Anthropology, 7,* 177-182.

Parrillo, V. N. (1991). The immigrant family: Securing the American dream. *Journal of Comparative Family Studies, 22,* 131-145.

Peterson, G., Cobas, J., Balcazar, H., & Amling, J. (1998). Acculturation and risk behavior among pregnant Mexican American females: A structural equation model. *Sociological Inquiry, 68,* 536-556.

Phinney, J. (1989). Stages of ethnic identity development in minority group adolescents. *Journal of Early Adolescence, 9,* 34-49.

Portes, A., & Rumbaut, R. G. (1996). *Immigrant America: A portrait.* Berkeley: University of California Press.

Portes, A., & Stepick, A. (1993). *City on the edge: The transformation of Miami.* Berkeley: University of California Press.

Redfield, R., Linton, R., & Herskovits, L. (1936). Memorandum on the study of acculturation. *American Anthropologist, 38,* 49-152.

Roer-Strier, D. (1997). In the mind of the beholder: Evaluation of coping styles of immigrant parents. *International Migration, 35,* 271-286.

Rogler, L. H., Cortes, D. E., & Malgady, R. G. (1991). Acculturation and mental health status among Hispanics: Convergence and new directions for research. *American Psychologist, 46,* 585-597.

Rosenberg, M. (1979). *Conceiving the self.* New York: Basic Books.

Rumbaut, R. G. (1996). The crucible within: Ethnic identity, self-esteem, and segmented assimilation among children of immigrants. In A. Portes (Ed.), *The second generation* (pp. 119-170). New York: Russell Sage.

Schmitz, P. (1997). Individual differences in acculturative stress reactions: Determinants of homesickness and psychosocial maladjustment. In M. Van Tilburg & A. Vingerhoets (Eds.), *Psychological aspects of geographic moves: Homesickness and acculturative stress* (pp. 103-117). The Netherlands: Tilburg University Press.

Sung, B. L. (1987). *The adjustment experience of Chinese immigrant children in New York City.* Staten Island, NY: Center for Migration Studies.

Thomas, T. (1995). Acculturative stress in the adjustment of immigrant families. *Journal of Social Distress and the Homeless, 4,* 131-142.

Tienda, M. (1984). Language, education, and the socioeconomic achievement of Hispanic origin men. *Social Science Quarterly, 65,* 519-536.

U.S. Department of Health and Human Services. (1988). *The adaptation of Southeast Asian refugee youth: A comparative study.* Washington, DC: Office of Refugee Resettlement.

Van Tilburg, M., & Vingerhoets, A. (1997). *Psychological aspects of geographical moves: Homesickness and acculturative stress.* The Netherlands: Tilburg University Press.

Waters, M. C. (1996). Ethnic and racial identities of second-generation black immigrants in New York City. In A. Portes (Ed.), *The new second generation* (pp. 171-196). New York: Russell Sage.

Zhou, M. (1997). Growing up American: The challenge confronting immigrant children and children of immigrants. *Annual Review of Sociology, 23,* 63-95.

Zhou, M., & Bankston, C. L., III. (1998). *Growing up American: How Vietnamese children adapt to life in the United States.* New York: Russell Sage.

16

Families and the Gay Community

Stressors and Strengths

KAREN L. WILCOX
KATHERINE R. ALLEN

Living Life as Gay or Lesbian

There are a variety of ways individuals choose to live their lives when they begin to make decisions about how to "be" in the world, while identifying to some degree as gay, lesbian, bisexual, or transgendered. Some people choose not to share their thoughts and feelings of attraction to members of the same gender with anyone else, while others shout it from the mountaintops. Some may choose to share information about themselves in subtle ways—by supporting organizations that work toward extending the rights of gay, lesbian, bisexual, and transgendered individuals, for example—yet still remain annonymous about their sexual orientation to the people they interact with in their daily lives.

Brian McNaught (1988) describes what he terms as "proud growls and courageous roars" as he gives examples of ways individuals can act indirectly to offer vitally important support. An example of a growl may be the gay student who "might not speak up in class during the morning discussion on homosexuality, but may walk across campus in the evening to the gay and lesbian support group meeting" (p. 73). This is just one example of how individuals and families may choose to deal with the stress of being in a gay or lesbian family. Adaptations are made daily as family members consider what their approach will be to living in families with gay, lesbian, bisexual, and transgendered members. There are variations among family members as their level of comfort fluctuates due to their personal experiences with their own sexual orientation and that of their sister, brother, mother, father, daughter, son, or grandparent.

Potentially, any family can be considered a gay or lesbian family because any family is likely to have at least one member who is gay, lesbian, or bisexual, if not now then perhaps at some time in the future. Gay and lesbian families are at the forefront of family structures and processes that are highly adaptable in a changing world (Allen & Demo, 1995). Where to begin discussing family variations by sexual orientation diversity is rather arbitrary. Families consist of individuals in relationships; they can have biological, marital, adoptive, and chosen ties. Families have identities, but the identity of any family is likely to differ from the identity of the individuals who constitute it. Gay and lesbian families offer a unique social location because family configuration and membership can change over time.

Until recently, family scholars have neglected to take sexual orientation seriously. There are many ways that the intersection of families and the gay community creates stress and just as many ways that this location creates and maintains strengths. In the publication *Our Families, Our Children* (Dispenza, 1999), the Lesbian and Gay Child Care Task Force documented anecdotal evidence of homophobia that included the following:

- Refusal to accept children from lesbian, gay, bisexual, and transgender (LGBT) families into child care.
- Biased attitudes expressed to children when they speak about their families.
- Demonstrated lack of understanding of the unique issues that children and LGBT families face on a day-to-day basis even when biased attitudes are not expressed or may not exist. (Dispenza, 1999, p. iv)

As a result of conducting interviews with 167 lesbian, gay, bisexual, and transgender parent/guardians and child care providers, the elements identified as positive aspects included provider staff awareness and enlightenment; family pride and self-pride; nondiscrimination policies, procedures, and practices; curriculum and environment that reflect and affirm all families and cultures; and communication that builds understanding (Dispenza, 1999, p. iv).

It is important to study the diversity of sexual orientation because, increasingly, our society is bringing these issues out of the closet. Each year, more and more young adults come out to their parents (Savin-Williams & Esterberg, 2000), and gay and lesbian issues are more visible in the media. The popularity of television programs featuring openly gay characters, such as MTV's *Real World, Friends, Will and Grace,* and *Dawson's Creek,* reveals the growing presence of sexual orientation in the media.

In this chapter, we begin by discussing issues affecting individuals and families to introduce questions and concerns reflected in the discussion of families and the gay community. Next we examine family-related stressors and strengths associated with the coming out process, addressing identity formation, self-disclosure, and support systems that are either available or absent from the experience. Then we look at families in which the adults are gay or lesbian, highlighting issues of partnership and parenting that are central to adult life experience regardless of sexual orientation. We also address the stressors and strengths associated with the aging process, particularly for older gay men and lesbians. Finally, we consider intervention strategies, policy implications, and future directions for research and advocacy relevant to strengthening families with gay, lesbian, bisexual, or transgendered members.

Researching Gay and Lesbian Families

Regardless of age, several issues surface in a variety of ways as individuals attempt to deal with their same-sex attraction and sexual orientation. Any discussion of sexual orientation must begin with a definition of *heterocentrism,* the belief in and practice of valuing heterosexuality as the norm (Herek, Kimmel, Amaro, & Melton, 1991). Anything that differs from heterosexuality is treated as subordinate to or deviant from the norm. Heterosexuality is taken as the assumed standard against which all sexual orientations and gender identities are compared. It prescribes that only men and women can and should be attracted to and sexually connected to each other. The implications of heterocentrism are that legal marriage is restricted to opposite sex partners and that family members who are gay and lesbian are legal strangers to each other. Homophobia, which is related to heterosexism, is the irrational fear and hatred of gay, lesbian, and bisexual people and is based on stereotype and myth (Blumenfeld, 1992; Pharr, 1988). Homophobia is a prejudice that is internalized by individuals through child-rearing practices and passed down intergenerationally. It is supported publicly by laws and de facto discrimination that lead to unequal treatment for lesbian, gay, and bisexual individuals and their families.

A second issue related to sexual orientation that cuts across current research is linked to identity. Forming, maintaining, and transforming one's sense of self necessitates continual exploration for individuals of all ages and sexual orientations as a result of changing life events and circumstances. As individuals encounter realizations throughout life about self-identification as gay, lesbian, bisexual, or heterosexual, they make choices about how to act, or not act, on their discoveries. Sexual orientation is a complex mix of many dimensions, including sexual attraction, sexual behavior, sexual fantasies, emotional preference, social preference, self-identification, lifestyle choice, and changes over time (Klein, 1990).

A third issue is that coming out is a vital and continual process that gay, lesbian, bisexual, and transgendered individuals face throughout the life course, from adolescence to young, middle, and later adulthood. Age cohort makes a difference in the expectations and acceptability of coming out because the history of the gay and lesbian rights movement has had an impact on the comfort level and openness of individuals and society (Allen, 1997; Boxer, Cook, & Herdt, 1991; Herdt & Boxer, 1993; Quam & Whitford, 1992; Savin-Williams, 1998). Examples of similarities found in regard to motives and fears considered in the coming out process at any age are a desire for honesty with self and others, a fear of rejection, the presence or lack of support, acceptance of self, and a fear of stigmatization and prejudice (Ben-Ari, 1995; Quam & Whitford, 1992; Savin-Williams, 1998). Coming out is not an event but a lifelong process (Allen, 1995). In Rhoads's (1995) 2-year ethnographic study of the coming out experiences of gay and bisexual college men, one student described coming out as "something that has a beginning but never really ends" (p. 69). Another participant commented that there are "different levels of 'outness' that people reach over time" (p. 69).

A fourth issue is that the degree of social support plays a significant role in the disclosure of sexual orientation to family and friends. Many studies show that the most feared and difficult stress lesbians and gay men face is how and when to reveal their sexual orientation to their families (Ben-Ari, 1995; Boxer et al., 1991; D'Augelli, 1991; Savin-Williams, 1998). The reaction of family members, especially parents, plays a significant role in the present and future relationships within the family (Ben-Ari, 1995; Savin-Williams, 1998; Savin-Williams & Dube, 1998; Strommen, 1989). Social support systems also play a part in the development of gay and lesbian identities (D'Augelli, 1991; Herdt & Boxer, 1993; Weston, 1991). Quam and Whitford (1992), for example, demonstrate that integration into a social environment offering support through service organizations and political organizations helps older adults adjust to the aging process.

A fifth issue is methodological. Information about sexual orientation and family relations needs to be integrated into general family research (Allen & Demo, 1995; Savin-Williams, 1998). Sexual orientation is a feature of all human experience, not simply a concern for gays and lesbians. Everyone has a sexual orientation, yet sexual orientation is typically ignored in studies of

family life. To gather empirical evidence on the lives of lesbians, gay men, bisexuals, and transgendered individuals, researchers must avoid the presump-
tion of universal heterosexuality and insist on access to diverse populations
and their families (Harry, 1983).

We turn now to specific stressors and strengths associated with sexual orientation diversity in families, using empirical studies and personal narratives
to explore critical issues that families with gay, lesbian, bisexual, or transgendered individuals confront. We build on our own research as family social
scientists and on our experiences as lesbians in academia and families to aug-
ment the scholarly material we present. Perhaps the most important contribution we can make in this chapter is to describe how we have firsthand experience of some of the events and processes in this chapter, thereby putting a
human face on what many students may encounter as a new or unfamiliar experience.

Stressors and Strengths in the Coming Out Process

Coming out is a multidimensional process that can take many forms. At stake
is one's sense of self and one's way of being in the world. Social stigma
and prejudice make it difficult to resolve the conflict between what a person
feels and the primarily negative information that he or she has been taught regarding sexual orientation. Allport (1958) describes prejudice as a negative
attitude based on overgeneralization or error. As young people, and now increasingly adults of all ages, struggle with issues of identity formation, gays
and lesbians explore and consider how claiming an identity as gay, lesbian,
bisexual, or transgendered may affect their relationships with family, friends,
and the larger community.

Identity exploration during adolescence and young adulthood can be a
stressful period because questions and challenges regarding independence
can conflict with expectations of parents and other family members
(D'Augelli, 1991). Identity formation among lesbian and gay youth adds a
layer of complexity (Herdt, 1989). These complex issues include recognition
of feelings of attraction toward same-sex individuals, decisions about ways
to deal with sexual orientation among family and friends, and the potential
consequences of sharing this information in both private and public ways.

Increasingly, coming out issues confront adults as they age. Both empirical
research and personal experience reveal that it is not uncommon for women
who have already raised families and lost husbands to death or divorce to

choose other women as life partners, thereby facing coming out issues in the second half of life. Coming out for the first time as an older lesbian or gay man may present particular challenges because members of one's former life may be harsh and rejecting, not understanding how a person can be straight one day and gay the next. Similarly, the gay community may not always be welcoming; the new arrival may be met with hostility or fear that his or her change of heart is only temporary (Friend, 1980).

Coming Out to Family and Friends

Although more young people are coming out to their parents within the increasingly accepting social climate of the late 20th and early 21st centuries, coming out is still a difficult process. Sharing this information with parents can be troublesome because, at some level, young people anticipate that their parents will reject them. The conflict between parental expectations of heterosexuality and revealing their lesbian, gay, or bisexual orientation to parents may result in fear that delays disclosure until one feels detached from the family of origin. Many young adults report that their recognition of feelings of same-sex attraction and self-identification as gay, lesbian, or bisexual occurred in early to late adolescence, yet they did not act on their feelings or disclose their identity to family until they left home (Ben-Ari, 1995; Martin, 1982; Savin-Williams, 1998).

With the difficulty of coming out to parents, it is understandable that young adults search for a way to relieve the burden of carrying a secret of such magnitude. The initial disclosure of gay or lesbian sexual identity is usually to a close friend who is trusted to offer support (D'Augelli & Hershberger, 1993). They test the waters and a degree of pressure is released about holding such a secret. It can be a relief to experience that someone is available to talk; as a result, a new sense of comfort exists about the ability to be oneself in the context of future interactions. Young adults may disclose their sexual orientation to parents through face-to-face conversations with one or both parents, by writing a letter, or by dropping hints through the language used in discussing relationships with friends. Disclosure to mothers usually occurs prior to disclosure to fathers (Savin-Williams, 1998). Mothers are perceived as more understanding and accepting than fathers.

Parents' initial reactions to their child's disclosure include a questioning of their potential responsibility through feelings of blame and guilt and a mixture of feeling shocked, disappointed, and angry. Savin-Williams and Dube (1998) described parental reactions to sons or daughters disclosing their gay, lesbian, or bisexual orientation in terms of the series of stages described by

Kubler-Ross (1969) to identify individuals coping with their own impending death. Parents, Families, and Friends of Lesbians and Gays (PFLAG), the largest support group of its kind, also related parental reaction to a developmental model of gradual acceptance of a child's difference. Parents may feel they have experienced a death through the loss of their hopes and dreams for their child to follow a normative life course, which actually means heterosexual marriage and parenthood. The developmental model of parental reactions that Savin-Williams and Dube (1998) present includes experiencing shock, denial and isolation, anger, bargaining, depression, and acceptance. All parents may not experience all of these stages and may experience them in a different order and to differing degrees, yet components of each stage are likely to occur. Empirical evidence is needed to test the mourning/loss stages as well as the differences between parents' initial reactions to a son or daughter coming out to them and the ways the parent-child relationship changes or stays the same over time across the life course. Whether the disclosure of sexual orientation is sudden or gradual may also create variations in parental reactions.

It is understandable that older parents of adult gay and lesbian children experience stress as they confront the unexpected challenge of learning that a child is gay. Socialization for parenting in adulthood does not prepare them to understand or accept this knowledge (Allen, Demo, Walker, & Acock, 1996) because having a gay, lesbian, or bisexual child is a nonnormative experience (Pillemer & Suitor, 1991) and is certainly not how most parents expect their children to "turn out" (Ryff, Schmutte, & Lee, 1996). For some parents, however, there are surprising results that actually strengthen their family. We conducted in-depth interviews, 2 to 3 hours in length, with 15 participants and attended monthly meetings of a support group for parents, families, and friends of lesbians and gay men for more than 1 year (Allen & Wilcox, 1996). We found that the process of coming to terms with having a gay child involved several transitions that eventually brought parents closer to becoming an activist on behalf of their child. A major transition was moving away from denial or complacency and toward political involvement and advocacy. Parents defined their current activism as being linked to past involvement in civil rights for other minority groups earlier in their lives. Following the initial experience of discomfort and struggle, parents eventually became mobilized as a result of the discrimination and social prejudice their children faced. Parents were motivated by the love for their children to speak out against oppression and to work for social change. They also experienced a process of coming out of denial about who their family really is. Parents saw activism as a way to keep their families together. They learned what is really important in their families, such as "supporting my child" and facing unresolved issues in their own lives such as alcoholism, homosexuality, and healing old wounds.

Coping With the
Fears and Risks of Coming Out

Ben-Ari (1995) found that the perception of being rejected by parents was the greatest fear in coming out to parents; the most frequent motive to do so was a need not to hide or not to live a lie. Especially during adolescence, many individuals are concerned about fitting in and being accepted by peers; the anticipation of being stigmatized and excluded from peer groups is a frightening reality to face. Risks that lesbian and gay youth face after disclosure include verbal and physical abuse, poor school performance, running away from home, substance abuse, criminal activity, and suicide attempts (Savin-Williams, 1994).

In general, victimization of lesbians and gay men has been found to be the most common form of bias-related violence, whether the victimization is the result of known or assumed lesbian or gay sexual orientation (Berrill, 1990; Comstock, 1991; Herek, 1989). Individuals can be beaten up just for looking gay. (An extreme example of victimization was the murder of Matthew Shepherd.) Pilkington and D'Augelli (1995) surveyed 194 lesbian, gay, and bisexual youth between the ages of 15 and 21 and found that most respondents had experienced some form of victimization because of their sexual orientation. They examined the specific social contexts in which antilesbian or antigay victimization occurred and found that no social environment (family, school, work, or community) was free from risk of harm.

Suicide is a very real risk associated with accepting a gay or lesbian identity. The National Center for Health Statistics (1993) reports that suicide is the third leading cause of mortality for adolescents in the United States. Lesbian, gay, and bisexual youth have been identified as being at an elevated risk for suicide (Remafedi, 1994). Approximately one third of youths dealing with gay identity issues have attempted suicide (Herdt & Boxer, 1993). Feelings of isolation and a struggle with the socialization that "homosexuality is wrong" lead to considering desperate measures to escape dealing with same-sex desires. Estimates of the number of gay and lesbian youth who commit suicide may be low because many have not disclosed their sexual orientation to anyone (Hershberger, Pilkington, & D'Augelli, 1997).

Finding Support From Family and Friends

Social support is needed from family and friends as gay, lesbian, or bi-sexual individuals search for ways to create understanding for themselves and others. Availability of accurate information about lesbians and gay men is critical to breaking down stereotypes that lead to antigay and antilesbian discrimination. The values held by family members play a vital role in their reactions to, and support of, the disclosure that a son, daughter, sister, or brother is gay or lesbian (Strommen, 1989). Gay youth report many benefits in disclosing their sexual orientation, including a greater sense of freedom and liberation, a sense of pride with being honest with oneself, and genuine acceptance from family members (Savin-Williams, 1998).

Social service providers agree that adult role models are needed to create a safe and comfortable environment for lesbian and gay youth (Martin, 1982). Adolescents and young adults need to see and identify a diverse array of gay and lesbian adults. This will encourage their own identity formation by dem-onstrating that there are a variety of examples of successful, happy, and ful-filled "people like me," and it will allow them to therefore see themselves as an integral part of the diversity that not only exists but thrives in communities across the United States.

Finding Support in School Environments

Understanding the attitudes of peers and school personnel toward gay men, lesbians, and bisexuals can play a significant role in creating a space that en-ables all members of a community to thrive. Simoni (1996) found in a study of college students that being younger, having less education, being male, and having less educated parents were associated with negative attitudes to-ward lesbians and gay men. Engstrom and Sedlacek (1997) studied a sample of university students to explore the attitudes of heterosexual students toward gay and lesbian peers when sexual orientation was not disclosed in social, academic, and family situations. They found that more intensive prejudicial attitudes toward gay male and lesbian students existed and that homopho-bic feelings toward gay men were more extreme by male students than by females.

Telljohann and Price (1993) conducted a qualitative study of 120 gay and lesbian youth (ages 14-21) from eight youth centers dispersed across geo-graphically diverse cities throughout the United States. They explored the reactions of peers, family members, physicians, and school personnel re-garding the awareness of gay and lesbian identity. The participants were also asked about (a) homosexuality in the curriculum and problems faced in school concerning sexual orientation; (b) individuals who had been helpful; and (c) the school's role in dealing with these issues. The results of this study indicated that support within the school community was weak or nonexistent. On the basis of their findings, the authors suggest the development of either support groups for gay and lesbian students or, at least, a referral network within the community; they also advocate taking a stronger stand against discrimination and abuse through education and policy adoption.

Lopez and Chism (1993) propose recommendations for instructors based on their study of the classroom concerns of gay and lesbian students in a large Midwestern university. An important point raised by lesbian and gay students who were studied is that each student, regardless of sexual orientation, has different needs and preferences about how topics and issues are dealt with, especially those in which they hold a personal stake. These researchers recommended that (a) teachers recognize that it is very likely that they do teach gay and lesbian students; (b) students are in the process of coming out to self and others during the college years and will vary as to what support they need; and (c) students will make their decision to identify as gay or lesbian only under conditions that appear safe to them. Students emphasized that professors should realize that gay and lesbian students judge professors' attitudes by what they say or do not say, how and if they respond to oppressive statements, and what they include or exclude from course content.

Just as support is needed for students to feel safe in coming out, the environment must also be safe for faculty members to do the same. The need for adult role models who are willing to be open about their sexual orientation as gay, lesbian, bisexual, or transgendered individuals is an essential part of reducing the stress that is involved for students both inside and outside the classroom. We have experienced the process of coming out to ourselves and to our students in the college classroom (see Allen, 1995, for an earlier narrative about coming out in a family studies classroom). In order to be open about such a personal and controversial issue as an instructor, there are many things to be considered. There are issues that may seem obvious in an instructor's decision to come out to his or her students and those that may not be apparent to someone who has not been faced with this situation.

The issues that are more readily apparent deal with job security and personal safety (Khayatt, 1992; Savin-Williams, 1993). Coming out as a teacher in a classroom setting presents the risk of losing one's job. Although there may be policies that prohibit discrimination based on sexual orientation in place at some schools, there is also always the possibility that job action will be taken under a premise other than sexual orientation. The ability to feel safe from verbal, emotional, and physical danger is also always an issue of concern, to some extent, because there is no real way for anyone to be protected from the possibility of being placed in danger—no matter what the cause of provocation.

Coming Out as a Faculty Member: Karen's Personal Narrative

I experienced coming out to my university class for the first time during the fall quarter of 1999. I was teaching a class on parenthood, and we had just discussed gay and lesbian parenting. I knew I had been trying to find a way to come out in the classroom for a number of years and had been through countless scenarios as to how that would occur. It seemed very "logical" to choose this time to share my coming out process with them, yet it was still very difficult to compose the words that would communicate to them what I wanted them to hear. My thinking about the implications of such a personal disclosure included wondering how the students would react at the time of my coming out to them, how other faculty and staff members at the institution may react, and whether or not the revelation of my sexual orientation as a lesbian would cause them to reconsider any of their previously held impressions of me as a faculty member or a person.

I decided to share my personal process of the decision making that was involved in my coming out to them to help demonstrate the complexity of the issue. I shared with them that I wanted to tell them about my own coming out process in order to assist them in understanding some of the concerns that gay and lesbian individuals have to deal with every day of their lives. I expressed to them that I had never done this in a class before and so I wasn't really sure how it would go. After telling them about how I came out to my family by writing them a letter, and bringing up some of the issues that were of concern to me, they began asking questions.

The questions they asked had to do with general issues of sexual orientation such as "When did you know you were a lesbian?" and "You can't really lose your job just because someone finds out you're a lesbian, can you?" to personal questions such as "Do you plan to have children?" and "Who will have them, you or your partner?" From my perspective, as I listened to the questions they were asking, it felt like they were in a safe place to address some of the questions they may have wondered about for a long time but never had been given the invitation to ask. Although it created a great deal of anxiety for me to come out to my class, it was accompanied by an even stronger sense of freedom and respect. I could take the risk involved to reveal this information to them, while they took the risk of asking questions and becoming involved in my process and theirs on a more personal level.

I asked them to write their reactions and reflections on the exit slips we have used throughout the quarter for purposes of attendance and to enable them to respond to the readings and class activities. The majority of the students wrote about the courage that it took for me to come out to the class, and they expressed their appreciation for the opportunity to learn about the issue of gay and lesbian lives in a more personal way. Many also wrote that they were honored to have been told this information. Creating space to be a role model and to offer authenticity about life issues was well worth taking the risk of coming out in class.

Stressors and Strengths in Lesbian and Gay Families

Research on gay and lesbian couples and families has greatly increased since the 1970s. In general, surveys indicate that between 45% and 80% of lesbians and between 40% and 60% of gay men are involved in a committed romantic relationship (Kurdek, 1995). In his review of 236 heterosexually married, 66 gay cohabiting, and 51 lesbian cohabiting couples, Kurdek (1998) also concluded that gay and lesbian partnerships have a great deal in common with heterosexual marriages. Kurdek found that the strength with which five dimensions of relationship quality (intimacy, autonomy, equality, constructive problem solving, and barriers to leaving) were linked to two relationship outcomes (the trajectory of change in relationship satisfaction and relationship dissolution over 5 years) was equivalent among the three types of couples, with only a few variations. Gay and lesbian couples reported more autonomy, fewer barriers to leaving, and more frequent relationship dissolution than married couples. Lesbian couples also reported more intimacy and equality in their relationships than the others. As Schwartz (1994) found in her research on heterosexual and gay or lesbian couples, same-sex couples tend to follow a model of best friendship rather than the role complementarity that is common in heterosexual partnerships.

Legal Stressors Confronting Lesbian and Gay Couples

Because it is disruptive to relationship stability, a major stressor for gay and lesbian partners is their lack of legal protection. Although many gay and lesbian couples have made long-term commitments to each other and many celebrate their union in a commitment ceremony in the presence of family and friends (Sherman, 1992), no state legally recognizes same-sex marriage.

The Defense of Marriage Act (DOMA), signed into law in 1995, defines marriage as a union between only one man and one woman and bans federal acknowledgment of marriages between a man and a man or a woman and a woman (Gallagher, 1996). Now 38 states have a state-level DOMA law. That means that if Hawaii does become the first state to recognize same-sex marriage, gay or lesbian couples getting married in Hawaii have limited chances of having their marriage recognized in their home state if they do not live in one of the other 11 reciprocating states. For example, a couple from Connecticut could travel to Hawaii, get married, and then petition the state for legal recognition, but a couple from Virginia would be barred from doing so.

The fundamental right to marry, regardless of the gender of the partners, is central to the legal case for same-sex marriage (Editors of the *Harvard Law Review*, 1990). Gays and lesbians are denied equality and civility when they are denied this basic right (Eskridge, 1996). Zicklin (1995) summarized the legal and financial advantages of state-sanctioned marriage that are denied same-sex partners: the right of inheritance if a spouse dies without a will; the right to Social Security survivor benefits; the right to include a legally married spouse on a partner's health insurance coverage; the right to immunity from having to testify against a spouse in a criminal proceeding; the right of residency for a foreign spouse of a U.S. citizen; and the right to visit one's spouse in government-run institutions such as prisons and hospitals (pp. 55-56).

The Challenges and Rewards of Gay and Lesbian Parenting

There is a notable shift in the literature on gay and lesbian parenting from a deficit model to a view emphasizing the strengths of such families in confronting the challenges and rewards that come their way. The lesbian and gay parenting movement took hold in the 1970s when gay men and lesbians became more intentional about having children in the context of a gay partnership (Pies, 1988). Donor insemination was one solution to the fertility problem lesbians face in getting pregnant. With the increase in AIDS among gay men in the 1980s, the initial enthusiasm with which alternative insemination was embraced necessarily dimmed as concern over transmitting the AIDS virus through insemination increased. Martin (1993), however, reports that the gay and lesbian parenting movement responded to this concern with increasing knowledge and the use of safe insemination practices.

Lesbian and gay families are increasing, however. In their 1990 publication, the editors of the *Harvard Law Review* concluded that "approximately three million gay men and lesbians in the United States are parents, and between eight and ten million children are raised in gay or lesbian households" (p. 119). There is every reason to believe that a "lesbian baby boom" is occurring given the unprecedented number of lesbians having children by choice in the context of their lesbian partnerships (Patterson, 1995). These planned lesbian families are changing the definition of *family* from the primacy of genetics to the primacy of deliberateness and intentionality in constructing emotional bonds and family ties (Stacey, 1996; Weston, 1991).

Rohrbaugh (1992) suggested a useful way to think about the diversity of gay- and lesbian-headed families that include dependent children. She identified three types of family structures: blended families, single-parent families, and couples having children together. Because most gay fathers and lesbian mothers became parents in the context of a heterosexual marriage, blended families are probably the most common type of family structure. Given the difficulty that gay men face in obtaining custody of children, most gay male stepfamilies are typically noncustodial households; children are not as likely to live with their fathers as with their mothers (Crosbie-Burnett & Helmbrecht, 1993).

In her groundbreaking review of 12 studies comparing children of lesbian or gay parents with children of heterosexual parents on the dimensions of the child's gender identity, gender role behavior, and sexual orientation, Patterson (1992) ushered in a new era of research on gay and lesbian parenting and outcomes for children. She demonstrated that the available empirical evidence reveals that children's development in gay or lesbian families does not differ from children's development in families headed by heterosexual parents. She also concluded that based on this empirical evidence, children of lesbian and gay parents have normal and satisfactory relationships with peers and with adults of both sexes. Instead of the pursuit of differences, with the heterosexist assumption that children automatically fare worse in gay or lesbian households, the empirical evidence, burgeoning in the 1990s, is that attention, love, and support are far more important ingredients in successful child rearing than the gender of one's parent.

In contrast to the deficit view in commonsense notions about diverse families, our view is that there are many strengths associated with gay and lesbian families. Researchers describe the following possibilities for providing a positive environment for child rearing in families headed by gay men or lesbians. First, Laird (1993) points out that children growing up in a multicultural environment learn to respect, empathize with, and tolerate the multicultural environments in which others live. Second, children can experience flexible interpretations of gendered behavior and intimate relationships by observing adults who are more free in their interpretations of gender roles and socialization (Blumstein & Schwartz, 1983; Schwartz & Rutter, 1998). Third, by living in an intentional family, children come to understand that families are based not simply on biological or genetic relationships but more so on love, self-definition, and choice (Laird, 1993; Weston, 1991). Fourth, as gay cultural centers emerge and become increasingly visible to society at large, children of gay and lesbian parents experience strong ties in the gay community that can deepen and support their family relationships (Allen, 1997; Herdt, 1992).

Stressors and Strengths Associated With Aging in the Gay Community

It is difficult to estimate the number of older gay men and lesbians because (a) there is a lack of agreement on what constitutes "old" (Lucco, 1987); (b) there is a lack of a clearly delineated definition of who is gay or lesbian (Berger, 1984); and (c) not all older lesbians and gay men are willing to reveal their sexual identity (Poor, 1982). The terms that older lesbians and gay men use to describe themselves are not always the same terms used in today's postmodern society. Kehoe (1988) asked a participant in her study of 100 lesbians over age 65, "What word do you prefer to use to describe your emotional and/or sexual preference?" (p. 46). One woman's response was "Anything but lesbian" (p. 46).

Members of birth cohorts from the earlier part of the 20th century exhibit a differing life experience from that of individuals growing up now (Friend, 1991). Choices that may be seen as adaptive for one generation in a specific sociohistorical context may become maladaptive for future generations (Adelman, 1991). Younger members of the gay and lesbian community who are activists should not look down on the choice of invisibility made by older members of the community. They should understand that (a) there were fewer options available in the context of the historical and societal framework and (b) the choice of being out carried with it a greater risk than it does today (Faderman, 1991). Until the mid-1970s, homosexuality was still classified as a mental disorder by the American Psychiatric Association and the American Psychological Association (Herek et al., 1991). Kochman (1993) emphasizes the importance of viewing older gays and lesbians as role models: "After all, we are the survivors. We lived, loved, worked, and cared for ourselves under the most prejudicial circumstances. We should be proud" (p. 98).

In the few studies about women and men who are aging, little attention was paid to older gays and lesbians until the mid-1970s (Jacobson & Grossman, 1996). Research also focuses more on gay men than on lesbians. The exclusion of older lesbians reflects a "triply invisible minority" due to the categories of gender, age, and sexual orientation (Kehoe, 1988).

The popular stereotype of older lesbians and gay men is very negative. Older gay men are regularly portrayed as depressed, lonely, oversexed, and living without the support of family and friends (Kelly, 1977). Older lesbians are typically portrayed as lonely, unattractive, and unemotional (Berger, 1982). On the contrary, studies conducted with older gay men have shown them to be psychologically well-adjusted, self-accepting, and adapting well to the aging process (Berger, 1982; Francher & Henkin, 1973; Friend, 1980; Kelly, 1977; Kimmel, 1978; Weinberg, 1970). Studies of older lesbians have also indicated that most are happy and well-adjusted to their lives and the aging process (Martin & Lyon, 1992; Raphael & Robinson, 1980).

Friend (1991) developed a model of identity formation for older gays and lesbians based on opposite ends of a continuum of potential cognitive and behavioral responses to heterosexism. At one end of the continuum are individuals whose identities conform to the stereotypes and exhibit internalized homophobia, termed "stereotypic older lesbian and gay people." He describes those who respond to heterosexism by reconstructing a positive and affirmative sense of self as "affirmative older lesbian and gay people." The group identified as "passing older lesbian and gay people" is characterized by having a strong investment in either passing as nongay or nonlesbian or not appearing to be stereotypically gay or lesbian. Under certain circumstances, some of these individuals will label themselves as lesbian or gay.

The population of older gays and lesbians is very diverse. Raphael and Meyer (1993) believed that studying the lives of older lesbians would enable them to learn about what their old age would be like. The women they talked to explained that the ideas they had while they were in their 50s and 60s about what they would like to be doing in their 70s and 80s did not end up being the story of their lives. As they got older, their ideas about how they wanted to live their lives changed along with them.

The difficulties faced by older gays and lesbians are most directly related to the stigma of being gay or lesbian. In his study of older gay men, Vacha (1985) found that "the discrimination that comes with aging is compounded by the discrimination that comes with being a homosexual" (p. 78). Respondents in Adelman's (1991) study who had not disclosed their sexual orientation to coworkers felt the need to work harder and achieve more because they were gay, which is a common method of adapting to being a member of a stigmatized group (Goffman, 1963). Some authors also suggest that the development of strategies to deal with being a member of a stigmatized group provides older gays and lesbians with more skills to help them cope with stigma associated with ageist assumptions (Francher & Henkin, 1973; Friend, 1980).

Older gays and lesbians are concerned with the same issues as other citizens: health care, transportation, housing, jobs and job training, retirement, the opportunity to make meaningful use of leisure time through recreational pursuits, body changes, loss of friends, lack of consistent mobility, and being old in a youth-oriented society (Kochman, 1993; Quam & Whitford, 1992; Raphael & Meyer, 1993). Quam and Whitford (1992) asked a question in their study about whether or not being gay or lesbian helps them adjust to the process of aging. Of the 80 individuals surveyed, 68% believed that being gay or lesbian was helpful because of the following reasons: Having a gay or lesbian identity allowed them to accept themselves as they are; they had a supportive community; the stress of being in a sexual and social minority helped to strengthen their beliefs and mental health; and their status forced them to plan more carefully for their future.

An older lesbian participant in Adelman's (1991) study stated, "I don't think anybody, if they cannot accept with good grace whatever they are, can be happy" (p. 22). The compilation of stories in *Long Time Passing: Lives of Older Lesbians* (Adelman, 1986) substantiated her finding that the most important factor for determining psychological well-being for older lesbians is the level of homophobia in society and in ourselves.

Reflections on Growing Older as a Lesbian: Katherine's Personal Narrative

Although much of the literature on women and aging emphasizes the negative aspects of growing old in a sexist society, I am finding that identifying as a lesbian has had a liberating effect on my experience of aging. Physical attractiveness and professional success used to be my obsessions in earlier years, but these external trappings of approval are no longer my main concerns. Now, I feel much more focused on my inner life of physical and emotional health, and I find deeper pleasures in participating fully as a parent, partner, and citizen. Although I came out at age 35, after a decade as a married woman, it has taken a long time, at least another decade, to accept that this is the life that feels most comfortable to me. Giving up heterosexual privilege

was a struggle, and not an easy one, because so many of the rewards associated with being an educated, professional woman are linked to one's ability to
court male approval. The coincidence of aging and a woman-centered life
makes a great deal of sense to me, providing a flexibility and freedom to define my life more by internal, rather than external, standards.

Perhaps the reward I most cherish of living such a life is the example I am
giving my children of "no secrets"—nothing to hide and nothing to be afraid
of. I am living the life I want to live so that they do not have to live it for me.
Generations of women before me have provided the opportunities that current generations have to act on our heart's desire and mind's choice. I am
aware that the opportunities I now experience toward such fulfillment and
freedom come at a price that was paid by those who came before me.
Knowing of their sacrifice makes it so much easier to relinquish some of my
own privilege, and that is another benefit of growing older in a woman-
centered life.

Future Directions:
Intervening Through Policy and Advocacy

What can we do individually and collectively to alleviate the stressors and expand the strengths of families with gay, lesbian, bisexual, and transgendered
members? Education about family diversity is critical to dismantling prejudices and stereotypes. Lifelong learning is essential for dealing with the rapid
social change that affects daily life. Schools are a place to open the conversation with children, parents, and teachers about sexual orientation diversity.
Teaching about the humanity of gays and lesbians in the schools is different
than teaching about their sexuality or sexual behavior. Instead, it involves
teaching them about the community of gay and lesbian people, their relationships, the biases and discrimination they face, and the need to teach children
early on to be tolerant and accepting of others. We cannot allow silence to
overcome our efforts to teach children about what many would consider to be
sensitive issues. Instruction in schools and communities, at all levels, is
needed because all families need to be validated: Some children grow up and
become gay or lesbian, some children have parents who are gay or lesbian,
and some children have relatives or friends who are gay or lesbian.

We all need to be concerned about the policies in our communities involving the legal and social rights and responsibilities of individuals and families
and work to dismantle present barriers. The participants in Dispenza's (1999)
study talked about personal steps they would take as they imagined a world of

enhanced quality of child care for LGBT parents and children and made statements such as "I'm going to get training in homophobia" and "I'm going to ask the question—'Do you see yourself reflected in this?' " One participant responded by saying, "It's important for me to deal with my stuff" (p. 24). It is important for all of us to recognize and deal with "our stuff" so that we can take advantage of the opportunity to educate ourselves and others and find ways to respect all individuals and families living in our communities.

DISCUSSION QUESTIONS

1. What are the challenges faced by gay and lesbian families?
2. What are heterocentrism, heterosexism, and homophobia? How are they related? Why are they so prevalent? How can they be counteracted?
3. What obligation does society have to address proactively the violence against gays, lesbians, and bisexuals, including the high suicide rate among teens dealing with being or feeling gay?
4. How would the world be different if gay, lesbian, and bisexual families had the same rights and privileges as heterosexual families?
5. How can policies in schools and workplaces be changed to be more inclusive?

SUGGESTED READINGS

Benkov, L. (1994). *Reinventing the family: The emerging story of lesbian and gay parents.* New York: Crown.
Bernstein, R. A. (1995). *Straight parents/gay children: Keeping families together.* New York: Thunder's Mouth Press.
Eskridge, W. N., Jr. (1996). *The case for same-sex marriage: From sexual liberty to civilized commitment.* New York: Free Press.
Patterson, C. J., & D'Augelli, A. R. (1998). *Lesbian, gay, and bisexual identities in families.* New York: Oxford University Press.
Savin-Williams, R. C., & Cohen, K. M. (Eds.). (1996). *The lives of lesbians, gays, and bisexuals: Children to adults.* Fort Worth, TX: Harcourt Brace.

REFERENCES

Adelman, M. (Ed.). (1986). *Long time passing: Lives of older lesbians.* Boston: Alyson.
Adelman, M. (1991). Stigma, gay lifestyles, and adjustment to aging: A study of later-life gay men and lesbians. In J. A. Lee (Ed.), *Gay midlife and maturity* (pp. 7-32). New York: Harrington Park.

Allen, K. R. (1995). Opening the classroom closet: Sexual orientation and self-disclosure. *Family Relations, 44,* 136-141.

Allen, K. R. (1997). Lesbian and gay families. In T. Arendell (Ed.), *Contemporary parenting: Challenges and issues* (pp. 196-218). Thousand Oaks, CA: Sage.

Allen, K. R., & Demo, D. H. (1995). The families of lesbians and gay men: A new frontier in family research. *Journal of Marriage and the Family, 57,* 111-127.

Allen, K. R., Demo, D. H., Walker, A. J., & Acock, A. C. (1996, November). *Older parents of gay and lesbian adult children.* Paper presented at the annual meeting of the National Council on Family Relations, Kansas City, MO.

Allen, K. R., & Wilcox, K. L. (1996, November). *Becoming an activist: Older parents of adult gay children.* Paper presented at the annual meeting of the Gerontological Society of America, Washington, DC.

Allport, G. (1958). *The nature of prejudice.* Garden City, NY: Doubleday.

Ben-Ari, A. (1995). The discovery that an offspring is gay: Parents', gay men's, and lesbians' perspectives. *Journal of Homosexuality, 30,* 89-112.

Berger, R. M. (1982). The unseen minority: Older gays and lesbians. *Social Work, 27,* 236-242.

Berger, R. M. (1984). Realities of gay and lesbian aging. *Social Work, 29,* 57-62.

Berrill, K. (1990). Anti-gay violence and victimization in the United States: An overview. *Journal of Interpersonal Violence, 5,* 274-294.

Blumenfeld, W. J. (Ed.). (1992). *Homophobia: How we all pay the price.* Boston: Beacon.

Blumstein, P., & Schwartz, P. (1983). *American couples.* New York: William Morrow.

Boxer, A. M., Cook, J. A., & Herdt, G. (1991). Double jeopardy: Identity transitions and parent-child relations among gay and lesbian youth. In K. Pillemer & K. McCartney (Eds.), *Parent-child relations throughout life* (pp. 59-92). Hillsdale, NJ: Lawrence Erlbaum.

Comstock, G. D. (1991). *Violence against lesbians and gay men.* New York: Columbia University Press.

Crosbie-Burnett, M., & Helmbrecht, L. (1993). A descriptive empirical study of gay male stepfamilies. *Family Relations, 42,* 256-262.

D'Augelli, A. R. (1991). Gay men in college: Identity processes and adaptations. *Journal of College Student Development, 32,* 140-146.

D'Augelli, A. R., & Hershberger, S. L. (1993). Lesbian, gay, and bisexual youth in community settings: Personal challenges and mental health problems. *American Journal of Community Psychology, 21,* 421-448.

Dispenza, M. (1999). *Our families, our children.* Seattle, WA: Child Care Resources.

Editors of the *Harvard Law Review.* (1990). *Sexual orientation and the law.* Cambridge, MA: Harvard University Press.

Engstrom, C. M., & Sedlacek, W. (1997). Attitudes of heterosexual students toward their gay male and lesbian peers. *Journal of College Student Development, 38,* 565-576.

Eskridge, W. N., Jr. (1996). *The case for same-sex marriage: From sexual liberty to civilized commitment.* New York: Free Press.

Faderman, L. (1991). *Odd girls and twilight lovers: A history of lesbian life in twentieth century America.* New York: Penguin.

Francher, S. J., & Henkin, J. (1973). The menopausal queen. *American Journal of Orthopsychiatry, 43,* 670-674.

Friend, R. A. (1980). GAYging: Adjustment and the older gay male. *Alternative Lifestyles, 3,* 231-248.

Friend, R. A. (1991). Older lesbian and gay people: A theory of successful aging. *Journal of Homosexuality, 20,* 99-118.

Gallagher, J. (1996, July 23). Love and war. *Advocate: The National Gay and Lesbian Newsmagazine,* pp. 22-28.

Goffman, E. (1963). *Stigma: Notes on the management of spoiled identity.* New York: Simon & Schuster.

Harry, J. (1983). Gay male and lesbian relationships. In E. D. Macklin & R. H. Rubin (Eds.), *Contemporary families and alternative life styles: Handbook on research and theory* (pp. 216-234). Beverly Hills, CA: Sage.

Herdt, G. (1989). Gay and lesbian youth: Emergent identities and cultural scenes at home and abroad. *Journal of Homosexuality, 17,* 1-42.

Herdt, G. (Ed.). (1992). *Gay culture in America.* Boston: Beacon.

Herdt, G., & Boxer, A. (1993). *Children of horizons: How gay and lesbian teens are leading a new way out of the closet.* Boston: Beacon.

Herek, G. M. (1989). Hate crimes against lesbians and gay men: Issues for research and policy. *American Psychologist, 44,* 948-955.

Herek, G. M., Kimmel, D. C., Amaro, H., & Melton, G. B. (1991). Avoiding heterosexist bias in psychological research. *American Psychologist, 46,* 957-963.

Hershberger, S. L., Pilkington, N. W., & D'Augelli, A. R. (1997). Predictors of suicide attempts among gay, lesbian, and bisexual youth. *Journal of Adolescent Research, 12,* 477-497.

Jacobson, S., & Grossman, A. H. (1996). Older lesbians and gay men: Old myths, new images, and future directions. In R. C. Savin-Williams & K. M. Cohen (Eds.), *The lives of lesbians, gays, and bisexuals* (pp. 345-373). Fort Worth, TX: Harcourt Brace.

Kehoe, M. (1988). Lesbians over 60 speak for themselves. *Journal of Homosexuality, 16,* 1-11.

Kelly, J. (1977). The aging male homosexual: Myth and reality. *Gerontologist, 17,* 328-332.

Khayatt, M. D. (1992). *Lesbian teachers: An invisible presence.* Albany: State University of New York Press.

Kimmel, D. C. (1978). Adult development and aging: A gay perspective. *Journal of Social Issues, 34,* 113-130.

Klein, F. (1990). The need to view sexual orientation as a multivariable dynamic process: A theoretical perspective. In D. P. McWhirter, S. A. Saunders, & J. M. Reinisch (Eds.), *Homosexuality/heterosexuality: Concepts of sexual orientation* (pp. 277-282). New York: Oxford University Press.

Kochman, A. (1993). Old and gray. In J. Adleman, R. Berger, M. Boyd, V. Doublex, M. Freedman, W. S. Hubbard, M. Kight, A. Kochman, M. K. R. Meyer, & S. M. Raphael (Eds.), *Lambda gray* (pp. 93-99). North Hollywood, CA: Newcastle.

Kubler-Ross, E. (1969). *On death and dying.* New York: Macmillan.

Kurdek, L. A. (1995). Lesbian and gay couples. In A. R. D'Augelli & C. J. Patterson (Eds.), *Lesbian and gay identities over the lifespan: Psychological perspectives on personal, relational, and community processes* (pp. 243-261). New York: Oxford University Press.

Kurdek, L. A. (1998). Relationship outcomes and their predictors: Longitudinal evidence from heterosexual married, gay cohabiting, and lesbian cohabiting couples. *Journal of Marriage and the Family, 60,* 553-568.

Laird, J. (1993). Lesbian and gay families. In F. Walsh (Ed.), *Normal family processes* (2nd ed., pp. 282-328). New York: Guilford.

Lopez, G., & Chism, N. (1993). Classroom concerns of gay and lesbian students. *College Teaching, 41,* 97-103.

Lucco, A. J. (1987). Planned retirement housing preferences of older homosexuals. *Journal of Homosexuality, 14,* 35-56.

Martin, A. (1993). *The lesbian and gay parenting handbook.* New York: HarperPerennial.

Martin, A. D. (1982). Learning to hide: The socialization of the gay adolescent. *Adolescent Psychiatry, 10,* 52-65.

Martin, D., & Lyon, P. (1992). The older lesbian. In B. Berzon (Ed.), *Positively gay* (2nd ed., pp. 111-120). Berkeley, CA: Celestial Arts.

McNaught, B. (1988). *On being gay.* New York: St. Martin's.

National Center for Health Statistics. (1993, January 7). Advance report of final mortality statistics, 1990. *Monthly Vital Statistics Report, 41.* Hyattsville, MD: U.S. Public Health Service.

Patterson, C. J. (1992). Children of lesbian and gay parents. *Child Development, 63,* 1025-1042.

Patterson, C. J. (1995). Families of the lesbian baby boom: Parents' division of labor and children's adjustment. *Developmental Psychology, 31,* 115-123.

Pharr, S. (1988). *Homophobia: A weapon of sexism.* Little Rock, AR: Chardon Press.

Pies, C. (1988). *Considering parenthood* (2nd ed. updated). San Francisco: Spinsters/ Aunt Lute.

Pilkington, N. W., & D'Augelli, A. R. (1995). Victimization of lesbian, gay, and bisexual youth in community settings. *Journal of Community Psychology, 23,* 34-56.

Pillemer, K., & Suitor, J. J. (1991). "Will I ever escape my child's problems?" Effects of adult children's problems on elderly parents. *Journal of Marriage and the Family, 53,* 585-594.

Poor, M. (1982). The older lesbian. In M. Cruikshank (Ed.), *Lesbian studies* (pp. 165-173). Old Westbury, NY: Feminist Press.

Quam, J. K., & Whitford, G. S. (1992). Adaptation and age-related expectations of older gay and lesbian adults. *Gerontologist, 32,* 367-374.

Raphael, S. M., & Meyer, M. K. R. (1993). Old lesbians seizing the moment, changing their world. In J. Adleman, R. Berger, M. Boyd, V. Doublex, M. Freedman, W. S. Hubbard, M. Kight, A. Kochman, M. K. R. Meyer, & S. M. Raphael (Eds.), *Lambda gray* (pp. 101-113). North Hollywood, CA: Newcastle.

Raphael, S. M., & Robinson, M. K. (1980). The older lesbian. *Alternative Lifestyles, 3,* 207-229.

Remafedi, G. (Ed.). (1994). *Death by denial: Studies of suicide in gay and lesbian teenagers.* Boston: Alyson.

Rhoads, R. A. (1995). Learning from the coming out experiences of college males. *Journal of College Student Development, 36,* 67-74.

Rohrbaugh, J. B. (1992). Lesbian families: Clinical issues and theoretical implications. *Professional Psychology: Research and Practice, 23,* 467-473.

Ryff, C. D., Schmutte, P. S., & Lee, Y. H. (1996). How children turn out: Implications for parental self-evaluation. In C. D. Ryff & M. M. Seltzer (Eds.), *The parental experience in midlife* (pp. 383-422). Chicago: University of Chicago Press.

Savin-Williams, R. C. (1993). Personal reflections on coming out, prejudice, and homophobia in the academic workplace. In L. Diamant (Ed.), *Homosexual issues in the workplace* (pp. 225-241). Washington, DC: Taylor & Francis.

Savin-Williams, R. C. (1994). Verbal and physical abuse as stressors in the lives of lesbian, gay male, and bisexual youths: Associations with school problems, running away, substance abuse, prostitution, and suicide. *Journal of Consulting and Clinical Psychology, 62,* 261-269.

Savin-Williams, R. C. (1998). The disclosure to families of same-sex attractions by lesbian, gay, and bisexual youths. *Journal of Research on Adolescence, 81,* 49-68.

Savin-Williams, R. C., & Dube, E. M. (1998). Parental reactions to their child's disclosure of a gay/lesbian identity. *Family Relations, 47,* 7-13.

Savin-Williams, R. C., & Esterberg, K. G. (2000). Lesbian, gay, and bisexual families. In D. H. Demo, K. R. Allen, & M. A. Fine (Eds.), *Handbook of family diversity* (pp. 197-215). New York: Oxford University Press.

Schwartz, P. (1994). *Peer marriage: How love between equals really works.* New York: Free Press.

Schwartz, P., & Rutter, V. (1998). *The gender of sexuality.* Thousand Oaks, CA: Pine Forge.

Sherman, S. (Ed.). (1992). *Lesbian and gay marriage: Private commitments, public ceremonies.* Philadelphia: Temple University Press.

Simoni, J. M. (1996). Pathways to prejudice: Predicting students' heterosexist attitudes with demographics, self-esteem, and contact with lesbians and gay men. *Journal of College Student Development, 37,* 68-76.

Stacey, J. (1996). *In the name of the family: Rethinking family values in the postmodern age.* Boston: Beacon.

Strommen, E. F. (1989). "You're a what?" Family member reactions to the disclosure of homosexuality. *Journal of Homosexuality, 18,* 37-58.

Telljohann, S. K., & Price, J. H. (1993). A qualitative examination of adolescent homosexuals' life experiences: Ramifications for secondary school personnel. *Journal of Homosexuality, 26,* 41-56.

Vacha, K. (1985). *Quiet fire: Memoirs of older gay men.* Trumansburg, NY: Crossing Press.

Weinberg, M. S. (1970). The male homosexual: Age-related variations in social and psychological characteristics. *Social Problems, 17,* 527-537.

Weston, K. (1991). *Families we choose: Lesbians, gays, kinship.* New York: Columbia University Press.

Zicklin, G. (1995). Deconstructing legal rationality: The case of lesbian and gay family relationships. *Marriage & Family Review, 21,* 55-76.

Author Index

Subject Index

About the Contributors

Katherine R. Allen is Professor of Family Studies at Virginia Polytechnic Institute and State University. She also has faculty appointments in the Center of Gerontology and the Women's Studies Program and chairs the Virginia Tech Academy of Teaching Excellence. She is the recipient of the William E. Wine Award for Excellence in Teaching from Virginia Tech and the Osborne Teaching Award from the National Council on Family Relations. Active in the National Council on Family Relations, she is a charter fellow and deputy editor of the *Journal of Marriage and the Family*. She is also the author of numerous articles and several books, including *Single Women/Family Ties: Life Histories of Older Women, Women and Families: Feminist Reconstructions* (with Kristine Baber), and *Handbook of Family Diversity* (with David Demo and Mark Fine). She received her PhD from Syracuse University.

Hector Balcazar is Professor and Division Director of Social and Behavioral Sciences, School of Public Health, Health Science Center at Fort Worth, University of North Texas. He specializes in the study of public health problems of Latinos and Mexican Americans and is currently the principal investigator on a project, funded by the Department of Health and Human Services, to study the use of perinatal, infant, and childhood health

435

services among high-risk Hispanic subgroups in Arizona. His publications have focused on perinatal and infant health outcomes, relationships between acculturation and Latino health problems, cardiovascular disease in Latinos, and border health issues. He received his PhD in International Nutrition at Cornell University.

Grace M. Barnes, Senior Research Scientist at the Research Institute on Addictions in Buffalo, New York, is the author of numerous articles focusing on adolescence and substance abuse. Selected publications include those in the *Journal of Youth and Adolescence,* the *Journal of Adolescent Research,* and the *Journal of Marriage and the Family.* She has also held the positions of principal investigator or coprincipal investigator for numerous grants investigating adolescent substance abuse. She received her PhD from the University at Buffalo, SUNY.

Suzanne Bartholomae is a PhD candidate in family science at the Ohio State University. Her research interests focus on the impact of economic stress on marital quality, and she has published in several journals, including *Family Relations* and *Consumer Interests Annual.*

Thomas L. Campbell is Professor of Family Medicine and Psychiatry at the University of Rochester School of Medicine. He has written extensively on the role of the family in medical practice and on the influence of families on health. His National Institute of Mental Health monograph, *Family's Impact on Health,* has been an influential review in this area. Other books he has coauthored include *Families and Health* (with William Doherty) and *Family-Oriented Primary Care* (with Susan McDaniel and David Seaburn). He is a board-certified family physician, a clinical member of the American Association of Marriage and Family Therapy, and a member of the board of the American Family Therapy Academy. He is also coeditor of *Families, Systems & Health: The Journal of Collaborative Family Healthcare* and chair of the Advisory Council of the Bayer Institute for Health Care Communication. He received his BA from Harvard College and his MD from Harvard Medical School.

Jeanne Joseph Chadwick is a doctoral student in the Family Studies Department at the University of Connecticut. She is also involved in marriage and family therapy practice at the Ackerman Institute and trains interviewers for a study focusing on depression at Yale University.

Margaret Crosbie-Burnett is Associate Professor in Counseling Psychology and Chair of the Department of Educational and Psychological Studies at the University of Miami (Florida). Her research, teaching, and scholarly work has focused on theory, instrument development, and policy related to stepfamilies and the development of instruments for the assessment of stepfamily adjustment. She was guest editor of a special issue of *Family Relations* on stepfamilies and was cochair of the Focus Group on Remarriage and Stepfamilies in the National Council on Family Relations. She received her PhD from Stanford University.

Adam Davey is Assistant Professor in the Department of Child and Family Development and a Fellow in the Institute for Behavioral Research at the University of Georgia. His research focuses on areas related to families and aging and, in particular, intergenerational exchange and research methodologies used to study older families. He has published in several scholarly journals, including *Journal of Family Psychology, Journals of Gerontology, Psychological Sciences,* and *Journal of Marriage and the Family,* and contributed several chapters to edited volumes. He teaches in areas related to research methodology and gerontology and families, and received his PhD from Pennsylvania State University.

David H. Demo is Professor and Chair in the Department of Human Development and Family Studies at the University of North Carolina–Greensboro. His research focuses on parent-child relationships with an emphasis on adolescence. He has published numerous articles in professional journals and is the coauthor or coeditor of several books, including *Handbook of Family Diversity* (with Katherine Allen and Mark Fine); *Parents and Adolescents in Changing Families* (with Anne-Marie Ambert); *Family Diversity and Well-Being* (with Alan C. Acock), which received the Choice Magazine Outstanding Book Award; and *Marriage and Family in Transition* (with John N. Edwards). He also serves on the editorial boards of several journals, including the *Journal of Marriage and the Family.* He received his PhD from Cornell University.

Michael P. Farrell is Professor of Sociology at the University at Buffalo, SUNY. His research focus is on families, friendships, and adolescence, including substance abuse, sexuality, and delinquency. He has secured several major grants from the Woman's Sports Foundation, the National Institute on Alcohol Abuse and Alcoholism, and the National Institute on Aging. He has published in leading journals, including the *Journal of Marriage and* *the Family,* the *Journal of Health and Social Behavior,* and the *Journal of Research on Adolescence.* He is also the author of *Men at Midlife* (with S. Rosenberg). He received his PhD from Yale University.

Mark A. Fine is Professor and Chair of the Department of Human Development and Family Studies at the University of Missouri–Columbia. His research and scholarly endeavors focus on intervention programs for families, and he has published extensively in professional journals and edited volumes. He has also coauthored or coedited three books: *Understanding and Helping Families: A Cognitive-Behavioral Approach* (with A. I. Schwebel), *A Manual for Conducting Even Start Program Evaluations* (with D. J. Polzella), and *Handbook of Family Diversity* (with David Demo and Katherine Allen). He is editor of the *Journal of Social and Personal Relationships* and associate editor of *Family Relations* and the *Journal of Marriage and the Family.* He received his PhD from Ohio State University.

Jonathan J. Fox is Assistant Professor in the Department of Consumer and Textile Sciences at the Ohio State University. His research focuses on consumer economics, family financial management, and financial socialization, and he has served as principal investigator for several projects in these areas. He has published in several professional journals, including *Financial Counseling and Planning, Consumer Interests Annual,* and *Family Relations.* He teaches in areas related to family financial management and methodology in family resource management. He received his PhD at the University of Maryland, where he won the Best Doctoral Dissertation Award from the American Council on Consumer Interests.

Lawrence H. Ganong is Professor of Nursing and Family Studies at the University of Missouri–Columbia. He has coauthored (with Marilyn Coleman) *Remarried Family Relations* and *Bibliotherapy With Stepchildren,* along with more than 100 articles in scholarly journals. His research interests include postdivorce family relationships, remarriage and stepparenting, intergenerational family responsibilities, and family stereotyping. He teaches in the areas of research methods, family dynamics, intervention, and family theories. He has also served on the editorial boards of several professional journals, including the *Journal of Marriage and the Family, Family Relations,* and the *Journal of Nursing.* He received his PhD from the University of Missouri.

Stephen M. Gavazzi is Associate Professor in the Department of Human Development and Family Science at the Ohio State University. He has established a research program that identifies the impact of family dynamics on adolescent development, psychopathology, and problem behavior. He has also been involved in the development and evaluation of several family-based programming efforts, including the psychoeducation group for families who have children with mood disorders, and created a program for families with adolescents known as the Growing Up FAST: Families with Adolescents Surviving and Thriving™ program, a program that has been modified for use with juvenile offenders and their families. He received his PhD in Family Studies at the University of Connecticut.

Richard J. Gelles holds the Joanne and Raymond Walsh Chair of Child Welfare and Family Violence in the School of Social Work at the University of Pennsylvania. He is the author or coauthor of 23 books and more than 100 articles and chapters on family violence. These include, among others, *The Violent Home, The Book of David: How Preserving Families Can Cost Children's Lives,* and *Intimate Violence in Families* (3rd ed.). In 1998, Secretary of Health and Human Services Donna Shalala appointed him to the Kinship Care Advisory Panel of the Administration for Children, Youth, and Families. He was also a member of the National Academy of Science's panel on "Assessing Family Violence Interventions" and vice president of the National Council on Family Relations. He received the Outstanding Contributions to Teaching Award from the American Sociological Association and has presented innumerable lectures to policy-making and media groups. He received his PhD from the University of New Hampshire.

Kathleen Mathieson is a PhD student in the Department of Sociology at Arizona State University. Her areas of interest are health, illness, medicine, health policy, and statistics. She is currently involved in a project to evaluate enrollment efforts for a state-funded child health insurance program in Arizona and is conducting research on self-health-care practices among older adults.

Katrina M. McClintic is a doctoral student in the Department of Educational and Psychological Studies at the University of Miami. She holds an MS in counseling from the Georgia State University.

Patrick C. McKenry is Professor in the Department of Human Development and Family Science and the Ohio Agricultural Research and Development Center at the Ohio State University. He also has adjunct appointments in the Department of African American and African Studies. His research focuses on families and stress, with particular interest in family conflict and violence, postdivorce adjustment, variations in coping by gender and race, and the role of conflict and violence in the coparenting process after divorce. He has published extensively in the marriage and family literature and coauthored or coedited with Sharon Price *Divorce, Families Across Time: A Life Course Perspective,* and both editions of *Families and Change: Coping With Stessful Events.* He is a member of the American Sociological Association and the National Council on Family Relations, where he has held several leadership positions. He has also been the recipient of three Ohio State University Awards for excellence in teaching and research. He received his PhD at the University of Tennessee and was a postdoctoral fellow at the University of Georgia.

Colleen I. Murray is Associate Professor of Human Development and Family Studies and the Interdisciplinary PhD Program in Social Psychology at the University of Nevada, Reno. Her research interests focus on family grief and media reporting of mass tragedies, bereaved parent–surviving sibling experiences, and theoretical and methodological issues in the study of families. She has published in leading family journals, including *Family Relations,* the *Journal of Early Adolescence,* and *Child and Adolescent Social Work.* She received her PhD from the Ohio State University.

Velma McBride Murry is Associate Professor in the Department of Child and Family Development and Faculty Fellow in the Institute for Behavioral Research at the University of Georgia. Her research focuses on the significance of multiple ecologies in explaining and predicting the linkages of family process, parenting, family relations, and positive outcomes of children and adolescents of color. She received her PhD at the University of Missouri–Columbia and was recently the recipient of the Osborne Award for Outstanding Teaching in Family Studies, presented by the National Council on Family Relations.

Barbara M. Newman is Professor of Human Development and Family Science at the Ohio State University. She has held several positions, including Professor and Chair of her home department and Associate Provost for Faculty Recruitment and Development at the Ohio State University. She has coauthored or coedited several books, including *Development Through Life: A Psychosocial Approach,* which has been translated into Japanese and Chinese; *Infancy and Childhood: Development and Its Contexts;* and *Development Through Life: A Case Study Approach.* She received her PhD from the University of Michigan.

Gary W. Peterson is Professor and Chair of Human Development at Washington State University, and former Professor and Chair of the Department of Sociology and the Department of Family Resources and Human Development at Arizona State University. His general areas of research and scholarly expertise are adolescent development within the context of families and parent-child relationships. He has explored these and other topics in articles and chapters within samples of middle-class, urban and low-income, and rural youth in the United States and has publications in many journals, including the *Journal of Marriage and the Family, Family Relations,* and the *Journal of Adolescent Research.* He is coeditor of the *Handbook of Marriage and the Family* (2nd ed.) and *Adolescents in Families* and editor of *Marriage and Family Review.* He received his PhD from Brigham Young University.

Sharon J. Price is Professor and Graduate Coordinator, and former Department Head, in the Department of Child and Family Development at the University of Georgia. She is also on the faculties of Gerontology and Women's Studies and has published extensively in professional journals. She and Patrick McKenry have coauthored and coedited *Divorce, Families and Change: Coping With Stressful Events* (1st ed.), and *Families Across Time: A Life Course Perspective.* Her present research focuses on the study of widows who live on family farms. She has won several teaching awards, including the Osborne Award, presented by the National Council on Family Relations, and the highest honor for teaching at the University of Georgia, the Josiah Meigs Award. She is active in several professional organizations and has served in many capacities, including president of the National Council on Family Relations. She received her PhD at Iowa State University.

Zhenchao Qian is Associate Professor in the Department of Sociology at Arizona State University. His research and publications focus on ethnic and minority families, with an emphasis on Asian families. He has published articles on interracial marriage, aspirations of adolescents, and mobility of workers. He teaches research methodology, statistics, and family courses. He received his PhD from the University of Pennsylvania.

Ronald M. Sabatelli is Professor of Family Studies at the University of Connecticut. His research has focused on the transition to parenthood, outcomes experienced in marriage, parent education for divorced parents, and interpersonal interaction in marriage. He has published in leading professional journals and edited volumes. He serves on the editorial boards of several professional journals, including the *Journal of Marriage and the Family,* the *Journal of Social and Personal Relationships,* and *Family Relations.* He received his PhD from the University of Connecticut.

Angie M. Schock is a PhD student in the Department of Human Development and Family Science at the Ohio State University. Her research interests include family programming and interventions for families with children and adolescents with mood disorders. In particular, her focus is on the role of fathers in the development and treatment of children's mental illness.

Karen L. Wilcox is Assistant Professor of Family Studies at Ohio University. She worked for several years as Assistant Dean of Students at Roanoke College, where she directed the Residence Life Program. She was the recipient of the 1997 Student of the Year Award from the National Council on Family Relations and teaches courses on family development, human sexuality, pluralistic lifestyles, death and dying, and family gerontology. Her research interests are in the areas of family diversity, adult sibling relationships, and parent–young adult relationships. She received her PhD from Virginia Polytechnic Institute and State University.